D0207755

Handbook of East German Drama

DDR–Studien/East German Studies

Richard A. Zipser, General Editor

Vol. 1

PETER LANG

New York · Bern · Frankfurt am Main · Paris

Herbert Lederer

Handbook of East German Drama

1945–1985

DDR Drama Handbuch

PETER LANG
New York · Bern · Frankfurt am Main · Paris

Library of Congress Cataloging-in-Publication Data

Lederer, Herbert
  Handbook of East German drama, 1945–1985=
DDR drama Handbuch, 1945–1985.

  (DDR-Studien=East German studies ; vol. 1)
  1. German drama—Germany (East)—Bio-bibliography.
2. German drama—20th century—Bio-bibliography.
3. Theater—Germany (East)—Bio-bibliography. I. Title.
II. Title: DDR drama Handbuch, 1945–1985. III. Series:
East German studies ; vol. 1.
PT3721.L43 1987   016.832′914′0809431   86-27775
ISBN 0-8204-0367-9
ISSN 0882-7095

CIP-Kurztitelaufnahme der Deutschen Bibliothek

Lederer, Herbert
Handbook of East German drama : 1945–1985=
DDR-Drama-Handbuch / Herbert Lederer.—New York ;
Bern ; Frankfurt am Main ; Paris ; Lang, 1987.
  (East German studies ; Vol. 1)

ISBN 0-8204-0367-9
NE: DDR-Studien

Printed by Weihert-Druck GmbH, Darmstadt (West Germany)

INTRODUCTION

1. Background.

Both quantitatively and qualitatively, the role of the theater in the cultural life of the German Democratic Republic (GDR) is remarkable. In a country of fewer than 17 million inhabitants and approximately the size of the state of Ohio, there are close to 100 professional acting companies, playing a full season of repertory theater. Many of them perform on a number of stages, often simultaneously. In addition, there are numerous workers' theaters and other amateur groups. Altogether, over 200 theatrical performances take place on any given day, attended every year by total audiences of about 10 million people. Even if one takes into account the number of foreigners in these audiences, especially in Berlin, the astonishing statistical fact remains that on the average every man, woman, and child in the GDR attends a play at least once every two years.

This truly amazing figure can be attributed to three causes: Organized group attendances and subscriptions account for a good percentage; tickets are very inexpensive, with prices for seats ranging from 1 to 15 Marks (cheaper than most movies); and on the whole, the artistic quality of the performances is consistently high. Enjoying generous financial support by the government (there are no private theaters in the GDR), job security for the ensembles, and the luxury of extensive rehearsal time, GDR stage productions today at least equal--and perhaps surpass--the best that West German, Swiss, and Austrian theaters have to offer.

The theater has always played a significant part in German cultural history. Unlike France or England, professional theater flourished not only in the capital, but in many provincial cities and smaller towns as well. In part, of course, this was due to the political structure of Germany: numerous independent principalities and municipalities vying with one another for cultural excellence. In addition, the stage has traditionally been viewed as an instrument for aesthetic, moral, and political education--more so than other mass media, which lack its effectiveness of live, collective group dynamics.

To be sure, these principles apply to some extent to all four German-speaking countries. It is probably safe to say, however, that none of them (nor, for that matter, any other nation) can equal the over-all theater density of the GDR, or the popularity and importance of the theater as an indispensable element of social life.

Obviously, not all theatrical offerings on GDR stages are by native authors. The major and minor classics of the German dramatical past are frequently part of the repertoire, as are the great dramatists of past centuries of other countries.

Works by Soviet writers and by playwrights from the other Socialist countries are often performed. Contemporary plays from the Third World and from Western countries (including the U.S.) also appear on GDR stages. But ever since the creation of the Soviet Zone of Occupation in 1945 and the beginning of the GDR as an independent state in 1949, a large percentage of the repertoire, season after season, has been devoted to plays by East German dramatists.

Only a very small number of these playwrights, however, are known in the West, and even fewer are performed there. Aside from famous authors like Bertolt Brecht, Friedrich Wolf, or Arnold Zweig, who wrote most of their plays before the end of World War II, not more than a handful of GDR dramatists are familiar even to experts on contemporary German drama. Foremost among them is Heiner Müller, arguably the most important living German-language playwright. Peter Hacks, who started his play-writing career in the Federal Republic, and Heinar Kipphardt, who left the GDR and wrote most of his dramas in the West, are of course widely known. Ulrich Plenzdorf achieved fame as the result of a single play, *"Die neuen Leiden des jungen W."* ("The New Sorrows of Young W."). Volker Braun's works are occasionally discussed in critical scholarship. But most Western scholars of German literature would be hard put to come up with more than perhaps a dozen names. Western literary journals often contain articles on GDR poets and prose authors, but only rarely on dramatists. Standard biographical and bibliographical reference books on contemporary German-language authors are a better, but not much better source of information. Even GDR lexica deal with only the most prominent authors.

2. General Principles.

The original aim of the research project, which led to this book, was to write an article (or at most a slim volume) presenting a comprehensive compilation of all GDR dramatists. At the outset, the most ambitious goal wich appeared attainable was relatively modest: to gather data on perhaps one hundred writers and their works. Much to everyone's surprise (this author and experts within the GDR itself included), the list grew and grew. It now contains some 700 names and over 3,000 titles.

Of course, not all of these are significant writers or worthwhile plays. A number of the authors were not professional dramatists at all; spurred on by contests and by general encouragement for home-grown artistic talent, they wrote one or two plays which were produced at some small theaters; after a few performances, they sank into well-deserved oblivion. But others were and are genuine playwrights, gifted craftsmen who authored well-made plays on important topics.

It is not the aim of this book, however, to make critical evaluations or to set arbitrary standards of any kind, be they literary, cultural, sociological, or political. Nor is this the place to trace the historical development of GDR drama. Instead, the purpose of this work is to serve as a reference source on who wrote what when, where and when it was first performed, and whether (and if so, where and when) it was published.

Absolutely complete coverage is, to be sure, an impossible dream. Despite all efforts, biographical data was unattainable for a number of minor writers. Similarly, performance information could not be ascertained in every single instance. Bibliographic data, while the most thorough, is probably also not one hundred percent complete.

To the extent possible, however, this volume represents an attempt to list all stage works written within the territory of the GDR from 1945 to 1985. In order to give an accurate picture of an author's work, plays written by GDR dramatists before 1945 are listed. (In a few instances, plays written in 1985, but premiered and/or published in early 1986, have also been included.) The term "stage works" is used to include dramas, comedies, one-act plays, fragments, scenes, juvenile theater, puppet plays, pantomimes, choral works, cantatas, and libretti for operas, operettas, musicals, and ballets. Film, radio, and TV scripts are not included; on the other hand, if a play is based on a previous work in one of these three genres, that fact is indicated.

All playwrights who lived and worked within the area of the GDR are listed, even if they came to the GDR from a different country or emigrated from the GDR. Residence, rather than nationality, is the deciding factor. (Brecht, after all, had an Austrian passport.) Composers appear as main entries only to the extent that they wrote, co-authored, or adapted their own libretti. Translators of foreign texts are normally not included, unless they also wrote plays of their own. Adaptations from foreign sources, however, are listed. To be sure, the dividing line between translations and adaptations is often vague.

3. Organization of Entries.

Authors are listed in alphabetical sequence by last name (or by their pseudonym, if that is more frequently used). Alternate forms of the name are shown in parentheses. Pseudonyms or real names are cross-referenced. In the alphabetization, the German *Umlaut* forms ä, ö, and ü are not resolved as ae, oe, and ue, unless the author uses that spelling. The German ß is alphabetized as ss and is spelled SS when a name is capitalized.

Date and place of birth and death are given, if known, using a sequence of day/month/year. If the name of a town has been changed, the currently used name is indicated where such information is available. In this section of the entry, names of towns are not abbreviated.

Biographical data, to the extent it was obtainable, is divided into three sections: important life dates, with the first year given in full, and subsequent years listed by the last two digits only; honors, prizes, and awards, again with only the first year cited in full; and other genres in which the author has published.

For each author, plays are arranged in chronological order, with the year (or years) of writing in the left margin. If the exact year of origin is unknown, the space is left blank and the sequence is approximate, usually by year of first performance. Works written outside of the GDR are also listed, to the extent that such information was obtainable.

German titles are shown in *bold italics*, with alternate title forms in brackets ‹ ›. An English translation of the title follows in *italics*, enclosed in parentheses ( ). No translation is given if the title consists of proper names with only articles or *und* added. Original German manuscript titles, if different from the final version, are indicated within quotation marks.

The type of play (e.g. drama, comedy, puppet play, etc.) is indicated in abbreviated form. (See List of Abbreviations.) The words Opera, Operetta, or Musical are used by themselves only if the composer also wrote (or participated in the writing of) the text; otherwise, the word Libretto follows. If the work is a revision of a previous title, a boldface cross-reference so indicates. If the title is a collective title for a series of one-acts, each individual title is listed separately, followed by a translation. Works written under a pseudonym are so identified.

Co-authors are listed, as are the sources on which the play is based. If the source was in a different genre, this fact is also cited, as is the author and title of the source (unless author or title are identical with the main entry). Composers are identified, if known and if different from the author.

Next, year and place of first performance are indicated. After 1945, Berlin always refers to East Berlin, unless otherwise indicated. If possible, the name of the theater is also identified for large cities, such as Berlin. If the play was performed under a different title, this is shown in quotation marks. If a play was first performed in a foreign language, the language is listed in parentheses, followed by the German premiere. On the other hand, if a play by a GDR author was later performed in English translation, this fact is also noted (except for Brecht, where such instances are too numerous).

Bibliographic information first cites publication in journals with name in *italics*, followed by year/issue number. Publication in the anthology series *Spectaculum* is listed by volume, followed by comma and year. Book titles are only listed if different from the main entry. Publishers which occur frequently (see special list) are indicated by name only; for others, the city is given. Subsequent listings of the same book (for another work by the same author) are identified by title and year only. Within the categories of journal and book publications, bibliographic entries are in chronological order. Secondary sources are not listed. No bibliographic information is given for Bertolt Brecht, since such data would (and indeed does) fill an entire volume of its own.

Since 1946, the Henschel Publishing Company has had sole performance rights for most plays written within the GDR. These works were printed as stage manuscripts and were not intended for general sale. They are therefore not identified in this volume as publications. They may, however, be available for performance or research purposes from Henschelverlag Kunst und Gesellschaft, Henschel Schauspiel, DDR 1040 Berlin, Oranienburger Straße 67/68.

A boldface cross-reference to a later version of a given play is given at the end of the entry, indicating year and title of revision.

4. Acknowledgments.

The information contained in this book was obtained from many different sources. For a number of authors, biographical data was found in such standard reference works as Kosch, *Deutsches Theaterlexikon* and *Deutsches Literatur Lexikon*; Kürschners *Deutscher Literaturkalender*; Albrecht et al., *Schriftsteller der DDR*; Trilse/Hammer/Kobel, *Theaterlexikon*; Arnold, *Kritisches Lexikon zur deutschsprachigen Gegenwartsliteratur*; Endres, *Autorenlexikon der deutschen Gegenwartsliteratur*; and others. For bibliographic information, the many-volumed sets of *Gesamtverzeichnis deutschsprachigen Schrifttums: 1911-1965* and its succesor, *Deutsche Bibliographie: Halbjahresverzeichnis*, 1966-1985, were extremely helpful. Performance information for the last eight years was found in the annual publication *Wer spielte was*.

Much of the remaining data, especially that pertaining to earlier first performances and to lesser-known playwrights, had to be dug out for each individual author and play. All issues of *Theater der Zeit* and *Theater heute* were searched; the Henschelverlag generously made its author contract files and other archival material accessible; materials in the Brecht Archiv and the archives of the Berliner Ensemble, Deutsches Theater, and the Nationaltheater in Weimar were made available; the files of the Schriftstellerverband, the Akademie der Künste, and the Verband der Theaterschaffenden yielded additional information; and letters of inquiry to the archivists of almost every theater in the GDR were in most instances answered courteously, though the information sought was not always obtainable. I am deeply grateful to all these organizations and to their staff members.

Beyond that, a great many individuals patiently gave of their time to answer questions in the area of their expertise. They are too numerous to list them all by name; however, I can not fail to mention Ilse Galfert, whose astounding memory and encyclopedic kowledge of all aspects of GDR theater enabled her to supply innumerable details. For her kindness, interest, and generosity, I owe her special heartfelt thanks.

I also wish to express my appreciation and gratitude for the financial support this project received from the University of Connecticut Research Foundation, from the National Endowment for the Humanities, and especially from the GDR Center of the International Theater Institute in Berlin, whose charming director, Mrs. Irene Gysi, extended repeated invitations to me to come to the GDR to conduct my research. Without this assistance, the present undertaking would never have come to fruition.

Furthermore, I am greatly indebted to Richard A. Zipser, the editor of the series DDR-STUDIEN/EAST GERMAN STUDIES, who suggested and supported the publication of this volume by Peter Lang. Finally, but most importantly, I want to thank my wife Eva for her careful proofreading, her valuable editorial and stylistic suggestions, and for her patience, understanding, and loving support during the long years of my involvement with GDR drama.

List of Abbreviations

AdK	Akademie der Künste der DDR (Academy of Arts, GDR)
Assoc	Association
asst	assistant
BE	Berliner Ensemble, Berlin
Bl	Ballet
Com	Comedy
d	der, des, etc. (the)
DDR	Deutsche Demokratische Republik (GDR)
DEFA	Deutsche Film Aktiengesellschaft (GDR Film Studio, Potsdam-Babelsberg)
Dr	Drama
Dsdn	Dresden
dt	deutsch- (German)
DT	Deutsches Theater, Berlin
FDGB	Freier Deutscher Gewerkschaftsbund (Free German Trade Union Association--GDR labor organization)
FDJ	Freie Deutsche Jugend (Free German Youth--GDR youth organization)
Fkft/M	Frankfurt am Main (FRG)
Fkft/O	Frankfurt an der Oder (GDR)
FRG	Federal Republic of Germany (West Germany)
GDR	German Democratic Republic
Gm	German
h.c.	honoris causa (honorary degree)
HS	Hochschule (University)
I.Lit	Institut für Literatur "Johannes Becher", Leipzig
int'l	international-
jg	jung- (young)
Juv	Juvenile play
Km.Op	Komische Oper, Berlin
KMSt	Karl Marx Stadt
KPD	Kommunistische Partei Deutschlands (German Communist Party)
Lib	Libretto
Lpzg	Leipzig
M	Music
Met	Metropol Theater, Berlin
MG	Maxim Gorki Theater, Berlin
Mgdbg	Magdeburg
MHS	Musikhochschule (Music Conservatory)
Mus	Musical
NdL	Neue deutsche Literatur
On	One-act play
Op	Opera
Opt	Operetta
Pant	Pantomime
POW	Prisoner of War

Pp	Puppet play
Pp.Th	Puppet theater
Pr	Premiere
Prof	Professor
Pseud	Pseudonym
rev	revised, revision
Sc	Scene
SED	Sozialistische Einheitspartei Deutschlands (German Socialist Unity Party--Socialist Party of GDR)
SPD	Sozialdemokratische Partei Deutschlands (German Social-Democratic Party)
Spec	*Spectaculum*, Frankfurt/Main: Suhrkamp
St.Op	Staatsoper, Berlin
TdZ	*Theater der Zeit*, Berlin: Henschelverlag
Th	Theater
Th.h.	*Theater heute*, Zurich: Orell Füssli & Friedrich Verlag
TiP	Theater im Palast, Berlin
Tr	Translation, translated, translator
Univ	University, Universität
USSR	Union of Soviet Socialist Republics
VB	Volksbühne, Berlin
vol	volume
W	West
WW	World War

Frequently occurring publishers:

Akademie - Akademieverlag, Berlin (GDR)
Aufbau - Aufbauverlag, Berlin (GDR)
Eulenspiegel - Eulenspiegel Verlag, Berlin (GDR)
Henschel - Henschelverlag, Berlin (GDR)
Reclam - Reclam Verlag, Leipzig (Note: The West German Reclam Verlag will be identified by the city Stuttgart.)
Suhrkamp - Suhrkamp Verlag, Frankfurt/M.

ABRAHAM, Peter
19 Jan 1926 Berlin/Neukölln –
After apprenticeship, worked two years for book dealer; 1959-
60 Film HS, Potsdam; since 60 dramaturg, GDR TV. 1973 FDGB
Prize and Erich Weinert Medal. Writes prose, TV and film
scripts, children's books.
1966   *Und das soll Liebe sein (And That's Supposed to Be
Love).* Com. Pr 1967 Potsdam.

ACHTEL, Ludwig   see Alexander KENT

ADDAMS, Peter   see Boris DJACENKO

ADERHOLD, Egon
17 Dec 1929 Neustadt –
Now lives in Birkenwerder. Writes novels and TV scripts.
1983   *Eros und Psyche.* Com. Pr 1983 Rostock.

ALBIG, Hans Georg
Director of literary center "Junge Autoren." Lives in Gera.
1980 Horst Salomon Prize. Writes prose.
1976   *Anstoß für Claudia (Scandal for Claudia).* Mus Lib (M
Friedrich-Wilhelm Tiller). Pr 1977 Gera.

ALBRECHT, Paul
Hamlet aus Wittenberg (Hamlet from Wittenberg). On.
Pr 1983 Wittenberg.
Die Martinsgans (A Goose for St. Martin's Day). On.
Pr 1983 Wittenberg.

ALLIHN, Jochen
Composer and librettist.
1961   *Ja, die Familie ‹O, diese Kinder› (Ah, the Family ‹Oh
These Children›).* Mus (with Heinz Kramer). Pr 1962
Fkft/O.
2 x Madeleine (Twice Madeleine). Mus.
*Verlobt ist nicht verheiratet (Engaged is Not Yet Mar-
ried).* Mus.
1963   *Ehe ungenügend (Marriage Unsatisfactory).* Mus. Pr
1964 Rostock.
1964   *Verflixter Alltag (Darned Everyday Routine).* Mus
(with Ursula Damm-Wendler and Horst-Ulrich Wendler).
Pr 1965 Rostock.
1970   *Die Zwickmühle (The Dilemma).* Mus (with Hans-Joachim
Preil). Pr 1971 Rostock.
1977   *Der Wolf und die sieben Geißlein (The Wolf and the Seven Goats).* Juv Mus (with Peter Ensikat; based on
Grimm). Pr 1978 Mgdbg.
1978   *Aladdin und die Wunderlampe (Aladdin and the Magic
Lamp).* Juv Mus (with Heinz Hall). Pr 1978 Zeitz.
1980   *Kalif Storch (Caliph Stork).* Juv Mus (with Holger
Eckert; based on Hauff). Pr 1981 Bernburg.

ALLIHN (cont'd)
1984   *Damals in Prag (That Time in Prague)*. Mus (with Hans-
         jörg Schneider and Brigitte Wulkow). Pr 1985 Erfurt.

AMBERGER, Wolfgang
12 Nov 1939 Berlin –
After high school, studied acting W. Berlin until 1960; since
then actor and stage director at various GDR theaters; after
72 member of ensemble Annaberg; 75-79 studied theater history
in Lpzg. Writes poetry and short prose.
1979   *Die Schlacht am Little-Big-Horn ‹Sitting Bull› (The
         Battle of Little Big-Horn)*. Dr. Pr 1979 Annaberg.

ANDERSON, Edith   (married name Schroeder)
30 Nov 1915 New York –
Worked as English teacher, cultural editor of "Daily Worker";
1943-47 railroad conductor; 47 married writer Max Schroeder,
moved to GDR; 67-68 editor with New York publisher; now lives
in Berlin. Translator, writes prose, children's books.
         Eine Rosine in der Sonne (A Raisin in the Sun). Dr
         (with B. Fuchs; tr from Lorraine Hansberry). Pr 1963.
         Der Herbstgarten (The Autumn Garden). Dr (with U.
         Püschel; tr from Lillian Hellman). Pr 1968.
1978   *Wo ist Katalin? (Where Is Katalin?)*. Dr. Pr 1979
         Weimar.

ANGERMÜLLER, Horst
1970   *Risiko (Risk)*. Dr. Pr 1970 Gera.

ARNOLD, Hans Dieter   (Pseud. John Ray ATKINSON)
7 May 1886 Magdeburg – 10 May 1961 Berlin
Retired teacher; lived in Berlin. Wrote short stories, novels, essays.
1931   *Alles um die Liebe (Everything for Love)*. Mus Lib.
1937   *Mühle im Schwarzwald (A Mill in the Black Forest)*.
         Opt Lib.
1946   *Er, sie und die anderen (He, She, and the Others)*.
         Mus Lib.
1947   *Die Dame aus Indien (The Lady from India)*. Opt Lib.
1947   *Das Blumenmädchen von Kanton (The Flower Girl of Can-
         ton)*. Opt Lib.
         Des Teufels Lustschloß (The Devil's Summer Castle).
         Op Lib (based on Kotzebue; M Franz Schubert).
         Der gestiefelte Kater (Puss in Boots). Juv Op Lib (M
         Gerhard Rosenfeld).

ATKINSON, John Ray see Hans Dieter ARNOLD

AUENMÜLLER, Hans
31 Oct 1926 Dresden –
1945-49 MHS Dsdn, then rehearsal conductor, Meiningen; 50-52
conductor and choir director Bernburg, since 72 Halberstadt.
Composer and librettist.
1962   *Das tapfere Schneiderlein (The Brave Little Tailor)*.
         Juv (based on Grimm).

AUENMÜLLER (cont'd)

1963   *Schneewittchen (Snow White)*. Juv (based on Grimm). Pr 1963 Halberstadt.

1964   *Frau Holle (Mother Holle)*. Juv (with Günter Kaltofen; based on Grimm). Pr 1965 Dessau.

1967   *Stadthauptmann Karst (Alderman Karst)*.   Dr. Pr 1968 Halberstadt.

1969   *Hans im Glück (Lucky Jack)*. Juv Mus (with Holger Ekkert; based on Grimm). Pr 1970 Zeitz.

1971   *Der Froschkönig (The Frog Prince)*. Juv (with Günter Kaltofen; based on Grimm). Pr 1972 Wittenberg.

1972   *Die Bremer Stadtmusikanten (The Town Musicians of Bremen)*. Juv Mus (with Hans-Hermann Krug; based on Grimm). Pr 1975 Altenburg.

1973   *Der gestiefelte Kater (Puss in Boots)*. Juv Mus (with Hans-Hermann Krug). Pr 1974 Halberstadt.

1976   *Tilla und der Burgvogt (Tilla and the Castle Steward)*. Juv Mus (with Hans-Hermann Krug; based on Georg Waldemar Pijet). Pr 1976 Halberstadt.

1978   *Der Bärenhäuter (The Man with the Bear Skin)*. Juv Op (with Bernd Wolff; based on Grimm). Pr 1978 Halberstadt.

1979   *Die feuerrote Blume (The Fiery Red Flower)*. Juv Mus. Pr 1980 Döbeln.

1983   *Komödianten‹welt› (‹The World of› Actors)*. Mus (with Bernd Wolff). Pr 1984 Halberstadt.

AUTENGRUBER, Ewald

1967   *Die Kinder des Kapitän Grant (Captain Grant's Children)*. Juv (with Andreas Rose; based on Jules Verne). Pr 1968 Th. d. jg. Garde, Halle.

BAETZ, Christian   see Friedrich WOLF

BAGDAHN, Alfred
>Das oberste Gesetz (The Highest Law). Dr. Pr 1955 Neustrelitz.

BAHR, Peter
1977   >Befragung Anna O. (Interrogation Anna O.). Dr (with Werner Buhss; based on TV play by Gerhard Stuchlik and Klaus Poche). Pr 1978 Rudolstadt.

BAIERL, Helmut (Johannes)
23 Dec 1926 Rumburg, Czechoslovakia –
After 1945,   farm worker; 49-51 studied Slavic languages in Halle;   51-55 Russian teacher in Köthen and Greifswald; 55-57 I.Lit Lpzg, then editor Lpzg; 59-67 dramaturg BE.   Member AdK since 1969, 70-74 Secretary for Literature and Language; 1961 and 70   National Prize of the GDR, 70 Erich Weinert Medal, 75 FDGB Prize,   76 Lessing Prize, 79 Goethe Prize Berlin,   80 Johannes Becher Medal. Translator, also writes film scripts.
>Das Liebespaar von Kiang-nan (The Lovers of Kiang-Nan). Dr (based on Chinese folk play; tr Miautse Yuan; M Siegfried Thiele). Lpzg: Hofmeister, 1958.
1952   >Ein Wegweiser (A Sign Post). On. Halle: Mitteldt. Verlag, 1952.
1952   >David der Glöckner (David, the Bell-Ringer). Com (based on Georg Kopanyi). Halle: Mitteldeutscher Verlag, 1953.
1953   >Die drei Irrtümer des Sebastian Fünfling (The Three Mistakes of Sebastian Fünfling). Com. Pr 1954. Halle: Mitteldt. Verlag, 1953. Lpzg: Hofmeister, 1959.
1954   >Gladiolen, ein Tintenfaß und eine bunte Kuh (Gladiolas, an Inkwell and a Colorful Cow). Three On: Gladiolen zum Geburtstag (Gladiolas for a Birthday); Mathematik und ein Tintenfaß (Mathematics and an Inkwell); Auf der Suche nach einer bunten Kuh (Searching for a Colorful Cow). Lpzg: Hofmeister, 1957. Henschel 1963.
1954   >Der Streit um J. S. Bach (The Quarrel about J. S. Bach). Com. Pr 1955. Lpzg: Hofmeister, 1955.
1955   >Eva und der Moralist. Com. Pr 1955.
1956   >Die Feststellung (The Statement). Dr. Pr 1957 Erfurt. Lpzg: Hofmeister, 1959. Stücke, Henschel 1968. Sozialistische Dramatik, Henschel 1968. Die ersten Schritte, Halle: Mitteldeutscher Verlag, 1985.
1956   >Tölpelhans und die gelehrten Brüder (Jack the Dunce and the Learned Brothers). Juv (based on Hans Christian Andersen; M C. E. Teichmann). Lpzg: Hofmeister, 1956.
1956   >Der rote Veit (Veit the Red). Juv. Lpzg: Hofmeister, 1957. Henschel 1962.

BAIERL (cont'd)

1961   *Frau Flinz (Mrs. Flinz)*. Com. Pr 1961 BE. Henschel 1964. *Stücke*, 1968.

1962   *Der dreizehnte (The Thirteenth)*. Dr (with Erwin Burghardt and Herbert Fischer). Pr 1962 Workers' Theater Treptow under title of "Geschichten vom dreizehnten". *Fünf Geschichten vom Dreizehnten*, Henschel 1963. *Stücke*, 1968. Rev 1970 as Schlag 13.

1963   *Kampf im Westen (Fight in the West)*. Dr (based on Vishnevsky).

1963-65 *Johanna von Döbeln (St. Joan of Döbeln)*. Com (with Manfred Wekwerth). Pr 1969 BE. *Sinn & Form* 1966/5 (scenes). *Stücke*, 1968. Rev 1975 as Die Abenteuer der Johanna von Döbeln.

1965   *Purpurstaub (Purple Dust)*. Com (with Hans-Georg Simmgen; tr from Sean O'Casey). Pr 1966 BE.

1966   *Mysterium buffo*. Dr (based on Vladimir Mayakovsky). Pr 1976 VB. *Sinn & Form* 1966/2 (1st act, "Der Kyffhäuser").

1967   *Der Stern wird rot (The Star Turns Red)*. Dr (tr from Sean O'Casey). Pr 1968 MG.

1969   *Der lange Weg zu Lenin (The Long Road to Lenin)*. Dr (based on film, "Unterwegs zu Lenin"). Pr 1970 Rostock. Henschel 1971.

1970   *Schlag 13 (Stroke 13)*. Dr (rev of Der dreizehnte). Pr 1971 Lpzg. *TdZ* 1971/10.

1971   *Kikeriki (Cock-a-Doodle-Dandy)*. Com (with Hans-Georg Simmgen; tr from Sean O'Casey).

1973   *...stolz auf 18 Stunden (Proud for 18 Hours)*. Dr. Pr 1973 BE. *TdZ* 1974/9. Aufbau 1975.

1974   *Die Lachtaube (The Laughing Turtledove)*. Com. Pr 1974 BE. *Sinn & Form* 1976/3. *TdZ* 1976/5. Aufbau 1975 (with ...stolz auf 18 Stunden).

1974   *Das Eden Hotel*. On. Pr 1975 BE.

1975   *Der Sommerbürger (The Summer Citizen)*. Com. Pr 1976 BE. *Sinn und Form* 1976/3. *TdZ* 1976/5.

1975   *Die Abenteuer der Johanna von Döbeln (The Adventures of St. Joan of Döbeln)*. Com (rev of Johanna von Döbeln.) Pr 1976 MG.

1978   *Rückspiele (Return Games)*. Com. Pr 1979 TiP.

1979   *Kirschenpflücken (Cherrypicking)*. Com. Pr 1979 Dsdn planned, cancelled. *TdZ* 1980/2.

1981   *Leo und Rosa*. Dr (with Karin Freiberg). Pr 1982 TiP. *NdL* 1982/5.

1983   *Ihr seid ein Grünhorn, Sir! (You Are a Greenhorn, Sir!)*. Juv (based on Karl May, "Winnetou"). Pr 1984 Th. d. Freundschaft, Berlin.

1983   *Die Erdenfahrt des Dr. Faust (The Earthly Journey of Dr. Faust)*. Pp. Pr 1984 Pp.Th., Berlin. *TdZ* 1984/4.

1983   *Der Vogtländer (The Man from Vogtland)*. Dr. Pr 1984 Gera.

   Die zweite Hochzeit (The Second Wedding). Dr (based on Yevgenyi Gabrilovitch).

BANKEL, Walter
Dramaturg Lpzg.
Aufführung verboten (Performance Prohibited). Dr. Pr
1951 Erfurt.

BARCKHAUSEN, Elfriede see Elfriede BRÜNING

BARTHEL, Kurt see KUBA

BARTSCH, Kurt
10 July 1937 Berlin –
Left school in 1954, worked in various jobs (coffin salesman,
stock clerk, office worker, publisher's assistant); 64-65 I.
Lit Lpzg; since 80 in West Berlin. Illustrator, writes prose
and poetry.
1969   *Orpheus in der Unterwelt (Orpheus in the Underworld).*
     Opt Lib (M Reiner Bredemeyer). Pr 1970 VB.
1973   *Der Bauch (The Belly).* Mus Lib. Pr 1974 VB (Part of
     program under collective title "Spektakel 2"). *TdZ*
     1977/6. *Der Bauch und andere Songspiele*, Aufbau 1977.
1976   *Die Goldgräber (The Gold Prospectors).* On. Pr 1976
     Schwerin. *TdZ* 1977/6. *Der Bauch...*, 1977.
1977   *Der Strick (The Rope).* On. Pr 1978 Budapest. *Der*
     Bauch..., 1977.
1977   *Warten auf Brecht (Waiting for Brecht).* Com.
1978   *Die Vögel (The Birds).* Com (based on Aristophanes).
1982   *Die Acharner oder Der private Frieden (The Acharnae*
     or A Private Peace). Com (based on Aristophanes). Pr
     1982 Schwerin.
     Geschichte eines Pferdes (The Story of a Horse). Dr
     (based on Leo Tolstoy and Mark Rosovsky; tr Thomas
     Reschke).

BAUER, Andreas
6 June 1906 Marienwerde –
Former Deputy Manager, Km.Op. Translator, writes poetry, libretti, children's books.
1956   *Sterne, Geld und Vagabunden (Stars, Money, and Vaga-*
     bonds). Mus Lib (with Erich Geiger; M Herbert Kawan).
1957   *Sensation in London.* Mus Lib (based on Mark Twain,
     "The Million Pound Banknote"; M Herbert Kawan). Pr
     1957 Rostock.
     Die Abenteuer der Mona Lisa (Mona Lisa's Adventures).
     Mus Lib (M Herbert Kawan).
     Die Witwe von Valencia (The Widow from Valencia).
     Com.
     Techtelmechtel (Hanky-Panky). Com.
     Frl. Reisebüro (Miss Travel Agency). Com.
     Die kluge Prinzessin (The Clever Princess). Juv.
     Die Prinzessin mit dem goldenen Stern (The Princess
     with the Golden Star). Juv.

BAUER, Friedhold
13 Apr 1934 Schweikershain -
1948-51 music school, then worked in furniture factory; after high school graduation, two years Th.HS Lpzg; 58-60 asst. dramaturg and director, Brandenburg; 61-66 editor, Henschelverlag. Lives in Berlin.

1966   *Baran ‹und die Leute im Dorf› (Baran ‹and the Village People›)*. Dr. Pr 1967 DT. *TdZ* 1966/24. Henschel 1968.
    Baran in Reinsdorf. Dr (different version of above?) Pr 1967 Erfurt.
1967   *König von Moskau (King of Moscow)*. Dr (based on Leonid Shukovitsky, "Der Ritt auf dem Delphin").
1968   *Der Schneeball (The Snowball)*. Dr (based on Vera A. Lyubimova). Pr 1968 Th. d. Freundschaft, Berlin.
1971   *Das Idol von Mordassow (The Idol of Mordassov)*. Com (based on Dostoyevsky, "Onkelchens Traum"). Pr 1972 Meiningen.

BAUER, Werner
12 Apr 1925 Reichenbach -
After high school, served in Army till 1945; 45-46 worked as carpenter; 46-56 teacher; 56-59 I. Lit Lpzg; 59-62 Instructor for German and Social Science. Writes children's books and chldren's radio plays.

1960   *Blast das Feuer an (Blow on the Fire)*. Dr (with Helmut Preißler).
1963   *Sind wir das? (Is That Us?)*. Five On: *Die Erkenntnis (The Knowledge)*; *Der Verbesserungsvorschlag (The Suggestion)*; *Die Kündigung (The Notice)*; *Weiberlist (Feminine Wiles)*; *Die Probe (The Rehearsal)*. Pr 1964.
1964   *Immer obenauf (Always on Top)*. Three On: Title play; *Kälberserenade (Calves' Serenade)*; *Wissen oder besser wissen (To Know or to Know Better)*. Pr 1965.

BAUMGART, Peter
Member, pantomime ensemble, DT.

1982   *Die Höllenfahrt des Doktor Faust (Doctor Faust's Descent into Hell)*. Pant (with Burkhart Seidemann). Pr 1962 DT.
1984   *Ver-rückt-wärts (Backward)*. Pant. Pr 1984 DT.

BECHER, Johannes R(obert)
22 May 1891 Berlin - 11 Oct 1958 Berlin
Studied medicine, philology, and philosophy; since 1912, contributor to journal *Die Aktion*; 13 editor of *Neue Kunst*; 33 emigration to USSR via Austria, Czechoslovakia, Switzerland, France; till 45 editor of anti-fascist journal *Internationale Literatur*; 45 return to Berlin, co-founder of Aufbau Verlag; 54 Minister for Culture. 1949 and 50 National Prize; 51 Dr. h.c. Humboldt Univ., Berlin, 51 Honorary Senator Univ. Jena, 52 Lenin Peace Prize, 53-56 President AdK. Wrote prose, poetry, essays.

1918   *Ikaros*. Dr. *Einakter und kleine Dramen*, Stuttgart: Reclam, 1968. *Gesammelte Werke*, vol. 8, Aufbau 1971.

BECHER (cont'd)
1918   *Hans im Glück (Lucky Jack)*. Dr.
1919   *Arbeiter, Bauern und Soldaten (Workers, Peasants, and
        Soldiers)*. Dr (rev 1924). Fkft/M: Taifun, 1924. *Ge-
        sammelte Werke*, vol. 8, 1971.
1931   *Der große Plan (The Great Plan)*. Dr. Vienna/Berlin:
        Agis, 1931. *Auswahl in 6 Bänden*, vol. 3, Aufbau 1971.
        Rev 1932.
1932   *Der große Plan und seine Feinde (The Great Plan and
        Its Enemies)*. Dr (with H. W. Hillers). Pr 1932 Jg.
        Volksbühne, Berlin. *Gesammelte Werke*, vol. 8, 1971.
1941   *Die Schlacht um Moskau (The Battle for Moscow)*. Dr.
        Pr 1942 Mexico. Rev 1945 as Winterschlacht. *Gesam-
        melte Werke*, vol. 8, 1971.
1942   *Das Führerbild (The Picture of the Führer)*. Dr. Mu-
        nich: Kurt Desch, 1946. Rev 1953 as Der Weg nach Füs-
        sen.
1945   *Winterschlacht (Winter Battle)*. Dr (rev of Die
        Schlacht um Moskau; M Hanns Eisler). Pr 1952 Prague.
        Aufbau 1953. Reclam 1960. *Werke in 3 Bänden*, vol. 2,
        Aufbau 1970. *Gesammelte Werke*, vol. 8, 1971. Rev
        1964 as Op, Die Passion des Johannes Hörder (M Jean
        Kurt Forest). Pr 1965 Stralsund.
1953   *Der Weg nach Füssen (The Road to Füssen)*. Dr (rev of
        Das Führerbild; M Paul Dessau). Pr 1956 MG. *Sinn und
        Form* 1953/1 (scenes). Berlin: Rütten & Loening, 1953.
        Gesammelte Werke, vol. 8, 1971.

BECK, Fritz see Fritz ERPENBECK

BECK, Rolf
1971   *Heinrich Heine: Dichter unbekannt (Heinrich Heine: Au-
        thor Unknown)*. Dr (with Claus Bremer). Pr 1972 Ro-
        stock.

BECKERT, Dieter
1980   *Kasper und die Farben (Punch and the Colors)*. Pp
        (with Peter Beckert). Pr 1981 Dsdn.

BEHLING, Heinz   see Heinz KAHLOW

BEJACH, Peter
20 April 1916 Berlin –
Actor, then director Dsdn, Neustrelitz, VB, Met. Writes for
radio and film.
1940   *Teuflische Wünsche (Devilish Wishes)*. Com.
1946   *Es war... (There was...)*. Dr.
1947   *Wetten, daß... (I'll Bet That...)*. Com.
        Man sollte nicht schwindeln (You Shouldn't Cheat).
        Mus Lib (M Modest Tabatchnikov).
        Träume vom Glück (Dreams of Happiness). Mus Lib.
1950   *Treffpunkt Herz (Meeting Place: The Heart)*. Mus Lib
        (M Herbert Kawan). Pr 1951 Met.

BEJACH (cont'd)

1952 *Ferien am Schneeberg (Vacation on Snow Mountain).* Mus Lib (M Herbert Kawan). Pr 1953 Rostock.

1953 *Jedes Jahr im Mai (Every Year in May).* Mus Lib (M Herbert Kawan). Pr 1954 Met.

1954 *Eine unmögliche Frau (An Impossible Woman).* Mus Lib (M Guido Masanetz). Pr 1954 Rostock.

1956 *Der Kuß der Juanita (Juanita's Kiss).* Mus Lib (based on Yevgenyi Shatunovsky; M Yuri Milyutin). Pr 1957 Moscow (in Russian); Gm Pr 1958 Dsdn.
Laßt mich doch singen (Let Me Sing). Opt Lib (M Gherase Dendrino).

1970 *Rotkäppchen von Grünau (Little Red Riding Hood of Grünau).* Mus Lib (M Siegfried Schäfer). Pr 1971 Meiningen.

1982 *‹Meine Geschichte mit› Aniko (‹My Story with› Aniko).* Mus Lib (M Manfred Grafe). Pr 1983 Erfurt.

BENDEY, Herbert

1952 *Aschenbrödel (Cinderella).* Juv (with Anna Süß and Susanne Dancker; based on Grimm). Pr 1952 Th. am Schiffbauerdamm, Berlin. Berlin: Jg. Welt, 1952.

BENECKE, Heinz-Martin

1979 *Der Soldat und das Feuerzeug (The Soldier and the Tinderbox).* Juv Mus Lib (based on Hans Christian Andersen; M Thomas Bürkholz). Pr 1979 Lpzg.

BERG, Alfred

1960 *Servus Peter (Hello Peter).* Mus Lib (with Helmut Bez and Jürgen Degenhardt; M Gerd Natschinski). Pr 1961 KMSt.

BERG, Jochen

1948 Bleicherode –

Worked as mechanic and male nurse. 1969-71 studied at Drama School Berlin; then worked as teamster, prop man. 1974 author's contract with DT. Writes prose, verse, film scripts.

1971 *Schwierigkeiten beim Hören von Musik (Difficulties With Hearing Music).* On.

1971 *Ein Theater wird vorgestellt (A Theater Is Introduced).* On.

1972 *Dave oder Warum rennst du gegen die Wand wenn die Tür offen ist? (Dave or Why Do You Run into the Wall When the Door Is Open?).* Com. Pr 1972 DT planned, cancelled. Reading 1978 Schwerin.

1973 *Wechsel (Change).* Dr.

1974 *Die Axt (The Axe).* Dr.

1975 *Strephart.* Dr.

1977 *Im Taurerland (In the Land of the Taurians).* Dr. Pr 1978 DT planned, cancelled. *TdZ* 1978/5. Rev 1982 as Iphigeneia.

1980 *Die Phoenizierinnen des Euripides (The Phoenician Women of Euripides).* Dr. Pr 1981 Stuttgart.

BERG (cont'd)

1981 *Orestes.* Dr. Pr 1982 Stuttgart.

1981 *Niobe.* Dr. Pr 1983 Stuttgart.

1982 *Iphigeneia.* Dr (rev of Im Taurerland). Pr 1982 Stuttgart.

1982 *Klytemnestra.* Dr. Reading 1982 Lpzg; Pr 1983 Stuttgart.

1983 *Niobe am Sipylos (Niobe on the Sipylos).* Dr. Pr 1984
Stuttgart.

BERGNER, Edith (nee Müller; also known as Edith Müller-Beeck)
19 Apr 1917 Pretzsch –
Studied agriculture, then nursing; worked as laboratory asst.
in Halle; after 1945 reporter in Hamburg, then moved to GDR.
1960 State Prize, 61, 64 & 66 FDGB Prize, 66 & 67 Prize for
Children's Radio Plays, 70 & 72 Halle Art Prize. Writes novels, children's books, radio plays.

1954 *Schwielenhans (Calloused Jack).* Juv.

1955 *Das Natternkrönlein (The Serpent's Crown).* Juv Mus
Lib (M Werner Hübschmann). Lpzg: Hofmeister, 1956.

1955 *Die goldene Gans (The Golden Goose).* Juv Mus Lib
(based on Grimm; M Werner Hübschmann). Lpzg: Hofmeister, 1956.

1956 *Katze und Maus in Gesellschaft (Cat and Mouse in So-
ciety).* Juv. Märchenth., Lpzg: Hofmeister, 1956.

1956 *König Drosselbart (King Thrushbeard).* Juv Mus Lib
(based on Grimm; M Werner Hübschmann). Lpzg: Hofmeister, 1956. *Kinderbühne,* Lpzg: Hofmeister, 1961.

1957 *Kennen Sie Pieferding? (Do You Know Pieferding?).*
Pp. *Puppenspiel,* Lpzg: Hofmeister, 1957.

1958 *Das Spiel von Irgendwer (The Play of Anyone).* Juv.
Lpzg: Hofmeister, 1958.

1962 *Das singende Pferdchen (The Singing Pony).* Juv Op Lib

1963 *..und wachsen wird der junge Wind (And the Young Wind
Will Grow).* Dr. Pr 1963 Halle.
Das tapfere Schneiderlein (The Brave Little Tailor).
Pp (with Joachim Seidel; based on Grimm).
Dornröschen (Sleeping Beauty). Pp (based on Grimm).

BERNHARDY, Werner (Pseud. for Werner TUMMELEY)
27 June 1918 Berlin –
After school, took evening courses in textile arts, worked as
costume designer, illustrator, and trick film animator. 1962,
63, 65 & 71 Silver Laurel for TV, 69 Golden Laurel, 71 Heinrich Greif Prize. Writes children's books, film, radio, and
TV scripts.

1947 ‹*Die Prinzessin und› Der Schweinehirt (‹The Princess
and› The Swineherd).* Juv(with Marja Steiner-Brühl;
based on Hans Christian Andersen). Pr 1949 Berlin.

1948 *Das tapfere Schneiderlein (The Brave Little Tailor).*
Juv (based on Grimm). Pr 1948 BE.

1950 *Was machen wir mit dem Kaiser? (What Shall We Do with
the Emperor?).* Juv. Pr 1951 Th. d. jg. Welt, Lpzg.

1951 *Die Schauerbude (The House of Thrills).* Juv.

1952 *Ein Polterabend (Shivaree).* Com. Pr 1952 DT.

BERTHOLD, Siegfried
Served as a career officer in National People's Army.
1963   *Postengang (Guard Duty)*. Dr. Pr 1964 Quedlinburg.
1967   *Hammer oder Amboß (Hammer or Anvil)*. Dr. Pr 1968 Quedlinburg.
1973   *Der Zwillingssoldat (The Twin Soldier)*. Juv. Pr 19-73 Halle.

BESELER, Horst
29 May 1925 Berlin –
Service in WW II, then American POW; 1945-47 film technician; 47-52 journalist and editor, now lives near Güstrow. 1957 Fontane Prize, 66 Erich Weinert Medal, 73 Fritz Reuter Prize, 82 National Prize. Writes prose, film scripts, children's books.
1951   *Die Moorbande (The Moor Gang)*. Juv (based on novel). Pr 1953 Th. d. Freundschaft, Berlin. Berlin: Kinderbuchverlag, 1952.

BESKE, Peter
1961   *Der Grenzgänger (The Border Crosser)*. Dr. Pr 1962 Workers' Theater Treptow.

BEYGANG, Hans-Joachim
1965   *Karl Stülpner*. Dr. Pr 1966 Annaberg.
1979   *Dornröschen (Sleeping Beauty)*. Juv (based on Grimm). Pr 1979 Quedlinburg.

BEZ, Helmut
28 Aug 1930 Sondershausen –
After high school, 1949-51 Drama School Erfurt; 51-66 actor in various theaters, film and TV; also director; since 66, lives in Berlin. 1977 GDR Radio Play Prize. Writes poetry, prose, radio and TV scripts.
1959   *Messeschlager Gisela (Gisela, the Hit of the Fair)*. Mus Lib (with Jürgen Degenhardt; M Gerd Natschinski). Pr 1960 Met.
1960   *Servus Peter (Hello Peter)*. Mus Lib (with Alfred Berg and Jürgen Degenhardt; M Gerd Natschinski). Pr 1961 KMSt.
1964   *Mein Freund Bunbury (My Friend Bunbury)*. Mus Lib (with Jürgen Degenhardt; based on Oscar Wilde, "The Importance of Being Earnest"; M Gerd Natschinski). Pr 1964 Met.
1964   *Der Mann, der Dr. Watson war (The Man Who Was Dr. Watson)*. Mus Lib (with Jürgen Degenhardt; based on Arthur Conan Doyle).
1965   *Urlaub mit Engel (Vacation with Angel)*. Mus Lib (with Jürgen Degenhardt).
1966   *Sie sind zauberhaft, Madame (You Are Enchanting, Madam)*. Mus Lib (with Jürgen Degenhardt).

BEZ (cont'd)

1967　*Kleinstadtgeschichten (Small Town Tales)*. Mus Lib (with Jürgen Degenhardt; based on Kotzebue, "Die deutschen Kleinstädter"). Pr 1967 Erfurt.

1967　*Froufrou*. Mus Lib (with Jürgen Degenhardt). Pr 1967 Erfurt.

1968　*Calamity Jane*. Mus Lib (with Jürgen Degenhardt).

1969　*Bretter, die die Welt bedeuten (The Stage Is the World)*. Mus Lib (with Jürgen Degenhardt; based on Schönthau "Der Raub der Sabinerinnen"; M Gerhard Kneifel). Pr 1970 Met.

1971　*Die Wette des Mr. Fogg (Mr. Fogg's Wager)*. Mus Lib (with Jürgen Degenhardt; based on Jules Verne, "Around the World in 80 Days"). Pr 1971 Lpzg.

1973　*Terzett (Trio)*. Mus Lib (with Jürgen Degenhardt; M Gerd Natschinski). Pr 1974 Lpzg.

1975　*Keep Smiling*. Mus Lib (with Jürgen Degenhardt; M Harry Sander). Pr 1976 Lpzg.

1976　*Casanova*. Mus Lib (with Jürgen Degenhardt; M Gerd Natschinski). Pr 1976 Met.

1976　*Zwiesprache halten (Holding a Conversation)*. On (based on radio play). Pr 1977 Mgdbg.

1977　*Jutta oder Die Kinder von Damutz (Jutta or The Children of Damutz)*. Dr (based on radio play). Pr 1978 Halle. *TdZ* 1978/10.

1977　*Liebhabereien (Flirtations)*. Com (with Jürgen Degenhardt). Pr 1978 Parchim.

1977　*Prinz von Preußen (Prince of Prussia)*. Mus Lib (with Jürgen Degenhardt; M Dieter Brand). Pr 1978 Erfurt.

1978　*Dobberkau ist da (Dobberkau is Here)*. Com. Pr 1978 Gera.

1978　*Nachruf (Obituary)*. On (based on radio play, "Spätvorstellung"). Pr 1985 Brandenburg.

1979　*Warmer Regen (Warm Rain)*. Com. Pr 1979 Zwickau. *TdZ* 1979/11.

1981　*Die verkehrte Welt (The Topsy-Turvy World)*. Com (based on Ludwig Tieck). Pr 1984 Greifswald. *TdZ* 1982/1.

BIELER, Manfred
3 July 1934 Zerbst –
Attended school in Anhalt, As (Czechoslovakia), Dessau; 52-56 studied German literature Humboldt Univ., Berlin; 56-60 worked for Deutscher Schriftstellerverband (*GDR Authors' Assoc.*); 1960 went to Canada as sailor on fishing vessel; 65 Prague, since 68 FRG; now lives in Munich. Writes prose, TV, radio and film scripts, parodies.

1962　*Die linke Wand (The Left Wall)*. Dr (based on radio play). Pr 1964 Mgdbg. *NdL* 1962/7. Radio version in *Drei Rosen aus Papier*, Reclam 1967.

1963　*Nachtwache (Night Watch)*. Dr (based on radio play). Pr 1964 VB. *NdL* 1963/8. *TdZ* 1964/11. Radio version in *Drei Rosen aus Papier*, 1967.

1968　*ZAZA*. Dr. Pr 1969 Tübingen.

BIGOTT, Gabriele
Dramaturg TiP.
1979   *Kippenberg.* Dr (based on novel by Dieter Noll). Pr
        1980 TiP. *TdZ* 1980/9.
1984   *Der Nullmensch (The Nonentity).* On. Pr 1984 TiP (part
        of program under collective title of "Männermonolo-
        ge").
1985   *Wie ein Theaterstück entsteht (How a Play Originates)*
        Com (based on Karel Capek). Pr 1985 TiP.

BILLERBECK-GENTZ, Fred   see Friedrich GENTZ

BILLING, Gerd
29 Dec 1932 Leipzig –
Studied journalism in Lpzg, received diploma 1954. Editor of
student journal *"Forum"'* till 63, then contributor to journal
"Weltbühne." Lives in Berlin, writes short stories, film and
TV scripts.
1968   *Das Uhrenständchen (The Little Clock Pedestal).* Com.
        Pr 1969 Rostock.
1971   *Vendetta.* Dr. Pr 1972 Rostock.
1972   *Der große Ferienscheck (The Big Vacation Check).* Com.
        Pr 1972 Rostock.

BISCHOFF, Karl-Heinrich ‹Karl-Heinz)   (Pseud. Veit BÜRKLE)
6 June 1900 Laichingen – ?
Book dealer and editor. Wrote prose.
1964   *Unter der Egge (Beneath the Harrow).* Dr.
1965   *Die gestohlene Weihnachtsuhr (The Stolen Christmas
        Clock).* Com. Pr 1965 Putbus.
1968   *Montague und Capulet.* Mus Lib (based on Shakespeare,
        "Romeo and Juliet"). Pr 1969 Stralsund.

BLACH, Erich
18 Apr 1907 Güstrow – 1972
Member Socialist youth group; later KPD, arrested 1933; medical orderly in WW II, Russian POW; after return home, studied
I.Lit Lpzg. 1964 Juvenile Book Prize, 71 First Prize for Contemporary Drama. Wrote poetry, prose.
1952   *Der Mensch lebt nicht vom Brot allein (Man Does Not
        Live by Bread Alone).* Dr. Pr 1953 Rostock.
1955   *Die Sturmflut (The Tidal Wave).* Dr. Pr 1955 MG.
1971   *Die Bernsteinbrigade (The Amber Brigade).* Com. Pr
        1972 Th. d. Freundschaft, Berlin.

BLANKENFELD, Martin   (Pseud. F. Willy SEYLER)
1959   *Tatort Warenhaus (Department Store Crime).* Dr (with
        Jan Michell, pseud. for Erich Geiger). Pr 1960 Dsdn.

BLANKENSTEIN, Walter
16 Dec 1929 Königsberg (now Kaliningrad, USSR) –
1948-51 studied singing; 48-53 asst stage director, KMSt; 53-
77 stage director Fkft/O, Plauen, Görlitz; now in Berlin.
1963   *Unberufen toi, toi, toi (Touch Wood!).* Com. Pr 1964
        Plauen.

BLASS, Helmut
1980   *Grabgeflüster ‹Gruftgeflüster› (Whispering in the Grave)*. Mus Lib (based on Lessing, "Die Matrone von Ephesus"). 1981 Wittenberg.
Na, diese Musketiere (Well, Those Musketeers). Mus Lib (M F. Couperin, A. Scarlatti, J. S. Bach)

BLUME, Horst
2 June 1920 Magdeburg –
1961   *Die Bewährung (The Probation)*. Dr. Pr 1963 Prenzlau.
1963   *Licht auf den Feldern (Light on the Fields)*. Dr (based on TV play).

BOBROWSKI, Johannes
9 Apr 1917 Tilsit – 2 Nov 1965 Berlin
Moved to Königsberg 1928, after high school studied art history; served in Army in WW II, then Russian POW; returned 49, editor for several publishers. 1962 Group 47 Prize, 65 Heinrich Mann Prize. Wrote prose, poetry.
       Das Tierhäuschen (The Animal Cottage). Juv (based on Samuil Marshak).
1972   *Lewins Mühle (Levin's Mill)*. Op Lib (based on novel, dramatized by Ingo Zimmermann; M Udo Zimmermann). Pr 1973 Dsdn. *TdZ* 1972/5. Lpzg: Dt. Verlag für Musik, 1973.
1974   *Litauische Claviere (Lithuanian Pianos)*. Op Lib (based on 1965 novel, dramatized by Gerhard Wolf; M Rainer Kunad). Pr 1976 Dsdn. *TdZ* 1975/9. Henschel 1975.

BODEIT, Gerhard
18 Jan 1921 Rostock –
1945 began studying German and art history in Kiel, Rostock, and Halle; then author's contract with Th. d. jg. Generation, Dsdn and Th. d. jg. Welt, Lpzg. 1963 and 64 Silver Laurel of GDR TV. Writes radio and TV scripts.
1947   *Brüderchen und Schwesterchen (Little Brother and Little Sister)*. Juv. Pr 1947 Dsdn.
1952   *Hänsel und Gretel*. Juv (based on Grimm).   Pr 1953 Lpzg.
1953   *Die Lichter von Rustawi (The Lights of Rustavy)*. Dr (based on Dadyany and Yevlakhov). Halle: Mitteldt. Verlag, 1953.
1956   *Tischlein deck dich (The Table, the Ass, and the Stick)*. Juv (based on Grimm). Pr 1956 Lpzg.
1963   *Wohin du gehörst (Where You Belong)*. Dr. Henschel 1963.
1964   *Zwei Sonnen über dem Feld (Two Suns Over the Field)*. Dr. Pr 1964.

BÖHME, Susanne
1977   *Eine Ferienfahrt ist fein (A Vacation Trip is Fine)*. Pp. Pr 1977 Mgdbg.

BOHNE, Monika

1979	*Vom Katerchen, das Stiefel trug (Puss in Boots)*. Pp. Pr 1979 Erfurt.
1980	*Die Prinzessin aus dem Birkenschloß (The Princess of the Birch Castle)*. Pp (based on Estonian fairy tale). Pr 1980 Erfurt.
	Spielwiese (Playground). Pp.
1984	*Don Quijote*. Pp (based on Cervantes). Pr 1984 Erfurt.
1985	*Schneeweißchen und Rosenrot (Snow-White and Rose-Red)* Pp (based on Grimm). Pr 1985 Erfurt.

BONHOFF, Otto
21 Feb 1931 Leipzig –
Attended Theater School Lpzg; also worked as journalist and editor. Lives in Selchow, writes prose, radio and TV scripts.

1972	*Besuch aus dem Nebel (A Visit Out of the Fog)*. Juv. Pr 1973 Th. d. Freundschaft, Berlin.

BONN, Karl Heinrich
1927 Thüringen –
After high school, studied law in Erlangen; 1956 moved to GDR, became teacher in Waltershausen.

1958	*Studenten (Students)*. Dr. Pr 1959 VB.
1963	*Ihre große Liebe (Her Great Love)*. Dr. Pr 1963 Zwickau.
1967	*Das letzte Wochenende (The Last Weekend)*. Dr (based on radio play). Pr 1968 Zwickau.
	Ein hoffnungsloser Fall (A Hopeless Case). Dr.

BORDE-KLEIN, Ingeborg (nee Hoyer; also uses name Inge BORDE)
18 Mar 1917 Berlin-Charlottenburg –
After high school in Hamburg and Bremen, studied music in Berlin; 1938 music teacher; after 45 puppeteer; president of lay puppet theater organization, vice-president of *Union Internationale des Marionettes*. 1955 Children's Literature Prize, 71 Alex Wedding Medal, 74 FDGB Prize, 74 and 79 Johannes Becher Medal.

1954	*Weihnachten im Wald (Christmas in the Forest)*. Juv. Lpzg: Hofmeister, 1954.
1954	*Die vier Jahreszeiten (The Four Seasons)*. Pp. *Puppenspiel*, Lpzg: Hofmeister, 1955.
1954	*Der Wettlauf (The Race)*. Pp (based on Grimm). *Puppenspiel*, 1955.
1956	*Das goldene Korn (The Golden Grain)*. Pp.
1957	*Die Schneekönigin (The Snow Queen)*. Pp (based on Hans Christian Andersen).
1958	*Vom Mäuschen, Vögelchen und der Bratwurst (The Little Mouse, the Little Bird, and the Sausage)*. Pp. Lpzg: Hofmeister, 1959.
1958	*Reingefallen (Gotcha!)*. Pp. Lpzg: Hofmeister, 1959.
1959	*Trombis Erdenreise (Trombi's Earth Journey)*. Juv. Henschel 1963.

BORDE-KLEIN (cont'd)

1959   *Wie Klauke die vier besiegt (How Klauke Conquers All Four)*. Pp. Lpzg: Hofmeister, 1960.

1960   *Frau Holle (Mother Holle)*. Juv (based on Grimm).

1961   *Wer fängt Hugo? (Who Catches Hugo?)*. Pp. Lpzg: Hofmeister, 1962.

1962   *Reisefieber (Travel Fever)*. Juv. Pr 1963.

1964   *Familie Morgenwind (The Morning Wind Family)*. Pp. Puppentheater, Henschel 1964.

1966   *Herr Märchen spielt Märchen (Mr. Fairy Tale Plays Fairy Tales)*. Juv (with B. Svaton). Pr 1966.

1973   *Sprengstoff für Santa Ines (Dynamite for Santa Inez)*. Mus Lib (with Karl Adolf; based on novel by Eduard Klein; M Guido Masanetz). Pr 1973 Wittenberg.

1977   *Tuppi Schleife und die drei Grobiane (Tuppi Schleife and the Three Ruffians)*. Pp (based on children's book by Inge Feustel). Pr 1978 Dessau.

1978   *Das Geschenk des Totems (The Totem's Gift)*. Pp. Pr 1978 Mgdbg.

1981   *Der freundliche Drache (The Friendly Dragon)*. Pp. Pr 1981 Berlin.

BORMANN, Arnold
20 Oct 1894 Berlin - ?
Engineer, editor, writer.

1946   *Biedermänner (Solid Citizens)*. Com.

1947   *Mein Freund, meine Frau (My Friend, My Wife)*. Com.

1947   *Maskerade von Liebe (Masquerade of Love)*. Mus Lib (M Ernst Peter Hoyer). Pr 1955 Met.

1947   *Liebe für Ingeborg (Love for Ingeborg)*. Com.

1947   *Es ist eine alte Geschichte (It's an Old Story)*. Dr.

1948   *Die Wünschelrute (The Divining Rod)*. Dr.

1948   *Der Chargierkran (The Loading Crane)*. Dr. Potsdam: Märkische Verlagsgesellschaft, 1949.

1949   *Der kluge Achmed (Clever Ahmed)*. Juv. Laienspiele, Halle: Mitteldt. Verlag, 1949.

1949   *Der goldene Kessel (The Golden Kettle)*. Juv. Laienspiele, 1949.

1956   *Ja, diese Biedermänner (Ah, These Solid Citizens)*. Com (rev of 1946?).

BOROWSKI, S.A.

1969   *Die steinerne Blume (The Stone Flower)*. Juv. Pr 1970 Quedlinburg.

1972   *Dornröschen (Sleeping Beauty)*. Juv (based on Grimm). Pr 1972 Quedlinburg.

1982   *Schneeweißchen und Rosenrot (Snow-White and Rose-Red)*. Juv (based on Grimm). Pr 1983 Quedlinburg.

1983   *Das Geheimnis des Kupferbergs (The Secret of Copper Mountain)*. Juv. Pr 1984 Quedlinburg.

BORTFELDT, Kurt
30 Apr 1907 Hamburg – 9 June 1981 Berlin
After high school, became actor; 1940–41 and 44–45 served in
Army; 57–60 Instructor at Film HS Potsdam. 1954 Karlovy Vary
Prize of Czechoslovakia, 63 & 64 Silver Laurel of GDR TV, 64
Arndt Medal. Wrote poetry, radio, TV and film scripts.

	Der verlorene Vater (The Missing Father). Com.
1935	*Kinder auf Zeit (Children on Credit).* Com. Pr 1936.
1936	*Sturz nach oben (Upward Fall).* Com. Pr 1937 Cottbus.
1936	*Zwillingskomödie (Comedy of Twins).* Com.
1937	*Trockenkursus (Dry Course).* Com. Pr 1938 Hamburg.
1942	*Dir zuliebe (For Your Sake).* Com (incidental M Mark Roland). Pr 1942.
1945	*Das leisere Leben (The Quieter Life).* Dr.
1946	*Der andere Don Quichote (The Other Don Quixote).* Dr.
1947	*Schießbudenfiguren (Shooting-Gallery Figures).* Dr. Pr 1949.
1948	*Südseemärchen (South Sea Fairy Tale).* Juv.
1949	*Prinzessin Rosinchen (Princess Raisinette).* Juv.
	Aschenputtel (Cinderella). Juv (based on Grimm).
1962	*Das ist Diebstahl (That's Theft).* Dr (based on novel by Marianne Bruns). *Laientheater*, Henschel 1963.
1967	*Variante B (Variation B).* Dr (based on Granin). Pr 1968.

BOSTROEM, Annemarie (first married name Annemarie Eisenlohr, second marriage Annemarie Hinze)
24 May 1922 Leipzig –
1940–44 studied literature and theater Univ Lpzg, Berlin, and
Vienna; 46–54 drama editor Aufbau Verlag. Writes poetry.

1948	*Die Kette fällt (The Chain Falls).* Dr. Pr 1948 Chemnitz (now KMSt). Lpzg: Rupert, 1949.
1957	*Die irdene Lampe (The Earthen Lamp).* Dr (based on B. Gargi). Pr 1958 Anklam.
	Das buntgescheckte Kalb (The Piebald Calf). Opt Lib (M Otto Vincze).

BÖTTCHER, Ilse   see Ilse NÜRNBERG

BÖTTCHER, Wolfgang
1909 –
Actor, stage director, writer; married to Ilse Nürnberg.

	Umzug ins Glück (Moving into Happiness). Mus Lib (M Milan Novak).
	Frühlingswalzer (Spring Waltz). Mus Lib (M Jenö Horvath).
	O die Mama (Oh That Mama). Mus Lib (based on Geza Baroti and Tomas Garai; M Zdenko Tamassy).
	Die Musterfrauen (The Model Wives). Mus Lib (M Istvan Sarközi).
1952	*Ehe eine Ehe eine Ehe wird (Before a Marriage Becomes a Marriage).* Mus Lib (with Ilse Nürnberg; M Benno Lipinski). Pr 1953 Lpzg.

BÖTTCHER (cont'd)

1954   *Zum Glück hat sie Pech (Luckily She's Unlucky)*. Mus Lib (with Ilse Nürnberg; M Conny Odd). Pr 1955 Rostock.

1956   *Der verlorene Schlaf (The Lost Sleep)*. Mus Lib (with Ilse Nürnberg; based on Friedrich Dietz; M Olaf Koch).

1958   *Don Juans Höllenfahrt (Don Juan's Descent into Hell)*. Mus Lib (with Ilse Nürnberg; M Conny Odd).

1959   *Der eingebildete Kranke (The Imaginary Invalid)*. Mus Lib (based on Moliere, "Le malade imaginaire"; M Helmut Heinze).

1960   *Der Diener zweier Herrn (The Servant of Two Masters)*. Mus Lib (with Fritz Wendel; based on Carlo Goldoni; M Joachim-Dietrich Link).

1961   *Hände hoch, Mr. Copper (Hands Up, Mr. Copper)*. Mus Lib (M Conny Odd). Pr 1962 Dsdn.

1963   *Zwei Schleier, drei Freier (Two Veils, Three Suitors)* Com (with Manfred Grafe). Pr 1963 Görlitz.

1964   *Die schöne Galathee (Beautiful Galathea)*. Mus Lib (based on Poly Henrion; M Franz von Suppe).

1966   *Irene und die Kapitäne (Irene and the Captains)*. Mus Lib (with Ilse Böttcher; M Conny Odd). Pr 1967 Dsdn. *TdZ* 1967/10.

1969   *Das Glas Wasser (The Glass of Water)*. Mus Lib (based on Eugene Scribe; M Horst Elsner). Pr 1970 Schwerin.

1969-70 *Von einem, der auszog, das Gruseln zu lernen (The Lad Who Set out to Learn Fright)*. Juv Op Lib (with Ilse Böttcher; based on Grimm; M Joachim-Dietrich Link). Pr 1970 Gera.

1971   *Wie die Wilden (Like Savages)*. Mus Lib (based on Sergey Mikhalkov; M Herbert Kawan). Pr 1971 Annaberg.

1971   *Frau Mohr hat ihre Schuldigkeit getan (Mrs. Mohr Has Done Her Duty)*. Mus Lib (with Ilse Böttcher; M Benno Lipinski). Pr 1972 Schwerin.

1977   *Die Schatzinsel (Treasure Island)*. Juv Op Lib (based on Robert Louis Stevenson; M Joachim-Dietrich Link). Pr 1978 Gera.

1977   *Lysistrata*. Mus Lib (M Paul Lincke). Pr 1978 Brandenburg.

1980   *Upstand in't Ollenheim (Revolt in the Old-Age Home)*. Com (written in Low German). Pr 1981 Schwerin.

1982   *Der Gast aus Paris (The Guest from Paris)*. Mus Lib (based on Ede Sziglieti, "Der Bart"; M Otto Vinczes). Pr 1983 Görlitz/Zittau.

BRANSTNER, Gerhard
25 May 1927 Blankenhain –
Served in WW II; 1945-47 POW France and Belgium; 49-56 studied philosophy in Jena, Berlin; then administrator and editor. Now lives in Berlin, writes prose, poetry, TV scripts.

1962   *Die Morgengabe (The Dowry)*. Op Lib (M Kurt Schwaen). Pr 1963 Fkft/O.

1964   *Die kleine Liebelei (The Little Love Affair)*. Lib.

1966   *Ein deutsches Schicksal (A German Fate)*. Lib.

BRANSTNER (cont'd)

     Des Jägers Wunderhorn (The Hunter's Magic Horn).
1976   *Die Kantine (The Canteen)*. Dr. Pr 1979 DT. Rostock: Hinstorff, 1977, 1981.
1977   *Der Himmel fällt aus den Wolken (Heaven Is Flabbergasted)*. Com (based on prose text). Pr 1984 Halle. Berlin: Der Morgen, 1977.
1983   *Du meine Tante (Oh, My Aunt)*. Com. Pr 1984 Halle.

BRASCH, Peter
1982   *Don Juan*. Dr. Reading 1982 Lpzg.

BRASCH, Thomas
1945 Westow, England –
Son of Jewish emigrants; returned GDR 1947; 56-60 Elite Cadet School of GDR Army; then worked as locksmith and printer; 64-65 studied journalism Univ Lpzg, expelled; 65-67 waiter, construction worker; 67-68 studied dramaturgy Film HS Potsdam; 68 arrested for distributing leaflets, sentenced to two years in prison; 71-72 worked in Brecht Archives; 76 moved to West Berlin; now lives in Zurich; film director. 1978 Ernst Reuter Prize, 1980 Frankfurt Literature Prize.

    Sie geht, sie geht nicht (She's Going, She's Not Going). Dr.
1970   *Das ‹beispielhafte› ‹Spiel vom› Leben und Tod des Peter Göring: Biografie eines glücklichen Bürgers (The ‹Exemplary› ‹Play about› Life and Death of Peter Göring: Biography of a Happy Citizen)*. Dr (with Lothar Trolle). Pr 1971, student production Berlin. Henschel 1971.
1974   *Der Schweinehirt (The Swineherd)*. Juv (based on Hans Christian Andersen).
1975   *Geschichten zum Erzählen (Stories to Be Told)*. Five On (based on Osvaldo Dragun): *Der Mann als Hund (Man as Dog)*, rev 1976 as Die argentinische Nacht; *Panchito und die Beulenpest (Panchito and the Bubonic Plague)*; *Das Zahngeschwür (The Abcessed Tooth)*; *Die Liebenden vom Tisch 10 (The Lovers from Table 10)*; *Der Fall des Professors Zorillo (The Case of Professor Zorillo)*. Pr 1976 VB.
1975   *Der Papiertiger (The Paper Tiger)*. Pr 1976 Austin, Texas. *Spec* 26, 1977. Suhrkamp 1977.
1976   *Die argentinische Nacht: Eine Hundetragödie (The Argentinian Night: A Dog's Tragedy)*. Dr (rev of Der Mann als Hund). Pr 1977 Tübingen. Fkft/M: Verlag der Autoren, 1977.
1976   *Hakims Geschichten (Hakim's Stories)*. Dr (based on Norberto Gavila). Pr 1976 Fkft/M. *Th.h.* 1978/8. Fkft/M: Verlag der Autoren, 1980.
1977   *Satyros oder Der vergötterte Waldteufel (Satyros or The Idolized Forest Sprite)*. Com (based on Goethe). Suhrkamp 1978.
1977   *Lovely Rita*. Dr. *Th.h.* 1977/2. *Spec* 28, 1978. Suhrkamp 1977.

BRASCH, Thomas (cont'd)

1977   *Rotter: Ein deutsches Märchen (Rotter: A German Fairy Tale)*. Dr. Pr 1977 Stuttgart. *Th.h.* 1977, special issue. Suhrkamp 1978. *Spec* 37, 1983.

1977-78 *Platonow*. Dr (based on Chekhov). Pr 1979 Freie Volksbühne, West Berlin. *Th.h.* 1979/2.

1978   *Herr Geiler (Mr. Geiler)*. Com (based on Goethe). *Satyros...*, 1978.

1978   *Lucie geh oder Das Unglück auf dem Theater (Lucy Go or The Misfortune in the Theater)*. Com. Pr 1979 Schillerth., West Berlin.

1979   *Lieber Georg: Ein Kunst-Eis-Läufer Drama aus dem Vorkrieg (Dear George: A Prewar Ice-Skater Drama)*. Dr. Pr 1980 Bochum. *Th.h.* 1980/2. *Spec* 30, 1979.

1979   *Bericht vom Sterben des Musikers Jack Tiergarten (Report of the Death of the Musician Jack Tiergarten)*. Dr.
Eulenspiegel. Com.
Pabst Urban VIII. (Pope Urban the Eighth). Dr.

1983   *Mercedes*. Dr. Pr 1983 Zürich. *TdZ* 1983/12. *Spec* 38, 1984.

BRAUN, Klaus Dieter

1970   *Des Kaisers neue Kleider (The Emperor's New Clothes)*. Juv (based on Hans Christian Andersen). Pr 1971 Quedlinburg.

1972   *Timur und sein Trupp (Timur and His Band)*. Juv. Pr 1973 Quedlinburg.

1973   *Aschenputtel (Cinderella)*. Juv (based on Grimm). Pr 1974 Quedlinburg.

BRAUN, Volker

7 May 1930 Dresden –

1957 printer; 58-59 construction worker; 59-60 machinist; 60-64 studied philosophy Lpzg; 65-66 dramaturgical asst. BE, 71-72 Lpzg, 72-77 DT, since 77 again BE. 1964 Erich Weinert Medal, 71 Heinrich Heine Prize, 80 Thomas Mann Prize. Writes prose, poetry.

1962-65 ‹Die Ballade vom› *Kipper Paul Bauch* (‹The Ballad of› *Dumper Paul Bauch*). Original title "Der totale Mensch" (*The Total Human Being*). Dr. *Forum* 1966/8. *Dt. Th. d. Gegenwart*, Suhrkamp 1967. Rev 1970-71 as Die Kipper.

1965   ‹Die› *Freunde* (‹The› *Friends*). Dr. Pr 1972 Karl Marx Univ, Lpzg. *Neue Stücke*, Henschel 1971.

1966   *Mink*. Fragment. Pr 1972 Lpzg.

1967-68 *Hans Faust*. Original title "Faust 3." Dr. Pr 1968 Weimar. Rev 1972 as Hinze und Kunze.

1969   *Lenins Tod (Lenin's Death)*. Dr. Pr 1970.

1969-78 *Schmitten (The Schmitt Woman)*. Dr. Pr 1982 Lpzg. *Th.h.* 1982/4. *TdZ* 1982/4. *Stücke 2*, Suhrkamp 1981. *Stücke*, Henschel 1983.

1970   *Arbeiter und Bauern (Workers and Peasants)*. Dr.

1970   *Gericht in Kronstadt (Judgment in Kronstadt)*. Dr.

BRAUN, Volker (cont'd)

1970–71   *Die Kipper   (The Dumpers)*. Dr (rev of Kipper Paul
Bauch). Pr 1972 Lpzg. *Sinn & Form* 1972/1. *Spec* 16,
1972. Aufbau 1972. *Stücke 1*, Suhrkamp 1975. *Drei
Stücke*, Henschel 1975. *Gedichte, Prosa, Stücke*, Halle: Mitteldt. Verlag, 1978. *Stücke*, 1983.

1972   *Hinze und Kunze*. Dr (rev of Hans Faust). Pr 1973
KMSt. *TdZ* 1973/3. *Spec* 19, 1973. *Drei Stücke*, 1975.
Stücke 1, 1975. *Stücke*, 1983.

1972–74 *Tinka*. Dr. Pr 1976 KMSt. *Drei Stücke*, 1975. *Stücke
1*, 1975. *Stücke*, 1983.

1975   *Guevara oder Der Sonnenstaat   (Guevara or The Sun
State)*. Dr. Pr 1976 Karl Marx Univ, Lpzg. *Th.h.* 19-
78/1. *Spec 27*, 1977. *Stücke 2*, 1981. *Stücke*, 1983.
Rev 1982 as Der Sonnenstaat.

1976–77 *Großer Frieden   (Great Peace)*. Dr. Pr 1979 BE. *TdZ*
1979/9. *Gedichte, Prosa, Stücke*, 1978. *Stücke 2*, 19-
81. *Stücke*, 1983. Engl. Pr 1983 Univ Essex, Engld.
(Tr Malcolm Griffith). Rev 1982 as Op (M Karl Otto
Treibmann).

1978–79 *Simplex Deutsch (German Simpleton)*. Dr. Pr 1980 BE.
TdZ 1980/7. *Stücke 2*, 1981. *Stücke*, 1983.

1980   *Der tugendhafte Taugenichts   (The Virtuous Good-for-
Nothing)*. Fragment. Pr 1981 Film HS, Potsdam.

1980–81 Dmitri ‹Demeter›. Dr (based on Schiller, "Demetri-
us"). Pr 1982 Bochum. *Stücke*, 1983. Schiller: *Deme-
trius* & Braun: *Dmitri*, Reclam 1984.

1981   *Totleben (Living Dead)*. Dr. Pr 1982 Schwerin.

1982   *Der Sonnenstaat (The Sun State)*. Dr (rev of Guevara
oder Der Sonnenstaat). Pr 1983 Lpzg. Reclam 1983.

1984   *Nibelungen*. Dr. Pr planned 1986 BE.

BRECHT, Bert(olt) (really Eugen Berthold Friedrich Brecht)
10 Feb 1898 Augsburg – 14 Aug 1956 Berlin
1917 began studying literature, philosophy, and medicine in
Munich; served as medical orderly in WW I; 18 member of Soldiers' Council; 19–23 resumed studies, then dramaturg and
stage director Munich; 24 Berlin, till 26 dramaturg under Max
Reinhardt at DT; 28 married Helene Weigel; 33 emigration via
Austria, Switzerland, France, Denmark, Sweden, Finland, Soviet Union to USA (41); 47 interrogation by House Un-American
Activities Committee, then returned to Europe, first Switzerland, 48 Berlin; 49 formed Berliner Ensemble. 1923 Kleist
Prize, 51 GDR National Prize, 54 Lenin Peace Prize; member
AdK, President PEN Center both FRG and GDR. Wrote poetry,
prose, essays.

1913–14 *Die Bibel (The Bible)*. On.
Der Fischzug   (The Fishing Expedition). On. Pr 1967
Heidelberg.
Das Leben des Konfutse (The Life of Confucius). On.
Der Ingwertopf (The Ginger Jar). On. Pr 1965 Heidel-
berg.

1918   *Trommeln in der Nacht ‹Spartakus› (Drums in the Night
‹Spartacus›)*. Dr. Pr 1922 Kammerspiele, Munich.

BRECHT (cont'd)

1918-22 *Baal*. Dr. Pr 1923 Lpzg. Op version M Friedrich Cerha.

1919 *Die Hochzeit ‹Die Kleinbürgerhochzeit› (The ‹Petty Bourgeois› Wedding)*. On (M Hans-Dieter Hosalla). Pr 1926 Fkft/M.

1919 *Der Bettler oder Der tote Hund (The Beggar or The Dead Dog)*. On. Pr 1965 Prenzlau.

1919 *Lux in tenebris*. On. Pr 1969 Essen.

1919 *Er treibt den Teufel aus (He Casts out the Devil)*. On. Pr 1975 Basel.

1919-22 *Gösta Berling*. Fragment (based on Selma Lagerlöf).

1920-32 *‹Der Untergang des Egoisten Johann› Fatzer (‹The Downfall of the Egotist Johann› Fatzer)*. Fragment. Pr 1967 Schaubühne, W. Berlin.

1921 *Garga ‹Im Dickicht› (Garga ‹In the Jungle›)*. Dr. Pr 1923 Residenzth., Munich. Rev 1924 as Im Dickicht der Städte.

1922 *Hannibal*. Fragment.

1923 *Leben Eduard des Zweiten von England (Life of Edward The Second of England)*. Dr (with Lion Feuchtwanger; based on Marlowe; M Hans-Dieter Hosalla). Pr 1924 Munich.

1924 *Im Dickicht der Städte (In the Jungle of the Cities)*. Dr (rev of Garga). Pr 1927 Darmstadt.

1924-25 *Das Elefantenkalb (The Elephant Calf)*. On (later made part of Mann ist Mann).

1926 *Mann ist Mann (A Man Is a Man)*. Dr (M Paul Dessau). Pr 1926 Darmstadt.

1927 *‹Das kleine› Mahagonny (‹The Little› Mahagonny)*. Mus Lib (M Kurt Weill). Pr 1927 Baden-Baden. Rev 1929 as Aufstieg und Fall der Stadt Mahagonny.

1928 *Die Dreigroschenoper (The Threepenny Opera)*. Op Lib (based on John Gay, "The Beggars' Opera"; M Kurt Weill). Pr 1928 Th. am Schiffbauerdamm, Berlin.

1929 *Aufstieg und Fall der Stadt Mahagonny (The Rise and Fall of the City of Mahagonny)*. Op Lib (rev of Das kleine Mahagonny; M Kurt Weill). Pr 1930 Lpzg.

1929 *Happy End*. Mus Lib (with Elisabeth Hauptmann; M Kurt Weill). Pr 1929 Th. am Schiffbauerdamm, Berlin.

1929 *Der Ozeanflug ‹Der Flug der Lindberghs› (The Flight across the Ocean ‹The Lindberghs' Flight›)*. Dr (based on radio play; M Paul Hindemith and Kurt Weill). Pr 1929 Baden-Baden.

1929 *Das Badener Lehrstück vom Einverständnis (The Baden Play of Acquiescence)*. On (M Paul Hindemith). Pr 19-29 Baden-Baden.

1929-30 *Der Brotladen (The Bakery Shop)*. Fragment. Pr 1967 BE.

1929-30 *Die heilige Johanna der Schlachthöfe (St. Joan of the Stockyards)*. Dr (M Hans-Dieter Hosalla). Pr 1959 Hamburg.

1929-30 *Der Jasager und Der Neinsager (The Yes-Sayer and The No-Sayer)*. Dr (M Kurt Weill). Pr 1930 Berlin.

BRECHT (cont'd)

1930   *Die Maßnahme (The Measure Taken)*. Dr (M Hanns Eisler). Pr 1930 Großes Schauspielhaus, Berlin.

1930   *Die Ausnahme und die Regel (The Exception and the Rule)*. Dr. Pr 1938 Givath Hazion, Palestine (in Hebrew); Gm. Pr 1956 Düsseldorf.

1930-32 *Die Mutter (The Mother)*. Dr (based on novel by Maxim Gorky; M Hanns Eisler). Pr 1932 Komödienhaus, Berlin.

1933   *Die sieben Todsünden ‹der Kleinbürger› (The Seven Deadly Sins ‹of the Petty Bourgeoisie›)*. Bl Lib (M Kurt Weill). Pr 1933 Paris.

1933-36 *Die Rundköpfe und die Spitzköpfe (The Round Heads and the Pointed Heads)*. Dr (M Hanns Eisler). Pr 1936 Copenhagen.

1934   *Die Horatier und die Curatier (The Horatians and the Curatians)*. Dr (M Kurt Schwaen). Pr 1958 Th. d. jg. Garde, Halle.

1935-38 *Furcht und Elend des dritten Reiches (Fear and Misery of the Third Reich; usually translated as The Private Life of the Master Race)*. Original title: "Deutschland: Ein Greuelmärchen" *(Germany: A Horror Tale)*. Dr (M Hanns Eisler). Pr 1938 Paris (seven scenes under title "99%"); full Pr 1948 DT.

1937   *Die Gewehre der Frau Carrar (Senora Carrar's Rifles)*. Dr (based on Synge, "Riders to the Sea"). Pr 1937 Paris.

1938-55 *‹Das Leben des› Galilei (‹The Life of› Galileo)*. Dr (M Hanns Eisler). Pr 1st version 1943 Zurich; 2nd version 1947 Los Angeles (in Engl.); 3rd version 1955 Cologne.

1938-42 *Der gute Mensch von Sezuan (The Good Woman of Setzuan)*. Dr (M Paul Dessau). Original title: "Die Ware Liebe." Pr 1943 Zurich.

1939   *Mutter Courage und ihre Kinder (Mother Courage and Her Children)*. Dr (M Paul Dessau). Pr 1941 Zurich.

1939   *Dansen oder Was kostet das Eisen? (Dansen or How Much Does the Iron Cost?)* Dr. Pr 1939 Stockholm (in Swedish); Gm. Pr 1967 Cologne.

1939-40 *Der Messingkauf (The Brass Purchase)*. Dialogues. Pr 1963 BE.

1939-40 *Das Verhör des Lukullus (The Trial of Lucullus)*. Dr (based on radio play). Pr 1947 Berkeley, Calif. Rev 1950 as Die Verurteilung des Lukullus.

1940   *Herr Puntila und sein Knecht Matti (Mr. Puntila and His Hired Hand Matti)*. Dr (based on Hella Wuolijoki; M Paul Dessau). Pr 1948 Zurich. Rev as Op "Puntila" (M Paul Dessau) Pr 1966 St.Op.

1940-41 *Flüchtlingsgespräche (Conversations of Two Refugees)*. Dialogues. Pr 1962 Munich.

1941   *‹Der aufhaltsame Aufstieg des› Arturo Ui (‹The Resistable Rise of› Arturo Ui)*. Dr (M Hans-Dieter Hosalla). Pr 1958 Stuttgart.

1941-43 *Die Gesichte der Simone Machard (The Visions of Simone Machard)*. Dr (with Lion Feuchtwanger; M Hanns Eisler). Pr 1957 Fkft/M.

BRECHT (cont'd)

1941-44 *Schwejk im zweiten Weltkrieg (Schweik in the Second World War)*. Dr (based on novel by Jaroslav Hasek; M Hanns Eisler). Pr 1957 Warsaw (in Polish); Gm. Pr 1958 Erfurt.

1941-45 *Der kaukasische Kreidekreis (The Caucasian Chalk Circle)*. Dr (M Paul Dessau). Pr 1948 Northfield, Minn. (in Engl.); Gm. Pr 1954 BE.

1945 *The Duchess of Malfi*. Dr (based on John Webster). Pr 1946 Univ of Boston (in Engl.).

1947 *Die Antigone des Sophokles (The Antigone of Sophocles)*. Dr (based on tr by Hölderlin). Pr 1948 Chur; rev version Pr 1951 Greiz.

1948-49 *Die Tage der Commune (The Days of the Commune)*. Dr (M Hanns Eisler). Pr 1956 KMSt.

1950 *Die Verurteilung des Lukullus (The Condemnation of Lucullus)*. Op Lib (rev of Das Verhör des Lukullus; M Paul Dessau). Pr 1951 St.Op.

1950 *Der Hofmeister (The Private Tutor)*. Dr (based on Jakob Michael Reinhold Lenz). Pr 1950 BE.

1951 *Herrnburger Bericht (Herrnburg Report)*. Choral work (originally written as radio play; M Paul Dessau). Pr 1951 DT.

1951-54 *‹Die Tragödie des› Coriolan (‹The Tragedy of› Coriolanus)*. Dr (based on Shakespeare). Pr 1962 Fkft/M.

1952 *Der Prozeß der Jeanne d'Arc zu Rouen 1431 (The Trial of Joan of Arc at Rouen 1431)*. Dr (based on 1931 radio play by Anna Seghers). Pr 1952 BE.

1952 *Urfaust*. Dr (based on Goethe).

1952 *Don Juan*. Com (based on Moliere). Pr 1952 Rostock.

1953-54 *Turandot oder Der Kongreß der Weißwäscher (Turandot or The Congress of the Whitewashers)*. Dr (based on Carlo Gozzi, tr by Schiller; M Hans-Dieter Hosalla). Pr 1967 BE.

1953-55 *Pauken und Trompeten ‹Der Werbeoffizier› (Drums and Trumpets ‹The Recruiting Officer›)*. Dr (based on Farquhar; M Rudolf Wagner-Regeny). Pr 1955 BE.

1955 *Büsching*. Fragment. Original title "Hans Garbe". Pr 1969 Zurich.
Das wirkliche Leben des Jakob Geherda (The Real Life of Jacob Geherda). Fragment. Pr 1983 Düsseldorf.

BREHMER, Joachim
1944 Chemnitz (now Karl Marx Stadt) –
After Polytechnical High School, became confectioner's apprentice, then director of youth club; 1969-74 member of Cultural Council of KMSt., also correspondence studies at I. Lit Lpzg; 74-76 literary adviser, Municipal Theater KMSt; now lives in Limbach-Oberfrohna. 1980 FDGB Prize. Writes prose and radio plays.

1972 *Das Mädchen Sabine (A Girl Called Sabine)*. Dr. Pr 1974 Halle.

1973 *Ein Mensch ist kein Schmetterling (A Person Is Not a Butterfly)*. Pr 1974 KMSt.

BREMER, Claus
11 July 1924 Hamburg –
Dramaturg. Now lives in Switzerland.
1971 *Heinrich Heine: Dichter Unbekannt (Heinrich Heine: Author Unknown).* Dr (with Rolf Beck). Pr 1972 Rostock.
1977 *Hier wird Geld verdient (Money Is Made Here).* Dr.

BRENDT, Edy see Eduard CLAUDIUS

BRENNECKE, ‹Al›bert
13 Dec 1898 Halberstadt – 31 Aug 1970 Halle/Saale.
Legal clerk and administrative asst.; 1917 military service; then laborer, payroll clerk in factory, union organizer; 24 member SPD; 33 director of agit-prop theater group; arrested, placed under police surveillance; unemployed, then sales clerk Mgdbg; 39 service in WW II; after 47 editor and publisher. Wrote prose, poetry, radio plays.
    Die letzte Stunde (The Last Hour). Dr. Pr 1920.
    Der Komet (The Comet). Dr. Pr 1920.
    Der Henker von Braunau (The Hangman of Braunau). Dr. Pr 1933.
1956 *Der lange Matz (The Tall Guy).* Dr. Pr 1958.

BRENNECKE, Wolf D.
28 Sep 1922 Magdeburg –
Service in WW II, then POW; transport worker, construction laborer, printer; since 1949 writer. 1950 Erich Weinert Medal. Writes prose, children's books, radio plays.
1950 *Zweimal Helden (Twice Heroes).* Com. Pr 1950.
1972 *Monk oder Wer dreht schon Tauben den Hals um? (Monk or Who Would Wring Pigeons' Necks?).* Com. Pr 1973.

BREZAN, Jurij (Pseud. Dusan SWITZ)
9 June 1916 Räckelwitz/Kamenz –
Studied economics; after 1933 member of illegal Sorbian resistance group; 37-38 emigration to Czechoslovakia and Poland; 38-39 in prison Dsdn, then military service; 45-48 Sorbian youth leader; since 49 independent writer in Bautzen. 1951, 52, 64, and 67 National Prize, 63 and 83 FDGB Prize; 73 Domowina Literature Prize; 59 and 62 Cisinski Prize; 64 PEN Center GDR, 65 AdK. Writes novels, short prose, poetry, TV plays, children's books, mostly in Sorbian language.
1955 *Zapotcatki.* Dr.
1960 *Marja Jancowa.* Dr.
1964 *Mannesjahre (Years of Manhood).* Dr (based on novel). Pr 1968 Dsdn.

BROCK, Rudolf Peter (Pseud. Peter KORB)
6 Aug 1916 Bismarckhütte – 26 Sep 1982 Berlin
Worked as mailman, then studied Theater HS Mannheim; military service, medical discharge 1942; 45-48 artistic director Halle Radio; after 49 editor; 55 studied I. Lit Lpzg; after 60 lived in Teltow near Berlin. 1970 Fontane Prize. Wrote children's books.

BROCK (cont'd)

1954   *Die kapitolinische Venus (The Capitoline Venus).* On (based on Mark Twain). Pr 1954.

1955   *Der Schweinehirt (The Swineherd).* Juv (based on Hans Christian Andersen). Pr 1955.

1956   *Paddy Glück (Lucky Paddy).* Dr.

BRODWIN, Stefan   see Slatan DUDOW

BROSCH, Alwin
23 Oct 1903 Neupaulsdorf (now Nove Pavlovice, Czechoslovakia) - ?
Actor and writer. Since 1953 lived in Putbus.

1937   *Die Mühle im Schwarzwald (The Mill in the Black Forest).* Mus Lib.

1937   *Die Glocken von Straßburg (The Bells of Strasbourg).* Opt Lib.

1938   *Hoheit die Liebe (Sovereign Love).* Opt Lib.

1942   *Fritze mit der Zipfelmütze (Freddy with the Pointed Cap).* Juv.

1942   *Der tapfere Zinnsoldat (The Brave Tin Soldier).* Juv (based on Hans Christian Andersen).

1942   *Hänsel und Gretel.* Juv (based on Grimm).

1947   *Annemarie.* Opt Lib.

1950   *Hans und der Zirkus ‹Hans und der Teppich› (Jack and the Circus ‹Jack and the Carpet›).* Juv. Pr 1950 Köthen.

1950   *Die Regentrude (Rain Trudy).* Juv (based on story by Theodor Storm). Pr 1950 Gera.

1954   *König Drosselbart (King Thrushbeard).* Juv (based on Grimm). Pr 1955 Th. d. jg. Generation, Dsdn.

BRÜNING, Elfriede   (married name Elfriede Barckhausen)
8 Nov 1910 Berlin -
Office clerk and publisher's secretary; 1930 became member KPD; 35 imprisoned; after 45 editor, since 50 writer; lives in Berlin. 1980 Berlin Goethe Prize. Writes TV plays, novels, children's books.

1964   *Die Heiratsanzeige (The Wedding Announcement).* Com. Pr 1965 Fkft/O.

1974   *Hochverrat (High Treason).* Dr. Pr 1975 Th. d. Freundschaft, Berlin.

1975   *Axel.* Juv. Pr 1975 Th. d. Freundschaft, Berlin.

BUDJUHN, Horst
30 July 1910 Bromberg -
Now lives in Switzerland. Writes scripts for film, TV, and radio.

1958   *Die zwölf Geschworenen (The Twelve Jurors).* Dr (based on TV play by Reginald Rose, "Twelve Angry Men"). Pr 1979 KMSt. Cologne: Kiepenheuer and Witsch, 1962.

1970   *Noahs Jeep.* Dr (with Robert Neumann).

1971   *Ein Zwischenfall (An Incident).* Dr.

BUHSS, Werner
Stage, radio, and TV director. Writes radio plays.
1977   *Befragung Anna O. (Interrogation Anna O.).* Dr (with Peter Bahr; based on TV play by Gerhard Stuchlik and Klaus Poche). Pr 1978 Rudolstadt.
1983   *Nina Nina tam kartina.* Dr (based on novel by Daniil Granin, "Das Gemälde"). Reading 1984 Lpzg.

BUNGE, Gudrun   see Hans BUNGE

BUNGE, Hans (Wolf)
Works in Brecht Archives.
1982   *HUAC - Der Fall Eisler ‹Das Eisler Verhör›* *(HUAC - The Eisler Case ‹The Eisler Interrogation›).* Dr (with Gudrun Bunge). Pr 1982 BE.

BÜRGER, Ernst
17 June 1928 Lörrach/Baden -
In Berlin since 1933, attended high school there; then lived two years in occupied Poland; 44 Air Force helper, 45 Russian POW; 46-48 completed school; 48-49 teaching asst., then studied German literature and theater history; since 52 teacher. Writes prose and TV scripts.
1948   *Jugend (Youth).* Dr. Pr 1959 Crimmitschau.
1972   *Veilchen für Dolly (Violets for Dolly).* Com. Pr 19-73 Th. d. Freundschaft, Berlin.

BURGER, Hanus
4 June 1909 Prague -
Studied in Prague, Hamburg; worked as set designer, dramaturg and stage director, first Fkft/M, then Bremen, Hamburg, later Prague, DT, Vienna (Th. in der Josefstadt); 1938 emigrated to USA, worked in Hollywood as film director; during WW II, service in US Army for three years; after war, TV director CBS, New York; returned to Europe, now lives in Czechoslovakia and GDR.
        Max und Moritz. Juv.
1936   *Tom Sawyers ‹großes› Abenteuer (Tom Sawyer's ‹Great› Adventure).* Juv (with Stefan Heym; based on Mark Twain). Pr 1937 Vienna. Rev version Pr 1952 Halle (Performance title: Abenteuer am Mississippi). Halle: Mitteldt. Verlag, 1953. Kassel: Bärenreiter, 1957.
1957   *Der Dudelsackpfeifer von Strakonitz oder Das Fest der Waldgeister (The Bagpiper of Strakonitz or The Festival of the Forest Spirits).* Juv (tr from Josef Kajetan Tyl).
1957   *Das starrsinnige Weib (The Stubborn Woman).* Juv (tr from Josef Kajetan Tyl; based on Czech folk tale).
1963   *La Farola.* Juv. Pr 1964 Th. d. Freundschaft, Berlin. *TdZ* 1964/14.

BÜRKLE, Veit   see Karl-Heinrich BISCHOFF

BUSCHMANN, Wolfgang
19 Dec 1943 Rittenberg –
Teacher, lives in Töblitz. Writes prose and children's books.
1982   *Die große Erfindung (The Great Invention).*   Pp (M Robert Linke). Pr 1985 KMSt.

CAMPE, Helmut   see Alfred KANTOROWICZ

CHANEL, Flacon   see Paul Herbert FREYER

CLAUDIUS, Eduard   (Pseud. Edy BRENDT; really Eduard SCHMIDT)
29 July 1911 Buer/Gelsenkirchen - 13 Dec 1975 Potsdam
At age 16, became correspondent for KPD Press; 1933 arrested,
34 emigration to Switzerland; 36 with Int'l Brigade to Spain,
39 returned illegally to Switzerland, arrested again; 39-45
with partisan brigade in Italy; 45 Head of Press Section in
Bavarian Ministry for Denazification, Munich; 47 moved to GDR
(Potsdam); 56-59 Consul for GDR in Syria, 59-61 Ambassador to
Vietnam. 1951 National Prize, 55 Literature Prize; 65 member
AdK. Wrote novels and short prose.
1951   *Die Söhne Garibaldis (The Sons of Garibaldi)*. Dr. Pr
       1952 Potsdam.

CLAUS, Manfred
9 Apr 1928 Plauen -
Studied pedagogy Dsdn, Humboldt Univ Berlin; 1969 Instructor,
later Prof. for Pedagogy Jena.
1981   *Zur letzten Rettung (The Last Rescue)*. Mus Lib (M
       Manfred Grafe). Pr 1982 Dsdn.

COLLIN, Christian   (Pseud. for Bodo HOMBERG)
4 Mar 1926 Rostock -
After high school, studied music, then served in WW II; 1945-
48 Russian POW; studied German, art and theater history, then
worked as journalist and radio reporter, since 57 for GDR TV.
1954 Gerhart Hauptmann Prize. Writes radio and TV scripts.
1951   *Odysseus (Ulysses)*. Dr. Pr 1952 Bochum.
1954   *Die Karriere (The Career)*. Dr.
1956   *Der verlorene Blick (The Lost Glance)*. Dr (based on
       TV play).
1957   *Die Heimkehr des verlorenen Vaters (The Return of the
       Missing Father)*. Dr (based on TV play).
1959   *Die Geier der Helen Turner (Helen Turner's Vultures)*.
       Com (based on TV play). Pr 1965 Erfurt.
1964   *Golf bei Sniders (Golf at the Sniders)*. Dr (based on
       TV play, "Der Neger Kuoli"). TdZ 1965/4.
1964   *Manana Manana*. Juv (based on TV play). Pr 1974 Th.
       d. Freundschaft, Berlin. *Sinn & Form* 1965/3-4.
1970   *Hochzeit einer Nonne (A Nun's Wedding)*. Com (based
       on novella by Conrad Ferdinand Meyer, "Plautus im Non-
       nenkloster"). Pr 1970.

CORRINTH, Curt
20 Feb 1894 Lennep/Rhineland - 27 Aug 1960 Berlin
Studied law Paris and Mgdbg, then literature and art history
Bonn; 1915-17 soldier in WW I, then editor in Berlin; began
writing plays 18; 33 arrested, plays prohibited; 34-36 again
editor; 39-40 dramaturg for UFA; after WW II book dealer;
since 55 GDR (Berlin). Wrote novels and film scripts.

CORRINTH (cont'd)

1918   *Der König von Trinador (The King of Trinador)*.   Dr.

1920   *Die Leichenschändung (The Desecration of Corpses)*. Dr.

1929   *Trojaner (Trojans)*. Juv. Pr 1929 Berlin. Rev 1955 as Die Sache Päker.

1930   *Sektion Rahnstetten (The Rahnstetten Section)*. Dr. Pr 1930 Berlin. Rev 1947.

1931   *Der Smaragdring (The Emerald Ring)*.   Dr.

1932   *Mann und Vaterland (Man and Fatherland)*. Dr. Pr 19-32.

1934   *Erstens kommt es anders (First of All Things Go Differently)*. Com. Pr 1935 Dt. Bühne, Bygdosz, Hungary.

1947   *Sektion Rahnstetten (The Rahnstetten Section)*. Dr (rev version)*.

1955   *Die Sache Päker (The Päker Affair)*. Juv (rev of Trojaner). Pr 1956 Th. d. Freundschaft, Berlin.

CZECH-KUCKHOFF, Ilse   (Pseud. Ilse PAUL-CZECH)
27 Jan 1908 Tichau (now Tichy, Poland) –
Writes film and radio scripts.

1938   *Die weiße Königin (The White Queen)*.   Dr.

1939   *Nie wieder... (Never Again...)*.   Com (with Hans Hansen)*.

1942   *Ein Mann mit Herz (A Man with Heart)*. Com. Pr 1953 Erfurt.

1949   *Du sollst dir kein Bildnis machen (Thou Shalt Not Make a Graven Image)*. Dr.

1953   *Die heiligen drei Affen (The Three Sacred Monkeys)*. Com.

CZECHOWSKI, ‹Karl› Heinz
7 Feb 1935 Dresden –
Was trained in graphic and advertising art; until 1958 technical draftsman; 58-61 studied I. Lit Lpzg, then literary adviser Mgdbg theater; editorial asst. Halle; now independent author. 1970 Berlin Goethe Prize, 77 Heinrich Heine Prize. Editor and essayist.

1968   *Maskerade (Masquerade)*. Dr (based on Mikhail J. Lermontov)*.

1969   *Das Märchen vom Kaiser und vom Hirten (The Tale of the Emperor and the Shepherd)*. Juv (based on Bosko Trifunovic). Pr 1969 Th. d. Freundschaft, Berlin.

1969   *König Drosselbart (King Thrushbeard)*. Juv (based on Grimm; incidental M Heinz Röttger). Pr 1969 Th. d. Freundschaft, Berlin. *TdZ* 1969/7.

1971   *Rumpelstilzchen (Rumpelstiltskin)*. Juv (based on Grimm). Pr 1971 Th. d. jg. Welt, Lpzg. *TdZ* 1972/8.

1978   *Die Novembernacht (The November Night)*. Dr (based on Stanislav Vyspiansky, tr by Gabriele Bock).

1983   *Der Meister und Margarita (The Master and Margarita)*. Op Lib (based on novel by Mikhail Bulgakov, tr Thomas Reschke; M Rainer Kunad). Pr 1986 Lpzg.

CZERWENKA, Rudi   (Pseud. Rudolf WENK)
27 Apr 1927 Breslau (now Wroclaw, Poland) –
Teacher, lives in Bad Sülze.   Writes children's books and TV
plays.
1982   *Rostocker Billerbogen (Rostock Picture Book).*   Two On
          (in Low German).   Pr 1983 Rostock.

D

DÄBRITZ, Fritz (Pseud. Jörg PETER)
20 Sep 1919 Reichstädt –
Writes poetry and children's books.
 Däumlings Abenteuer (Tom Thumb's Adventures). Pp.
 Frau Holle (Mother Holle). Pp (based on Grimm).
 Kasper und Nixi (Punch and Nixi). Pp.
 Das tapfere Schneiderlein (The Brave Little Tailor). Pp (based on Grimm).
1981 *Das Seepferdchen (The Little Sea Horse)*. Pp.

DAMM-WENDLER, Ursula
31 Mar 1922 Dresden –
Actress; married to Horst-Ulrich Wendler. Writes TV scripts.
1955 *Der Hausgeist (The Household Spirit)*. Pp.
1957 *Der Wundertopf (The Miracle Pot)*. Pp.
1958 *Das Zauberkochbuch (The Magic Cookbook)*. Pp.
1958 *Wiedersehn am Wochenende (Weekend Reunion)*. Com (with Horst-Ulrich Wendler).
1959 *Wirbel unter einem Dach (Turmoil under One Roof)*. Com. Pr 1961 Dsdn/Radebeul.
1963 *Die Fehde des Michael Kohlhaas (The Feud of Michael Kohlhaas)*. Dr (with Horst-Ulrich Wendler; based on novella by Heinrich Kleist). Pr 1963 Quedlinburg.
1964 *Verflixter Alltag (Darned Everyday Routine)*. Mus Lib (with Horst-Ulrich Wendler; M Jochen Allihn). Pr 1965 Rostock.
1965 *Die drei Musketiere (The Three Musketeers)*. Mus Lib (with Horst-Ulrich Wendler; based on Alexander Dumas). Pr 1966 Quedlinburg. Part II 1969 under title of Die vier Musketiere.
1968 *Für fünf Groschen Urlaub (Vacation for Five Cents)*. Mus Lib (with Horst-Ulrich Wendler). Pr 1969 Met.
1969 *Die vier Musketiere (The Four Musketeers)*. Dr (with Horst-Ulrich Wendler; based on Alexander Dumas). Part II of Die drei Musketiere. Pr 1970 Rudolstadt.
1970 *Die Abenteuer der Musketiere (The Adventures of the Musketeers)*. Juv. Pr 1971 Th. d. jg. Generation, Dsdn.
1973 *Letzter Ausweg Heirat (Last Alternative Marriage)*. Mus Lib (with Horst-Ulrich Wendler). Pr 1974 Dsdn.
1975 *Tschüß bis Freitag (See You Friday!)* Mus Lib (with Horst-Ulrich Wendler). Pr 1976 Parchim.
1983 *Herbstgewitter (Autumn Thunderstorm)*. Mus Lib (M Henry Krtschil). Pr 1983 Dsdn.

DANCKER, Susanne
1952 *Aschenbrödel (Cinderella)*. Juv (with Anna Süß and Herbert Bendey; based on Grimm). Pr 1952 Th. am Schiffbauerdamm, Berlin. Berlin: Jg. Welt, 1952.
1961 *Fliegenfängergeschichte (Story of a Fly Catcher)*. Juv. Pr 1962 Th. d. jg. Generation, Dsdn.
 Die Schweinekirmes (The Hog Fair). Mus Lib (with Eva Fritzsche; M Eberhard Schmidt).

DECHANT, Lutz
1948 Jena –
1967-71 studied Film HS Potsdam/Babelsberg; 71-82 actor and stage director, Th. d. Freundschaft, Berlin; 82-85 studied I. Lit Lpzg, then returned to Th. d. Freundschaft.

1978   *Paul und Maria.* Juv. Pr 1978 Th. d. Freundschaft, Berlin.

1980   *Disko mit Oskar (Disco with Oscar).* Juv. Pr 1980 Th. d. Freundschaft, Berlin.

1985   *Icke bin doch Icke (I Am Still Me).* Juv. Pr 1985 Th. d. Freundschaft, Berlin.

DEGENHARDT, Jürgen (Pseud. Hans HARDT)
21 Oct 1930 Dresden –
Journalist, stage director; lives in Erfurt. 1980 Erfurt Culture Prize. Writes poetry, essays, songs, film scripts.

1959   *Messeschlager Gisela (Gisela, the Hit of the Fair).* Mus Lib (with Helmut Bez; M Gerd Natschinski). Pr 19-60 Met.

1961   *Servus Peter (Hello Peter).* Mus Lib (with Alfred Berg and Helmut Bez; M Gerd Natschinski). Pr 1961 KMSt.

1961   *Musik ist mein Glück (Music Is My Happiness).* Mus Lib.

1962   *Die schwarze Perle (The Black Pearl).* Opt Lib. Pr 1962 Erfurt.

1963   *Die Frau des Jahres (Woman of the Year).* Revue.

1964   *Mein Freund Bunbury (My Friend Bunbury).* Mus Lib (with Helmut Bez; based on Oscar Wilde, "The Importance of Being Earnest"; M Gerd Natschinski). Pr 19-64 Met.

1964   *Der Mann, der Dr. Watson war (The Man Who Was Dr. Watson).* Mus Lib (with Helmut Bez; based on Arthur Conan Doyle).

1965   *Urlaub mit Engel (Vacation with Angel).* Mus Lib (with Helmut Bez).

1966   *Sie sind zauberhaft, Madame (You Are Enchanting, Madam).* Mus Lib (with Helmut Bez).

1967   *Kleinstadtgeschichten (Small Town Tales).* Mus Lib (with Helmut Bez; based on Kotzebue, "Die deutschen Kleinstädter"). Pr 1967 Erfurt.

1967   *Die Gondolieri (The Gondoliers).* Opt Lib (based on Gilbert & Sullivan).

1967   *Froufrou.* Mus Lib (with Helmut Bez). Pr 1969 Erfurt.

1968   *Calamity Jane.* Mus Lib (with Helmut Bez).

1969   *Bretter, die die Welt bedeuten (The Stage Is the World).* Mus Lib (with Helmut Bez; based on Schönthau "Der Raub der Sabinerinnen"; M Gerhard Kneifel). Pr 1970 Met.

1971   *Die Wette des Mr. Fogg (Mr. Fogg's Wager).* Mus Lib (with Helmut Bez; based on Jules Verne, "Around the World in 80 Days"). Pr 1971 Lpzg.

1973   *Terzett (Trio).* Mus Lib (with Helmut Bez; M Gerd Natschinski). Pr 1974 Lpzg.

DEGENHARDT (cont'd)

1975   *Keep Smiling.* Mus Lib (with Helmut Bez; M Harry Sander). Pr 1976 Lpzg.

1976   *Casanova.* Mus Lib (with Helmut Bez; M Gerd Natschinski). Pr 1976 Met.

1977   *Liebhabereien (Flirtations).* Com (with Helmut Bez). Pr 1978 Parchim.

1977   *Prinz von Preußen (Prince of Prussia).* Mus Lib (with Helmut Bez; M Dieter Brand). Pr 1978 Erfurt.

1979   *Berlin, wie es weint und lacht (Berlin, Laughing and Crying).* Revue (based on Kalisch).

1980   *Die schöne Helena (Helen of Troy).* Opt Lib (new adaptation; M Jacques Offenbach).

1981   *Ein Fall für Sherlock Holmes (A Case for Sherlock Holmes).* Mus Lib (based on Arthur Conan Doyle, "The Hound of the Baskervilles"; M Gerd Natschinski). Pr 1982 Erfurt.

1982   *Zauber der Melodie (The Magic of Melody).* Revue.

DEICKE, Günther
21 Oct 1922 Hildburghausen –
Served in Navy in WW II, then English POW; 1945-47 farm worker in FRG; 47 moved to GDR; became cultural editor, 51-52 Aufbau Verlag, then *NdL* and Verlag der Nation. Member AdK since 1969; 1964 Heinrich Heine Prize, 70 and 73 National Prize, 82 Order of Merit. Writes poetry.

    Wo steckst du, Bursche? (Where Are You, Fellow?). Dr (with Günter Jänicke; based on Vera Panova).
    Schwanda, der Dudelsackpfeifer (Schwanda the Bagpiper). Op Lib (with Gustav Just; M Leos Janacek).

1959   *Ein Tagebuch für Anne Frank (A Diary for Anne Frank).* Dr (with J. Hellwig).

1961   *Wenn der Wacholder blüht (When the Juniper Blooms).* Oratorio Lib (M Ruth Zechlin). Pr 1961.

1962   *Reineke Fuchs (Reynard the Fox).* Op Lib (M Ruth Zechlin). Pr 1968 Th. d. Freundschaft, Berlin. *NdL* 1968/8.

1963   *Was ihr wollt ‹Die Schiffbrüchigen von Illyrien› (What You Will ‹The Shipwrecked of Illyria›).* Mus Lib (based on Shakespeare, "Twelfth Night"; M Klaus Fehmel). Pr 1963 Th. d. Freundschaft, Berlin.

1965   *Esther.* Op Lib (based on novella by Bruno Apitz; M Robert Hanell). Pr 1966 St.Op. *TdZ* 1966/6.

1972   *Reiter der Nacht (Riders of the Night).* Op Lib (based on novel by Peter Abrahams, "The Path of Thunder"; M Ernst H. Meyer). Pr 1973 St.Op. *TdZ* 1973/6.

1973   *Meister Röckle (Master Jacket).* Juv Op Lib (based on Ilse and Vilmos Korn, "Meister Hans Röckle und Meister Flammfuß"; M Joachim Werzlau). Pr 1976 St.Op. Lpzg: Edition Peters, 1978.

1980   *Das Chagrinleder (Grained Leather).* Op Lib (based on novel by Honore de Balzac, "La peau de chagrin"; M Fritz Geißler). Pr 1981 Weimar.

1982   *Die schwarze Kabale (The Black Intrigue).* Op Lib based on Mikhael Bulgakov; M Fritz Geißler).

DENGER, Alfred (Fred)
12 June 1920 Darmstadt – 30 Oct 1983 Hohegeiß
Merchant, book dealer, later actor and author; moved to FRG.
Wrote novels, radio, TV, and film scripts.
1945   *Wir heißen euch hoffen (We Bid You Hope)*. Dr. Pr 19-
       46 DT.
1946   *Die Pest (The Plague)*. Dr (based on "The Pied Piper
       of Hamelin"). Pr 1964 Potsdam.
1946   *Bikini*. Dr. Pr 1948 Göttingen.
1947   *Hunger*. Dr. Pr 1947 Remscheid.
1952   *Drachen steigen gegen den Wind (Kites Rise against
       the Wind)*.
1957   *Langusten ‹Marie vom Hinterhof› (Crayfish ‹Marie from
       the Backyard›)*. Dr. Pr 1957 Bremen.
1958   *Ebbe und Sündflut (Ebb and Flood)*. Dr.
       *Die Trauben werden nicht süßer (The Grapes Aren't Get-
       ting Any Sweeter)*. Com.
       *Das Wetter von Kiebitzwinkel (The Weather of Kiebitz-
       winkel)*. Com.
1970   *Wenn der Thunfisch tickt (When the Tuna Ticks)*. Com.

DINKELMANN, Kurt
1974   *Dann wollen wir einmal wieder! (Let's Do It Again!)*.
       Com. Pr 1974 Rostock.

DITTRICH, Paul-Heinz
1982   *Die Verwandlung (Metamorphosis)*. Op (with Frank
       Schneider; based on story by Franz Kafka). Pr 1983
       Metz.

DJACENKO, Boris   (Pseud. Peter ADDAMS)
10 Sep 1917 Riga (Estonia) – 14 Apr 1975 Berlin
Worked as sailor and fisherman, then correspondence study of
philosophy Riga; 1940 arrested in France, interned Le Vernet;
brought to Germany as slave laborer, escaped, worked illegally in Berlin; 45 joined Soviet troops; after WW II appointed
Mayor of Leest; later moved to Berlin, became author. Wrote
prose.
       *Hans Bockums Höllenfahrt (Hans Bockum's Descent into
       Hell)*. Juv.
1950   *Dschungel (Jungle)*. Dr. Pr 1951 Dsdn.
1951   *Menschen an der Grenze (People at the Border)*. Dr.
       Pr 1951 Neue Bühne, Berlin.
1952   *Die feuerrote Blume (The Fiery Red Flower)*. Juv
       (based on Russian fairy tale). Pr 1953 Th. d. Freund-
       schaft, Berlin.
1962   *‹Doch› Unterm Rock der Teufel (‹But› The Devil under
       the Skirt)*. Com. Pr 1966 Lpzg. Eulenspiegel, 1966.
       Rev version Pr 1968 VB.

DOMMA, Ottokar   see Otto HAUSER

DORNATH, Heinz   see Heinz HELM

DORNBERGER, Paul
31 Aug 1901 Zeitz - 2 Dec 1978 Berlin
1933 sent to prison for underground activities; 36-46 emigration to Czechoslovakia, England, Canada; actor, dramaturg, director of theater club "Die Möwe," Berlin; editor. Wrote novels.

1941   *Tagesbefehl 333 (Order of the Day No. 333)*. Dr. Pr 1942 London.
1943   *Der Überläufer (The Deserter)*. Dr. Pr 1943 London.
1955   *Das eiserne Büffelchen (The Little Iron Buffalo)*. Juv (based on novel by Alex Wedding). Pr 1958 Th. d. jg. Garde, Halle.
1956   *Der treue Prinz von Behramgur (The Faithful Prince of Behramgur)*. Juv. Pr 1957 Th. d. jg. Welt, Lpzg.

DÖRNER, Karin
1977   *Auguste, die Weihnachtsgans (Augusta, the Christmas Goose)*. Pp (based on story by Friedrich Wolf). Pr 1977 Halle.

DORNIK, Miklaws
1974   *Die Junggesellensteuer (The Bachelors' Tax)*. Com. Pr 1975 Bautzen (in Sorbian language).

DOROWA, Almut (married name Ballhaus)
30 May 1916 Weimar -
Dancer and choreographer.
    Hänsel und Gretel. Juv (based on Grimm). Pr 1966 Eisenach.

DÖRWALDT-KÜHL, Edith
1967   *Ballade vom Glück (The Ballad of Happiness)*. Op Lib (M Kurt Schwaen). Pr 1967 Staatsoper, Dsdn.

DRESCHER, Piet (Peter)
14 Jan 1946 Brüx (Czechoslovakia) -
Book dealer. Writes novels.
1964   *Belli, Maxe und Gespenster (Belli, Max and Ghosts)*. Juv Mus Lib (M Hans Jürgen Wenzel). Pr 1965 Th. d. jg. Garde, Halle.
1966   *Ein Student kommt an (A Student Arrives)*. Com. Pr 1967 Lpzg.
1967   *Das blaue Licht (The Blue Light)*. Juv. Pr 1967 Parchim.

DREWNIOK, Heinz
1949 Gliwice, Poland -
Moved to GDR in 1957. After high school, Drama School Rostock; then actor, director, dramaturg at various theaters; studied theater history Lpzg, then artistic director Workers' Theater Gotha; guest lecturer Rostock and Music Conservatory Lpzg; since 1981 actor and dramaturg Dsdn. Writes short stories and radio plays.
    Harlekin und Colombine (Harlequin and Columbine). Juv.
    Besuch in Muchowiec (Visit in Mukhoviets). Dr.

DREWNIOK (cont'd)

     Platzkonzert (Open-Air Concert). Dr.

     Der Namensvetter (The Namesake). Dr (based on Granin).

1979   *Die Jungs (The Boys).* Dr. Pr 1981 Dsdn. *TdZ* 1982/3.

1980   *Szenen aus dem Thüringer Wald* (Scenes from the Thuringian Forest). Three On: *Karl und Kasimir,* Pr 1981 Dsdn as part of program under collective title "Anregung"; *Waldesruh (Forest Peace),* Pr 1983 Karl Marx Univ, Lpzg; *Egon ist da (Egon Is Here),* Pr 1984 Senftenberg. *TdZ* 1981/5.

1981   *Wenn Georgie kommt... (When Georgie Comes...).* Com. Pr 1983 Dsdn. *TdZ* 1983/2.

     Der Pförtner (The Doorkeeper).

1982   *Die Jäger (The Hunters).* On (addition to Szenen aus dem Thüringer Wald). Pr 1983 Potsdam.

1982   *Stefan und Franziska.* Dr.

     Die Nackten (The Naked Ones). On. Reading 1983 Dsdn.

1983   *Simplizius Simplizissimus.* Dr (based on novel by Grimmelshausen). Pr 1984 Dsdn.

1983   *Überall ist Heiterkeit (There Is Cheerfulness Everywhere).* On (addition to Szenen aus dem Thüringer Wald). TV Pr 1984 under title "Spielgefährten". Pr 1985 Gera.

1983   *Alles im Haus (Everything in the House).* Com. Pr 1984 Dsdn.

1984   *Teamwork.* Dr. Pr 1985 Lpzg.

1984   *Auf und ab (Up and Down).* Dr. Pr 1985 Dsdn.

1985   *Tod und Leben des Martin Röder (Martin Röder's Death and Life).* Dr. Pr 1986 Lpzg.

1985   *Der Tüchtige (The Capable Man).* Dr. Pr 1986 Quedlinburg.

DRÖGE, Ernst Wolf

     Die glückliche Insel (The Happy Island). Com. Pr 1948 Burgstadt.

DUDELSACK, Wendelin   see Kurt Arnold FINDEISEN

DUDOW, Slatan   (Pseud. Stefan BRODWIN)
30 Jan 1903 Zaribrod, Bulgaria (now Yugoslavia)- 12 July 1963 Fürstenwalde
High school Sofia until 1919; 22 began study of theater history Berlin; then training as actor; stage and film experience under direction of Leopold Jessner, Fritz Lang, G. W. Pabst; 27-29 theater studies USSR; 30-32 worked with Bertolt Brecht on films "Kuhle Wampe" and "Dreigroschenfilm," as well as plays such as "Die Maßnahme", "Mann ist Mann" and "Die Mutter"; 35 emigration to France and Switzerland; 46 return to Berlin, directed films. 1950 and 55 National Prize; 55 AdK. Wrote film scripts.

1939   *Der Feigling (The Coward).* Com. Pr 1948 DT.

1941   *Der leichtgläubige Thomas (The Credulous Thomas).* Com.

DUDOW (cont'd)
1943   *Das Narrenparadies (Fools' Paradise).* Com.
1946   *Der Weltuntergang (The End of the World).* Com.
1956   *Der Hauptmann von Köln (The Captain from Cologne).*
         Com (with Michael Tschesno-Hell; based on film). Pr
         1959 Lpzg. Henschel 1956.

EBEL, Karl-Albert
> *Die Eselskomödie (The Donkey Comedy)*. Com (based on Plautus). Pr 1967 Straßfurt.

EBERT, Gerhard A.
Theater historian, critic, Deputy Director of Drama School, Berlin.
1977   *Der wilde Mann (The Wild Man)*. Com. Pr 1978 Parchim.

EBERT, Günther
19 Feb 1925 Meerane –
Attended trade school; 1942-45 service in WW II; American POW until 47; 48-49 editor "Volksstimme," 49-51 book dealer, 51-52 editor, literary critic in Berlin; 57-58 I.Lit Lpzg. 1968 and 82 Fritz Reuter Prize. Writes essays, children's books.
> *Es war eine Mutter (There Was a Mother)*. Juv.
1981   *Der Spielmann ist da (The Minstrel Is Here)*. Juv. Pr 1982 Greifswald.
1984   *Wie Hund und Katze (Like Cat and Dog)*. Juv. Pr 1985 Greifswald.

ECKE, Felix   see Ralph WIENER

ECKERT, Holger
2 Nov 1903 Schneidemühl (now Poland) –
1923-28 studied law Berlin and Göttingen, received law degree; 33 moved to Berlin; wrote for various newspapers and periodicals; 35-38 lived in England, then returned to Germany; studied acting and singing; actor at various theaters in Berlin, Görlitz, Quedlinburg. Writes prose.
> *Meine Frau ist keine Frau für mich (My Wife Is Not the Right Woman for Me)*. Com. Pr 1955 Wittenberg.
> *Bijou*. Mus Lib (with Peter Hansen).
1966   *Der Tote kommt zu Gast (The Dead Man Comes Visiting)*. Com. Pr 1968 Zeitz.
1967   *Eine Frau mit Vergangenheit (A Woman with a Past)*. Mus Lib (with Heinz Vogt; based on Oscar Wilde, "Lady Windermere's Fan"). Pr 1969 Annaberg.
1968   *Die Bremer Stadtmusikanten (The Town Musicians of Bremen)*. Juv (based on Grimm). Pr 1969 Zeitz.
1969   *Das tapfere Schneiderlein (The Brave Little Tailor)*. Juv (based on Grimm). Pr 1969 Zeitz.
1969   *Hans im Glück (Lucky Jack)*. Juv Mus Lib (based on Grimm; M Hans Auenmüller). Pr 1970 Zeitz.
1973   *Die Zauberburg (The Magic Castle)*. Juv Mus Lib (M Henry Kaufmann). Pr 1975 Bernburg.
1977   *Die Hexe Bimbambulla (Bimbambulla, the Witch)*. Juv. Pr 1978 Zeitz.
1979   *So ein Theater (What an Act)*. Mus Lib (M Henry Kaufmann). Pr 1979 Zeitz.
1980   *Kalif Storch (Caliph Stork)*. Juv Mus Lib (based on Wilhelm Hauff; M Jochen Allihn). Pr 1981 Bernburg.

ECKERT, Wolfgang
20 Apr 1935 Meerane –
After various occupations, 1960-63 I.Lit Lpzg, then librarian in Meerane. 1974 Hans Marchwitza Prize. Writes novels, short stories, TV plays.
1970   *Schienenballade (Ballad of the Rails)*. Dr. Pr 1971 Rostock.

EGER, Steffen
1966   *Karl Stülpner*. Dr. Pr 1967 Annaberg.

EHRHARDT, Rolf
1978   *Die Heinzelmännchen (The Elves)*. Juv (with Rosemarie Ehrhardt). Pr 1979 Eisleben.

EIDAM, Klaus
23 May 1926 Chemnitz (now Karl Marx Stadt) –
After high school, served in WW II; after 1946 actor in Bernburg, Straßfurt, Greitz, also dramaturg; 51-54 Chief Dramaturg Landesbühnen Sachsen, 55-58 Th. d. Freundschaft, Berlin; since 63 head of theater section of music publisher "Lied der Zeit."
1946   *Himmeldonnerwetter (Good Heavens!)*. Revue. Pr 1946.
1946   *Schneewittchen (Snow White)*. Juv (based on Grimm). Pr 1947 Stralsund.
1949   *Der fliegende Teppich (The Flying Carpet)*. Juv (based on "The 1001 Nights"). Pr 1952 Th. d. jg. Welt, Lpzg.
1950   *Der silberne Pfeil (The Silver Arrow)*. Juv.
1951   *Der letzte Häuptling (The Last Chieftain)*. Juv.
         Nasreddin in Buchara. Com (based on Leonid Solovyev).
1952   *Die Hochzeit des Figaro (The Marriage of Figaro)*. Com (based on Beaumarchais). Pr 1953.
1953   *Der Ochse von Kulm (The Ox of Kulm)*. Com (based on W. K. Schweickert). Pr 1954.
1955   *Zäpfel Kerns Abenteuer (Zäpfel Kern's Adventures)*. Juv (based on Collodi and Bierbaum). Pr 1956 Stralsund.
1956   *Der Lügner (The Liar)*. Com (based on Goldoni). Pr 1957.
1957   *Der Fall Schandauer (The Schandauer Case)*. Dr.
1958   *Münchhausen*. Com. Pr 1958. Rev 1959 as Pp.
1960   *Die Schatzinsel (Treasure Island)*. Juv (based on Robert Louis Stevenson). Pr 1963 Th. d. jg. Garde, Halle.
1961   *Scharfe Schau und schlimme Schurken (Sharp Inspection and Sly Scoundrels)*. Revue.
1961   *Rund ist die Welt (The World Is Round)*. Opt Lib (M W. Heicking). Pr 1961.
1962   *Orpheus in der Unterwelt (Orpheus in the Underworld)*. Opt Lib (new adaptation; M Jacques Offenbach).
1962   *Die Lästerschule (School for Slander)*. Com (based on Sheridan, "School for Scandal"). Pr 1962.
1963   *Maria Tudor*. Dr (based on Victor Hugo).
1963   *System Kuckuck (The Cuckoo System)*.

EIDAM (cont'd)

1963   *Urlaub ins Glück (Vacation into Happiness).* Opt Lib (M Stefan Kerst). Pr 1963 Lpzg.

1964   *Die Banditen (The Bandits).* Opt Lib (based on Meilhac and Halevy; M Jacques Offenbach). Pr 1964 Lpzg.

1965   *Tod am Morgen (Death in the Morning).* Dr. Pr 1965 Putbus.

1967   *Connie und der Löwe (Connie and the Lion).* Mus Lib (M Rolf Zimmermann). Pr 1968 Halle. *TdZ* 1969/6.

1969   *Mit 60 fängt das Leben an (Life Begins at 60).* Mus Lib (M Rudi Werion). Pr 1970 Halle.

1970   *Der tapfere kleine Schneider (The Brave Little Tailor).* Pp (based on Grimm).

1970   *Showboat.* Mus Lib (based on Edna Ferber and Oscar Hammerstein; M Jerome Kern). Pr 1972 Plauen.

1971   *O la la Mademoiselle.* Mus Lib (based on Charles Lecocq, "La Fille de Madame Angot"; M Conny Odd). Pr 1972 Lpzg.

1975   *Frohes Wochenende (Happy Weekend).* Mus Lib (with Klaus Winter; M Rolf Zimmermann). Pr 1976 Halle.

1976   *Reise mit Joujou (A Trip with Joujou).* Mus Lib (based on Guy de Maupassant; M Robert Hanell). Pr 1976 Gera.

1976   *Geld wie Heu (Money to Burn).* Mus Lib (M Rudi Werion). Pr 1977 Met.

      Mirandolina. Com (based on Goldoni).

1979   *Das Fräulein wird Minister ‹Hoftheater› (Miss Minister of State ‹Putting on an Act at Court›).* Mus Lib (based on Margit Gaspar; M Rolf Zimmermann).

1981   *Des Königs Datsche oder Nackenstützen für Badewannen (The King's Dacha or Neck Braces for Bathtubs).* Mus Lib (with Klaus Winter; M Martin Hattwig). Pr 1982 Halle.

1981   *Babettes grüner Schmetterling (Babette's Green Butterfly).* Mus Lib (M Robert Hanell). Pr 1982 Weimar. *TdZ* 1983/1.

1981   *Gehobene Unterhaltung (High-Class Conversation).* Com.

1982   *Ein Mann zum Heiraten (A Man for Marrying).* Com. Pr 1983 Parchim.

EISENLOHR, Friedrich
28 May 1889 Freiburg im Breisgau - 18 Oct 1954 Berlin
Journalist, dramaturg, editor.

1947   *Die Hochzeitsreise (The Honeymoon).* Dr (based on novel by De Coster). Pr 1948 Schwerin.

EISLER, Hanns
6 July 1898 Leipzig - 6 Sep 1962 Berlin
Composer; studied in Vienna under Arnold Schönberg; 1924-33 Berlin, then emigration to Austria, Holland, Belgium, France, England, Denmark, USA; 48 return to Vienna; 50 Prof. at MHS Berlin. 1948 National Prize for GDR national anthem (text by Johannes R. Becher).

1952   *Johann Faustus.* Dr with M. Pr 1974 Tübingen. *Sinn & Form* 1952/6. *Th.h.* 1974/5. Aufbau 1952. Henschel 1983.

EISLER (cont'd)
1962   *Kalifornische Ballade (California Ballad)*. Dr with M
        (based on text by Ernst Ottwalt). Pr 1970 MG.

ELBERS, Martin
1963   *Das Brigadekind (The Child of the Brigade)*. Com (with
        Eugen Schaub). Pr 1963 Halle.

ENDER, Roland
        Glücklich, aber verheiratet (Happy but Married). Com.
1976   *Das Wunschkind (The Ideal Child)*. Com. Pr 1977 Wit-
        tenberg.
1978   *Frauen sind Männersache (Women are a Man's Business)*.
        Com. Pr 1978 Wittenberg.
1981   *Lachen Sie einfach mit (Just Join in the Laughter)*.
        Com. Pr 1982 Wittenberg.

ENDERS, Horst
23 Oct 1921 Beiersdorf -
Attended engineering school; 1940 Army service, 44-47 POW; 51
textile engineer, later vocational teacher; 59 dramaturg Rostock, since 63 TV dramaturg. Writes radio and TV plays.
1956   *Victory-Day*. Dr (based on Guy de Maupassant). Pr 19-
        57 Gera.
1957   ‹*Stützpunkt*› *Trufanowa* (‹*Stronghold*› *Trufanova*). Dr.
        Pr 1958 Altenburg.
1958-59 *Das Haus im Schatten (The House in the Shadows)*. Dr
        (based on TV play). Pr 1960 Rostock.
1960   *Ankerplatz (Anchorage)*. Dr (based on I. Shtok). Pr
        1961 Rostock.
1961   *Eine Million für ein Lächeln (A Million for a Smile)*.
        Com (based on Anatoly Sofronov). Pr 1961 Rostock.
1966   *Warschauer Konzert (Warsaw Concerto)*. Dr. Pr 1967
        Rostock. *TdZ* 1967/8.
1967   *Das neue Kapitel (The New Chapter)*. Dr (with Horst-
        Ulrich Wendler). *TdZ* 1967/21.
1970   *Dissonanzen (Dissonances)*. Dr. Pr 1970 Greifswald.
1975   *Namensgebung (Christening)*. Dr. Pr 1976 Th. d. jg.
        Generation, Lpzg.

ENDLER, Adolf
10 Sep 1930 Düsseldorf -
After various careers, became journalist in FRG; came to GDR
in 1955; 55-57 I. Lit Lpzg, then editor, critic, translator;
now lives in Berlin; married to Elke Erb. Writes prose and
poetry.
1972   *Krali Marko*. Juv (based on I. Teofilov). Pr 1973.
1973   *Das bucklige Pferdchen (The Humpbacked Pony)*. Juv
        (with Elke Erb; based on poem by O. Yerzhov). Pr 19-
        73 Th. d. Freundschaft, Berlin. *TdZ* 1973/3.
1976   *Ramayana*. Juv (with Elke Erb; based on Indian epic,
        adapted by Walter Ruben). Pr 1976 Th. d. Freund-
        schaft, Berlin.

ENGELMANN, Heinz

1961   *Der Ketzer aus Nola (The Heretic from Nola)*. Dr. Pr 1962 Crimmitschau.

ENSIKAT, Peter

1941 Finsterwalde –

Graduated high school 1959; then until 62 training as actor at Th. HS Lpzg; 62-65 actor and asst. stage director, Th. d. jg. Generation, Dsdn; 65-75 Th. d. Freundschaft, Berlin. 19-85 Lessing Prize. Writes for cabaret, film, and TV.

   Das Rübchen (The Little Carrot). Juv (with Horst Hawemann; based on Pavel Malyarevsky).

1965   *Die Prinzessin und der Schweinehirt (The Princess and the Swineherd)*. Juv (based on Hans Christian Andersen). Pr 1965 Th. d. jg. Generation, Dsdn.

1967   *Gavroche*. Juv (based on Victor Hugo). Pr 1967 Th. d. jg. Generation, Dsdn.

1968   *Dornröschen (Sleeping Beauty)*. Juv (based on Grimm; incidental M Hans-Jürgen Noack). Pr 1969 Th. d. jg. Generation, Dsdn. Rev 1980.

1969   *Tschintschraka oder Das große Abenteuer eines kleinen Gauklers (Tshintshraka or The Great Adventure of a Little Conjurer)*. Juv (with Horst Hawemann; based on Russian fairy tale by Georgyi Nakhutsrishvily). Pr 1970 Th. d. Freundschaft, Berlin.

1976   *Vasantasena*. Mus Lib (based on Indian motifs; M Guido Masanetz). Pr 1978 Met.

1977   *Der Wolf und die sieben Geißlein (The Wolf and the Seven Goats)*. Juv Mus Lib (based on Grimm; M Jochen Allihn). Pr 1978 Mgdbg.

1978   *Die Bremer Stadtmusikanten (The Town Musicians of Bremen)*. Juv (based on Grimm). Pr 1980 Potsdam. *TdZ* 1979/6.

1978   *Spuk in der Bibliothek (Ghosts in the Library)*. Com. Pr 1979 Rostock.

1979   *Das tapfere Schneiderlein (The Brave Little Tailor)*. Juv (based on Grimm; incidental M Rainer Lischka). Pr 1980 Th. d. jg. Generation, Dsdn.

1979   *Bürger schützt eure Anlagen oder Wem die Mütze paßt (Citizens Protect Your Parks or If the Cap Fits)*. Com (with Wolfgang Schaller). Pr 1982 Stralsund. Henschel 1983.

1980   *Von Tisch und Bett (Legally Separated)*. Com. Pr 19-81 Met.

1980   *Hase und Igel (The Hare and the Hedgehog)*. Juv Mus Lib (based on Grimm; M Bernd Wefelmeyer). Pr 1982 Th. d. Freundschaft, Berlin.

1981   *Frech wie Oskar (Fresh Like Oscar)*. Juv (with Heinz Kahlau and Erich Schlossarek). Pr 1982 Fkft/O.

1983   *Dreiklang (Three-Part Harmony)*. Juv Mus Lib (M Bernd Wefelmeyer). Pr 1983 Th. d. Freundschaft, Berlin.

1984   *Was soll das ganze Theater?   (What Is This Act For?)* Cabaret. Pr 1985 VB.

ERB, Elke   (married name Elke Endler)
18 Feb 1938 Scherbach/Eifel –
In GDR since 1949; 57-58 and 59-63 studied history, German
literature, and Slavic languages in Halle; in-between industrial worker; later editor; lives in Berlin. Writes poems, essays, translations.
1968   *Mein spöttisches Glück (My Ironic Fortune)*. Dr (based
        on Leonard Malyudin). Pr 1970 Rostock.
1973   *Das bucklige Pferdchen (The Humpbacked Pony).* Juv
        (with Adolf Endler; based on poem by O. Yerzhov). Pr
        1973 Th. d. Freundschaft, Berlin. *TdZ* 1973/3.
1976   *Ramayana*. Juv (with Adolf Endler; based on Indian e-
        pic, adapted by Walter Ruben). Pr 1976 Th. d. Freund-
        schaft, Berlin.
        Die Heirat (The Marriage). Com (tr from Nicolai Go-
        gol).
        Boris Godunov. Dr (tr from Alexander Pushkin).
        Bruder Aljoscha (Brother Alyosha). Dr (based on no-
        vel by Dostoyevsky, "The Brothers Karamazov").

ERGE   see Emil Rudolf GREULICH

ERPENBECK, Fritz (Pseud. Fritz BECK, Helmut FRANCKE)
6 Apr 1897 Mainz – 7 Jan 1975 Berlin
Worked as locksmith and plumber; 1915-18 served in WW I, then
training as actor in Osnabrück until 21; later actor, dramaturg, and stage director in various theaters; 27 joined KPD;
31-33 journalist and editor; 33 emigration to Prague, then
with wife (Hedda Zinner) to Soviet Union; member National Committee "Freies Deutschland"; 45 returned to Berlin, editor of
various journals; 59 Chief Dramaturg VB.   1956 Lessing Prize.
Wrote short stories, novels, theater criticism, essays.
1949   *Der Tiefstapler (Living below One's Means)*. Com (un-
        der pseud. Fritz Beck). Pr 1950 Weimar.
1959   *Zimmer ‹Nr.› 13 (Room ‹No.› 13)*. On (under pseud.
        Helmut Francke). Pr 1960 VB.

ERPENBECK, Hedda   see Hedda ZINNER

ESCHNER, Eugen
1937 Zawaby, Poland –
1947 moved to Freiberg (Saxony); 54-56 studied Th. HS Lpzg;
acting engagements Wismar, Greifswald, MG, and Th. d. Freundschaft, Berlin; since 76 independent author.
1957   *Das Untier von Samarkand (The Monster of Samarkand)*.
        Juv (with Peter Hacks and Anna E. Wiede). Pr 1957
        Th. d. Freundschaft, Berlin. *Märchendramen*, Henschel
        1980.
1972   *Die Kristallkugel (The Crystal Ball)*. Juv (based on
        Grimm). Pr 1973 Brandenburg.
1973   *König Jorg (King Jorg)*. Juv. Pr 1974 Th. d. jg. Ge-
        neration, Dsdn. *TdZ* 1974/4. *Märchendramen*, Henschel
        1980.

ESCHNER (cont'd)

1976   *Frühlingskapriolen (Spring Capers)*. Juv (based on short story by Vladimir Tendriakov, "Frühlingswirbel"). Pr 1978 Th. d. Freundschaft, Berlin.

1979   *Lilith*. Dr (incidental M Peter Rabenalt).

1981   *Undine*. Juv. Pr 1982 Th. d. Freundschaft, Berlin. *TdZ* 1982/2.

EYLT, Ernst   see Peter HACKS

FABIAN, Gerhard
15 June 1930 Hamburg -
Theater historian, dramaturg; lives in Lpzg. Writes poetry, radio plays.
1957 ‹*Geschichten um*› *Marie Hedder* (‹*Stories about*› *Marie Hedder*). Dr. Pr 1958 Greifswald.
1959 *Die Stärkeren (The Stronger Ones).* Dr. Pr 1959 Dessau. Leipzig: Hofmeister, 1960.
1961 *Die Füchse (The Foxes).* Lib.
1972 *Menschenskind, Nikolka! (Man Oh Man, Nicky!).* Juv. Pr 1972 Halle.
1977 *Gardeschütze Mattrosow (Guardsman Mattrosov).* Juv (based on novel by P. Skurba). Pr 1977 Halle.

FASSDAUBE, Hans   see John STAVE

FAUST, Bernhard
13 Mar 1879 Greußen - 22 Feb 1963 Dresden
Graduate engineer; wrote novels and short stories.
1948 *Bindegarn (Twine).* Dr. Pr 1950 Parchim.

FELKEL, Günter
5 Aug 1921 Dresden -
1941-45 served in WW II; deserted shortly before end of war; 45 founded little theater, "Dresden Künstlerstudio"; director and announcer for Radio Dresden. Writes poetry, novels, radio plays.
1947 *Unsterbliche Flamme (Eternal Flame).* Dr. Pr 1948 Görlitz.
1948 *Belastungsprobe* ‹*Die tausend Tapferen*› *(Stress Test* ‹*The Thousand Brave Ones*›). Dr. Pr 1951 Neue Bühne, Berlin.
1949 *Der Aufstand (The Uprising).* Dr. Pr 1949.
1949 *Die Welle (The Wave).* Dr. Pr 1949 Steelworks Riesa.
1953 *Oel* ‹*Der Kampf um Erdöl*› *(Oil* ‹*The Struggle for Petroleum*›). Dr. Pr 1953 Schwerin.
1955-58 *Narkose (Anaesthesia).* Dr. Pr 1958 Erfurt.
1959 *Affentheater (Monkeyshines).* Dr.

FENSCH, Eberhard
1928 -
Journalist; 1958-63 director, broadcast studio Rostock, then director GDR Radio, Berlin.
1968 *Original Anregung aus Betrieben der DDR (Original Stimulation from GDR Concerns).* Sc (part of program of short pieces under collective title of "Anregung I"). Pr 1969 Halle.
1970 *Anregung II (Stimulation II).* Sc (part of program of short pieces under collective title. Pr 1970 Halle.

FEUSTEL, Gotthard
1979   *Hirsch Heinrich (Henry the Stag).* Pp (based on children's book by Fred Rodrian). Pr 1980 Pp.Th., Berlin.
1980   *Der doppelte Schatten (The Double Shadow).* Pp (based on Indian folk tale). Pr 1980 Pp. Th., Berlin.
1981   *Kasper und Iwanuschka (Punch and Little Ivan).* Pp. Pr 1981 Pp. Th., Berlin.
1982   *Kleine Ente Namenlos (The Little Nameless Duck).* Pp (with Ilsolde Stark). Pr 1983 Pp Th., Berlin.

FINCK, Wolfgang
1963-64 *Reifeprüfung (Final Examination).* Dr. Pr 1964 Parchim

FINDEISEN, Kurt Arnold (Pseud. Wendelin DUDELSACK)
15 Oct 1883 Zwickau - 18 Nov 1963 Dresden
Attended Pedagogical Institute and Univ. Dsdn; then became grade school teacher; 1915-18 medical orderly; 25-33 worked for Central German Radio, 34 dismissed by Nazis. 1929 Lessing Prize. Editor, wrote prose and radio scripts.
1933   *Ein deutsches Herz (A German Heart).* Dr. Pr 1934 Dsdn.
1937   *Das Spiel vom Prinzenraub (The Play about the Abducted Prince).* Juv. Pr 1937 Dsdn.
1951   *Das Spiel vom Pumphut (The Play about the Borrowed Hat).* Juv.

FINK, Walter
1967   *Käte Kerri.* Dr (based on novel by Irma Harder, "Die Spatzen pfeifens schon vom Dach").

FISCHBORN, Gottfried
1936 –
1955-59 studied theater history; 59-61 dramaturg Meiningen; since 61 Prof. Th. HS Lpzg. Writes essays, criticism, radio and TV plays.
1971   *Mildernde Umstände: keine (Extenuating Circumstances: None).* Dr (based on Leonid Gorbachov, "Keine Begnadigung"). Pr 1971 Altenburg. *TdZ* 1972/2.
1974   *Löser oder Die Todesspirale (Löser or The Death Spiral).* Dr. Reading 1974 Halle; Pr 1977 Meiningen.

FLECHSIG, Horst
1981   *Tristan und Isold.* Com (based on Hans Sachs). Pr 1982 Rudolstadt.

FLEGEL, Walter
17 Nov 1934 Freiburg (now Swiebodzice, Poland) –
After high school, three years military academy Dsdn, then artillery officer; 1960-63 I. Lit Lpzg, then began writing. 19-61 and 69 State Prize, 72 Theodor Körner Prize. Writes radio and TV plays, prose.
1973   *Draufgänger (Daredevils).* Juv. Pr 1974 Th. d. jg. Generation, Dsdn.
1974   *Soldaten (Soldiers).* Dr.

FLIEG, Helmut   see Stefan HEYM

FOCKE, Gerd   (Pseud. as journalist: Jens SIMON)
7 Apr 1927 Leipzig –
At age 17, drafted into Labor Service; after 1946, actor, dramaturg; 53-57 Chief Dramaturg Nordhausen; 60-64 stage director Th. d. jg. Garde, Halle; since 64 dramaturg GDR TV.

1954   *Sie tragen wieder Ritterkreuz (They Are Wearing Knights' Crosses Again)*. Dr.

1957   *Gaunerballade (Scoundrels' Ballad)*. Com.

1958   *Gefährliches Schweigen (Dangerous Silence)*. Dr. Pr 1959 Nordhausen.

1959   *Skandal um Meegeren (Scandal about Meegeren)*. Dr. Pr 1959 Nordhausen.

1963   *Weißt du, wo du zu Hause bist? (Do You Know Where Home Is?)*. Juv. Pr 1963 Th. d. jg. Garde, Halle.

1967   *Fronten (Fronts)*. Dr. Pr 1968.

1968   *Signal auf Rot (Red Signal)*. Dr (based on Otto Gotsche).

1971   *Die Pariserin (The Parisian Woman)*. Dr (based on Henri Becque).

1974   *Fünfmal die Drei (Five Times Three)*. Com. Pr 1974 Gera.

1975   *Der große Coup des Waldi P. (Waldi P.'s Great Coup)*. Juv. Pr 1976 Parchim.

1977   *Gefrühstückt wird um acht (Breakfast Is at Eight)*. Com. Pr 1979 Wittenberg.

        Ein verrückter Einfall (A Crazy Idea). Com (with Carl Lauffs). Pr Wittenberg.

1983   *Rinaldo Rinaldini*. Dr. Pr 1984 Quedlinburg.

FOELLBACH, Lena   (nee Benedix)
19 May 1916 Braunsdorf –
Worked as plant manager in Cuxhaven, Dsdn, Wiesbaden; 1946-52 went with husband to USSR; later editor Friedrich Hofmeister Verlag, Lpzg; studied at Theater Institute Lpzg, then moved to Rostock; now lives in FRG. Writes children's books, children's TV and radio plays.

        Kaspar und das Wahrheitstuch (Punch and the Cloth of Truth). Pp.

1956   *Schneeweißchen und Rosenrot (Snow-White and Rose-Red)*. Juv Mus Lib (based on Grimm; M Carl-Ernst Ortwein). Lpzg: Hofmeister, 1956.

1961   *Ein halbes Jahr geht schnell vorbei (Half a Year Goes By Quickly)*. Juv. Pr 1962 Th.d. jg. Welt, Lpzg.

1962   *So eine reizende Familie (Such a Charming Family)*. Com. Pr 1962 Rostock.

1963   *Großvater, wo steckst du? (Grandfather, Where Are You Hiding?)*. Juv Mus Lib (M Carl-Ernst Ortwein). Pr 1963 Th. d. jg. Welt, Lpzg.

1969   *Das Märchen vom salzigen Quell (The Tale of the Salty Spring)*. Juv. Pr 1969 Greifswald. Rev 1981 as *Die Geschichte von Liebe und Salz*.

FOELLBACH (cont'd)
1973   *Die drei Schwestern (The Three Sisters)*. Juv Op Lib.
1974   *Jahresringe (Annual Circles)*.   Dr. Pr 1974 Rostock.
        TdZ 1974/11.
1976   *Es war einmal kein König (Once Upon a Time There Was
        No King)*. Juv (based on fairy tale). Henschel 1977.
1977   *Das gläserne Glöckchen (The Little Glass Bell)*. Pp.
        Pr 1978 Halle.
1978   *Die beiden Geschenke (The Two Gifts)*.   Pp (with Rolf
        Thieme). Pr 1978 Halle.
1979   *Kapitän Pudelmütze (Captain Pompon-Cap)*. Pp. Pr 19-
        79 KMSt.
1980   *Der habgierige Richter (The Greedy Judge)*. Juv. Pr
        1981 Pionierth., Schwerin.
1981   *Die Geschichte von Liebe und Salz (The Tale of Love
        and Salt)*. Juv Op Lib (rev of Das Märchen vom salzi-
        gen Quell; M Kurt Dietmar Richter). Pr 1982 Halber-
        stadt.

FOREST, Jean Kurt
2 Apr 1909 Darmstadt - 2 Mar 1975 Berlin
Started playing violin at four, first concert at six; studied
Conservatory Wiesbaden; 1926-29 concertmaster for various or-
chestras; 30-34 solo violist; 34-38 emigrated to France, returned to Germany; 39 Music Director Braunschweig Th.; drafted 40, deserted to Red Army; 48-56 conductor GDR Radio and
TV, then independent composer and librettist.
1959   *Der Arme Konrad (Poor Conrad)*. Op (based on Fried-
        rich Wolf).
1959   *Die Fischer von Niezow (The Fisherman of Niezow)*. Opt
        (with Hedda Zinner).
1960   *Tai Yang erwacht (Tai Yang Awakens)*. Op (with Walter
        Pollatschek; based on Friedrich Wolf). Pr 1960 St.Op.
1963   *Wie Tiere des Waldes (Like the Animals in the Woods)*.
        Op (based on Friedrich Wolf).
1964   *Die Passion des Johannes Hörder (The Passion of Jo-
        hannes Hörder)*. Op (based on Johannes Becher, "Win-
        terschlacht"). Pr 1965 Stralsund.
1967   *Die Blumen von Hiroshima (The Flowers of Hiroshima)*.
        Op (based on novel by Edita Morris). Pr 1967 Weimar.

FÖRSTER-STAHL, Heidemarie   see Heidemarie STAHL

FRANCKE, Helmut   see Fritz ERPENBECK

FRANK, Elisabeth   see Hedda ZINNER

FREESE, Rudolf
3 June 1914 Nowawes -
Editor.
1949   *Das stärkere Gesetz (The Stronger Law)*. Dr. Pr 1949
        Eisenach.

FREIHEIT, Peter
14 June 1940 Breslau (now Wroclaw, Poland) –
After 1945, member Halle Boys' Choir, took cello instruction; later studied composition Halle Conservatory; 65 cellist Altenburg Th., then member Handel Festival Orchestra Halle; artistic director Th. d. jg. Garde, Halle; since 80 conductor Halle Chamber Ensemble. Composer and librettist.

1981   *Der Bär (The Bear)*. Op (based on Chekhov). Pr 1982 Halle.

1984   *Der Heiratsantrag (The Marriage Proposal)*. Op (based on Chekhov). Pr 1984 Halle.

FREITAG, Franz
21 June 1925 Lassan/Wolgast –
Son of Communist worker family; parents arrested 1933 and tried for high treason; served in WW II, then Russian POW; after 46 farm worker, smith, municipal administrator; 59-60 and 65-67 I.Lit Lpzg; since 62 lives as independent writer in Neustrelitz. 1963 and 72 Fritz Reuter Prize. Writes TV and cabaret texts.

1961   *Sozialistischer Frühling (Socialist Spring)*. Cantata. Pr 1961.

1963   *Verschwörung um Hannes (Conspiracy about Hannes)*. Com. Pr 1963 Meiningen. *TdZ* 1963/14.

1964   *Sorgenkinder (Problem Children)*. Com. Pr 1964 Neustrelitz. *TdZ* 1965/6.

1965   *Ehekrach und heiße Noten (Marital Squabble and Hot Music)*. Mus Lib. Pr 1966.

1967   *Der Egoist*. Com. Pr 1968 Neustrelitz.

1968   *Ellermann macht alles (Ellermann Does Everything)*. Com. Pr 1969 Anklam.

1970   *Memoiren eines Aktivisten (Memoirs of an Activist)*. Dr. Pr 1971.

1973   *Die Zwillinge (The Twins)*. Pr 1973.

FREITAG, Manfred
4 June 1934 Reichenbach –
1954 worked as assistant librarian KMSt; 55 joined People's Police; 56-60 studied dramaturgy Film HS Potsdam, since then script writer for DEFA. 1965 Documentary Film Prize, Lpzg. Writes prose, film and TV scripts.

1966   *Seemannsliebe (Sailor's Love)*. Mus Lib (with Joachim Nestler; M Günter Hauck). Pr 1967 MG. *TdZ* 1967/15. Henschel 1968.

1971   *Tandem oder Moralisches Rezept für doppelte Eheführung (Tandem or Moral Recipe for Bigamy)*. Com (with Joachim Nestler). Pr 1971 Brandenburg.

FRENZEL, Klaus
     Das Feuerzeug (The Tinderbox). Pp (based on Hans Christian Andersen). Pr Schwerin.
     Hänsel und Gretel. Pp (based on Grimm). Pr Schwerin.
     Hilfe, ich bin der Kaspar (Help, I am Punch). Pp. Pr Schwerin.

FRENZEL (cont'd)
> *Großvater und Enkel besuchen den Schnee (Grandfather and Grandson Visit the Snow).* Pp. Pr Schwerin.

1982 *Vom Fischer und seiner Frau (The Fisherman and His Wife).* Pp (based on Grimm). Pr 1983 Schwerin.

1983 *Pinkus.* Juv. Pr 1984 Schwerin.

FREYER, Paul Herbert   (Pseud. Flacon CHANEL, Claus JÜRGENS)
4 Nov 1920 Crimmitschau – 13 Aug 1983 Berlin
1936 worked as a seaman; 47 dramaturg Crimmitschau, 51 Chief Dramaturg Gera, later MG; 55 Managing Director Th. Plauen, after 56 General Manager KMSt Theaters; since 60 lives in Berlin. Ernst Arndt Medal. Wrote prose and TV scripts.

1950 *Der Pfad der Irrenden (The Path of the Bewildered).* Dr. Pr 1960 Crimmitschau.

1951 *Auf verlorenem Posten (On a Lost Outpost).* Dr. Pr 1951 Neue Bühne, Berlin.

1952 *Der Dämpfer (The Damper).* Com. Pr 1953 Gera.

1953 *Kornblumen (Cornflowers).* Dr. Pr 1954 Meiningen.

1954 *Die Straße hinauf (Up the Street).* Dr. Pr 1954 Dessau.

1954 *Schiff auf großer Fahrt (Ship at Full Speed).* Juv. Pr 1954 Halle.

1955 *Die wilden Schwäne (The Wild Swans).* Juv (with Fred Lanzendorf; based on Hans Christian Andersen). Pr 1955 Plauen. Lpzg: Hofmeister, 1955.

1956 *Wenn man Freunde hat (If You Have Friends).* Dr (under pseud. Claus Jürgens). Pr 1957 KMSt.

1957 *Brokat aus Frankreich (Brocade from France).* Com (under pseud. Flacon Chanel). Pr 1958 KMSt.

1960 *Karl Marx.* Dr.

1961 *Das Amulettt (The Good-Luck Charm).* Dr. Pr 1962 Magdeburg.

1964 *Die Zeit der Hoffnung (The Time of Hope).* Dr. Pr 1964 Dsdn.

1966 *Der Hausmeister (The Building Superintendent).* Com.

1967 *Familiensonntag (Family Sunday).* Com. Pr 1968.

1968 *Nachbarn (Neighbors).* Dr. Pr 1968 Greifswald.

FRICKE, Jürgen
1964 *Das zweite Gesicht (Second Sight).* Dr. Pr 1965 Gera.

1969 *Das Geschenk (The Gift).* Juv. Pr 1969 Th. d. jg. Generation, Dsdn.

FRIEDRICH, Karl
20 Jan 1920 Stockheim –
Studied at Dsdn Conservatory; 1930 violinist Dsdn Philharmonic; 61 Instructor for violin Dsdn MHS. Composer.
1960-62 *Tartuffe.* Op (based on Moliere). Pr 1964 Dsdn.

FRIES, Hans Joachim (Heinz)
24 Mar 1919 Hohenneudorf/Berlin –
Writes cabaret and song texts.
1953 *Zwecks späterer Heirat (Future Intentions: Marriage).* Com. Pr 1955 Güstrow.

FRIES (cont'd)

1955   *Sappho in Paris*.   Mus Lib (M Wilhelm Licht).   Pr 1956 Güstrow.

1970   *Ringtausch (Exchange of Rings)*.   Mus Lib.   Pr   1972 Parchim.

FRITZSCHE, Eva

    Die Schweinekirmes (The Hog Fair).   Mus Lib (with Susanne Dancker; M Eberhard Schmidt).

FÜHMANN, Franz

15 Jan 1922 Rochlitz (now Rokytnice, Czechoslovakia) - July 1984 Berlin

Drafted while still in school; Russian POW, returned home 19-49; after 50 lived in Berlin as independent author. Member AdK; 1956 Heinrich Mann Prize, 57 National Prize, 63 Johannes Becher Prize, 64 FDGB Prize, 70 Barlach Medal, 72 Lion Feuchtwanger Prize. Wrote poetry, novels, short stories, children's books, essays, radio plays, film scripts.

1956   *Lidice*.   Cantata (M Ruth Zechlin).   Pr 1958 Berlin.

1984   *Die Schatten (The Shadows)*.   Dr (based on radio play; adapted by students at School of Drama, Berlin).   Pr 1985 Studio Theater "bat," Berlin.

G

GABRIEL, Gerhard
> *Steffel und der Zauberhut (Steffel and the Magic Hat).*
> Juv. Pr 1971 Zeitz.
1978   *Der Schatz in der Zauberhöhle (The Treasure in the Magic Cave).* Juv. Pr 1979 Zeitz.

GANGRAIN, Wolf   see Wolfgang Rainer GERLACH

GASSAUER, Karl
1973   *Der verspielte Scheidungsgrund (Lost Grounds for Divorce).* Com. Pr 1973 MG.
1983   *Casanova auf Schloß Dux (Casanova at Dux Castle).* Com (based on TV play). Pr 1986 Fkft/M.

GAY, Fritz
27 May 1907 Gera - 23 May 1969 Dresden
Studied literature and art history; wrote poetry, prose, essays.
> *Das Pinguinenei (The Penguin Egg).* Juv.
1958   *Die Schuhe der Zarin (The Tsarina's Shoes).* Pp (based on Gogol).
1960   *Der Wildtöter (The Deer Slayer).* Pp (based on James Fenimore Cooper). Pr 1962 Greiz.
1964   *Das tapfere Schneiderlein (The Brave Little Tailor).* Juv (based on Grimm). Pr 1964 Dsdn.

GEIGER, Erich (Pseud. Jan MICHELL)
12 Jan 1924 Karlsruhe -
Studied medicine; then became stage and TV director, dramaturg; now lives in Steinburg (FRG). Writes prose and TV scripts.
1950   *Bei Mirandolina (At Mirandolina's).* Mus Lib (based on Goldoni; M Herbert Kawan).
1956   *Sterne, Geld und Vagabunden (Stars, Money, and Vagabonds).* Mus Lib (with Andreas Bauer; M Herbert Kawan).
1956   *Lucius Sulla.* Op Lib (M Mozart).
1958   *Geiger, Gauner und Geschäfte (Fiddlers, Scoundrels, and Deals).* Com. Pr 1959 Vidin, Bulgaria.
1959   *Tatort Warenhaus (Department Store Crime).* Dr (under pseud. Jan Michell; with Martin Blankenfeld). Pr 19-60 Dsdn.
1979   *Fremde Federn (Borrowed Plumes).* Dr (based on Guy de Maupassant).
1979   *Terrorfalle (Terror Trap).* Dr.
1979   *Erdbebenernte (Earthquake Harvest).* Dr.

GEISSLER, Fritz
16 Sep 1921 Wurzen - 1983 Bad Sauer
After high school, violinist in Lpzg; served in WW II, POW in England; 1948-53 MHS Dsdn, Berlin; since 53 Instructor,then Professor MHS Lpzg. Composer and librettist.

GEISSLER (cont'd)
1970   *Der zerbrochene Krug (The Broken Jug)*. Op (with Christian Geißler; based on Kleist). Pr 1971 Lpzg.
1972   *Der verrückte Jourdain (Crazy Jourdain)*. Mus (based on Mikhail Bulgakov). Pr 1973 Rostock. Rev version Pr 1979 Gera.

GENG, Heinz
1966   *Das tapfere Schneiderlein (The Brave Little Tailor)*. Juv (based on Grimm). Pr 1966 Döbeln.

GENTZ, Friedrich (also known as Fred BILLERBECK-GENTZ)
22 June 1903 Dühringsdorf - ?
Actor, dramaturg; during Nazi period, Editor-in-Chief, Zentralverlag Berlin. Wrote prose, poetry.
1934   *Opposition der Erde (Opposition of the Earth)*. Dr. Pr 1934 Erfurt.
1935   *Francis Bacon*. Dr. Pr 1936 Lübeck.
1937   *Heimdalls Erneuerung (Heimdall's Revival)*. Choral work.
1938   *Pässe nach Deutschland (Passports for Germany)*. Dr. Pr 1938 Stralsund.
        Befreiung (Liberation). Dr.
1950   *Liebe ist nicht immer blind (Love Is Not Always Blind)*. Com. Pr 1951 Mgdbg.
1956   *Pilot Herzog*. Dr. Pr 1956 Greiz.

GERISCH, Klaus
15 June 1936 Stollberg -
Electrician's apprentice, then attended Sports Academy Werda; later became artistic director of cabaret "Hornissen"; lives in Cottbus. Johannes Becher Medal. Writes short stories and novels.
1964   *Doch der Vierzehnte (But the Fourteenth)*. Dr.
1971   *Das Jahr und Katrin (The Year and Katrina)*. Dr (based on novel, publ. Rostock: Hinstorff, 1972). Pr 1974 Cottbus.

GERLACH, Friedrich
? Bremen - 17 Mar 1984 Berlin
Protestant minister; actor and manager of amateur theater group.
1970   *Die Herren des Strandes (Masters of the Beach)*. Juv with M (based on short story by Jorge Amado; M Georg Katzer). Pr 1971 Th. d. Freundschaft, Berlin.

GERLACH, Harald
7 Mar 1940 Bunzlau (now Boleslawiecz, Poland) -
Moved to Thüringen 1945; completed high school 58 Meiningen, then various occupations, including stage technician and later stage manager; 70-79 literary advisor Erfurt Th.; 79-83 stage director Stendal. Writes poetry, cabaret texts, prose.
1969   *Das kalte Herz (The Cold Heart)*. Juv (based on Wilhelm Hauff). Pr 1969 Erfurt.

GERLACH, Harald (cont'd)
1974   *Rodaer Ballade (The Ballad of Roda)*. Cantata Text. Pr 1974.
1975-78 *Der Preis (The Prize)*. Op Lib (M Karl Ottomar Treibmann). Pr 1980 Erfurt.
1976   *Till*. Juv (based on Grigory Gorin). Pr Erfurt. *‹Vier› Szenen (‹Four› Scenes): Stufen (Steps); Westerplatte (Western Plateau); Der Fakir; Barrikade (Barricade)*. Spiele, Aufbau 1983.
1979   *Die Straße (The Street)*. Dr. Pr 1979 Erfurt. *TdZ* 1980/5. Spiele, 1983.
1980   *Der Pfahl (The Stake)*. Com. Spiele, 1983.
1982   *Held Ulysses (Ulysses, the Hero)*. Dr (based on Holberg, "Ulysses von Ithaka"). Pr 1982 Erfurt.
1983   *Der Idiot*. Op Lib (based on Dostoyevsky; M Karl Ottomar Treibmann). Spiele, 1983.
1983   *Scherz, Satire, Ironie und tiefere Bedeutung (Jest, Satire, Irony, and Deeper Meaning)*. Op Lib (based on Grabbe; M Karl Ottomar Treibmann). Pr 1986 Erfurt.
1983   *Die Schicht (The Shift)*. Juv. Pr 1984 Erfurt. *TdZ* 1984/9.

GERLACH, Wolfgang Rainer   (Pseud. Wolf GANGRAIN)
1978   *Das tapfere Schneiderlein (The Brave Little Tailor)*. Juv Mus Lib (written under pseudonym Wolf Gangrain; based on Grimm; M Hans Ostarek). Pr 1979 Stendal.
1981   *Detektiv Tom (Detective Tom)*. Juv. Pr 1981 Stendal.

GERSCH, Christel
Translator; lives in Berlin as independent author.
1979   *Jacques und sein Herr oder Die Willkür des Autors (Jacques and His Master or The Author's Caprice)*. Com (based on novel by Denis Diderot). Pr 1980 Weimar.
1980   *Der Geizige (The Miser)*. Com (tr from Moliere).
1983   *Lorenzaccio*. Com (tr from Alfred de Musset).
1984   *Einer macht den Hansel (He Who Plays the Fool)*. Com (based on Georges Feydeau, "Le dindon").

GERSCH, Tilmann
1965 –
After high school, became stagehand DT.
1982   *Sisyphos*. Dr. Reading 1984 Lpzg.

GERSTER, Ottmar
29 June 1897 Braunfels – 31 Aug 1969 Leipzig
Served in WW I; 1919-21 Conservatory Fkft/M; 21-24 violinist Fkft Symphony Orch., later concertmaster and music teacher; 47 Prof., 48-51 Director, MHS Weimar; 52-62 Prof. MHS Lpzg. Since 1950 AdK; 51-60 President of Assoc'n. of German Composers; 51 Nat'l Prize; 56 Lpzg Art Prize. Composer and librettist.
1933   *Madame Lieselotte*. Opt. Pr 1933 Essen.
1936   *Enoch Arden oder Der Möwenschrei (Enoch Arden or The Cry of the Seagulls)*. Op (with Karl von Levetzow; based on poem by Tennyson). Pr 1936 Düsseldorf.

GERSTER (cont'd)

1941 *Die Hexe von Passau (The Witch of Passau)*. Op (with Richard Billinger). Pr 1941 Düsseldorf.

1949 *Das verzauberte Ich (The Enchanted Self)*. Op. Pr 19-49 Wuppertal.

1960 *Der fröhliche Sünder (The Cheerful Sinner)*. Op (based on comedy by Leonid Solovyov). Pr 1963 Weimar.

GILBRICHT, Walter
24 Oct 1891 Chemnitz (now Karl Marx Stadt) - 13 Aug 1974 Leipzig
Public school teacher Lpzg; later author and editor. Wrote prose and radio plays.

1931 *Großstadt mit einem Einwohner (The Metropolis with One Inhabitant)*. Com.

1932 *Oliver Cromwells Sendung (Oliver Cromwell's Mission)*. Dr.

1935 *Michael Kohlhaas.* Dr (based on Kleist).

1936 *Marie Charlotte Corday.* Dr.

1937 *Spartanische Suppe (Spartan Soup)*. Com.

1938 *Letizia (Letitia)*. Dr.

1939 *Abraham Lincoln.* Dr (rev 1955 as Das Amerika Abraham Lincolns).

1940 *Die Gallwespe (The Gall Wasp)*. Com.

1940 *Erbe seiner selbst (His Own Heir)*. Com.

1941 *Ulysses daheim (Ulysses at Home)*. Com.

1942 *Der große Helfer (The Great Helper)*. Dr.

1943 *Die Schuhe unterm Bett (The Shoes under the Bed)*. Com.

1953 *Der Tod des Matrosen Hassein (The Death of the Sailor Hassein)*. Dr.

1955 *Das Amerika Abraham Lincolns (The America of Abraham Lincoln)*. Dr (rev of Abraham Lincoln). Pr 1955 Lpzg.

GLOWALLA, Klaus
15 Nov 1924 Neibenburg -
Actor and stage director at Quedlinburg, Dsdn/Radebeul, and Mgdbg.

 Mordprozeß Consolini (The Consolini Murder Trial). Dr. Pr 1960 Mgdbg.

GÖRLICH, Günther
6 Jan 1928 Breslau (now Wroclaw, Poland) -
At age 17, Russian POW; after return home, joined GDR Police 1950; studied pedagogy, became home tutor, later editor; 58-61 I. Lit Lpzg; lives in Berlin. 1960 and 66 FDGB Prize, 62 Erich Weinert Medal, 71 National Prize. Writes prose, childrens's books, TV plays.

1958 *Wilhelm Rochnow ärgert sich (Wilhelm Rochnow Is Annoyed)*. Dr (based on TV play). Pr 1961.

1961 *Die Ehrgeizigen (The Ambitious Ones)*. Juv (with Hans-Dieter Schmidt; based on novel). Pr 1962 Th. d. Freundschaft, Berlin. Rev 1970 as Den Wolken ein Stück näher.

GÖRLICH (cont'd)
1962   *Goldene Hände (Golden Hands).* Dr.
1963   *Egon und das achte Weltwunder (Egon and the Eighth
        Wonder of the World).* Juv (with Hans-Dieter Schmidt;
        based on novel by Joachim Wohlgemuth). Pr 1965 Th. d.
        jg. Welt, Lpzg.
1970   *Den Wolken ein Stück näher (A Little Closer to the
        Clouds).* Juv (rev of Die Ehrgeizigen; with Hans Die-
        ter Schmidt). Pr 1971 Th. d. jg. Welt, Lpzg. Berlin:
        Kinderbuchverlag, 1971.
1983   *Die Chance des Mannes (A Man's Chance).* Dr (based on
        novel). Reading 1984 Rostock.

GOERTZ, Heinrich
15 May 1911 Duisburg –
Lived in GDR 1946-61; now FRG.
        Das Donnerwetter (The Thunderstorm). Dr.
1946   *Peter Kiewe.* Dr. Pr 1946 DT.
1949   *Das Institut des Herrn Maillard (Mr. Maillard's Insti-
        tute).* Dr (based on Edgar Allan Poe). Pr 1950 Güst-
        row.
1950   *Das Leben ist kein Traum (Life Is No Dream).* Dr. Pr
        1951 Th. am Schiffbauerdamm, Berlin.
1962   *Der Dachboden (The Attic).* Dr.
1969   *Die Antigone des Sophokles (Sophocles' Antigone).* Dr
        (with Herbert Kreppel).

GORRISH, Walter (real name Walter KAISER)
22 Nov 1909 Barmen – 19 Jan 1981 Berlin
Laborer, joined KPD 1931; 33 emigration to Holland, Belgium,
France, Spain; became officer in Int'l Brigade; 40 arrested,
three years imprisonment for high treason; 43 sent to front
in punishment battalion, deserted to Red Army; since 45 in
Berlin. 1961 National Prize. Wrote prose and film scripts.
1960   *Revolte der Gefühle (Revolt of the Feelings).* Dr. Pr
        1960 Schwerin.

GOSSE, Peter
6 Oct 1938 Leipzig –
1956-62 studied engineering Moscow; 68-70 worked as engineer;
71-73 I.Lit Lpzg; since 73 author and Lecturer I. Lit Lpzg.
1969 Literature Prize Halle, 73 Literature Prize Lpzg; lives
in Lpzg. Writes essays, poetry, radio plays.
1969   *Anregung I (Stimulation I).* Contributor to evening of
        short pieces under collective title. Pr 1969 Halle.
1970   *Kleine Gärten - große Leute (Small Gardens - Big
        People).* Com (with Christoph Hamm, Joachim Nowotny,
        Hans Pfeiffer, Helmut Richter). Pr 1971 Lpzg.
1980   *Leben lassen (Let Live).* Dr (based on radio play).
        Pr 1984 Lpzg.
1982   *Palmyra.* Dr. Reading 1982 Lpzg. *TdZ* 82/12.

GOTSCHE, Otto
3 July 1904 Wolferode –
1918-21 worked as plumber; 21 joined KPD youth movement; 23 arrested and imprisoned for high treason; 27 traveled to USSR; 33 sent to concentration camp; after 45 municipal and regional administrator; since 1960 Central Committee SED; member AdK. 1958 National Prize, 59 FDGB Prize, 64 Prize of FDJ; now lives in Berlin. Writes prose, essays.
1961   *Unser kleiner Trompeter (Our Little Trumpeter).* Juv (based on novella). Rev 1962 as Juv Mus Lib by Hans Albert Pederzani (M Jean Kurt Forest). Pr 1963 Th. d. Freundschaft, Berlin. *TdZ* 1963/22.

GOZELL, Rolf
1935 –
1951 worker in chemical factory, then went back to school; 58-65 studied engineering, worked as engineer; 65-68 I.Lit Lpzg, since then author. Writes prose, film and TV scripts.
1961   *Aufgesang (First Stanza).* Dr. *Junge Kunst* 1962/8.
1970   *Der Aufstieg von Edith Eiserbeck (The Rise of Edith Eiserbeck).* Dr. Pr 1970 Zwickau. *TdZ* 1970/10.

GRABNER, Hasso
21 Oct 1911 Leipzig – 3 Apr 1976 Leipzig
After school, worked in bookstore; 1930 joined KPD; anti-Nazi resistance, arrested; nine years prison, concentration camp, punishment battalion; after 45 administrator GDR Radio; since 58 independent author in Werda. 1959 FDGB Prize, 68 Literature Prize Lpzg and Children's Book Prize, 69 Fontane Prize. Wrote prose, children's books, radio and TV plays.
1958   *Die Sieger (The Victors).* Dr.
1964   *Dimitroff.* Cantata.

GRAF, Marie-Louise   see Marie-Louise KENDZIA

GRAFE, Manfred
25 May 1935 Löbau –
Studied composition and conducting at Conservatory Schwerin and MHS Dsdn; orchestra and chorus conductor in Meißen, Görlitz and since 1970 Dsdn.
1959   *Hampelmann Schönbunter (The Multi-Colored Jumpingjack).* Juv Op (with Gisela Schwarz-Marell).
1963   *Zwei Schleier, drei Freier (Two Veils, Three Suitors)* Com (with Wolfgang Böttcher). Pr 1963 Görlitz.
       Der Bauer im Fegefeuer (The Peasant in Purgatory). Op (based on Hans Sachs).
1978   *Herkules und die Frauen (Hercules and the Women).* Mus (with Helmut Müller and Gerhard Hartmann). Pr 1979 Dsdn.
1981   *Zur letzten Rettung (The Last Rescue).* Mus (with Manfred Claus). Pr 1982 Dsdn.
1982   *‹Meine Geschichte mit› Aniko (‹My Story with› Aniko).* Mus (with Peter Bejach). Pr 1983 Erfurt.
1985   *König Karotte (King Carrot).* Opt (with Helmut Müller; based on Jacques Offenbach). Pr 1986 Nordhausen.

GRATZIK, Paul
30 Nov 1935 Lindenhof (now Gizycko, Poland) –
1954 carpenter; 55–56 construction worker in Ruhr area (FRG); returned to GDR, worked in coal mine; 63–66 Institute for Pedagogy, Weimar, then educator; 68 I.Lit Lpzg, then again construction worker; now lives in Berlin. 1980 Heinrich Mann Prize. Writes radio and TV scripts.

1965   *Unruhige Tage (Restless Days).* Dr.
1967   *Malwa.* Dr (based on story by Maxim Gorky). Pr 1968 Potsdam.
1968   *Umwege: Bilder aus dem Leben des jungen Motorenschlossers Michael Runa (Detours: Scenes from the Life of Young Motor Mechanic Michael Runa).* Dr. Pr 1970 Dsdn. *TdZ* 1971/2. *Neue Stücke*, Henschel 1971. *Drei Stücke*, Rostock: Hinstorff, 1977.
1969   *Warten auf Maria (Waiting for Maria).* Com.
1971   *Der Kniebist (The Hairsplitter).* Com. Pr 1972 Potsdam.
1974   *Das Märchen von einem, der auszog, das Fürchten zu lernen (The Tale of a Lad Who Set Out to Learn Fear).* Dr. Pr 1975 Rathen.
1975   *Handbetrieb(Manual Operation).* Dr. Pr 1976 VB. *Drei Stücke*, 1977.
1977   *Lisa.* Dr. Pr 1979 BE. *Drei Stücke*, 1977.
1980   *Transportpaule (Paul the Teamster).* Dr (with Rudolf Koloc; based on novel). Pr 1981 Schwerin (scenes); full Pr 1984 Mgdbg.
1981   *Die Axt im Haus (The Axe in the House).* Dr (based on story by Martin Stade, "Der Präsentkorb"). Pr 1984 VB.

GREEF, Hertha
1953   *Mann und Frau im Essigkrug (Man and Wife in the Vinegar Jug).* Juv Op Lib (based on fairy tale by Ludwig Bechstein; M Joachim-Dietrich Link). Pr 1956 Th. d. Freundschaft, Berlin.
1955   *Schneeweißchen und Rosenrot (Snow-White and Rose-Red).* Juv (based on Grimm). Pr 1956 Brandenburg.

GRESSMANN, Uwe
1 May 1933 Berlin – 30 Oct 1969 Berlin
Raised in orphanage and foster home; worked in various unskilled and skilled labor occupations; self-educated; also artistically talented; frequently ill with TB. Wrote poetry.
    ‹*Der alte und der neue› Faust (‹Old and New› Faust).* Dr fragment (based on Goethe).

GREULICH, Emil Rudolf   (Pseud. ERGE)
6 Oct 1909 Berlin –
1924–28 printer; 29 joined KPD; after 33 in anti-Nazi underground; 39 arrested, 40 imprisoned for high treason; 42 punishment battalion; 43–45 American POW; 46 editor in Berlin, 48 Director of cabaret "Frischer Wind." 1968 Goethe Prize Berlin, 71 Erich Weinert Medal. Writes cabaret texts, film scripts, stories.

GREULICH (cont'd)
>   *Wurzelpeter (Peter with the Roots).*   Juv. Pr 1953
>   Güstrow.

GRIESBACH, Rudi
14 June 1916 Brekerfeld –
Attended high school Hamburg, then MHS Cologne; served in WW
II, Russian POW until 49; 49-50 Hamburg, then GDR; Prof. MHS
Dsdn; music dramaturg Dsdn Th. Composer and librettist.
1953   *Kleider machen Leute (Clothes Make the Man).* Bl (with
>   Anni Peterka; based on story by Gottfried Keller). Pr
>   1954 Met.
1955   *Schneewittchen (Snow White).* Bl (with Anni Peterka;
>   based on Grimm). Pr 1956 Met.
1958   *Kolumbus.* Op. Pr 1961 Workers' Opera, Niedersedlitz.
>   *Die Weibermühle (The Women's Mill).* Opt.
1960   *Marike Weiden.* Op. Pr 1960 Weimar.
1963   *Der Schwarze, der Weiße und die Frau (The Black Man,
>   the White Man, and the Woman).* Mus. Pr 1963 Dsdn.
1977   *Reineke Fuchs (Reynard the Fox).* Bl (based on Dutch
>   chapbook, "Reyneke de vos"). Pr 1978 Görlitz.
1982   *Aulus und sein Papagei (Aulus and His Parrot).* Op.
>   Pr 1982 Radebeul.
>   *Samson.* Bl.

GROHMANN, Gottfried
>   *Husarenstreiche ‹Kurier der schwarzen Jäger› (Dare-
>   deviltries ‹Courier of the Black Fusiliers›).* Dr. Pr
>   1967 Rathen.

GROLZ, Helmut
1968   *Porträt eines Helden (Portrait of a Hero).* Dr.

GRÖSCHKE, Gerhard
1948 Finkenheerd –
Left school in tenth grade to become electrician; later studied at Th.HS Lpzg; 1973-74 dramaturg Stendal, then Fkft/O.
1985 Kleist Prize. Writes poetry, prose, children's radio
plays.
1977   *Hochwasser (Flood).* Dr. Pr 1978 DT. *TdZ 1978/4.*
1979   *Die ungewöhnliche Königstochter (The Unusual Prin-
>   cess).* Juv. Pr 1980 Fkft/O.
1980   *Hermann oder Einesteils Vernunft (Herman or On the
>   One Hand Reason).* Dr. Pr 1982 Fkft/O.
1983   *Die Frau da draußen und der Mann (The Woman Out There
>   and the Man).* Dr. Pr 1984 Lpzg.
1984   *Augenblick im Tunnel (A Moment in the Tunnel).* Dr.
>   Pr 1985 Fkft/O.

GROSS, Jürgen
1946 Brandenburg –
Attended Sports Institute Brandenburg; 1965-67 stage hand,
then member of an amateur theater; later asst. stage director
GDR TV; 67-71 studied theater history Humboldt Univ, Berlin;

GROSS (cont'd)
then dramaturg and stage director KMSt., 71-74 Meiningen; 74-77 Lecturer, Humboldt Univ; since 78 author's contract MG; lives in Neuenhagen.

1966   *Vietnam Rhapsodie.* Dr.

1968   *Ein Gespenst geht um (Ghost A-Haunting).* Dr.

1969   *Der gewöhnliche Skandal (The Usual Scandal).* Dr (based on Günter Wallraff).

1970-71 *Die Schlacht um Helena (The Battle for Helen of Troy).* Com (based on Holberg).

1971   *Guter Rat kommt über Nacht (Good Advice Comes Overnight).* Com.

1972   *Neue Bekanntschaft (A New Acquaintance).* Com.

1973   *Napoleon oder Die hundert Tage (Napoleon or The Hundred Days).* Dr (with Horst Ruprecht; based on Dietrich Christian Grabbe).

1974   *Die Stadt der Kinder (The City of Children).* Juv (based on Mikhailkov).

1976-79 *Trampelpfade ‹Der Trampelpfad - Szenen keiner Ehe› (Hiking Trails ‹The Hiking Trail - Scenes of No Marriage›).* Dr (based on novel by Daniil Granin, "Regen in einer fremden Stadt"). Pr 1977. *Neue DDR Dramatik*, Henschel 1981.

1976-79 *Geburtstagsgäste (Birthday Guests).* Dr. Pr 1980 MG. *TdZ* 1980/4. *Stücke*, Henschel 1984.

1976-80 *Die Parteibraut (The Party Bride).* Dr.

1977   *Match.* Dr. Pr 1978 MG. *TdZ* 1978/11. *Stücke*, 1984.

1977-81 *Blinder Eifer (Blind Zeal).* Three On: *Bruno der Erste (Bruno the First); John Blake; Lieben Sie Tschaikowski? (Do You Like Tchaikovsky?)* Pr 1981 Dessau.

1979   *Denkmal (Monument).* Dr. Pr 1983 KMSt. *TdZ* 1983/9. *Stücke*, 1984.

1981   *Revisor oder Katze aus dem Sack (The Inspector or Cat out of the Bag).* Com.

1981   *Die Diebin und die Lügnerin (The Thief and the Liar).* Com. Pr 1982 Dsdn. *TdZ* 1982/6.

1981-83 *Motzek.* Dr.

1982   *Chatyn.* Dr. Rev 1985 as Asche im Mund.

1982   *Herr Plim (Mr. Plim).* Dr.

1985   *Asche im Mund (Ashes in the Mouth).* Dr (rev of Chatyn).

GRUBERT, Peter
Editor, Henschel Verlag, Berlin.

1960   *Bewährungsfrist (Probationary Period).* Dr (with Klaus Behrens). Pr 1960.

       Kabelwerk Oberspree (Cable Works Upper Spree River). Dr. *Dokumentationen zum Arbeitertheater*, Henschel 1962.

       Inuk jagt die Sonne (Inook Chases the Sun). Dr (based on Henry Beissel, "Inook and the Sun").

1982   *Die kleine Hexe, die nicht böse sein konnte (The Little Witch Who Couldn't Be Wicked).* Juv (based on Maria Clara Machado). Pr 1984 Eisenach.

GRUCHMANN-REUTER, Margret
1908 -
> *Muß das sein? (Does That Have to Be?).* Com (with E-
> rich Heller).
1959 *Alwin der Letzte (Alvin the Last).* Com (with Erich
> Heller).
1960 *Das geht auf keine Kuhhaut (That Boggles the Mind).*
> Com (with Erich Heller). Pr 1960 Meiningen.

GRÜNBERG, Karl
5 May 1891 Berlin - 1 Feb 1972 Berlin
Unskilled laborer; served in WW I; 1919 participated in revolution as member of Soldiers' Council; 20 joined KPD, worked
for journal "Die rote Fahne"; 28-31 trips to USSR; 33-34 imprisoned concentration camp Sonnenburg; after 45, editor of
newspaper "Tägliche Rundschau." 1953 National Prize. Wrote
short stories.
1928 *Der politische Raritätensammler (The Political Curio
> Collector).* Dr.
1928 *Ein lehrreicher Lehrvertrag (An Educational Teacher's
> Contract).* Dr.
1928 *Molochs Wohnungsnot (Moloch's Housing Shortage).* Dr.
1928 *Warum Herr von Itzenplitz kommunistisch wählte (Why
> Mr. Itzenplitz Voted Communist).* Dr.
> *Brennende Ruhr (The Burning Ruhr).* Dr.
> *Schattenquartett (Quartet of Shadows).* Dr.
1948 *Golden fließt der Stahl (Golden Flows the Steel).*
> Dr. Pr 1950 Nordhausen. Berlin: Neues Leben, 1950.
1954 *Elektroden (Electrodes).* Dr. Pr 1954 Cottbus.

GUDDAT, Rolf
1930-1959
1957 *Mord an der Grenze (Murder at the Border).* Dr. Pr
> 1958 Greifswald.

GÜNTHER, Egon
30 Mar 1927 Schneeberg -
Apprentice locksmith, then became technical draftsman; served
in WW II, then POW in Holland, escaped; 1948-51 studied pedagogy, German literature and philosophy in Lpzg, then teacher
in Halle; after 58 dramaturg and film director DEFA. 1972 National Prize. Editor, writes prose, film scripts.
1953 *Till.* Op Lib (M Gerhard Wohlgemuth).
1955 *Fünf Spiele (Five Plays).* Juv (based on Grimm).
1957 *Die Abenteuer des tapferen Schneiderleins (The Adven-
> tures of the Brave Little Tailor).* Juv Op Lib (based
> on Grimm; M Kurt Schwaen). Pr 1962 Th. d. jg. Garde,
> Halle.
1957 *Das gekaufte Mädchen (The Purchased Girl).* Com
> (based on Plautus, "Mercator"). Pr 1960 Stendal.
1962 *Jetzt und in der Stunde meines Todes (Now and in the
> Hour of My Death).* Dr (based on film). Pr 1962 Ro-
> stock.
1963 *Schießen Sie nicht! (Don't Shoot!).* Com. Pr 1963
> Lpzg.

GÜNTHER, Egon (cont'd)
1970   *Kampfregel oder Die merkwürdigen Umstände der Marqui-*
        se von O. (Rule of Combat or The Strange Circumstan-
        ces of the Marquise of O.). Com (based on novella by
        Kleist). Pr 1972 Neustrelitz. Eulenspiegel 1970.

GÜNTHER, Horst
        Die Geschichte vom Mäuschen (The Story of the Little
        Mouse). Pp (based on Kim Meshkov).
1979   *Schneeweißchen und Rosenrot (Snow-White and Rose-Red).*
        Juv (based on Grimm). Pr 1979 Schwedt.
1980   *Nashorn und Giraffe (Rhinoceros and Giraffe).* Pp. Pr
        1981 Halle.
1983   *Der Teufel mit den 3 goldenen Haaren (The Devil with*
        the Three Golden Hairs). Pp (with Frieder Simon). Pr
        1984 Halle.
1984   *Froschkönig (The Frog Prince).* Pp (based on Grimm).

GÜNTHER, Jens-Uwe
18 Apr 1937 Magdeburg –
1959-64 studied music at Lpzg; 64-67 orchestra conductor, Erfurt, 67-74 Weimar; since 74 independent composer and librettist.
        Der überlistete Dieb (The Outsmarted Thief). Juv Mus
        (with Klaus Karina). Pr 1967 Zeitz.
        Das ist unser Jahr (This Is Our Year). Cantata (with
        Werner Voigt). Pr 1970 Weimar.
        Villon kommt über Paris (Villon Comes by Way of Pa-
        ris). Mus (with Hans Holdsch). Pr 1971 Gera.
1975   *Scherz, List und Rache (Jest, Ruse, and Revenge).* Mus
        (based on Goethe).
1977   *Macette.* Mus (with Heide Kirmße; based on Mathurin
        Regnier). Pr 1979 Weimar.
1980   *Dona Juanita.* Op (based on novel by Eberhard Panitz,
        "Die sieben Affären der Dona Juanita"). Pr 1981 Stral-
        sund.
1981   *Der erklärte Weiberfeind (The Sworn Misogynist).* Op
        (based on Lessing, "Der Misogyn"). Pr 1981 Weimar.
1982   *Georg Büchner.* Op.
1982   *Sonnen am Horizont (Suns on the Horizon).* Bl. Pr 19-
        83 Erfurt.
1985   *Lautlose Vögel (Silent Birds).* Op. Pr 1986 Erfurt.

GÜNTHER, Johann   see Günther RÜCKER

GÜNTHER, Lothar
1 Mar 1947 Leipzig –
After high school, became locksmith; 1967-68 worked for newspapers Lpzg; 68-72 studied journalism Karl Marx Univ., Lpzg,
71-76 editor univ. paper Halle; 76-79 I.Lit Lpzg, then dramaturg Th. d. jg. Welt, Lpzg.
1978   *Zugvögel nisten spät (Birds of Passage Nest Late).* Dr.
        Pr 1979 Stralsund.
1980   *Der Spatzenturm (The Tower of Sparrows).* Juv. Pr 19-
        81 Th. d. jg. Welt, Lpzg.

GÜNTHER, Lutz
>*Goldsucher in den Rocky Mountains (Gold Prospectors in the Rocky Mountains).* Dr. Pr 1972 Radebeul.

GUSTMANN, Egbert
1969   *Episoden aus der Ehe der Doris B. (Episodes from the Marriage of Doris B.).* Dr. Pr 1969 Parchim.
1971   *Glückwunsch, Paul (Congratulations, Paul).* Dr. Pr 1972 Parchim.

GÜTTINGER, Hans
1978   *Stoffel und der Zauberhut (Stoffel and the Magic Hat).* Juv. Pr 1979 Bernburg.

HAAS, Henn
26 Feb 1907 Riga –
1945-52 dancer and choreographer, dance theaters Weimar and
Erfurt; 52-57 choreographer, FDGB dance ensemble; since 57
Halle. FDGB Prize.
1967   *Kontraste (Contrasts)*.   Mus Lib (with Adolf Spicker-
           mann).   Pr 1968 Halle.
1978   *Die Froschzarin (The Frog Tsarina)*.   Bl Lib (with Ma-
           thias Nilius).   Pr 1978 Halle.

HAASE, Gisela
1981   *Der gestiefelte Kater (Puss-in-Boots)*.   Pp.   Pr 1982.

HABECK-ADAMEK, Anne
1930 Massow –
Lived in Weimar until 1951, then studied journalism in Berlin;
worked as editor for GDR Radio. Writes prose, poetry, radio
and TV scripts.
1978   *Ein Augenblick ist mein gewesen (A Moment Was Mine)*.
           Dr (based on correspondence between Olga Knipper and
           Anton Chekhov).   Pr 1979 Rostock.   Henschel 1985.

HACKS, Anna E‹lisabeth›   see Anna E. WIEDE

HACKS, Peter   (Pseud. Ernst EYLT)
21 Mar 1928 Breslau (now Wroclaw, Poland) –
Finished high school 1945 Wuppertal; then studied sociology,
philosophy, literature and theater history Munich; Dr.phil.
51; married author Anna E. Wiede; worked for Munich radio and
theaters until 55, then went to GDR; 60-63 dramaturg DT. Member GDR Pen Center and AdK; 1956 Lessing Prize, 65 Weiskopf
Prize, 71 GDR Critics' Prize, 74 and 77 National Prize, 81
Heinrich Mann Prize. Writes prose, essays, children's books,
radio and TV plays.
1951   *Kasimir der Kinderdieb (Casimir, the Child Thief)*.
           Juv.   Stage ms. Munich: Dreimaskenverlag.
1953   *Das Volksbuch vom Herzog Ernst oder Der Held und sein*
           Gefolge (The Chapbook of Duke Ernest or The Hero and
           His Retinue).   Dr.   Pr 1961 Mannheim.   *Th.h.* 1961/9.
           Spec 8, 1965. *Theaterstücke*, Aufbau 1957. *Fünf Stücke*,
           Suhrkamp 1965. *Stücke*, Reclam 1972. *Ausgewählte Dra-*
           men 2, Aufbau 1976.
1954   *Columbus oder Die Eröffnung des indischen Zeitalters*
           (Columbus or The Opening of the Indian Era).   Dr.   Pr
           1955 Kammerspiele, Munich. *NdL* 1955/2 (scenes 3-7).
           Theaterstücke, 1957. *Fünf Stücke*, 1965. "The Opening
           of the Indian Era" (Engl. tr J. R. Rose), *Modern Int'l*
           Drama 1970/1.   Rev 1970 as Columbus oder Die Weltidee
           zu Schiffe.
1955   *Die Schlacht bei Lobositz (The Battle at Lobositz)*.
           Com.   Pr 1956 DT.   *Theaterstücke, 1957. Fünf Stücke*,
           1965. *Dt. Th. d. Gegenwart 1*, Suhrkamp 1967. *Ausge-*
           wäählte Dramen 1, Aufbau 1971.

HACKS (cont'd)

1956   *Die Geschichte eines alten Wittibers im Jahre 1632 (The Story of an Old Widower in the Year 1632).* Com (based on radio play). *Sinn & Form* 1956/2 (radio version). Lpzg: Hofmeister, 1958.

1956   *Der Held der westlichen Welt (The Hero of the Western World).* Com (with Anna Wiede; based on J. M. Synge, "Playboy of the Western World"). Pr 1956 BE. Reclam 1961.

1957   *Der Müller von Sans-Souci (The Miller of Sans-Souci).* Com. Pr 1958 DT. *NdL* 1958/2. *TdZ* 1958/5. *Fünf Stücke*, 1965. *Stücke*, 1972. *Ausgewählte Dramen 3*, Aufbau 19-81.

1957   *Die Kindermörderin (The Child Murderess).* Dr (based on Heinrich Leopold Wagner). Pr 1959 Wuppertal. *Junge Kunst* 1957/2. *Zwei Bearbeitungen*, Suhrkamp 1963. *Stücke nach Stücken 1*, Aufbau 1965. Stuttgart: Klett, 1981. Rev version Pr 1965 Wittenberg.

1957   *Das Untier von Samarkand (The Monster of Samarkand).* Juv (with Eugen Eschner and Anna E. Wiede). Pr 1957 Th. d. Freundschaft, Berlin. *Märchendramen*, Henschel 1980.

1958   *Die Uhr geht nach (The Clock is Slow).* Dr.

1959   *Die Sorgen und die Macht (Worries and Power).* Dr (original title "Bricketts"). Pr 1960 Senftenberg. Rev version Pr 1962 DT. *Fünf Stücke*, 1965. *Ausgewählte Dramen 2*, 1976.

1959   *Die blaue Akte (The Blue File).* Dr (under pseud. Ernst Eylt; with Friedrich Karl Kaul; based on novel by Kaul, "Der blaue Aktendeckel"). Pr 1960 Quedlinburg.

1960   *Die Trickbetrügerin und andere merkwürdige Begebenheiten (The Deceitful Woman and Other Strange Occurrences).*

1961   *Moritz Tassow.* Com. Pr 1965 VB. *Sinn & Form* 1965/6. *Th.h.* 1965/2. *Ausgewählte Dramen 1*, 1971. *Vier Komödien*, Suhrkamp 1971.

1962   *Der Frieden (Peace).* Com (based on Aristophanes; incidental M Andre Asriel). Pr 1962 DT. *Zwei Bearbeitungen*, 1963. *Stücke nach Stücken 1*, 1965.

1963   *Polly oder Die Bataille am Bluewater Creek (Polly or The Battle of Bluewater Creek).* Com (based on John Gay; incidental M Andre Asriel). Pr 1965 Halle. *Sinn & Form* 1965/3-4. *Stücke nach Stücken 1*, 1965. *Stücke nach Stücken: Bearbeitungen 2*, Suhrkamp 1965. Henschel 1966.

1964   *Die schöne Helena (Helen of Troy).* Mus Lib (based on Meilhac and Halevy; M Jacques Offenbach and Herbert Kawan). Pr 1964 DT. *Stücke nach Stücken 1*, 1965. *Stücke nach Stücken: Bearbeitungen 2*, 1965.

1964-66 *König Heinrich IV. (King Henry the Fourth).* Dr (tr from Shakespeare). Pr 1970 Schillerth., West Berlin.

1965   *Der Mann, der bei Schirocco kam (The Man Who Came with the Desert Wind).* Com (under pseud. Ernst Eylt; with Anna E. Wiede). Pr 1967 Altenburg.

HACKS (cont'd)

1965   *Der Schuhu und die fliegende Prinzessin* *(The Shoohoo and the Flying Princess)*.   Juv (with Uta Birnbaum; based on children's book; incidental M Hans-Dieter Hosalla). Pr 1966 Drama School, Berlin.   Eulenspiegel 1966. Frankfurt/M: Insel, 1973. Rev as Juv Op Lib (M Udo Zimmermann). Pr 1976 Dsdn.

1965   *Rote Rosen für mich (Red Roses for Me)*.   Dr (tr from Sean O'Casey).

1965-66 *Margarete in Aix*.   Com.   Pr 1969 Basel. *Kürbiskern* 1966/1. *TdZ* 1967/2. *Th.h.* 1971/9. *Vier Komödien*, 19-71. Eulenspiegel 1974. *Ausgewählte Dramen 2*, 1976.

1967   *Amphytrion*. Com.   Pr 1968 Göttingen.   *Th.h.* 1968/3. *Spec* 13, 1970. Eulenspiegel 1969. *Vier Komödien*, 19-71. *Ausgewählte Dramen 1*, 1971.

1968   *Prexaspes*. Dr. Pr 1976 Dsdn. *TdZ* 1975/2. *Th.h.* 19-76/5. *Ausgewählte Dramen 2*, 1976. Düsseldorf: Claassen, 1978. *Sechs Dramen*, Aufbau 1978.

1969   *Omphale*. Com. Pr 1970 Fkft/M. *Sinn & Form* 1970/4. *Th.h.* 1970/5. *Vier Komödien*, 1971. *Ausgewählte Dramen 1*, 1971. "Omphale" (Engl. tr Andre Lefevere), *Dimensions* 1973/3. Rev 1972 as Op (M Siegfried Matthus). Pr 1976 Weimar. *Oper*, Aufbau 1975. Lpzg: Dt. Verlag für Musik, 1977.

1970   *Columbus oder Die Weltidee zu Schiffe (Columbus or The Global Idea on Shipboard)*. Dr (rev of Columbus oder Die Eröffnung des indischen Zeitalters). Pr 1975 Zaragoza. *Ausgewählte Dramen 1*, 1971. *Stücke*, 1972.

1971   *Numa*. Dr. *Sechs Dramen*, 1978.

1971   *Seneca‹s Tod› (Seneca‹'s Death›)*.   Dr. Pr 1980 DT. *NdL* 1978/6. *Sechs Dramen*, 1978. *Ausgewählte Dramen 3*, 1981.

1972   *Noch einen Löffel Gift, Liebling? (Another Spoonful of Poison, Darling?)*. Op Lib (based on Saul O'Hara, "Risky Marriage"; M Siegfried Matthus). Pr 1972 Km. Op. *TdZ* 1972/7. Lpzg: Dt. Verlag für Musik, 1972. *Oper*, 1975.

1972   *Adam und Eva (Adam and Eve)*. Com. Pr 1973 Dsdn. *Th.h.* 1972/12. *Sinn und Form* 1973/1. Reclam 1976. Düsseldorf: Claassen, 1976. *Sechs Dramen*, 1978. *Ausgewählte Dramen 3*, 1981.

1973   *Das Jahrmarktsfest zu Plundersweilen (The Plundersweilen Fair)*. Com (based on Goethe). Pr 1975 DT. *Th.h.* 1975/12. Aufbau 1976. Munich: Deutscher Taschenbuchverlag, 1981. *Stücke nach Stücken 2*, Aufbau 1985. "Market Day at Plundersweilen" (Engl. tr Julian Hilton and Hanne Boenisch), *Gambit* 1982/39-40.

1973   *Die Vögel (The Birds)*. Op Lib (based on Aristophanes; M Thomas Hertel). Pr 1981 Dsdn. *Oper*, 1975. *Stücke nach Stücken 2*, 1985.

1974   *Ein Gespräch im Hause Stein über den abwesenden Herrn von Goethe (A Conversation in the Stein Household about the Absent Mr. Goethe)*. Com. Pr 1976 Dsdn. *Ausgewählte Dramen 2*, 1976. *Sechs Dramen*, 1978. Engl.

HACKS (cont'd)

Pr 1980 New York, under title "Charlotte" (tr Uta Hagen and Herbert Berghof).

1975   *Die Fische (The Fishes).* Dr. Pr 1978 Göttingen. *TdZ* 1978/1. *Sechs Dramen*, 1978. *Ausgewählte Dramen 3*, 19-81.

1975   ‹*Und*› *Rosie träumt* (‹*And*› *Rosie Is Dreaming).* Dr (based on Hrosvita von Gandersheim). Pr 1975 MG. In *Das Jahrmarktsfest...*, 1976 and 1981. *Stücke nach Stücken 2*, 1985.

1978   *Armer Ritter (Poor Knight).* Juv. Pr 1978 Göttingen. *TdZ* 1979/3. *Märchendramen*, Henschel 1980.

1979   *Pandora.* Dr (based on Goethe). Pr 1982 Göttingen. *NdL* 1980/9. Aufbau 1981. *Stücke nach Stücken 2*, 1985.

1979-80 *Musen (Muses).* Four On: *Charlotte Hoyer; Charlotte Stieglitz; Cosima von Bülow; Schmeckebier.* Pr 1983 Mgdbg. *Ausgewählte Dramen 3*, 1981.

1980   *Die Binsen (The Bulrushes).* Com. Pr 1985 TiP. Aufbau 1986 (with *Fredegunde*).

1981   *Und lieben, Götter, welch ein Glück (Oh Gods, What Happiness It Is to Be in Love).* Pp (based on Goethe). Pr 1981 Naumburg.

1982   *Barby.* Com (with Rudi Strahl; based on Strahl, "Er ist wieder da"). Pr 1983 Halle. *NdL* 1983/6. *Stücke nach Stücken 2*, 1985.

1982   *Das musikalische Nashorn (The Musical Rhinoceros).* Juv Op Lib. Pr 1982 TiP.

1983   *Die Kinder (The Children).* Juv. Pr 1984 Greifswald.

1983   *Maries Baby (Mary's Baby).* Juv.

1984   *Fredegunde.* Dr. Aufbau 1986 (with *Die Binsen*). *Plusmacher Ernst oder Der Held und sein Kapital (Ernest the Profiteer The Hero and His Capital).* Fragment.

HAHN, Gustav

1955   *Frau Holle (Mother Holle).* Juv (based on Grimm). Pr 1957 Altenburg.

HAHNFELD, Ingrid
19 Sept 1937 –
Actress, lives in Mgdbg. Writes poetry, prose, radio plays.

1981   *Vom Aberheiner (Heiner the But-Sayer).* Pp. Pr 1982 Mgdbg.

HALL, Heinz

1962   *Der große und der kleine Klaus (Big Claus and Little Claus).* Juv (based on Hans Christian Andersen). Pr 1962 Rostock.

1963-64 *Küssen verboten (No Kissing).* Mus Lib (with Hans Peter; M Manfred Nitschke). Pr 1964 Rostock. *TdZ* 1964/20.

1965   *Millionär wider Willen (The Reluctant Millionaire).* Mus Lib (M Manfred Nitschke). Pr 1965 Rostock.

1968   *Ein Strom, der Liebe heißt (A River Called Love).* Mus Lib (M Manfred Nitschke). Pr 1969 Rostock.

HALL, Heinz (cont'd)

1970   *Ein Stern in Stockholm (A Star in Stockholm)*. Com. Pr 1971 Rostock.

1971   *Sommersonnabendsonntag (Summer Weekend)*. Mus Lib (M Manfred Nitschke). Pr 1972 Rostock.

1974   *Auf glattem Parkett (On Slippery Grounds)*. Mus Lib (M Manfred Nitschke). Pr 1974 Plauen.

1978   *Aladdin und die Wunderlampe (Aladdin and the Magic Lamp)*. Juv Mus Lib (M Jochen Allihn). Pr 1978 Zeitz.

HALL, Jan   see Maurycy JANOWSKI and Heinz KUFFERATH

HAMM, Christoph
1933 Riesa - 25 Feb 1986 Leipzig
1952-56 studied theater history; 56-60 dramaturg and stage director, Lpzg; since 81 staff member AdK.

1958   *Sturm aus den Sonnen (Storm from the Suns)*. Dr. Pr 1958.

1966   *Zehn Tage, die die Welt erschütterten (Ten Days That Shook the World)*. Dr (based on John Reed). Pr 1967 Lpzg.

1970   *Kleine Gärten - große Leute (Small Gardens - Big People)*. Com (with Peter Gosse, Joachim Nowotny, Hans Pfeiffer, Helmut Richter). Pr 1971 Lpzg.

1981   *Gatt*. Dr (with Gotthard Müller; based on novel by Erich Neutsch, "Auf der Suche nach Gatt"). Pr 1982 Lpzg. *TdZ* 1982/5.

HAMMEL, Claus
4 Dec 1932 Parchim -
High school in Demmin, then took voice instruction in Berlin; after 1955, studied theater history; 55-57 theater critic for "Neues Deutschland", 57-58 *NdL*, 58-68 "Sonntag"; 69-72 literary advisor DT, since then Rostock; lives in Berlin and Althagen. 1967 Erich Weinert Medal, 68 Lessing Prize, 74 SecondPrize Drama Competition, 76 FDGB Prize, 79 National Prize.

1957   *Hier ist ein Neger zu lynchen (There Is a Negro to Be Lynched Here)*. Dr (based on play by Hans Henny Jahnn, "Straßenecke"). *NdL* 1957/7.

1961   *Fischerkinder (Fishermen's Children)*. Dr (based on novel by Herbert Nachbar "Die Hochzeit von Länneken"). Pr 1962 Rostock.

1962-64 *Wer einmal aus dem Blechnapf frißt (Once You've Eaten from a Tin Plate)*. Dr (based on novel by Hans Fallada). *TdZ* 1965/14.

1963   *Frau Jenny Treibel oder Wo sich Herz zu Herzen find't (Mrs. Jenny Treibel or Where Two Hearts Find Each Other)*. Com (based on novel by Theodor Fontane). Pr 1964 MG. *TdZ* 1964/10. *Komödien*, Aufbau 1969.

1963-64 *Um neun an der Achterbahn (Nine o'Clock at the Roller Coaster)*. Com. Pr 1964 MG. *TdZ* 1964/18. Henschel 1966. *Sozialistische Dramatik*, Henschel 1968. *Komödien*, 1969.

HAMMEL (cont'd)

1966   *Ein Yankee an König Artus' Hof (A Yankee at the Court of King Arthur)*. Com (based on novel by Mark Twain, "A Connecticut Yankee at King Arthur's Court"). Pr 1967 Erfurt. *TdZ* 1966/10. Henschel 1967. *Komödien*, 1969. Rev version Pr 1982 Rostock.

1967   *Morgen kommt der Schornsteinfeger (The Chimney Sweep Is Coming Tomorrow)*. Com. Pr 1967 Erfurt. *Forum* 1967/19. *Komödien*, 1969. *Neue Stücke*, Henschel 1971.

1970   *Le Faiseur oder Warten auf Godeau (Le Faiseur or Waiting for Godeau)*. Com (based on novel by Balzac, "Mercadet"). Pr 1970 DT. *Sinn und Form* 1971/1. Eulenspiegel 1972.

1974   *Rom oder Die zweite Erschaffung der Welt (Rome or The Second Creation of the World)*. Com. Pr 1975 Rostock. *TdZ* 1975/3. Aufbau 1976.

1976   *Das gelbe Fenster, der gelbe Stein (The Yellow Window, the Yellow Stone)*. Dr. Pr 1977 Rostock. *TdZ* 1977/3.

1977   *‹Überlegungen zu› Feliks D. (‹Reflections about› Felix D.)*. Pr 1978 Rostock.

1979   *Humboldt und Bolivar oder Der neue Kontinent (Humboldt and Bolivar or the New Continent)*. Dr. Pr 1979 Rostock. *TdZ* 1979/8. Aufbau 1980.

1981   *Die Preußen kommen (The Prussians are Coming)*. Com. Pr 1981 Rostock. *TdZ* 1981/9.

1982   *Mensch Marx ‹Hommage a Marx› (Marx, the Human Being ‹Homage to Marx›)*. Cantata. Pr 1983 Rostock.

1983   *Lokomotive im Spargelbeet (The Locomotive in the Asparagus Bed)*. Com. Pr 1984 Rostock. *TdZ* 1984/12.

HANELL, Robert
2 Mar 1925 Tsosl, Czechoslovakia –
Studied music in Teplice, 1943 became choir director there, 44 conductor Meiningen, 45–48 Zwickau; 48–50 music director Görlitz, 50–52 Gera, 52–55 again Görlitz, 56–64 Km.Op; since 65 conductor Berlin Radio Orchestra; guest conductor, St.Op. 1967 National Prize, 81 Goethe Prize Berlin. Composer.

1947   *Der Bettler von Damaskus (The Beggar of Damascus)*. Op. Pr 1947 Zwickau.

1948   *Die Gnomenwette (The Wager of the Gnomes)*. Op. Pr 1949 Meiningen.

1950   *Cecil*. Op.

1951   *Die Spieldose (The Music Box)*. Op (based on Georg Kaiser). Pr 1957 Erfurt.

1962   *Dorian Gray*. Op (based on Oscar Wilde, "The Picture of Dorian Gray"). Pr 1962 Dsdn.

1964   *Oben und unten (Upstairs and Downstairs)*. Op (based on Johann Nestroy, "Zu ebener Erde und im 1. Stock"). Pr 1964 Mgdbg.

1965   *Esther*. Op (with Günther Deicke; based on novella by Bruno Apitz). Pr 1966 St.Op. *TdZ* 1966/6.

1969   *Die griechische Hochzeit (The Greek Wedding)*. Op (based on story by Herbert Otto). Pr 1969 Lpzg.

HANELL (cont'd)

1974   *Fiesta.*   Op   (based on novel by Prudencio De Pereda). Pr 1975 Weimar.

1976   *Reise mit Joujou (A Journey with Joujou).*   Mus (with Klaus Eidam; based on Guy de Maupassant).   Pr 1976 Gera.

1981   *Babettes grüner Schmetterling (Babette's Green Butterfly).*   Mus (with Klaus Eidam).   Pr 1982 Weimar.   *TdZ* 1983/1.

HARDT, Hans   see Jürgen DEGENHARDT

HARNISCH, Klaus

1933 -

Opera stage director Schwerin, Dsdn-Radebeul, Senftenberg; 1973-81 Head Dramaturg Music Theater Halle.

1983   *Büchner.*   Op Lib (M Friedrich Schenker).   Pr 1983 Schwerin.   *TdZ* 1983/6.

HARTMANN, Gerhard

1931 Potsdam -

    Der große Held Tartarin   (Tartarin,   the Great Hero). Mus Lib   (based on 1872 novel, "Tartarin de Tarascon" by Alphonse Daudet; M Rainer Lischka).   Pr Dsdn.

    Jeff und Andy.   Lib.   Pr 1971 Dsdn.

1973   *Das alltägliche Wunder (The Ordinary Miracle).* Op Lib (based on Yevgenyi Schwarz, "Das gewöhnliche Wunder"; M Gerhard Rosenfeld).   Pr 1973 Stralsund.

1977   *Der Mantel   (The Overcoat).*   Op Lib (based on Nikolai Gogol; M Gerhard Rosenfeld).   Pr 1978 Weimar.

1978   *Herkules und die Frauen (Hercules and the Women).* Mus Lib   (with Helmut Müller;   M Manfred Grafe).   Pr 1979 Dsdn.

1980   *Das Spiel von Liebe und Zufall   (The Game of Love and Chance).* Op Lib (based on Pierre de Marivaux, "Le jeu de l'amour et du hazard";   M Gerhard Rosenfeld).   Pr 1980 Potsdam.   *TdZ* 1980/12.

1983   *Copernicus.* Op Lib (M Jan F. Fischer). Pr 1984 Mgdbg.

1984   *Friedrich und Montezuma.*   Op Lib   (M   Gerhard Rosenfeld).

HASTEDT, Regina

23 Oct 1921 Flöha -

1936-39 worked as photographer, then attended Academy for Graphic Arts, Lpzg;   after 45 press photographer for "Volksstimme" Lpzg; 47 director of Radio Chemnitz (now KMSt).   1959 and 62 FDGB Prize.   Writes prose.

1954   *Wer ist hier von gestern   oder Hausfrau gesucht   (Who Is Here from Yesterday or Housewife Wanted).*   Mus Lib (M Hans Krug).   Pr 1955 KmSt.

1964   *Poltermanns Söhne (Poltermann's Sons).*   Com.

HAUFE, Jochen

1967   *Maria Theresia Schulze.*   Dr.   Pr 1968 Cottbus.

HAUPTMANN, Elisabeth   (Pseud. Catherine ÜX, Dorothy LANE)
20 June 1897 Peckelsheim - 20 Apr 1973 Berlin
Until 1922 teacher; then secretary and translator in Berlin;
28 joined KPD; 28-34 collaborated with Bert Brecht on various
plays, among them Dreigroschenoper, Mahagonny, and especially
Happy End; 33 emigration to France and USA; 35-40 college
teacher in St. Louis, 41-48 writer in New York and Los Angeles; married Paul Dessau; 48 returned to Berlin; after 54 dramaturg BE. 1961 Lessing Prize. Wrote prose, radio plays.

1929   *Happy End*. Mus Lib (under pseud. Dorothy Lane; with
       Bert Brecht; M Kurt Weill). Pr 1929 Th. am Schiffbau-
       erdamm, Berlin.
1951   *Tanker Nebraska*. Dr (tr from H. Tank). Pr 1951 BE.
1952   *Die erste Reiterarmee (First Cavalry Army)*. Dr (based
       on W. Vishnevsky). Pr 1952 Anhalt.
1953   *Potiphars Haus (Potiphar's House)*. Dr (tr from Alan
       Max and Lester Cole). Pr 1955 Altenburg.
1953   *Colonel Foster ist schuldig (Colonel Foster is Guil-
       ty)*. Dr (based on R. Vaillant).
1954   *Hirse für die Achte (Millet for Eight)*. Dr (with Man-
       fred Wekwerth; based on Chinese folk play). Pr 1963
       Brandenburg. *Sinn & Form* 1954/4.
1954   *Mutter Riba (Mother Riba)*. Dr (tr from David Berg).
       Pr 1955 DT.
1960   *Zwei Herren aus Verona (Two Gentlemen from Verona)*.
       Com (with Benno Besson; based on Shakespeare). Pr 19-
       60 Greifswald.
1961   *Optimistische   Tragödie (Optimistic   Tragedy)*. Dr
       (based on Vsevolod Vishnevsky).
1962   *Volpone oder Der Fuchs (Volpone or The Fox)*. Com (with
       Benno Besson; based on Ben Jonson). Pr 1963 Potsdam.

HAUSER, Harald
17 Feb 1912 Lörrach -
Studied law in Freiburg and Berlin; 1931 trip to Moscow; 32
joined KPD; 33 emigration to France, fought in Volunteer Regi-
ment of French Army and in underground resistance; after 45
editor for various newspapers and journals; now lives in Berlin. 1959 Lessing Prize, 60 National Prize. Writes stories,
film and TV scripts.

1951   *Prozeß Wedding (Trial in Wedding)*. Dr. Pr 1953 DT.
1953   *Am Ende der Nacht (At the End of the Night)*. Dr. Pr
       1955 Mgdbg. Henschel 1959. *Sozialistische Dramatik*,
       Henschel 1968. *Die ersten Schritte*, Halle: Mitteldt.
       Verlag, 1986.
1956-57 *Im himmlischen Garten (In the Heavenly Garden)*.   Dr
       (incidental M Guido Masanetz). Pr 1958 Lpzg.
1959   *Häschen Schnurks (Schnurks the Bunny)*.   Juv Mus Lib
       (with Helga Korff-Edel; M Guido Masanetz).   Pr 1960
       Th. d. Freundschaft, Berlin. Halle: Postreiter, 1966.
1960   *Weißes Blut (White Blood)*. Dr. Pr 1960 Lpzg. Hen-
       schel 1961.
1961   *Night Step ‹Nitschewo›*.   Com (original title: "Spuk
       auf Frankenhöhe"). Pr 1962 Rostock.

HAUSER (cont'd)

1962 *Der Große und der Kleine Buddha (Great Buddha and Little Buddha).* Juv. Pr 1965 Th. d. Freundschaft, Berlin.

1964 *Barbara.* Dr. Pr 1964 Rostock. Rev version Pr 1967 VB.

1970 *Wem gehören die Sterne? (To Whom Do the Stars Belong?).* Com. Pr 1970 Wittenberg.
Im Schatten des Turmes (In the Shadow of the Tower). Dr. Pr 1977.

HÄUSER, Otto (Pseud. Ottokar DOMMA)
20 May 1924 Schankau –
Editor, Eulenspiegel Verlag, Berlin. Writes short stories.

1970 *Vom braven Schüler Ottokar Domma (Ottokar Domma, the Well-Behaved Pupil).* Com (based on short story). Pr 1970 Mgdbg. (Part of program entitled "Anregung 11").

1976 *Ottokar Dommas Elternabend (Ottokar Domma's Parents Night).* Com (based on short story). Pr 1977 Mgdbg.

HAWEMANN, Horst
4 Feb 1940 –
After school, worked as locksmith; became actor in workers' theater; 61-62 studied Th. HS Lpzg; 62-66 studied directing in Moscow; 66-78 stage director, Th. d. Freundschaft, Berlin; since 78 independent author. 1969 Erich Weinert Medal and FDJ Prize; 70 Berlin Goethe Prize.

Das Rübchen (The Little Carrot). Juv (with Peter Ensikat; based on Pavel Malyarevsky).

1969 *Tschintschraka oder Das große Abenteuer eines kleinen Gauklers (Tshintshraka or The Great Adventure of a Little Conjurer).* Juv (with Peter Ensikat; based on Russian fairy tale by Georgyi Nakhutsrishvily). Pr 19-70 Th. d. Freundschaft, Berlin.

1977 *Tschapai... Tschapai... Tschapajew.* Dr (based on novel by Furmanov). Pr 1977 Th. d. Freundschaft, Berlin. *TdZ* 1977/10.

1978 *Kokori.* Juv (based on Joaquin Gutierrez). Pr 1979 Th. d. Freundschaft, Berlin.

1979 *Der Aschenstocherer oder Kopf ist das Beste (The Ash Poker or Heads Is Best).* Juv (based on Russian fairy tale by Georgyi Nakhutsrishvily). Pr 1980 Th. d. Freundschaft, Berlin.

1980-81 *Sekondeleutnant Aberdehr (Second Lieutenant Aberdehr).* Com (with Christoph Hein). Pr 1981 Das Ei, Berlin.
Spiel vor dem Feind (Playing before the Enemy). Dr (with Christel Hoffmann; based on Mikhail Svetlov).

1984 *König Drosselbart und das Mädchen Prinzessin (King Thrushbeard and the Girl Princess).* Juv (based on Grimm). Pr 1985 Th. d. Freundschaft, Berlin.

1985 *Die Katze (The Cat).* Juv. Pr 1986 Th. d. Freundschaft, Berlin.

HEIDUCZEK, Werner
24 Nov 1926 Hindenburg (now Zabrze, Poland) -
After high school, served in WW II; then Russian POW; 1945
farm worker, 46 teacher's asst.; then studied pedagogy and
German literature Halle and Potsdam; 61-64 German language instructor Bulgaria and Herder Institute, Lpzg. 1964 Artur
Becker Medal; 1969 Heinrich Mann Prize, Händel Prize, Halle,
and Johannes Becher Medal. Writes prose, children's books, radio plays.

1958   *Jule findet Freunde (Julie Finds Friends)*. Juv (based
       on short story). Pr 1959 Th. d. Freundschaft, Ber-
       lin.
1961   *Leben - aber wie? (Living - But How?)* Juv. Pr 1961
       Th. d. jg. Garde, Halle.
1968   *Die Marulas*. Dr (based on novel "Abschied von den En-
       geln"). Pr 1969 DT.
1971-72 *Mark Aurel oder Ein Semester Zärtlichkeit (Marcus Au-
       relius or One Semester of Tenderness)*. Dr. Pr 1977
       Neustrelitz. Berlin: Neues Leben, 1971. Fkft/M: Fi-
       scher, 1975.
1973   *Roswitha*. Dr. Pr 1974 Lpzg.
1974   *Maxi oder Wie man Karriere macht (Max Or How to Make
       a Career)*. Dr. Pr 1974 Lpzg. *Im Querschnitt*, Halle:
       Mitteldt. Verlag, 1976.
1975   *Das andere Gesicht (The Other Face)*. Dr. Pr 1976
       Lpzg. *Im Querschnitt*, 1976.
1978   *Jana und der kleine Stern (Jana and the Little Star)*.
       Pp (based on children's book; M Klaus-Dieter Adoma-
       tis). Pr 1983 Pp.Th., Berlin.
1984   *Der Gast aus Saadulla (The Guest from Saadulla)*. Com.
       Pr 1985 Lpzg.

HEIMANN, Josef
1965   *Pferdediebe in Arkansas (Horse Thieves in Arkansas)*.
       Dr (based on story by Friedrich Gerstäcker, "Die Re-
       gulatoren des Arkansas"). Pr 1966 Rathen.

HEIN, Christoph
1944 Heinzendorf (now Bagno, Poland) -
High school in West Berlin; moved to GDR in 1960; worked in
book store; then assistant director VB; 67-71 studied philosophy Univ Lpzg and Berlin; 71-79 dramaturg and author at VB;
lives in Berlin. 1982 Heinrich Mann Prize; 83 W. Berlin Critics Prize. Writes short prose, radio plays.
       Der fliegende Arzt (The Flying Doctor). Com (with
       Brigitte Soubeyran; based on Moliere).
1973   *Vom Furz (The Fart)*. Com (tr of anonymous French
       farce). Pr 1975 Basel.
1973   *Schlötel oder Was solls? (Schlötel or What's Up?)*
       Com. Pr 1974 VB (Part of program under collective
       title "Spektakel 2"). *Cromwell und andere Stücke*, Auf-
       bau 1981.
1974   *Vom hungrigen Hennecke (Hungry Hennecke)*. Juv. Pr
       1974 VB (Part of program under collective title "Spek-

        takel 2").

HEIN (cont'd)

1974   *Lasalle oder Die Genesis*. Dr. Rev 1979 as Lasalle
        fragt Herrn Herbert nach Sonja.

1976   *Brittanicus*. Dr (tr from Jean Racine).

1977   *John D. erobert die Welt (John D. Conquers the World)*.
        Revue (based on Friedrich Wolf). Pr 1979 Neustrelitz.

1978   *Cromwell*. Dr. Pr 1980 Cottbus. *TdZ* 1978/7. *Crom-
        well...*, 1981.

1979   *Lasalle fragt Herrn Herbert nach Sonja (Lasalle Asks
        Mr. Herbert about Sonya)*. Dr (rev of Lasalle oder Die
        Genesis). Pr 1980 Düsseldorf. *Cromwell...*, 1981.

1980   *Der neue Menoza oder Die Geschichte des kumbanischen
        Prinzen Tandi (The New Menoza or The Tale of the Cum-
        ban Prince Tandi)*. Com (based on J. M. R. Lenz). Pr
        1982 Schwerin. *TdZ* 1982/2. *Cromwell...*, 1981.

1980-81 *Sekondeleutnant Aberdehr (Second Lieutenant Aber-
        dehr)*. Com (with Horst Hawemann). Pr 1981 Das Ei,
        Berlin.

1980-82 *Die wahre Geschichte des Ah Q (The True Story of Ah
        Q)*. Com (based on short story by Lu Xun). Pr 1983 DT.
        TdZ 1983/10. Darmstadt: Luchterhand, 1984.
        Ossoki - Ossokin. Com. Pr Neustrelitz.
        Der Herr Haysaemon (Mr. Haysaemon).

HEINRICHS, Eckart

1965   *Die braven Börgers von Kreihenbarg (The Good Citizens
        of Kreihenbarg)*. Com (based on August von Kotzebue).
        Pr 1965 Schwerin.

1967   *Frau Holle (Mother Holle)*. Juv (based on Grimm). Pr
        1967 Zeitz.
        Diese Eh' döggt nix (This Marriage Isn't Working).
        Mus Lib (in Low German; based on Imre Kertesz, "Ehe
        ungenügend"; M Peter Fenyes).

HEINZE, Herbert

1961   *Die schwarze Madonna (The Black Madonna)*. Dr (with
        Armin Karl). Pr 1962 Neustrelitz.

HEINZE, Kurt   see Peter NELL

HELFRICHT, Klaus

1978   *Die Bremer Stadtmusikanten (The Town Musicians of Bre-
        men)*. Juv (based on Grimm). Pr 1978 Meiningen.

HELLER, Erich
1913 - 1964
        Muß das sein? (Does That Have to Be?) Com (with Mar-
        gret Gruchmann-Reuter).

1959   *Alwin der Letzte (Alvin the Last)*. Com (with Margret
        Gruchmann-Reuter).

1960   *Das geht auf keine Kuhhaut (That Boggles the Mind)*.
        Com (with Margret Gruchmann-Reuter). Pr 1960 Meinin-
        gen.

HELLWIG, Gerd Gunthart
1977   ‹Kasper und› Die kluge Bauerntochter (‹Punch and› The
          Clever Farmer's Daughter). Com. Pr 1978 Wittenberg.

HELM, Heinz   (Pseud. Heinz DORNATH)
27 Mar 1929 –
Lives in Berlin.
1982   Dienstreisegeschichten (Tales from a Business Trip).
          Com. Pr 1983 Wittenberg.

HENKELS, Hans
1962   Geschichten meiner Frau (Stories of my Wife). Com
          (with Hans Peter and Ralph Wiener). Pr 1962 Rostock.

HENTSCHEL, Sibylle
27 May 1938 Radebeul –
Set designer. Lives in Dsdn.
1978   Pellkartoffel (Potatoes In Their Jackets). Juv (with
          Beate Morgenstern; based on radio play). Pr 1981 Th.
          f. jg. Zuschauer, Mgdbg. TdZ 1982/11.

HEROLD, Annemarie   see Heide WENDLAND

HEROLD, Gottfried
8 May 1929 Weißbach –
Until 1955 technical draftsman; then editorial asst. "Sächsi-
sche Zeitung"; now independent author, lives in Dsdn; married
to Heide Wendland. 1961 Erich Weinert Medal. Writes poetry,
prose, children's books, and TV scripts.
1963   Der Liebe ist kein Wind zu kalt (No Wind Is Too Cold
          for Love). Com (with Heide Wendland; based on story,
          "Der rothaarige Widerspruch"). Pr 1964 Bautzen.

HERRMANN, Klaus
4 Aug 1903 Gruben – 22 Apr 1972 Erfurt
Studied history, German literature, and sociology in Jena and
Berlin; critic and editor for "Neue Bücherschau"; 1929–32
radio work, Berlin; 33–45 in Bavaria, worked as translator;
after 45 writer for "Neue Zeitung"; from 49 on in GDR; lived
in Weimar. 1952 member PEN Club. Wrote historical novels.
1930   Die Götterwitwe (The Divine Widow). Com. Pr 1947
          Bielefeld.
1931   Die Prüfungen Hiobs (The Trials of Job). Com.
1932   Vorstadttragödie (Suburban Tragedy). Dr.
1935   Augustus Potter. Com.
1939   Georg der Gerechte (George the Just). Dr.
1940   Im Himmel und auf Erden (In Heaven and on Earth).
          Com. Pr 1941 DT.
1946   Büchner. Dr. Pr 1946 DT.
1954   Salto Mortale (Flying Somersault). Dr.
          Der Befreier (The Liberator). Com.
          Die tote Zeit (Dead Time). Dr.
1962   M. M. greift ein (M. M. Intercedes). Dr. Pr 1962
          Cottbus.

HERTEL, Thomas
Composer and librettist.
1980   *Leonce und Lena.* Op (with Karla Kochta; based on Georg Büchner). Pr 1981 Greifswald.

HERZ, Joachim
15 June 1924 Dresden –
Studied at Music Conservatory Dsdn and Berlin; 1951 stage director Radebeul Op., 53 Km.Op; 1959-76 managing director Lpzg Op., 77-80 again Km. Op.; since 81 chief director, Dsdn Op. 1985 National Prize.
1964   *Zwerg Nase (Nose the Dwarf).* Juv (based on Wilhelm Hauff). Pr 1964 Nordhausen.
        Ein Maskenball (A Masked Ball). Op Lib (new adaptation; M Verdi).
        Die Macht des Schicksals (The Power of Destiny). Op Lib (new adaptation with Klaus Schlegel; M Verdi).
1981   *La Bohème.* Op Lib (new adaptation with Klaus Schlegel; M Puccini).
        Der Bajazzo (The Clown). Op Lib (new adaptation with Kurt Seipt; M Leoncavallo).

HERZKA, Peter-Maria
        Hänsel und Gretel. Juv (based on Grimm).
1963   *Der gestiefelte Kater (Puss in Boots).* Juv. Pr 1963 Zeitz.
1964   *Das Feuerzeug (The Tinderbox).* Juv (based on Hans Christian Andersen). Pr 1964 Zeitz.

HERZOG, Alfred
9 June 1895 Elbing – 15 Oct 1973 Berlin
Journalist, stage director, theater manager. Wrote prose, radio and TV plays.
1930   *Krach um Leutnant Blumenthal (Trouble with Lieutenant Blumenthal).* Com. Pr 1930 Berlin.
1931   *Und wen verurteilen Sie? (And Whom Do You Condemn?).* Com.
1932   *Das Mädel von der Grenze (The Girl from the Border).* Dr.
1933   *Kampf um Gott (Struggle over God).* Dr.
1934   *Der Mann ohne Heimat (The Man without a Homeland).* Dr. Rev 1951 as Menschen ohne Heimat.
1936   *Eine Frau verliert die Maske (A Woman Loses Her Mask).* Com.
1950   *Der Karneval von Nikolsburg (The Nicholsburg Carnival).* Dr.
1951   *Menschen ohne Heimat (People without a Homeland).* Dr (rev of Der Mann ohne Heimat).
1954   *Ohne uns (Without Us).* Dr.
        Der Stab (The Staff). Juv. Pr 1981 Th. d. jg. Generation, Dsdn.

HEYM, Stefan   (Real name Helmut FLIEG)
10 Apr 1913 Chemnitz (now Karl Marx Stadt) –
Studied literature and journalism; 1933 emigrated to Czechoslovakia, where he worked as journalist, then USA; studied at
Univ of Chicago, worked as dishwasher, waiter, salesman, language teacher; 37-39 editor of "Deutsches Volksecho"; 43-45
in American Army; served with occupation troops in Germany;
52 to GDR, now lives in Berlin. 1956 FDGB Prize, 59 National
Prize; 79 expelled from Schriftstellerverband (*GDR Authors'
Association*). Writes novels, short stories, essays; since 70,
works published in FRG only.
1934   *Gestern. Heute. Morgen (Yesterday. Today. Tomorrow).*
         Dr. Pr 1935 Chicago. *Das Wort* 1937/3.
1935   *Die Hinrichtung (The Execution).* Dr.
1936   *Tom Sawyers ‹großes› Abenteuer (Tom Sawyer's ‹Great›*
         Adventure).   Juv (with Hanus Burger; based on Mark
         Twain). Pr 1937 Vienna. Rev version Pr 1952 Halle
         (Performance title: Abenteuer am Mississippi). Halle:
         Mitteldt. Verlag, 1953. Kassel: Bärenreiter, 1955.

HIRSCH, Rudolf
17 Nov 1907 Krefeld –
After high school, worked in and later took over father's
shoe store; 1931 joined KPD; 33 emigration to Holland; 34 returned to Germany, worked in underground; 37 emigrated to Palestine, worked in shoe factory; 49 returned to GDR; after 50
court reporter; married to writer Rosemarie Schuder; lives in
Berlin. 1982 Order of Merit. Writes prose and children's
books.
1963   *Aktion Polarkuß (Mission Polar Kiss).* Juv.
1966   *Die vergifteten Hunde (The Poisoned Dogs).* Juv.

HLADIK, Rita
1984   *Und der August, der bist du (Eenie-Meenie-Minie-Moe).*
         Juv Mus Lib (M Matthias Nilius). Pr 1984 Th. d. jg.
         Garde, Halle.

HOCKE, Wolfgang
Composer and librettist.
1962   *Rote Nelken (Red Carnations).* Mus. Pr 1963 Meinin-
         gen.
1977   *Ein Vogel wollte Hochzeit machen (The Wedding of the*
         Birds). Juv Mus. Pr 1978 Meiningen.
1981   *Der Wettlauf zwischen Hase und Igel (The Race between*
         the Hare and the Hedgehog). Juv Mus. Pr 1982 Meinin-
         gen.
1983   *Der Halsabschneider (The Cutthroat).* Op (based on
         Lope de Vega). Pr 1984 Meiningen.
1985   *Sechse kommen durch die Welt (The Six Servants).* Juv
         Mus (based on Grimm). Pr 1986 Meiningen.

HOERNING, Walter
     Ein gewisser Herr Wolf (A Certain Mr. Wolf). Pr 1968 Wittenberg.

HOFFMANN, Eugen Ferdinand
16 Oct 1885 Ruhrort - ?
Merchant; lived in Görlitz as independent author. Wrote short stories.
1953   *Hochzeit in Luxemburg (Wedding in Luxembourg)*. Dr.

HOFFMANN, Max K.
1980   *August Cäsar (Augustus Caesar)*. Com. Pr 1981 Potsdam.

HOFFMANN, Walter
1976   *Amphitruo oder Eine lange Nacht (Amphitryon or A Long Night)*. Op Lib (based on Plautus; M Peter Freiheit). Pr 1977 Bernburg.

HOFMEIER, Anni
     Die Zaubersuppe (The Magic Soup). Juv. Pr 1948 VB.

HÖHER, Wolfgang
Editor, Mgdbg.
1954   *Unternehmen Rakete (Project Rocket)*. Dr. Pr 1955 Magdeburg.

HOLDSCH, Hans
Actor, Gera.
     Villon kommt über Paris (Villon Comes by Way of Paris). Mus Lib (with Jens-Uwe Günther). Pr 1971 Gera.
1974   *Anna ‹Hier liegt der Hund begraben› (Anna ‹There's the Rub›)*. Dr (based on novel by Ludwig Turek, "Anna Lubitzke"). Pr 1974 Gera.

HOLTZ-BAUMERT, Gerhard
25 Dec 1927 Berlin -
After high school, anti-aircraft helper, then soldier in WW II; deserted, American POW; escaped and returned to Berlin; 1950-51 studied pedagogy; 51-58 editor of children's magazines; 58-59 I. Lit Lpzg; 60-62 Secretary of GDR Authors' Assoc., 70 Secretary-General for Children's Literature. 1970 Heinrich Heine Prize. Writes children's books.
1976   *Trampen nach Norden (Hiking Up North)*. Juv. Pr 1979 Mgdbg.

HOMBERG, Bodo   see Christian COLLIN

HONIGMANN, Barbara
12 Feb 1949 Berlin -
1967 studied theater history Berlin, then became dramaturg Brandenburg; since 75 independent author in Berlin. Writes prose.

HONIGMANN (cont'd)
1979   *Das singende springende Löweneckerchen   (The Little Singing, Pouncing Lion Cub).* Juv. Pr 1981 Zwickau. TdZ 1980/1.
1979   *Der Schneider von Ulm (The Tailor of Ulm).* On (based on folk tale). Pr 1984 Fkft/M. *TdZ* 1981/12.
1980   *Don Juan.* On. Pr 1984 Fkft/M. *TdZ* 1981/12.
        Die Holz-Eisenbahn (The Wooden Train). Juv (based on Lev Ustinov; tr Nelly Drechsler).
1984   *Die Schöpfung (The Creation).* On. Pr 1985 Munich.

HORN, Heinz
        Schulleiter Fleming   (School Principal Fleming). Dr. Pr 1951 Borna.

HORN, Rudolf
1930 actor, then stage director in Meißen, Konstanz, Görlitz, Lpzg; also acting coach.
        Sturmvögel (Storm Birds). Dr (based on novella by Maxim Gorki, "Die Mordwinin"). Pr 1951 Radebeul.

HORNAWSKY, Gerd
10 Nov 1939 Suhl –
1945 moved to suburb of Lpzg; 58-63 studied chemistry Jena; Dr. of chemistry, works in Institute of Veterinary Medicine, Berlin. Writes poetry, stort stories, cabaret texts.
1973   *Lord Arthurs pflichtbewußtes Verbrechen (Lord Arthur's Conscientious Crime).* Mus Lib (based on Oscar Wilde, "Lord Arthur Savile's Crime"; M Bernd Wefelmeyer). Pr 1975 Plauen.
1984   *Nachlaß oder Ein Besuch für die Vergangenheit ‹Das Duell› (Literary Remains or A Visit for the Past ‹The Duel).* Dr (based on radio play, "Die Büchner Papiere"). Reading 1984 Lpzg. Pr 1986 Rudolstadt.

HORNBOGEN, Chris
21 Apr 1912 Messeburg –
Lives in Oberhof. Writes poetry, songs, short prose, fairy tales.
1980   *Muschebubu.* Juv Mus Lib (M Henry Krtschil). Pr 1981 Meiningen.

HUBERT, Gerhard
1981   *Ali Baba und die vierzig Räuber (Ali Baba and the Forty Thieves).* Juv. Pr 1982 Quedlinburg.

HÜLLWECK, Karl
13 May 1905 Dessau –
1924-29 studied psychology and theology Univ. Kiel, Munich, Jena; after 32 Protestant minister; 58 guest preacher Capri, Italy; 64 and 66 Sweden; since 70 lives in Dessau-Mildensee. Writes poetry, short stories.
1948   *Der todesmüde Tod (Dead-Tired Death).* Dr.

HÜLLWECK (cont'd)

1949   *Sie hatten sonst keinen Raum in der Herberge* (There Was No Other Room in the Inn). Dr.

1953   *Vorderhuus, Hinterhuus und der wahre Hintergrund* (Front Building, Rear Building and the Real Background). Dr.

HUSS, Hans   see Gustav von WANGENHEIM

IRMER, Hans-Joachim
>   *Eine Reise auf den Mond (A Trip to the Moon).* Op Lib
>   (new adaptation; M Jacques Offenbach).

1983   *Polenblut (Polish Blood).* Opt Lib (based on Leo Stein;
>   M Oscar Nebdal). Pr 1983 Potsdam. Rev version Pr 19-
>   85 Stralsund.

ISEGRIMM, Dr.   see Friedrich WOLF

JÄCKEL, Gerhard   (Pseud. Alfred PALISANDER)
17 Nov 1922 Halle -
After high school, service in WW II; 1945-47 teacher of German and English, Lpzg; after 47 reporter and editor for newspapers and radio; now lives in Berlin. Writes radio and TV
plays, criticism.
1962   *Die Wahnmörderin ‹Mordsache Mergel› (The Insane Mur-*
>   *deress ‹The Mergel Murder Case›).* Dr (with Ottomar
>   Lang; based on TV play). Pr 1962 Halle. *TdZ 1963/20.*
1973   *Musik aus der Kiste oder Ein Kindergeburtstag (Music*
>   *Out of the Box or A Child's Birthday).* Mus Lib. Pr
>   1973.
1979   *Der Kriminalfall (The Criminal Case).* On (based on
>   radio play; dramatized by Elke Tasche). *Neumann: 2 x*
>   *klingeln,* Lpzg: Zentralhaus für Kulturarbeit der DDR,
>   no date.

JAKOBSOHN-LASk, Berta   see Berta LASK

JAKOBS, Karl-Heinz
20 Apr 1929 Kiauken (now Poland) -
1945 brief war service, then various jobs; 48 began engineering studies in evening; later became editorial asst. and journalist; 56 I.Lit Lpzg; travel to Poland, Soviet Union, Far
East, Africa; 58-80 independent author in Berlin; since 1981
FRG. 1972 Heinrich Mann Prize. Writes prose, poetry, radio,
TV, and film scripts.
1964   *Die Fontäne (The Fountain).* Dr.
1965   *Die Heimkehr des verlorenen Sohnes (The Return of the*
>   *Prodigal Son).* Dr. Pr 1968 Mgdbg.
1975   *Rauhweiler.* Com. Pr 1976 Stralsund. *TdZ 1976/10.*
>   *Salzberger (Salt Miners).* Dr. Pr 1976 Stralsund.

JAKSCH, Bärbel
Dramaturg, Schwerin.
1978   *Franziska Linkerhand.* Dr (with Heiner Maaß; based on
>   1973 novel fragment by Brigitte Reimann). Pr 1978
>   Schwerin. *TdZ 1978/6.*
1980   *Das siebte Kreuz (The Seventh Cross).* Dr (with Heiner
>   Maaß; based on novel by Anna Seghers). Pr 1981 Schwe-
>   rin. *TdZ 1981/4.*
1980   *Kippenberg.* Dr (with Heiner Maaß; based on novel by
>   Dieter Noll). Pr 1981 Schwerin.

JAKSCH (cont')
1981   *Berlin Alexanderplatz (Alexander Square, Berlin).* Dr
(with Heiner Maaß; based on novel by Alexander Döb-
lin). Pr 1981 VB. *TdZ* 1981/11.

JANOWSKI, Maurycy   (Pseud. with Heinz Kufferath: Jan HALL)
1919 - 1973
Studied painting and art history; worked as editor of various
publications; dramaturg Rostock; after 1962 dramaturg DEFA.
1957   *Alarm in Pont l'Eveque.* Mus Lib (with Heinz Kufferath; M Conny Odd). Pr 1958 Erfurt. Rev 1970 as Gangster lieben keine Blumen.
1959   *Der Instrukteur soll heiraten (The Instructor Is Supposed to Get Married).* Com (with Heinz Kufferath).
1961   *In Frisco ist der Teufel los (All Hell Is Loose in
Frisco).* Mus Lib (with Otto Schneidereit; based on
Schneidereit's play, "Wer braucht Geld?"; M Guido Masanetz). Pr 1962 Met.
*Der Professor kommt um sechs ‹Knirps und das Zirkus-
pferd› (The Professor Comes at Six ‹Tiny and the Circus Horse›).* Juv Mus Lib (with Heinz Kufferath; based
on M. Lvovsky, "Kristall KS"; M Siegfried Matthus).
1968   *Karambolage (Collision).* Mus Lib (based on film, "Ge-
liebte weiße Maus"; M Conny Odd). Pr 1969 Gera. *TdZ*
1970/1.
1970   *Gangster lieben keine Blumen (Gangsters Don't Like
Flowers).* Mus Lib (rev of Alarm in Pont l'Eveque;
with Heinz Kufferath; M Conny Odd). Pr 1970 Rostock.
1973   *Man liest kein fremdes Tagebuch (You Don't Read Someone Else's Diary).* Mus Lib (M Conny Odd). Pr 1974
Met.

JIRSCHIM, Susanne
1981   *Till Eulenspiegel.* Juv. Pr 1982 Th. d. jg. Generation, Dsdn.

JOSTAU, Jakob   see Josef STAUDER

JUNG, Ilse
Contributor, *Tägliche Rundschau.*
1946   *Wo ist der Weg? (Where is the Path?)* Dr. Pr 1946.

JUNGNICKEL, Rudolf
3 Feb 1922 Frankfurt am Main -
After high school, received training as teacher; 1946-47 dramaturg in Nordhausen; 47 went to FRG, dramaturg Boppard; then
journalist and editor in Bonn, Fkft/M; now lives in West Berlin. Writes essays, poetry, radio plays.
1945   *Heinrich von Kleist‹s Tod› (‹The Death of› Heinrich
von Kleist).* Dr. Pr 1946 Nordhausen. Boppard: Die
Pforte, 1947.
1946   *Im Schatten des Kaisers (In the Emperor's Shadow).*
Dr. Pr 1947 Nordhausen (cancelled after three performances).
1952   *Der Weg zum Vesuv (The Road to Mt. Vesuvius).* Dr.

JUNGNICKEL (cont'd)

1954 *Gewissen und Gewalt (Conscience and Power)*. Dr. Coburg: Veste, 1954.

1966 *Die Schaukel oder Das Mädchen aus Caen (The Swing or The Girl from Caen)*. Dr. Pr 1966 Fränkisches Th., Massbach.

JÜRGENS, Claus   see Paul Herbert FREYER

JUST, Gustav

16 June 1921 Reinowitz (now Rynovice, Czechoslovakia) – Attended German high school with Czech language instruction; 1940–45 served in German Army; then moved to GDR; 46–48 teacher; later journalist and editor of "Sonntag"; lives in Berlin. Translator.

1964 *Das schwedische Zündholz (The Safety Match)*. Com (based on Chekhov). Pr 1964 Altenburg.
      Schwanda, der Dudelsackpfeifer (Schwanda, the Bagpiper). Op Lib (new adaptation; with Günther Deicke; M Leos Janacek).

KADEN, Stefan
1976-84 student at MHS Dsdn.
1984   *Prinzessin Hochmut (The Arrogant Princess).* Juv Op
       (based on Grimm, "King Thrushbeard"). Pr 1985 MHS
Dsdn.

KAHLAU, Heinz
6 Feb 1931 Drewitz/Potsdam -
Until 1948 unskilled laborer, then tractor driver; began writing in 50's; after 53, Brecht student; lives in Berlin. Member PEN Center; 1962 Heinrich Greif Prize, FDGB Prize, 63 Heinrich Heine Prize, Erich Weinert Medal, 71 Goethe Prize Berlin, 72 Lessing Prize, 81 Johannes Becher Prize, 85 National Prize. Writes poetry, songs, film and TV scripts.
1962   *Jones' Familie (The Jones Family).* Com. Henschel
       1962.
1964   *Das Märchen von der alten Straßenbahn Therese (The
       Tale of Theresa, the Old Streetcar).* Juv (with Hans-
       Dieter Schmidt; based on Ota Hofmann and Jan Gerstel).
       Pr 1964 Th. d. jg. Welt, Lpzg. *TdZ* 1966, spec'l issue.
1965   *Ein Krug mit Oliven (A Jug of Olives).* Juv (based on
       a tale from "The 1001 Nights"). Pr 1966 Th. d. Freund-
       schaft, Berlin. *TdZ* 1966/15.
1967   *Der gestiefelte Kater (Puss in Boots).* Juv. Pr 1967
       Th. d. Freundschaft, Berlin. Aufbau 1968.
1969   *Der Musterschüler (The Model Pupil).* Com. Pr 1969
       Th. d. Freundschaft, Berlin. *TdZ* 1969/12.
1971   *Die kluge Susanne (Clever Susan).* Juv. Pr 1972 Th.
       d. Freundschaft, Berlin. Aufbau 1972.
1972   *Das Eiszapfenherz (The Icicle Heart).* Juv. Pr 1972
       Th. d. jg. Generation, Dsdn. Dsdn: Kinderbuchverlag,
       1973.
1973   *Das Durchgangszimmer (The Connecting Room).* Mus Lib
       (based on story by Renate Holland-Moritz; M Bernd We-
       felmeyer). Pr 1973 Halle.
1978   *Die Galoschenoper (The Rubbers Opera).* Com (based on
       John Gay, "The Beggars' Opera"; incidental M Reiner
       Bredemeyer). Pr 1979 DT. *Tasso und die Galoschen,*
       Aufbau 1980.
1979   *Torquato Tasso.* Com (based on Goldoni). *Tasso und
       die Galoschen,* 1980.
1981   *Frech wie Oskar (Fresh Like Oscar).* Juv (with Peter
       Ensikat and Erich Schlossarek). Pr 1982 Fkft/O.
1982   *Zille-Heinrich.* Op Lib (M Joachim Werzlau).
1984   *Auweia und Ratzbatz (Ouchy and Ratty-Pile).* Pp (M
       Hermann Nahring). Pr 1985 Pp. Th., Berlin.

KAHLOW, Heinz   (Pseud. Heinz BEHLING)
5 July 1924 Rostock -
Raised in Danzig (now Gdansk, Poland); after high school, service in WW II; English POW; after return home, studied acting in Rostock; 1950 dramaturg and director, Radio Berlin; 54 editor of satiric periodical "Eulenspiegel"; since 57 lives

KAHLOW (cont'd)
in Berlin. Writes essays, children's books, poetry, scripts
for cabaret, film, and TV.

1960   *Adieu Olivia (Good-bye Olivia)*. Mus Lib (based on TV
       play "Fräulein mit Courage"; M Günter Hauk). Pr 1960.
       Zwischen Dünen und Daunen (Between Dunes and Down).
       Com. Pr 1968 Rostock.

1969   *Die nackte Wahrheit (The Naked Truth)*. Com (based on
       TV play). Pr 1970 Schwerin.

1976   *Kennen Sie Kahlow? (Do You Know Kahlow?)* Revue (with
       Wilfried Schmidt). Pr 1977 Mgdbg.

1977   *Karl Stülpner*. Dr. Pr 1977 Annaberg.

1977   *Das Decameronical (The Decameron Musical)*. Mus Lib
       (M Gerd Natschinski). Pr 1979 Halle. Henschel 1977.

1983   *Planet der Verliebten (The Planet of Lovers)*. Mus Lib
       (based on story by Gyula Fekete; M Gerd Natschinski).
       Pr 1984 Met.

KAISER, Walter   see Walter GORRISH

KALTOFEN, Günter
12 July 1927 Erfurt –
After high school, served in WW II 1943-45, became POW; 46-50
studied German and philosophy in Jena and Lpzg; Dr. phil. 50,
then dramaturg 50-51 Meißen, 51-54 Lpzg, 54-62 GDR TV, Berlin. 1960 GDR Art Prize. Writes children's books, TV and
film scripts.

1946   *Die Reise in das Märchenland (The Journey into Fairy-
       Tale Land)*. Juv. Pr 1947.

1951   *Hans im Glück (Lucky Jack)*. Juv (based on Grimm). Pr
       1951.

1952   *Die Bremer Stadtmusikanten (The Town Musicians of Bre-
       men)*. Juv (based on Grimm). Pr 1954 Stralsund.

1956   *Rumpelstilzchen (Rumpelstiltskin)*. Juv Op Lib (based
       on Grimm; M Wolfgang Huth). Pr 1959 Halberstadt.

1957   *Schneewittchen (Snow White)*. Juv (based on Grimm).
       Pr 1960 Quedlinburg.

1961   *Die goldene Gans (The Golden Goose)*. Juv (based on
       Grimm; incidental M Wolfgang Huth). Pr 1962 Rostock.

1962   *Märchen aus Märchen (Fairy Tales from Fairy Tales)*.
       Juv (based on Sak and Kusnetsov). Pr 1962 Döbeln.

1964   *Frau Holle (Mother Holle)*. Juv (based on Grimm; in-
       cidental M Hans Auenmüller). Pr 1965 Dessau.

1965   *Zwerg Nase (Nose the Dwarf)*. Juv Op Lib (based on Wil-
       helm Hauff; M Wolfgang Huth). Pr 1965 Zwickau.

1966   *Der gestiefelte Kater (Puss in Boots)*. Juv. Pr 1966
       Lpzg.

1967   *Aladdin und die Wunderlampe (Aladdin and the Magic
       Lamp)*. Juv (incidental M Wolfgang Huth). Pr 1967 Hal-
       berstadt. Rev version Pr 1971 Zwickau.

1968   *Tischlein deck dich (The Table, the Ass and the
       Stick)*. Juv (based on Grimm; incidental M Wolfgang
       Huth). Pr 1968 Th. d. jg. Welt, Lpzg.

1968   *Till Eulenspiegels Streiche (Till Eulenspiegel's
       Pranks)*. Juv. Pr 1969 Halberstadt.

KALTOFEN (cont'd)

1969   *Das kalte Herz (The Cold Heart)*. Juv (based on Wilhelm Hauff). Pr 1969 Quedlinburg.

1970   *Das tapfere Schneiderlein (The Brave Little Tailor)*. Juv (based on Grimm). Pr 1970 Lpzg.

1970   *Münchhausen auf Artemis (Munchhausen on Artemis)*. Juv (with Hans Pfeiffer). Pr 1971 Lpzg.

1971   *Der Froschkönig (The Frog Prince)*. Juv (based on Grimm; incidental M Hans Auenmüller). Pr 1972 Wittenberg.

1974   *Die Nachtigall (The Nightingale)*. Juv (based on Hans Christian Andersen). Pr 1975 Halberstadt.

1975   *Die schwarze Mühle (The Black Mill)*.

1976   *Salut an alle. Marx (Regards to Everyone, Marx)*. Dr (with Hans Pfeiffer). Pr 1976 Halle. *TdZ 1976/7*.

1977   *Heines letzte Liebe (Heine's Last Love)*. Dr (with Hans Pfeiffer). Pr 1977 TiP.

KANT, Hermann
14 June 1926 Hamburg –
Worked as electrician; then served in WW II, POW in Poland 1945-49; 49-56 studied German literature in Greifswald, then in Berlin; 56 research asst. Humboldt Univ., Berlin; worked briefly as editor; then became independent author; lives in Berlin. Since 1962 AdK; Vice-President and (since 78) President, GDR Authors' Assoc.; 62 and 67 Heinrich Mann Prize, 63 FDGB Prize, 66 Erich Weinert Medal, 68 Händel Prize Halle, 73 National Prize. Writes prose.

1964   *Die Aula (The Auditorium)*. Dr (collective dramatization; based on novel). Pr 1968 Halle.

1975-76 *Impressum (Imprint)*. Dr (collective dramatization; based on novel). Pr Halle.

KANTOROWICZ, Alfred   (Pseud. Helmut CAMPE)
12 August 1899 Berlin - 27 Mar 1979 Hamburg
Served in WW I, then studied law until 1923; 24-33 journalist and editor, Berlin; joined KPD 31; 33 emigrated to France; 36-38 Int'l Brigade Spain, then returned to France, where he was interned; 41 USA; 47 returned to GDR as Prof. for literature, Humboldt Univ, Berlin; after 57 lived in FRG. Wrote essays, prose, criticism.

1929   *Erlangen*. Dr.

1950   *Die Verbündeten (The Allies)*. Dr.

KARGE, Manfred
Actor, stage director, 1961 asst. director BE.

1981   *Jacke wie Hose (It's All the Same)*. Dr. Pr 1982 Bochum.

KARL, Armin
1961   *Die schwarze Madonna (The Black Madonna)*. Dr (with Herbert Heinze). Pr 1962 Neustrelitz.

KASTNER, Roland
Writes children's radio plays, film scripts.
1983   *Der Pferdehändler (The Horse Trader)*. Com (with Chris-
        tian Martin). Reading 1984 Lpzg.

KAUL, Friedrich Karl
21 Feb 1906 Posen (now Poznan, Poland) - 16 Apr 1981 Berlin
Studied law in Berlin and Heidelberg, worked as attorney; member KPD 1935-36; 37 emigration to USA; 45 returned to GDR;
after 60 Prof. Humboldt Univ., Berlin. 1960 National Prize.
Wrote prose, radio plays, film scripts.
1959   *Die blaue Akte (The Blue File)*. Dr (with Ernst Eylt,
        pseud. for Peter Hacks; based on novel, "Der blaue Ak-
        tendeckel"). Pr 1960 Quedlinburg).

KEISCH, Henryk
24 Feb 1913 Moers -
Critic and essayist; lives in Berlin. 1938 Heine Prize, 57
National Prize. Writes poetry, short prose, film, radio, and
TV scripts.
1962   *Boulevard Durand*. Dr (tr from Armand Salacrou).
1968   *Hochverratsaffäre (A Case of High Treason)*. Dr.
1969   *Ein toller Tag ‹Wenn Figaro Hochzeit macht› (A Mad
        Day ‹When Figaro Gets Married›)*. Com (based on Beau-
        marchais, "Le marriage de Figaro"). Pr 1970.

KELLER, Herbert
1922 Berlin -
Attended Th.HS, Berlin, then director and manager at various
theaters, such as Eisleben, Cottbus, VB.
1958   *Begegnung 1957 (Encounter 1957)*. Dr. Pr 1958 Zwickau.
        Lpzg: Hofmeister, 1960.

KENDZIA, Marie-Louise   (Married name Marie-Louise GRAF)
8 Nov 1926 Strasbourg -
Dr. phil., now lives in Munich. Writes children's books and
children's TV shows.
1949   *Tobias Ahoi! (Ahoy, Toby!)*. Juv. Pr 1950 Th. d. jg.
        Generation, Dsdn.

KENT, Alexander   (Real name Ludwig ACHTEL)
17 Sep 1929 Halle -
After high school, studied history in Halle 1950-55; since 57
dramaturg GDR Radio, Berlin. Writes radio and TV plays.
1960   *Karriere (Career)*. Dr. Pr 1961.

KERNDL, Rainer
27 Nov 1928 Bad Frankenhausen -
1943-45 lived with parents in occupied Poland; drafted while
still in school, POW; after return, graduated high school 48,
then worked as journalist and theater critic, especially for
newspaper "Neues Deutschland." 1961 Erich Weinert Medal, 64
and 78 FDGB Prize, 65 Lessing Prize, 72 National Prize and
Goethe Prize Berlin, 75 and 77 Order of Merit. Writes prose,
radio and TV plays.

KERNDL (cont'd)
1960   *Damals vor 15 Jahren (Fifteen Years Ago).* Dr.
1961   *Schatten eines Mädchens (The Shadow of a Girl).* Dr.
        Pr 1961 MG. Henschel 1962. *Stücke,* Henschel 1972.
1962   *Seine Kinder (His Children).* Dr. Pr 1963 MG. *TdZ*
        1963/18. Henschel 1965. *Sozialistische Dramatik,* Hen-
        schel 1968. *Stücke,* 1972.
1965   *‹Ein› Plädoyer für die Suchenden (‹A› Plea for the
        Seekers).* Dr. Pr 1966 Lpzg. *TdZ* 1965/18. *Stücke,*
        1972.
1966   *Die seltsame Reise des Alois Fingerlein (The Strange
        Journey of Alois Fingerlein).* Dr. Pr 1967 MG. Hen-
        schel 1968. *Stücke,* 1972. Henschel 1979 (with *Die
        lange Ankunft des Alois Fingerlein).*
1967   *Der verratene Rebell (The Betrayed Rebel).* Dr. Pr 19-
        68 Bautzen. *TdZ* 1967/2. Rev 1968 as Doppeltes Spiel.
1968   *Zwei in einer kleinen Stadt (Two People in a Small
        Town).* Com. Pr 1969 Freiberg.
1968   *Doppeltes Spiel (Double-Dealing).* Dr (rev of Der ver-
        ratene Rebell). Pr 1969 Rostock. *Stücke,* Henschel
        1983.
1969   *Ich bin einem Mädchen begegnet (I Met a Girl).* Dr.
        Pr 1969 Dsdn. *TdZ* 1970/2. *Stücke,* 1972.
1970   *Wann kommt Ehrlicher? (When is Ehrlicher Coming?)* Dr.
        Pr 1971 MG. *TdZ* 1972/1. *Stücke,* 1972.
1972-75 *Nacht mit Kompromissen (A Night with Compromises).*
        Dr. Pr 1976 Rostock. *TdZ* 1973/11. *Stücke,* 1983.
1973   *Jarash: Ein Tag im September (Jarash: A Day in Sep-
        tember).* Dr. Pr 1974 Rostock. *Stücke,* 1983.
1975   *Die wilde Rotte (The Wild Gang).* Dr. *TdZ* 1975/11.
1977   *Der vierzehnte Sommer (The Fourteenth Summer).* Dr.
        Pr 1977 KMSt. *TdZ* 1977/5. *Stücke,* 1983.
1979   *Die lange Ankunft des Alois Fingerlein (The Long Ar-
        rival of Alois Fingerlein).* Dr. Pr 1979 MG. *TdZ* 19-
        79/1. In *Die seltsame Reise des Alois Fingerlein,*19-
        79.
1982   *Der Georgsberg (Mt. George).* Com. Pr 1984 MG.

KEYN, Ulf
1972   *Kein Mensch lebt zweimal (Nobody Lives Twice).* Dr.
        Pr 1972 Dsdn/Radebeul.
1975   *Zeit der Störche (The Season of the Storks).* Dr (with
        Helmut Windisch). Pr 1976 Neustrelitz.

KILZ, Hans Otto
1953   *Der Querkopf ‹Tomaten und Stahl› (The Pigheaded One
        ‹Tomatoes and Steel›).* Dr. Pr 1954 KMSt.

KIPPHARDT, Heinar
8 Mar 1922 Heidersdorf - 18 Nov 1982 Munich
Studied philosophy, theater history and medicine (psychiatry)
in Bonn, Cologne, Königsberg, Breslau, Düsseldorf; then doctor in various hospitals, including Univ. Psychiatric Clinic
Charité, West Berlin; 1950 went to GDR; 50-59 chief dramaturg
DT; 59 returned to FRG as dramaturg Düsseldorf, 68-73 Kammer-

KIPPHARDT (cont'd)

spiele, Munich. Member FRG PEN Center, W. German Academy of Performing Arts; 1953 GDR National Prize, 67 Prix Italia, 77 Literature Prize Bremen.

1952   *Entscheidungen (Decisions)*. Scenes. Pr 1952 DT.

1953   *Varianten einer Szene (Variations of a Scene)*. Scene (planned for inclusion in Shakespeare dringend gesucht). *TdZ* 1953/9.

1953   *Shakespeare dringend gesucht (Shakespeare Urgently Needed)*. Com. Pr 1953 DT. Suhrkamp 1954. *Stücke 1*, Suhrkamp 1973. *Theaterstücke 1*, Cologne: Kiepenheuer & Witsch, 1978.

1956   *Der ‹staunenswerte› Aufstieg des Alois Piontek (The ‹Amazing› Rise of Alois Piontek)*. Com. Pr 1956 DT. Henschel 1956. *Theaterstücke 1*, 1978.

1958   *Esel schrein im Dunkel (Donkeys Cry in the Dark)*. Com (based on novel by Ilya Ilf and Yevgenyi Petrov, "12 Stühle"). Rev 1960 as Die Stühle des Herrn Szmil.

1960   *Die Stühle des Herrn Szmil (Mr. Szmil's Chairs)*. Com (rev of Esel schrein im Dunkel). Pr 1961 Wuppertal. *Jg. dt. Th. von heute*, Munich: Langen Müller, 1961. *Stücke 1*, 1973. *Theaterstücke 1*, 1978.

1960   *Der Hund des Generals (The General's Dog)*. Dr (based on short story). Pr 1962 Kammerspiele, Munich. Suhrkamp 1963. *Stücke*, Henschel 1970. *Stücke 1*, 1973. *Theaterstücke 1*, 1978. *Theaterstücke*, Aufbau 1982.

1962   *Bartleby*. Dr (based on Melville).

1962-64 *In der Sache J. Robert Oppenheimer (In the Matter of J. Robert Oppenheimer)*. Dr. Pr 1964 Kammerspiele, Munich. *Th.h.* 1964/11. *Spec* 7, 1964. Suhrkamp 1965. Fkft/M: S. Fischer, 1971. *Stücke 1*, 1973. *Theaterstücke 1*, 1978. *Theaterstücke*, 1982. Reinbek: Rowohlt, 1982. Engl. tr. London: Methuen, 1967.

1964-65 *Joel Brand: Die Geschichte eines Geschäfts (Joel Brand: The Story of a Business Deal)*. Dr (based on TV play). Pr 1965 Kammerspiele, Munich. *Dt. Th. d. Gegenwart 1*, Suhrkamp 1965. *Stücke 2*, Suhrkamp 1974. *Theaterstücke 2*, Cologne: Kiepenheuer & Witsch, 1981. *Theaterstücke*, 1982.

1966   *Die Nacht, in der der Chef geschlachtet wurde (The Night When the Boss Was Slaughtered)*. Com. Pr 1967 Stuttgart. *Stücke 2*, 1974. Rev version 1980. *Theaterstücke 2*, 1981. *Theaterstücke*, 1982.

1967   *Die Soldaten (The Soldiers)*. Dr (based on J. M. R. Lenz). Pr 1968 Düsseldorf. Suhrkamp 1978. Fkft/M: Fischer 1971. *Theaterstücke 2*, 1981. *Theaterstücke*, 1982.

1969   *Sedanfeier (Commemoration of Sedan)*. Dr. Pr 1970 Kammerspiele, Munich. *Stücke 2*, 1974. *Theaterstücke 2*, 1981.

        Das tote Tal (The Dead Valley). Dr (based on Alexander Kron).

KIPPHARDT (cont'd)

1978   *März: Ein Künstlerleben (März: An Artist's Life)*. Dr (based on novel and TV play). Pr 1980 Düsseldorf. Cologne: Kiepenheuer & Witsch, 1980. *Theaterstücke 2*, 1981. *Theaterstücke*, 1982.

1978-82 *Bruder Eichmann (Brother Eichmann)*. Dr. Pr 1983 Munich. *Kursbuch* 1978/51. *Th.h.* 1982/13. Reinbek: Rowohlt, 1983. Henschel 1984. Aufbau 1985.
    Der Prinz von Homburg (The Prince of Homburg). Dr (based on Kleist).

KIRCHNER, Annerose

2 Sep 1951 Leipzig –

Worked as typist, stenographer, newspaper typesetter; 1976-79 I.Lit Lpzg; lives in Gera. Writes poetry,short prose, children's radio shows.

1983   *Die goldene Gans (The Golden Goose)*. Juv Op Lib (based on Grimm; M Günter Schimm). Pr 1983 Gera.

KIRSCH, Rainer

17 July 1934 Döbeln –

Studied history and philosophy in Halle and Jena; after 1957 worked in print shop, then chemical factory; 58-68 married to Sarah Kirsch; 63-65 I.Lit Lpzg; now lives in Berlin as independent author; 73 expelled from SED. 1965 Erich Weinert Medal (with Sarah Kirsch). Writes poetry, translations, essays, radio plays.

1961   *Teddy Honigmaul und der Zauberer (Teddy Honeymouth and the Magician)*. Pp. Pr 1961 Lpzg.

1962   *Bruno der Unsichtbare (Bruno the Invisible)*. Juv Mus Lib (based on Korostylev and Ivoskyi; M Siegfried Tiefensee). *Kinderstücke*, Henschel 1962.

1963   *Wir freuen uns auf den Wind von morgen (We Look Forward to Tomorrow's Wind)*. Cantata.

1966   *Der Soldat und das Feuerzeug (The Soldier and the Tinderbox)*. Juv (based on Hans Christian Andersen). Pr 1967 Erfurt. Rev 1975 as Das Feuerzeug.

1967   *Pathetique ‹Pathetische Sonate› (The Pathetique Sonata)*. Dr (based on Nicolai Kulish). Pr 1967.

1968   *Cyrano aus Bergerac (Cyrano de Bergerac)*. Com (based on Edmond Rostand; tr Gisela Naumann). Pr 1969 Potsdam.

1970   *Münchhausen*. Com with Bl (M Rainer Kunad). Pr 1971 Weimar.

1971   *Die Schule der Frauen (The School for Wives)*. Com (based on Moliere, "L'ecole des femmes"; tr Gisela Naumann). Pr 1973 Anklam.

1972   *Schwitzbad (Steambath)*. Com (based on Vladimir Mayakovsky). Pr 1977 Schwerin. Fkft/M: Verlag der Autoren, 1973. Henschel 1977. Reclam 1978.

1972   *Geschichte von der vergessenen Puppe (The Story of the Forgotten Doll)*. Juv (based on Alfonso Sastre). Pr 1973 Lpzg.

KIRSCH, Rainer (cont'd)

1972-73 *Heinrich Schlaghands Höllenfahrt (Heinrich Schlag-hand's Journey to Hell)*. Com. *TdZ* 1973/4.

1973 *Der Stein des Glücks (The Lucky Stone)*. Dr (based on Carlos Reyes). Pr 1978 Rudolstadt.

1973 *Die Pantherfrau (The Panther Woman)*. Com. Pr 1974 Kleine Komödie, Berlin.

1974 *Das Land Bum-Bum oder Der lustige Musikant (Boom-Boom Land or The Jolly Musician)*. Juv Op Lib (based on Ronald Dobrovenskyi, "Hinter dem Violinschlüssel"; M Georg Katzer). Pr 1978 Km.Op. *TdZ* 1978/12.

1975 *Das Feuerzeug (The Tinderbox)*. Juv Mus Lib (rev of Der Soldat und das Feuerzeug; based on Hans Christian Andersen; M Dankwart Pfeiffer). Pr 1980 Karlsruhe. Eulenspiegel 1978. Fkft/M: Verlag der Autoren, 1982.

1977 *Die Wanze (The Bedbug)*. Com (based on Vladimir Mayakovsky). Pr 1978 Meiningen.

1977 *Von einem, der auszog, das Fürchten zu lernen (The Lad Who Set Out to Learn Fear)*. Com (based on Grimm). Reinbek: Rowohlt, 1978.

1978 *Der entfesselte Prometheus (Prometheus Unbound)*. Dr (based on Shelley). Lpzg: Insel, 1979.
  Der Bürger als Ehrenmann (The Bourgeois as Gentleman). Com (with Gerhard Neumann; based on Moliere, "Le bourgeois gentilhomme").

1982 *Frau Holle (Mother Holle)*. Juv (based on Grimm). Pr 1983 Th. d. jg. Generation, Dsdn.

1984 *Nachtasyl (Night Shelter)*. Dr (based on Maxim Gorki). Pr 1985 Schwerin.

KIRSCH, Sarah (nee Bernstein)
16 Apr 1935 Limlingerode –
After high school, worked in sugar factory, then studied biology Halle; 1958-68 married to Rainer Kirsch; 63-65 I. Lit Lpzg; 68-77 lived in Berlin, then moved to FRG. 1965 Erich Weinert Medal (with Rainer Kirsch). Writes poetry.
    Die Igeltreppe (The Hedgehog Staircase). Juv Mus Lib (M Georg Katzer).

1963 *Die betrunkene Sonne (The Drunken Sun)*. Juv Mus Lib (based on radio play; M Tilo Medek). Pr 1969 Brandenburg.

KLEEMANN, Roderich
1968 *Umtausch gestattet (Exchange Permitted)*. Com. Pr 1969 Zeitz.

KLEINEIDAM, Horst
23 June 1932 Gebhardsdorf (now Giebultow, Poland) –
Worked as a weaver, then carpenter; 1951 went to FRG, worked as coal miner in Ruhr area, construction worker in Cologne, began writing; 58 returned GDR; 63-65 I. Lit Lpzg. 1963 FDGB Prize, 69 Erich Weinert Medal.

1958 *Rebellion der Söhne (The Sons' Rebellion)*. Dr.

1959 *Die Offensive*. Dr. Pr 1960 Lpzg. Lpzg: Hofmeister, 1959.

KLEINEIDAM (cont'd)

1962   *Der Millionenschmidt (Schmidt, the Millionaire)*. Dr. Pr 1962 Lpzg. *TdZ* 1963/12.

1967   *Von Riesen und Menschen (Giants and People)*. Dr. Pr 1967 Dsdn. *TdZ* 1968/15. *Sozialistische Dramatik*, Henschel 1968.

1968   *Barfuß nach Langenhanshagen (Barefoot to Langenhanshagen)*. On. Pr 1968 Halle.

1969   *Der verlorene Sohn (The Prodigal Son)*. On. Pr 1969 Lpzg.

1969   *Susanne oder Ein Stern erster Größe (Susan or A Star of the First Magnitude)*. On. Pr 1969 Lpzg.

1969   *Auf dem Feldherrnhügel (On the Commander's Hill)*. On. Pr 1969 Quedlinburg.

1971   *Die Hochzeit in Tomsk (The Wedding in Tomsk)*. Com. Pr 1972 Schwerin.

1973   *Polterabend (Shivaree)*. Dr. Pr 1974 Eisenach. *TdZ* 1973/12.

1974   *Hinter dem Regenbogen (Behind the Rainbow)*. Dr. Pr 1975 Dsdn. *1525: Dramen zum deutschen Bauernkrieg*, Aufbau 1975.

1975   *Schlachtfest (Hog Butchering Celebration)*. Dr. Pr 1976 Görlitz/Zittau.

1977   *Karaseck*. Dr. Pr 1977 Görlitz/Zittau.

KNAUP, Andreas

   Die Säulen des Memnon (Memnon's Columns). Dr (incidental M Thomas Bürkholz).

1980   *Von einem, der auszog, das Fürchten zu lernen (The Lad Who Set Out to Learn Fear)*. Juv Mus Lib (based on Grimm; M Thomas Bürkholz). Pr 1981 Lpzg.

1981   *Sechse kommen durch die Welt (The Six Servants)*. Juv Mus Lib (based on Grimm; M Thomas Bürkholz). Pr 1982 Rostock.

1982   *Marie und ein Hans im Glück (Marie and A Lucky Jack)*. Rock Op Lib (M Thomas Bürkholz). Pr 1983 Rostock.

1983   *Rockballade (Rock Ballad)*. Op Lib (M Thomas Bürkholz). Pr 1983 Lpzg.

1985   *Carmagnole*. Mus Lib (M Thomas Bürkholz). Pr 1986 Lpzg.

KNAUTH, Joachim
5 Jan 1931 Halle –
1950–55 studied law and German literature, Univ Halle; 55–56 dramaturg Meißen, 56–62 DT, since then lives as independent author in Berlin. Writes radio, TV, and film scripts.

1954   *Heinrich VIII. oder Der Ketzerkönig (Henry the Eighth or The Heretic King)*. Com. Pr 1955 Schwerin. *TdZ* 1955/6 (scenes). Henschel 1960.

1956   *Der Tambour und sein Herr König (The Drummer and His Majesty the King)*. Dr. Pr 1957 Gera.

1958   *Wer die Wahl hat (A Difficult Choice)*. Com. Pr 1958 DT.

KNAUTH (cont'd)

1958   *Neuland unterm Pflug (Virgin Land under the Plow).* Dr (with T. I. London; based on novel by Mikhail Sholokhov). Pr 1958 Lpzg.

1959   *Der entfesselte Wotan (Wotan Unbound).* Com (based on Ernst Toller). Pr 1959.

1960   *Die sterblichen Götter (The Mortal Gods).* Com (based on radio play). Pr 1960. *TdZ* 1965/16.

1960   *Badenweiler Abgesang (The Badenweiler Final Chorus).* Com. *TdZ* 1965/16.

1961   *Die Kampagne (The Campaign).* Com. Pr 1963 Gera. *Stücke*, Henschel 1973.

1964   *Die Soldaten (The Soldiers).* Dr (based on J. M. R. Lenz). Pr 1970 Nordhausen.

1965   *Die Weibervolksversammlung (The Women's Assembly).* Com (based on Aristophanes). Pr 1972 Göttingen. *Stücke nach der Antike*, Henschel 1969. *Stücke*, 1973.

1965-66 *Aretino oder Ein Abend in Mantua (Aretino or An Evening in Mantua).* Dr. Pr 1966 Gera. *Stücke*, 1973.

1967   *Wie der König zum Mond wollte (How the King Wanted to Get to the Moon).* Juv (based on Persian fairy tale). Pr 1971 Mgdbg. *Vier Theatermärchen*, Henschel 1981.

1968   *Der Maulheld (The Braggart).* Com (based on Plautus, "Miles gloriosus"). Pr 1970 Göttingen. *Stücke*, 1973.

1969   *Der Prinz von Portugal (The Prince of Portugal).* Juv. Pr 1973 Halle. *TdZ* 1973/1. *Stücke*, 1973. *Vier Theatermärchen*, 1981.

1969-70 *Die Nachtigall (The Nightingale).* Juv (based on Hans Christian Andersen). Pr 1974 Vienna. *Stücke*, 1973. *Vier Theatermärchen*, 1981.

1971-73 *Bellebelle oder Der Ritter Fortune (Bellebelle or Fortune the Knight).* Juv (based on Marie Catherine d'Aulnoy). Pr 1974 Meiningen. *NdL* 1974/4. *Vier Theatermärchen*, 1981.

1975   *Lysistrata.* Com (based on Aristophanes). *Siebtens: Stiehl ein bißchen weniger (Seventh: Steal a Little Less).* Com (with Gerhard Neumann; based on Dario Fo).

KNIETZSCH, Karl Christian
12 Feb 1935 Dresden --
Worked as post office employee, waiter, film extra; after 1956 journalist, film critic, later assistant director for film and stage. Writes radio and TV plays, film scripts.

1970   *Der Sohn des Sheriffs (The Sheriff's Son).* Juv. Pr 1972 Rudolstadt.

1978   *Einer rechnet ab ‹Conchos Land› (Someone Settles the Accounts ‹Concho's Land›).* Juv Mus Lib (M Andreas Höhne). Pr 1979 Görlitz/Zittau.

KOCH, Ellen
1969   *Der liebe Gott hat Ausgang (The Good Lord's Day Off).* Dr. Pr 1970 Erfurt.

KOCH, Günter

1965   *Mordsache Brisson (The Brisson Murder Case)*. Dr. Pr 1965 KMSt.

1968   *Alibi vor Mitternacht (Alibi before Midnight)*. Dr. Pr 1968 Dsdn/Radebeul.

KOCH, Jurij

15 Sep 1936 Horka –

After high school, studied journalism Karl Marx Univ., Lpzg, then dramaturgy Th.HS, Lpzg. Writes prose and poetry (mostly in Sorbian language), translations, film scripts.

1968   *Unter sieben Brücken (Under Seven Bridges)*. Dr (based on novel). Pr 1970 Bautzen (in Sorbian).

1971   *Die letzte Prüfung (The Final Test)*. Juv. Pr 1972 Bautzen (in Sorbian); Gm Pr 1973 Bautzen.

1976   *Landvermesser (The Surveyor)*. Dr (based on story). Pr 1977 Halle. *TdZ* 1977/12.

1981   *Jagar Bagala*. Dr. Pr 1982 Bautzen (in Sorbian).

1982   *Das große Glück (The Great Fortune)*. Dr. Pr 1983 Bautzen (in Sorbian).

KOCHTA, Karla

1980   *Leonce und Lena*. Op Lib (based on Georg Büchner; M Thomas Hertel). Pr 1981 Greifswald.

KOEBEL-TUSK, Eberhard

1953   *Die Männer von Schilling-Reede (The Men from the Schilling Shipyard)*. Dr.

KOEPPEL, Jochen

28 Jan 1930 Delitzsch –

Actor and author; lives in Berlin. 1959 FDGB Prize.

1958   *Heiße Eisen (Hot Irons)*. Dr. Pr 1959 Greiz. Lpzg: Hofmeister, 1959. Henschel 1962.

1960   *Die Sache mit dem Fußball (The Thing about the Soccer Ball)*. Juv. Pr 1961 Th. d. Freundschaft, Berlin.

1961   *Die Behlings*.

1962   *Peter und der Kaktus (Peter and the Cactus)*. Juv. Pr 1962 Th. d. Freundschaft, Berlin.

KOERBL, Jürg-Michael   (until 1976 known as Jürg-Michael NEU-MANN)

15 July 1950 Stendal –

Transport worker and ship's stoker; then stage hand, actor, stage manager, director, Hans Otto Th., Potsdam. Writes radio plays.

1974   *Im Garten (In the Garden)*. Dr.

1975   *Ambrosio tötet die Zeit (Ambrosio Kills Time)*. Juv (based on Fauquez).

1975   *Heißer Stern (Hot Star)*. Dr. Pr 1976 Potsdam.

1975-77 *Alles oder etwas (Everything or Something)*. Dr. Pr 1981 Fkft/O.

1976   *Die Grenze (The Border)*. Dr.

1977-79 *Immanuel Kleist*. Dr.

KOERBL (cont'd)

1978   *Zirkus von hinten oder Die Russen kommen (Circus from the Back or The Russians Are Coming).* Dr. Pr 1982 Dsdn. *TdZ* 1980/9.

1978   *Familie (Family).* Dr.

1978   *Little Girl ‹Die Jungfrau von Orleans› (The Maid of Orleans).* Com.

1978   *Es wird, wie es bleibt (Things Will Be As They Remain).* Com.

1980   *Der Doppelmord in der Rue Morgue (The Double Murder in the Rue Morgue).* Dr (based on Edgar Allan Poe). *Kriminalstücke,* Henschel 1986.

1980   *Ein Auto zum Heiraten (A Car for Getting Married).* Com.

1981   *Walter, Hagen, Gunther und Hildegund.* Dr (based on the Nibelung legend).

1982   *La Mandragola.* Com (based on Niccolo Machiavelli). Pr 1982 Stendal.

KÖHLER, Erich
28 Dec 1928 Karlsbad (now Karlovy Vary, Czechoslovakia) –
After apprenticeships with baker and tailor, worked on farm in Mecklenburg; after WW Il traveled through FRG and Holland, returned GDR 1950; 58-61 I.Lit Lpzg.; now lives near Cottbus. 1964 FDGB Prize. Writes prose.

1970   *Die Lampe (The Lamp).* On. Pr 1970 DT.

1971   *Der Geist von Cranitz (The Spirit of Cranitz).* Dr. Pr 1972 VB. *TdZ* 1972/7.

1973   *Das Zauberpferdchen (The Magic Pony).* Juv. Pr 1975 Th. d. Freundschaft, Berlin. *Sinn & Form* 1973/4.

1974   *Vietnamesische Legende (Vietnamese Legend).* Juv. Pr 1975 Th. d. Freundschaft, Berlin.

1977   *Das kleine Gespenst (The Little Ghost).* Juv. Pr 1977 Th. d. Freundschaft, Berlin.

1982   *Der verwunschene Berg (The Bewitched Mountain).* Dr (based on film story, "Hartmut und Joana"). Reading 1983 Potsdam. *TdZ* 1983/3. Pr 1986 VB.

KOHLER, Siegfried
2 Mar 1927 Meißen –
1945-55 studied at MHS, Dsdn and Univ, Lpzg; 57-63 music librarian Humboldt Univ, Berlin; 63-68 artistic director, GDR record company; since 69 Prof. of Composition, Univ. Dsdn. Musicologist and composer.

1962   *Der Richter von Hohenburg (The Judge of Hohenburg).* Op. Pr 1963 Brandenburg.

KOHLHAASE, Wolfgang
31 Mar 1931 Berlin –
After 1947 journalist; 50-51 dramaturg DEFA. Member AdK, GDR PEN Center; 1954 and 68 National Prize, 73 Erich Weinert Medal. Writes prose, radio and TV plays, film scripts.

1968   *Fisch zu viert (Fish for Four).* Com (with Rita Zimmer; based on radio and TV play). Pr 1970 Th. d. jg. Generation, Dsdn.

KOHLHAASE (cont'd)
1970   *Ein Trompeter kommt   (A Bugler's Coming)*. Com (based on radio play). Pr 1972 Rostock. Radio version in *Hörspiele* 11, Henschel 1972.

KOLLHOFF, Helga
        Der Prinz und die Rose (The Prince and the Rose). Pp.
1980   *Marie und der Nußknacker   (Marie and the Nutcracker)*. Pp (based on E.T.A. Hoffmann). Pr 1980 Pp.Th., Berlin.
1982   *Die Stellung ist kampflos zu halten   (The Position Is to Be Held without a Fight)*. Pp (based on Russian tales). Pr 1983 Neubrandenburg.

KÖLLINGER, Bernd
1935 -
Historian; lives in Berlin.
        Bernardo Albas Haus   (Bernardo Alba's House). Bl Lib (M Hans-Dieter Hosalla).
        Schwarze Vögel (Black Birds). Bl Lib (with Tom Schilling; M Georg Katzer). Pr Km.Op.
        Wahlverwandtschaften   (Elective Affinities).   Bl Lib (with Tom Schilling; based on Goethe; M Franz Schubert).
1980   *Ein neuer Sommernachtstraum (A New Midsummer Night's Dream)*. Bl Lib (M Georg Katzer). Pr 1981 Km.Op.
1983   *Die magische Nacht (The Magic Night)*. Bl Lib (M Beethoven). Pr 1984 Km.Op.

KOLOC, Rudolf
1980   *Transportpaule   (Paul, the Teamster)*. Dr (with Paul Gratzik; based on novel by Gratzik). Pr 1981 Schwerin (scenes); full Pr 1984 Mgdbg.

KÖNIGSBERGER, Klaus
1982   *Der letzte Mohikaner (The Last of the Mohicans)*. Juv (with Klaus M. Pastowski; based on James Fenimore Cooper). Pr 1983 Eisenach.

KÖNIGSDORF, Helga
1939 -
Prof. of Mathematics in Berlin. Writes stories.
1984   *Pi.* On. Pr 1984 TiP (part of program under collective title of "Männermonologe").

KÖNNER, Alfred
2 Dec 1921 Altschalkendorf (now Siotkowice, Poland) -
After high school, service in WW II, British POW; 1945 worked as farmer, teamster, construction worker; 46-49 studied pedagogy Berlin, became language and literature teacher; after 59 editor; lives in Berlin. Writes children's books, criticism, translations.
1969   *Der Räuberhase   (The Robber Rabbit)*. Juv Op Lib (M Klaus Fehmel). Pr 1973 Th. d. Freundschaft, Berlin.
1975   *Weder Katz   noch Maus   (Neither Cat   Nor Mouse)*. Juv Mus Lib (M Klaus Fehmel). Pr 1976 Pp.Th., Berlin.

KÖNNER (cont'd)
1978   *Der Stiefelgeist (The Spirit of the Boots)*. Pp. Pr
        1978 Pp. Th., Berlin.
1984   *Pfefferchen (Little Pepper)*. Pp.

KORB, Irene
7 June 1923 Dsdn - 10 Dec 1978 Potsdam
Studied acting in Dsdn; after 1947 actress at various Berlin
theaters, also film and TV.
1966   *Das ‹Spiel vom› Mädchen Ming Ming (The ‹Play about
        the› Girl Ming Ming)*. Juv   (based on a Far-Eastern
        fairy tale). Pr 1966 Th. d. jg. Welt, Lpzg.
1975   *Die goldene Kuh (The Golden Cow)*. Juv (with Hans-
        Erich Korbschmitt). Pr 1976 Th. d. jg. Welt, Lpzg.
1976   *Tausend Dollar Lösegeld (A Thousand Dollars Ransom)*.
        Juv (with Hans-Erich Korbschmitt; based on story by
        Walter Kaufmann, "Kidnapping in Manhattan"). Pr 1977
        Th. d. jg. Welt, Lpzg.

KORB, Peter   see Rudolf Peter BROCK

KORBSCHMITT, Hans-Erich
1975   *Die goldene Kuh (The Golden Cow)*. Juv (with Irene
        Korb). Pr 1976 Th. d. jg. Welt, Lpzg.
1976   *Tausend Dollar Lösegeld (A Thousand Dollars Ransom)*.
        Juv (with Irene Korb; based on story by Walter Kauf-
        mann, "Kidnapping in Manhattan"). Pr 1977 Th. d. jg.
        Welt, Lpzg.

KORF, Rudolf ‹Rudi›
        *Eduard un de lütten Sünd'n (Edward and the Little
        Sins)*. Com (in Low German; with Anke Neumann).
1973   *Kein Hüsing (No Home)*. Dr (in Low German). Pr 1974
        Schwerin.
1976   *Unkel Jakob und Unkel Jochen (Uncle Jake and Uncle
        Joe)*. Com (in Low German; based on Fritz Reuter).
        Pr 1977 Schwerin.
        *Ut Großmudddings Honnigpott (Out of Grandma's Honey
        Jar)*. Com (in Low German). Pr Schwerin.
        *Nebenan wohnen andere Leute (There are Other People
        Living Next Door)*. Com (incidental M Klaus-Jürgen
        Schletterein). Pr Schwerin.

KORN, Ilse   (nee Ilse TRUÖL)
23 Apr 1907 Dresden - 15 June 1975 Kleinmachnow
1925-27 studied library science Lpzg; 33-44 in anti-fascist
underground; 44 arrested, together with husband Vilmos Korn;
45 librarian; 51-52 worked in Ministry of Education; after 52
independent author, contributor to children's periodicals. 19-
64 Fontane Prize (with Vilmos Korn). Wrote children's books,
radio, TV, and film scripts.
1962   *Mohr und die Raben von London (Mohr and the Ravens of
        London)*. Dr (with Vilmos Korn and Hans-Dieter Schmidt;
        based on novel and film).   Pr 1973 Th. d. jg. Welt,
        Lpzg.

KORN, Ilse (cont'd)

1968   *Meister Hans Röckle und Meister Flammfuß (Master Jack Jacket and Master Flamefoot).* Juv (with Vilmos Korn). Pr 1974. *NdL* 1973/3. Rev 1973 as Juv Op under title of Meister Röckle (Lib Günther Deicke; M Joachim Werzlau). Pr 1976 St.Op.

KORN, Nina

1973   *Der Freier als Jagdhund (The Suitor as a Hound Dog).* Juv. Pr 1977 Th. d. jg. Welt, Lpzg.

KORN, Vilmos (Pseud. KORVIL)

3 Apr 1899 Kikinda (now Yugoslavia) - 6 Nov 1970 Kleinmachnow
Volunteer in WW I, became officer in 1916; 18 member of Soldiers' Council, then union secretary; 23 arrested for striking, then unemployed; joined KPD 31; worked in anti-fascist underground; 44 arrested with wife Ilse Korn; 45-50 worked in Ministry of Education, 49-58 member of People's Chamber; lived in Berlin. 1964 Fontane Prize (with Ilse Korn).

1946   *Das Segel des Colon (Colon's Sail).* Dr.
1960   *Aber wenn der Schleier fällt (But When the Veil Falls).* Dr (based on TV play).
1962   *Mohr und die Raben von London (Mohr and the Ravens of London).* Dr (with Ilse Korn and Hans-Dieter Schmidt; based on novel and film). Pr 1973 Th. d. jg. Welt, Lpzg.
1963   *Münzers Tod (Münzer's Death).* Dr. Pr 1964.
1968   *Meister Hans Röckle und Meister Flammfuß (Master Jack Jacket and Master Flamefoot).* Juv (with Ilse Korn). Pr 1974. *NdL* 1973/3. Rev 1973 as Juv Op under title of Meister Röckle (Lib Günther Deicke; M Joachim Werzlau). Pr 1976 St.Op.

KÖRNER, Thomas

1976   *R. Hot bezw. Die Hitze (R. Hot or The Heat).* Op Lib (based on J. M. R. Lenz, "Der Engländer"; M Friedrich Goldmann). Pr 1977 St.Op.
1978   *Leonce und Lena.* Op Lib (based on Georg Büchner; M Paul Dessau). Pr 1979 St.Op.

KÖRNER-SCHRADER, Paul (real name Karl SCHRADER)

25 Apr 1900 Wedderstedt - 18 May 1962 Berlin
1918 served in WW I; 19 member Soldiers' Council, joined KPD; 21 arrested; worked illegally under name Paul Körner in various jobs; wrote for Communist newspapers, arrested repeatedly; 1939 service in WW II; after 45 independent author in Berlin. Wrote for amateur theater groups.

1949   *Erwischt (Caught).* Dr.
1950   *Die Angsthasen (The 'Fraidycats).* Dr. Berlin: Die Freie Gewerkschaft, 1950.
1950   *Da schaut der Ochs zum Fenster raus (The Ox Looks out of the Window).* Juv.
1951   *Der Spiegel (The Mirror).* Juv. Halle: Mitteldeutscher Verlag, 1951.

KORVIL   see Vilmos KORN

KOSK, Jan
1979   *Frühlingsgewitter (Spring Thunderstorm).* Dr. Pr 1980
        Bautzen (in Sorbian).

KRAMER, Heinz
1958   *Madame Cyprienne.* Mus Lib (based on Victorien Sar-
        dou). *Ja oder nein,* Berlin: Lied d. Zeit, 1959.
1961   *Ja, die Familie ‹O, diese Kinder› (Ah, the Family ‹Oh
        These Children›).* Mus Lib (M Jochen Allihn). Pr 19-
        62 Fkft/O.
        Fräulein Mama (Miss Mother). Mus Lib (M John See-
        berg).

KRAUSE, Hans
22 Mar 1924 Berlin –
After school, served in WW 1I until 1943; 2 years military
prison; 45 joined KPD; 48 acting school, 50 actor DT, after
51 cabaret actor; 58-63 director cabaret "Die Distel," Berlin;
editor of humor section, *Neues Deutschland*; lives in Berlin.
Writes poems, songs, cabaret sketches, stories, TV scripts.
1979   *Ich bin nicht meine Tante (I'm Not My Aunt).* Com. Pr
        1980 Wittenberg.

KRAUTZ, Bodo
        Netze an Bord (Nets on Board). Dr (with Johannes Wer-
        da). Pr 1953 Stralsund.
        Jan Suschka. Op Lib (M Dieter Nowka).

KRENGEL-STRUDTHOFF, Inge‹borg›   (also writes under name of
Inge‹borg› STRUDTHOFF)
8 Sep 1920 Berlin –
Dr. phil., dramaturg, translator; now lives in W. Berlin.
1945   *Zwei Hände (Two Hands).* Dr (based on Mary Hayley-
        Bell).
1946   *Unsere Großeltern nannten es Liebe (Our Grandparents
        Called It Love).* Com.
1947   *Das Haus am Strom (The House by the River).* Dr (based
        on E. P. and R. Denham).
1947   *Ein Inspektor kommt (An Inspector Calls).* Dr (tr from
        J. B. Priestley).
1948   *Der Gast (The Guest).* Dr. Pr 1949 Wernigerode.
1949   *Der Schicksalsacker (The Fateful Field).* Dr. Pr 1950
        Parchim.
1950   *Der taube Acker (The Barren Field).* Dr (rev of a-
        bove?).

KRUG, Hans-Hermann
1972   *Die Bremer Stadtmusikanten (The Town Musicians of Bre-
        men).* Juv Mus (based on Grimm; M Hans Auenmüller).
        Pr 1975 Altenburg.
1973   *Der gestiefelte Kater (Puss in Boots).* Juv Mus (M
        Hans Auenmüller). Pr 1974 Halberstadt.

KRUG (cont'd)

1976   *Tilla und der Burgvogt (Tilla and the Castle Steward).* Juv Mus (based on G. W. Pijet; M Hans Auenmüller). Pr 1976 Halberstadt.

1985   *Der kleine Muck (Little Muck).* Juv Mus (based on Wilhelm Hauff; M Hans Auenmüller). Pr 1986 Halbertstadt.

KRÜGER, Wolfgang

1963   *Der König des Böhmerwalds (The King of the Bohemian Forest).* Dr (based on novel by Rudolf Kalcik). Pr 1964 Rathen.

KRUPKAT, Günter

5 July 1905 Berlin –

After high school, studied engineering, then worked as technician; later became journalist, radio and film dramaturg; joined KPD 1932, worked in anti-fascist underground; drafted 40, deserted 45; after WW II, again journalist, then independent author in Berlin. Wrote stories, TV plays.

1960   *AR 2 ruft Ikarus (AR 2 Calling Icarus).* Dr. Pr 1960.

1961   *Der Fall Denziger (The Denziger Case).* Dr. Pr 1962.

1963   *Karibische Nacht (Caribbean Night).* Dr. Pr 1964 Th. d. jg. Welt, Lpzg.

1964   *Begegnung bei Nacht (Encounter at Night).* Dr. Pr 1964 Zwickau.

KUBA   (real name Kurt BARTHEL)

8 June 1914 Garnsdorf – 12 Nov 1967 Frankfurt am Main

1928-32 painter; 33 emigration to Prague, Vienna, Yugoslavia, USSR; 41 by way of Poland to England, where he was interned; 46 GDR, worked as editor; after 50 member People's Chamber, 54-67 Central Committee SED; after 56 lived in Warnemünde; 57-67 Chief Dramaturg, Rostock. National Prize 1949, 58, 59, and 64; 57 FDGB Prize, Erich Weinert Medal; 60 Dr. h.c. Rostock. Wrote poetry, prose, film scripts.

1959   *Meine junge alte Stadt (My Young Old City).* Opt Lib (based on W. Maas and M. Chervinsky). Pr 1960.

1959   ‹*Die Legende von› Klaus Störtebeker (‹The Legend of› Klaus Störtebeker).* Dr (incidental M Günter Kochau). Pr 1959 Rügen. Lpzg; Hofmeister, 1959.

1961   *Dantons Tod (Danton's Death).* Dr (based on Georg Büchner). Pr 1962 Rostock.

1962   *Nabucco.* Op Lib (new adaptation; M Verdi). Pr 1963 Rostock.

1963   *Terra incognita.* Dr. Pr 1964 Rostock. *TdZ* 1965/2. Rostock: Hinstorff, 1965. *Sozialistische Dramatik,* Henschel 1968.

1965   *Ein Hauch von Romantik (A Breath of Romance).* Mus Lib (based on W. Mankowitz, "Make Me an Offer"). Pr 1966 Rostock.

1966   *Ich sehn' den Tag herbei (I Long for the Day).* Mus Lib (based on B. Owen, "The Matchgirls"; M T. Russell). Pr 1967 Rostock.

1967   *Unbesiegbares Vietnam (Invincible Vietnam).* Dr (based on Uptal Dutt). Pr 1967 Rostock.

KUBERSKI, Angela
>*Die versäumte Verpflichtung (The Missed Obligation)*. On (based on radio play by Arne Leonhardt). *Neumann: 2 x klingeln*, Lpzg: Zentralhaus für Kulturarbeit, n.d.

KUBSCH, Hermann Werner
11 Feb 1911 Dresden - 15 July 1983 Dresden
Studied art Dsdn; 1930 joined KPD; became member of cabaret "Linkskurve"; 33 arrested and sent to concentration camp; 42 drafted; 45-49 director of Dsdn cabaret "Eulenspiegel"; 49-50 dramaturg DEFA. Wrote stories, film scripts, literary criticism.

1947	*Ende und Anfang (The End and the Beginning)*. Dr. Pr 1948 Dsdn.
1948	*Ferien auf dem Lande (Vacation in the Country)*. Juv.
1949	*Die ersten Schritte ‹Unser täglich Brot› (The First Steps ‹Our Daily Bread›)*. Dr. Pr 1949 Dessau.
1954	*Das Mädchen auf dem Traktor (The Girl on the Tractor)*. Choral work (M A. Ott).

KÜCHENMEISTER, Claus
7 Sep 1930 Berlin -
1949-50 studied Th. Institute, Weimar; 50-51 worked for DEFA; 51-55 studied under Brecht at BE, then became instructor at Film HS Babelsberg. 1965 Erich Weinert Medal, National Prize; together with wife Wera, Children's Literature Prize 58 and 59, FDGB Prize 71. Writes film scripts, radio plays, children's books.

1951	*Frau Holle (Mother Holle)*. Juv (with Wera Küchenmeister; based on Grimm). Pr 1952 Altenburg. Berlin: Kinderbuchverlag, 1954. Lpzg: Hofmeister, 1959. Henschel 1964.
1952	*Hans Pfriem oder Kühnheit zahlt sich aus (Hans Pfriem or Boldness Pays)*. Com (with Wera Küchenmeister; based on Martino Hayneccio). Pr 1953.
1952	*Waldfest der Tiere (The Animals' Forest Festival)*. Juv (with Wera Küchenmeister). Pr 1952 BE. Berlin: Kinderbuchverlag, 1954. Lpzg: Hofmeister, 1959.
1957	*Damals 18/19 (The Way It Was in 1918/19)*. Dr (with Wera Küchenmeister; based on radio play). Pr 1958 Th. d. Freundschaft, Berlin. *NdL* 1958/10.
1964	*Die Stunde Null (The Zero Hour)*. Dr. *NdL* 1964/5 (scenes).
1969	*Pinocchios Abenteuer (The Adventures of Pinocchio)*. Juv Op Lib (with Wera Küchenmeister; based on Carlo Collodi; M Kurt Schwaen). Pr 1970 Zwickau. *TdZ* 1971/1.
1980	*Der Streit um die Puppe (The Quarrel over the Doll)*. Juv (with Wera Küchenmeister; based on Victor Carvajal). Pr 1981 Th. d. Freundschaft, Berlin.
1983	*Der ABC Stern (The Alphabet Star)*. Juv Op Lib (with Wera Küchenmeister; based on children's book; M Kurt Schwaen). Pr 1984 Lpzg.

KÜCHENMEISTER, Claus (cont'd)
1985   *Craqueville oder Die unscbuldige Sünderin (Craque-
        ville or The Innocent Sinner).* Op Lib (with Wera Kü-
        chenmeister; M Kurt Schwaen). Pr 1986 Brandenburg.

KÜCHENMEISTER, Wera   (nee Wera Skupin)
18 Oct 1929 Berlin –
1949-50 studied Th. Institute Weimar; 50-54 studied under
Brecht at BE, then dramaturg DEFA and MG Th; later worked in
Ministry of Culture as secretary of Film Council. 1967 Critics' Prize, 1968 Erich Weinert Medal; together with husband
Claus, Children's Literature Prize 58 and 59, FDGB Prize 71.
Writes children's books. (All plays listed below written together with Claus Küchenmeister--see above).
1951   *Frau Holle.*
1952   *Hans Pfriem oder Kühnheit zahlt sich aus.*
1952   *Waldfest der Tiere.*
1957   *Damals 18/19.*
1969   *Pinnocchios Abenteuer.*
1980   *Der Streit um die Puppe.*
1983   *Der ABC Stern.*
1985   *Craqueville oder Die unschuldige Sünderin*

KUCKHOFF, Armin Gerd
13 Mar 1912 Munich –
Studied at Th. HS Aachen, then Pedagogical Institute Halle,
became teacher; after 1945 dramaturg DT and Th. am Schiffbauerdamm, Berlin; taught at Th. HS Weimar and Lpzg; Rector Lpzg
61-69.
        König Drosselbart (King Thrushbeard). Juv (with Ma-
        rie Otto; based on Grimm). Pr 1947 Th. am Schiffbau-
        erdamm, Berlin.

KUCKSHOLM, Heinz
        Anständige Menschen (Decent People). Dr. Pr 1948
        Burg.

KUFFERATH, Heinz   (Pseud. with Maurycy Janowski: Jan HALL)
22 Sep 1920 –
Lives in Berlin. 1971 Rostock Culture Prize; 71 GDR Medal of
Merit.
1957   *Alarm in Pont l'Eveque.* Mus Lib (with Maurycy Janow-
        ski; M Conny Odd. Pr 1958 Erfurt. Rev 1970 as Gang-
        ster lieben keine Blumen.
1959   *Der Instrukteur soll heiraten (The Instructor is Sup-
        posed to Get Married).* Com (with Maurycy Janowski).
        *Der Professor kommt um sechs ‹Knirps und das Zirkus-
        pferd› (The Professor Comes at Six ‹Tiny and the Cir-
        cus Horse›).* Juv Mus Lib (with Maurycy Janowski;
        based on M. Lvovsky, "Kristall KS"; M Siegfried Matt-
        hus).
1970   *Gangster lieben keine Blumen (Gangsters Don't Like
        Flowers).* Mus Lib (rev of Alarm in Pont l'Eveque;
        with Maurycy Janowski; M Conny Odd). Pr 1970 Rostock.

KUHN, Fritz
3 Jan 1918 Dresden –
After high school, served in World War II; since 1945 worked
as optician; lives in Dresden.

1956   *Der künstliche Mond geht auf (The Artificial Moon Is
Rising).* Com. Pr 1957 Fkft/O.

1956   *Leicht bewölkt, vorwiegend heiter (Partly Cloudy, Pre-
dominantly Fair).* Com. Pr 1956 Halberstadt.

1957   *Venezianisches Glas (Venetian Glass).* Dr. Pr 1957
Rostock.

1959   *Kredit bei Nibelungen (Credit with the Nibelungs).*
Com. Pr 1960 KMSt. Henschel 1968.

1960   *David und Batsheba.* Dr. Pr 1960.

1970   *Interview der verlorenen Söhne (Interview of the Prodigal Sons).* Dr. Pr 1971.

1972   *Wiederkehr eines Briefträgers (A Mailman's Return).*
Com. Pr 1973.
   Die Gnadenlosen (Those without Mercy). Dr.

KÜHNE, Hans J.
3 Feb 1928 Halberstadt –
1944 anti-aircraft helper; 45-47 finished school; 48 became
teacher; since 52 school principal in Heym. Writes short stories.

1958   *Aufregung um Teigmenger (Excitement about Dough Mix-
ers).* Dr. Pr 1958 Rostock.

1960   *Die Tannenkippe (The Fir See-Saw).* Dr. Pr 1960 An-
klam planned, then cancelled.
   Die Prämie (The Premium).
   Sitzenbleiben (Failing the Grade).

KUHNERT, Reinhard Frieder
29 Jan 1954 Berlin –
Actor, stage director; lives in Berlin.

1973   *Senora Sempre widerfährt Gerechtigkeit (Senora Sempre
Receives Justice).* Dr. Pr 1973 Mgdbg.

1976   *Jäckels Traum (Fool's Dream).* Com. Pr 1981 Brandenburg. TdZ 1981/7.

1977   *Eine schöne und lustige neue Aktion vom ernsthaften
Narren Hans Clauert (A Beautiful and Funny New Adventure of the Serious Fool Hans Clauert).* Com.

1978   *Die Zensurenschlacht (The Censorship Battle).* Com.
Pr 1979 Mgdbg.

1979   *Der Umweg (The Detour).* On. Pr 1980 Schwerin.

1979   *Im Trocknen (Safe).* On. Pr 1980 Schwerin.

1979   *Der Nächste (Next).* On.

1979   *Die Baumaschine (The Construction Machine).* On.

1979   *Wie man sich bettet (You've Made Your Bed).* On.

1980   *Der Heldentod (The Hero's Death).* Com. Reading 1982
Lpzg.

1982   *Vollpension (Full Room and Board).* Com. Pr 1982 Brandenburg.

1983   *Die Lösung (The Solution).* Com. Pr 1984 Schwedt.

KUNAD, Rainer
24 Oct 1936 Chemnitz (now Karl Marx Stadt) -
Studied Conservatory Dsdn 1955-56, MHS Lpzg 56-59; then became instructor at Conservatory Zwickau; 60-74 music director
Dsdn Th; since 74 Dsdn Op. and Prof. MHS Dsdn. Composer and
librettist.

1959   *Bill Brook*. Dr with M (based on story by Wolfgang Bor-
chert). Pr 1964 Dsdn/Radebeul.

1963   *Old Fritz*. Op (based on Rolf Schneider, "Der Mann aus
England"). Pr 1965 Dsdn/Radebeul.

1968   *Maitre Pathelin oder Die Hammelkomödie (Master Pathelin or The Mutton Comedy)*. Op (with Horst-Ulrich Wendler; based on his play, "Wer zuletzt lacht..."). Pr
1969 Dsdn. Lpzg: Peters, 1968.

1970   ünchhausen. Com with Bl (with Rainer Kirsch). Pr
1971 Weimar.

1971   *Bilder der Liebe ‹Wir aber nennen Liebe lebendigen
Frieden› (Images of Love ‹But We Call Love Living
Peace›)*. Bl Cantata (with Georg Maurer). Pr 1972
Dsdn.

1974   *‹Die Versuchung des› Sabellicus (‹The Temptation of›
Sabellicus)*. Op. Pr 1974 Dsdn.

1975   *Schweyk*. Op (based on novel by Hasek).

1977   *Vincent*. Op (based on Alfred Matusche, "Van Gogh").
Pr 1979 Dsdn.

1982   *Amphytrion*. Op (with Ingo Zimmermann). Pr 1984 St.
Op.

KUNERT, Günter
6 Mar 1929 Berlin -
1945-47 studied applied art in Berlin; 47 began writing for
humor periodical "Eulenspiegel"; 49 joined SED; 72 guest professor, Univ of Texas, Austin; 74-75 guest lecturer, Univ of
Warwick, England; 77 expelled from SED; since 79 lives in
Itzehoe, FRG. 1962 Heinrich Mann Prize, 73 Johannes Becher
Medal. Writes poetry, prose, radio and film scripts.

1958   *Vom König Midas (King Midas)*. Juv Cantata (M Kurt
Schwaen).

1961   *Die Weltreise im Zimmer (A Trip around the World in
One's Room)*. Juv Op Lib (M Kurt Schwaen). Pr 1962.

1980   *Futuronauten (Futuronauts)*. Dr. Pr 1981 Hannover.

KUNKEL, Erhard
1962   *Das tapfere Schneiderlein (The Brave Little Tailor)*.
Juv (based on Grimm). Pr 1963 Schwerin.

1963   *Das Märchen vom Bären Mischa (The Tale of Misha, the
Bear)*. Juv (with Heinrich Schmidt). Pr 1963 Schwerin.

1967   *Die Regentrude (Rain Trudy)*. Juv (based on story by
Theodor Storm). Pr 1967 Schwerin.

1971   *Die Schatzinsel (Treasure Island)*. Juv (based on Robert Louis Stevenson). Pr 1972 Neustrelitz.

1978   *Die Abenteuer der drei Musketiere (The Adventures of
the Three Musketeers)*. Dr (based on Alexander Dumas).
Pr 1979 Neustrelitz.

KUNKEL (cont'd)

1980   *Reise um die Erde in 80 Tagen (Around the World in 80 Days)*. Juv (based on Jules Verne). Pr 1980 Neustrelitz.

1985   *Die Abenteuer des braven Soldaten Schwejk (The Adventures of the Good Soldier Schweyk)*. Com (based on novel by Hasek). Pr 1986 Neustrelitz.

KUNZELMANN, Gerhard Heinz

No longer lives in GDR.

   Der Bauerngeneral (The Peasant General). Dr. Pr 1952 Greiz.

   Spione des Kaisers (The Emperor's Spies). Dr. Pr 1952 Greiz.

KUPSCH, Joachim

18 Oct 1926 Leipzig --

Soldier in WW II, then POW; after 1945 bricklayer, worked for radio and theater in Lpzg; 55-57 I. Lit Lpzg; 57-62 studied German literature Univ. Lpzg. Writes novels, stories, film scripts.

1953   *König für einen Tag (King for a Day)*. Com. Pr 1953 Zwickau.

KURZBACH, Herbert

1950   *Rebell Stülpner (Stülpner, the Rebel)*. Dr. Pr 1950 Th. d. jg. Generation, Dsdn.

KURZBACH, Paul

13 Dec 1902 Hohndorf - ?

1925-28 studied Lpzg Conservatory, then became music teacher; 39-45 military service and POW; after 45 taught at MHS KMSt. 1968-72 Vice-President of GDR Composers' Association; independent composer in KMSt.

1947   *Susanna*. Op. Pr 1948 Mgdbg.

1955   *Thomas Müntzer*. Op. Pr 1955 Mgdbg.

1957   *Tyl Claas ‹Tyl Klaas›*. Op (based on folk tale of Till Eulenspiegel). Pr 1958 Görlitz.

KYPKE, Peter Günter

1963   *Die Rheumakur (The Rheumatism Treatment)*. Com. Pr 1964 Schwerin.

1973   *Faule Eier (Rotten Eggs)*. Com. Pr 1973 Schwerin.

LAMBRECHT, Christine
1949 -
Cosmetician; lives in Dessau. Writes prose.
1984   *Männerbekanntschaften*   *(Male Acquaintances)*.   Dr. Pr
         1985 Halle.

LANE, Dorothy   see Elisabeth HAUPTMANN

LANG, Alexander
24 Sep 1941 Erfurt -
1964-66 attended School of Drama, Berlin; 66-69 actor, first
MG, then BE; since 69 actor and stage director, DT; 85-86
guest director St.Op. 1985 National Prize.
1968   *Die Zwerge (The Dwarfs)*. Com. Pr 1968 BE.
1974   *Die Stühle (The Chairs)*. Com. Pr 1974 VB (Part of
         program under collective title "Spektakel 2").
1976   *Das Biest des Monsieur Racine oder Das Wunder der
         Phantasie (Monsieur Racine's Beast or The Miracle of
         Imagination)*. Com (based on children's book by Tomi
         Ungerer). Pr 1977 DT.
1981   *Die traurige Geschichte von Friedrich dem Großen (The
         Sad History of Frederick the Great)*. Dr (based on
         fragment by Heinrich Mann). Pr 1982 DT. *Sinn & Form*
         1958/2-3 (original fragment). *Abenteuer Theater*, Hen-
         schel 1983.

LANG, Ottomar
1926 Schleusingen -
Attended high school Meiningen; 1944-46 Army service, POW; 47
teacher, then studied dramaturgy; 49-50 dramaturg Meiningen,
since 60 dramaturg for GDR TV.
         Der Damm (The Dam). Bl Lib.
1954   *Robert und Bertram*. Com (with Gerd Hecker; based on
         Gustav Raeder and Alfred Strässer).
1962   *Die Wahnmörderin ‹Mordsache Mergel› (The Insane Mur-
         deress ‹The Mergel Murder Case›)*. Dr (with Gerhard
         Jäckel; based on TV play). Pr 1962 Halle. *TdZ* 1963/
         20.
1970   *Rächer, Retter und Rapiere (Revengers, Rescuers, and
         Rapiers)*. Dr. Pr 1971 Quedlinburg.
1975   *Spartacus*. Dr. Pr 1976 Quedlinburg.

LANGE, Friedrich
6 Aug 1898 Flöha - 19 Jan 1976 Leipzig
Worked as a mechanic; 1917-19 served in WW I; 22-24 traveling
salesman, then journalist; 39-45 served in WW II, then journalist again; 47-51 worked for Radio Lpzg and Dsdn. Wrote
prose.
1949   *Der Triebriemen (The Drive-Belt)*. Dr. Pr 1950.
1950   *Projekt Goliath ‹Krach um Goliath› (Project Goliath
         ‹Argument about Goliath›)*. Juv. Pr 1951 Kamenz.
1953   *Meine Florentinerin (My Florentine Woman)*. Com. Pr
         1953 Plauen.

LANGE, Friedrich (cont'd)
1960   *Das Ehekollektiv (The Marriage Collective)*. Com. Pr
         1961.
1961   *Wenn das Eis bricht (When the Ice Breaks)*. Dr. Pr
         1961.

LANGE, Hanns ‹Johannes›
6 Oct 1891 Dresden - ?
Studied voice; 1912 tenor Dsdn Opera; after 27 voice teacher,
then director of Opera School, Dsdn; from 50 until retirement
Managing Director, State Opera of Saxony, Dsdn/Radebeul.
1970   *Die Schwitzkur (The Steam Treatment)*. Juv.
         Puppenhokuspokus (Puppet Magic). Pp (M Robert Linke).
1981   *Puppenzirkus (Puppet Circus)*. Pp (M Robert Linke).
         Pr 1982 KMSt.
1982   *Märchen aus der Truhe (Fairy Tale out of the Trunk)*.
         Pp (M Robert Linke). Pr 1983 KMSt.

LANGE, Hartmut
31 Mar 1937 Berlin –
1941-45 lived with family in occupied Poland; 46 returned to
Berlin; 55 left school, worked as occasional laborer; 57 began studies at Film HS Potsdam, expelled 60; 60-65 dramaturg
DT; then via Yugoslavia to West Berlin; dramaturg and stage
director various West Berlin theaters.
         Der Tartüff. Com (with Benno Besson; tr from Moli-
         ere). Pr DT 1963.
1960   *Senftenberger Erzählungen oder Die Enteignung (Senf-
         tenberg Tales or The Expropriation)*. Dr. Dt. Th. d.
         Gegenwart 2*, Suhrkamp 1967. *Theaterstücke 1960-1972*,
         Reinbek: Rowohlt, 1972.
1962-63 ‹*Leben und Tod des Herrn*› *Marski (‹Life and Death of
         Mr.› Marski)*. Com. Pr 1964 DT planned, cancelled;
         Pr 1966 Fkft/M. *TdZ* 1965/12. *Th.h.* 1966/9. Suhrkamp
         1965. *Theaterstücke*, 1972.
1964-67 *Der Hundsprozeß--Zwischenspiel--‹Stalin als› Herakles
         (The Dog Trial--Interlude--‹Stalin as› Hercules)*. Dr.
         Pr 1968 Schaubühne, West Berlin. Suhrkamp 1968. *The-
         aterstücke*, 1972.
1967   *König Johann (King John)*. Dr (based on Shakespeare).
         Pr 1969 Fkft/M. *Theaterstücke*, 1972.
1968   *Die Gräfin von Rathenow (The Countess of Rathenow)*.
         Com (based on Kleist novella, "Die Marquise von O.").
         Pr 1969 Cologne. *Th.h.* 1969/9. Suhrkamp 1969. *The-
         aterstücke*, 1972. Reinbek: Rowohlt, 1973.
1969-71 *Die Ermordung des Aias oder Ein Diskurs über das Holz-
         hacken (The Murder of Aias or A Discourse about Chop-
         ping Wood)*. Dr. Pr 1974 Schillerth., W. Berlin. Ber-
         lin (W): Wagenbach, 1971. *Theaterstücke*, 1972. Rein-
         bek: Rowohlt, 1973.
1971   *Trotzki in Coyoacan*. Dr. Pr 1972 Hamburg. *Th.h.* 19-
         72/3. Fkft/M: Verlag der Autoren, 1971. *Theaterstücke*,
         1972.

LANGE, Hartmut (cont'd)

1972　*Staschek oder Das Leben des Ovid (Stashek or The Life of Ovid).* Dr. Pr 1973 Stuttgart. *Theaterstücke*, 1972.

1973　*Jeppe vom Berge (Jeppe from the Mountain).* Com (based on Ludvig Holberg). Pr 1975 Stuttgart.

1974　*Jenseits von Gut und Böse oder Die letzten Stunden der Reichskanzlei (Beyond Good and Evil or The Last Hours of Hitler's Chancellery).* Dr. Pr 1975 Bremerhaven.

1975　*Vom Werden der Vernunft oder Auf der Durchreise nach Petersburg (The Coming of Reason or On the Way to Petersburg).* Dr. Pr 1976 W. Berlin.

1976　*Frau von Kauenhofen.* Dr. Pr 1977 W. Berlin.

1978　*Pfarrer Koldehoff (Parson Koldehoff).* Dr. Pr 1979 West Berlin.

　　　Der Drache (The Dragon). Juv (based on Yevgenyi Schwarz).

　　　Der Alchimist. Dr (based on Ben Jonson).

LANGE, Johannes　see Hanns LANGE

LANGE, Katrin
27 Nov 1942 Berlin –
Studied theater history Lpzg, Dr. phil. 1965; dramaturg KMSt 65, MG 71, various other theaters; now lives in Berlin. 1972 Radio Play Award. Writes radio scripts.

1978　*Frau Fischer Ilsebill ‹Die Sterne vom Himmel runter› (Ilsebill, the Fisherman's Wife ‹Wanting the Stars from the Sky›).* Juv. Pr 1979 Rostock. *TdZ* 1979/9.

1979　*Die Lerche, Tagverkünderin (The Lark, Harbinger of the Day).* Dr.

1983　*‹Die› Havarie (‹The› Explosion).* Dr (based on radio play). Pr 1985 Weimar. *TdZ* 1984/11.

1984　*Willi und die anderen (Willy and the Others).* Dr. Pr 1986 Rostock.

LANGE, Rainer R.
1917 – ?
Served in WW II; 1946-48 lived in Hamburg, then moved to GDR (Mecklenburg); actor, stage director, dramaturg at various theaters, mainly Th. d. Freundschaft, Berlin.

1963　*Tatort Lehrerzimmer (Scene of Crime: Teachers' Room).* Juv (with Manfred Streubel; based on 1960 novel by W. K. Schweickert). Pr 1964 Th. d. Freundschaft, Berlin. *TdZ* 1964/8.

LANZENDORF, Fred
1955　*Die wilden Schwäne (The Wild Swans).* Juv (based on Hans Christian Andersen). Pr 1955 Plauen. Lpzg: Hofmeister, 1955.

LANZER, Robert　see Rudolf LEONHARD

LASK, Berta   (Pseud: Gerhard WIELAND;   married name Berta JACOBSOHN-LASK)
17 Nov 1878 Wadowice (Poland) - 28 Mar 1967 Berlin
1901 married physician, became active in women's movement; 23 joined KPD; 25 traveled to Soviet Union; 33 arrested, then e-migrated to USSR; after return became author in Berlin. Wrote prose and poetry.

1910   *Die Päpstin (The Female Pope)*. Dr. Pr 1911.
1911   *Auf dem Hinterhof, vier Treppen links (In the Rear Courtyard, Fourth Floor Left)*. Dr. Pr 1912. Rev 19-32 as *Auf dem zweiten Hof, fünf Treppen*.
1914   *In Jehudas Stadt (In Yehuda's City)*. Dr. Pr 1914.
1920   *Senta*. Dr. Pr 1921.
1922   *Die Toten rufen (The Dead Are Calling)*. Choral work. Pr 1923.
1923   *Der Weg in die Zukunft (The Road to the Future)*. Choral work. Pr 1923. Lpzg: Wallmann, 1923.
1923   *Mitternacht (Midnight)*. Dr.
1925   *Die Befreiung (The Liberation)*. Dr. Pr 1925 Berlin.
1925   *Thomas Müntzer*. Dr. Pr 1925 Eisleben. Berlin: Ver-einigung int'l.Verlagsanstalten, 1925. *1525: Dramen zum dt. Bauernkrieg*, Aufbau 1975.
1926   *Weihe der Jugend (Consecration of Youth)*. Choral work. Berlin: Verlag für Arbeiterdichtung, 1927. Lpzg: Fi-scher, 1927. Rev 1956.
1927   *Leuna 1921*. Dr. Berlin: Int'l. Arbeiterverlag, 1927. Rev 1961 as Leuna.
1927   *Giftgasnebel über Sowjetrußland (Poison Gas Cloud o-ver Soviet Russia)*. Dr. Pr 1927 Kassel.
1932   *Auf dem zweiten Hof, fünf Treppen (In the Second Courtyard, Fifth Floor)*. Dr (rev of Auf dem Hinter-hof, vier Treppen links).
1936   *Johann der Knecht (John the Hired Man)*. On. Pr 1936 Moscow.
1938   *Vor dem Gewitter (Before the Thunderstorm)*. Dr. Pr 1938 Moscow.
1956   *Weihe der Jugend (Consecration of Youth)*. Choral work (rev).
1961   *Leuna*. Dr (rev of Leuna 1921). Pr 1963 Halle. Ber-lin: Dietz, 1961.

LATCHINIAN, Sewan
1964 -
Actor, Schwerin Th.
        Grabbes Grab (Grabbe's Grave). Dr (based on novel by Thomas Valentin, "Grabbes letzter Sommer"). *Tempera-mente* 1985/2.

LATZSCH, Monika
29 Dec 1930 -
Reporter and editor; now lives in Rostock. 1984 Kuba Medal. Writes short prose.
        Der Vorhof (The Front Courtyard). Com.
1981   *Ein Häuschen mit Butler (A Cottage with Butler)*. Com. Pr 1981 Rostock. *TdZ* 1981/1.

LÄTZSCH (cont'd)
1982   *Der Mann des Jahres   (The Man of the Year)*. Com. Pr
        1985 Rostock.

LEBINSKY, Horst
Actor Senftenberg, DT; now stage director, Fkft/O.
        Das tapfere Schneiderlein   (The Brave Little Tailor).
        Juv (based on Grimm). Pr 1966 Senftenberg.
1978   *Schwejk*. Dr (based on novel by Jaroslav Hasek, "The
        Adventures of the Good Soldier Schweik"). Pr 1980
        Fkft/O.

LEBRECHT, Georg and Hans
Joint pseudonyms for two stage directors at VB.
1973   *Villa Matuschek oder Die quälenden Wände (The Matu-
        schek Villa or The Tormenting Walls)*. On. Pr 1974
        VB (Part of program under collective title "Spektakel
        2").
1974   *Der Einbruch oder Die Tragödie vom Tod der liebeskran-
        ken Melisande (The Burglary or The Tragic Death of
        the Lovesick Melisande)*. On. Pr 1974 VB (Part of pro-
        gram under collective title "Spektakel 2").

LEIDNER, Susanne
1961   *Der Hase und der Igel ‹Der Wettlauf zwischen dem Ha-
        sen und dem Igel› (‹The Race between› The Hare and
        the Hedgehog)*. Juv. Pr 1962 Greiz.

LEONHARD, Rudolf   (Pseud. Robert LANZER)
27 Oct 1889 Lissa (now Leszno, Poland) - 19 Dec 1953 Berlin
Studied philosophy and law Univ. Jena, Berlin, and Göttingen;
1914 volunteered for military service; later court-martialed
as pacifist; 18-19 participated in revolution; worked as author and editor in Berlin; wrote for journal "Weltbühne"; 27
went to France, where he was interned 39; escaped, member of
underground; 44 in Paris again; 50 returned to Berlin. Wrote
poetry, prose, radio and film scripts.
1919   *Die Vorhölle (Purgatory)*. Dr. Pr 1919 Tribüne, Berlin.
1925   *Segel am Horizont (Sails on the Horizon)*. Dr. Pr 19-
        25 VB. Berlin: Die Schmiede, 1925.
1927   *Tragödie von heute (Today's Tragedy)*. Dr. Berlin:
        Die Schmiede, 1927.
1936   *Führer & Co.* Com. Paris: Editions du Phenix, 1936.
1941-45 *Geiseln (The Hostages)*. Dr (originally written in
        French). Pr 1946 Hebbelth., W. Berlin. Baden-Baden:
        Pallas, 1947. Reclam, 1952, 1960.
1947   *Anonyme Briefe (Anonymous Letters)*. Com.

LEONHARDT, Arne
20 Apr 1931 Chemnitz (now Karl Marx Stadt) - 1985 Karl Marx
Stadt
After school, worked as drill operator until 1950; 51-53 studied pedagogy; 53-58 teacher, also journalist; 58-61 I. Lit
Lpzg, then independent author in KMSt. 1967 Erich Weinert Medal, 71 FDGB Prize. Wrote prose, radio plays.

LEONHARDT (cont'd)
1967   *Der Abiturmann (The Graduate).* On (based on radio
        play). Pr 1969 KMSt. *TdZ* 1969/5. *Neue Stücke,* Hen-
        schel 1971.
1968   *'s ist Feierabend (Quitting Time).* Dr (based on ra-
        dio play). Pr 1970 Potsdam.

LEWIN, Waldtraut
8 Jan 1937 Wernigerode –
Studied German literature, Latin, theater history; dramaturg
and stage director, Halle and Rostock; now lives in Berlin.
Lion Feuchtwanger Prize, 1982 Radio Play Prize. Writes bio-
graphies, translations, adaptations of Händel operas, novels,
stories, radio plays.
1978   *Rosa Laub (Pink Leaves).* Rock Op Lib (M Horst Krü-
        ger). Pr 1979 Rostock.
1982   *Zaubersprüche (Magic Incantations).* Rock Op Lib (M
        Horst Krüger). Pr 1983 Rostock. *TdZ* 1982/7.

LIEBENBERG, Günter
1967   *Elf unter einem Dach (Eleven under One Roof).* Com
        (with Ruth Liebenberg). Pr 1967 Schwerin.
1968   *Vör de Dör een Auto (A Car in Front of the Door).* Com
        (in Low German). Pr 1969 Schwerin. Rev 1974 as Vor
        der Tür ein Auto.
1969   *Rook in Düwels Kök (Smoke in the Devil's Kitchen).*
        Com (in Low German; with Ruth Liebenberg). Pr 1970
        Schwerin.
1972   *Schreie im Kamin (Screams in the Fireplace).* Com.
        Pr 1973 Rudolstadt.
1974   *Vor der Tür ein Auto (A Car in Front of the Door).*
        Mus Lib (High German rev of Vör de Dör een Auto; M
        Klaus Hofmann). Pr 1974 Wittenberg.
1977   *Sommer, See und schwarze Betten (Summer, Sea, and
        Black Beds).* Mus Lib (M Klaus Hofmann). Pr 1978 Wit-
        tenberg.
1980   *Lassen wir uns ein bißchen scheiden (Let's Get Di-
        vorced a Little).* Mus Lib (M Klaus Hofmann). Pr 19-
        81 Wittenberg).
1983   *Ach du liebe Liebe (Isn't Love Lovely?).* Mus Lib (M
        Klaus Hofmann). Pr 1984 Wittenberg.

LIEBIG, Dieter
1951 Daubitz –
After school, studied theology in Lpzg and Naumburg 1970-76;
since 80 parson in Deutsch-Ossig. Writes for amateur church
theater groups.
        Das Lächeln der Freiheit (The Smile of Freedom). Dr
        (based on a novella by Vsevolod Ivanonov).
        König von Preußen (King of Prussia). Dr (based on a
        novel by Jochen Klepper).
        Grünes Requiem (Green Requiem). Dr.
        Nonnenmacher (The Nun-Maker). Dr. *TdZ* 1983/12.

LILJEBERG, Jörg
Actor at various theaters; also stage director Greifswald and
Dsdn; now managing director, Bautzen Th.
1966   *Die Schneekönigin (The Snow Queen)*. Juv (based on
        Hans Christian Andersen). Pr 1966 Th. d. jg. Garde,
        Halle.
1968   *Thyl Ulenspiegel, Geist von Flandern (Till Eulenspie-
        gel, Spirit of Flanders)*. Juv. Pr 1969 Th. d. jg.
        Garde, Halle.

LINDNER, Otto
8 Dec 1893 Falkenstein - 4 August 1983 Dresden
Wrote poetry, novels, short stories.
1937   *Rokkok soll sterben (Rokkok Must Die)*. Juv. Dsdn:
        Burdach, 1937.
1938   *Heimkehr aus Luzon (Return from Luzon)*. On.
1939   *Die Jungen von Nyk (The Boys from Nyk)*. Juv.
1942   *Der Sternenbaum (The Star Tree)*. Juv.
1943   *Prinzessin Tausendschön (Princess Thousandfold Fair)*.
        Juv (based on Grimm, "Snow White").
1948   *Die Nürnberger Nachtigall (The Nightingale of Nurem-
        berg)*. Com.
1949   *Der Schützenkönig (The Champion Marksman)*. Dr. Pr
        1950 Plauen.
1952   *Der Herr aus England (The Man from England)*. On.
1953   *Komplicen (Accomplices)*. On.
1956   *Trütschler*. Dr.

LINDOW, Rainer
23 Apr 1942 Berlin -
Stage director; lives in Potsdam. Writes novels, radio plays,
film scripts.
1983   *Rumpelstilz (Rumpelstiltskin)*. Juv (based on Grimm).
        Pr 1983 Potsdam.

LINK, Joachim-Dietrich   (Pseud. Benno LIPINSKI)
18 Oct 1925 Magdeburg -
Attended MHS Lpzg; 1948-50 rehearsal pianist, Lpzg; 50-57 orchestra conductor Lpzg, Weimar; 57-69 music director Greitz
and Gera; 69-75 orchestra conductor Km.Op; since 75 teacher
of opera at MHS Berlin. Composer and librettist.
1951   *Wer seine Frau lieb hat (If You Love Your Wife)*. Mus
        (with Josef Stauder). Pr 1952 Lpzg. Henschel 1956.
1952   *Ehe eine Ehe eine Ehe wird (Before a Marriage Becomes
        A Marriage)*. Mus (written under pseud. Benno Lipins-
        ki; with Wolfgang Böttcher and Ilse Nürnberg). Pr
        1953 Lpzg.
1953   *Mann und Frau im Essigkrug (Man and Wife in the Vine-
        gar Jug)*. Juv Op (with Hertha Greef; based on fairy
        tale by Ludwig Bechstein). Pr 1956 Th. d. Freund-
        schaft, Berlin.
        Das Krautlein Wahrheit (The Truth Herb). Juv Op.
1958   *Karaseck*. Op.

LINK (cont'd)

1960   *Der Diener zweier Herrn (The Servant of Two Masters).* Mus (with Wolfgang Böttcher and Fritz Wendel; based on Carlo Goldoni).

1967   *Juana.* Op. Pr 1968 Gera.

1969-70 *Von einem, der auszog, das Gruseln zu lernen (The Lad Who Set Out to Learn Fright).* Juv Op (with Ilse and Wolfgang Böttcher; based on Grimm). Pr 1970 Gera.

1971   *Frau Mohr hat ihre Schuldigkeit getan (Mrs. Mohr Has Done Her Duty).* Mus (written under pseud. Benno Lipinski; with Ilse and Wolfgang Böttcher). Pr 1972 Schwerin.

1974   *Die Prinzessin auf der Erbse (The Princess and the Pea).* Juv Op (with Friedrich Schmidt-Behrens; based on Hans Christian Andersen). Pr 1974 Gera.

1977   *Die Schatzinsel (Treasure Island).* Juv Op (with Wolfgang Böttcher; based on Robert Louis Stevenson). Pr 1978 Gera.

1979   *Pluft, das Geisterlein (Pluft, the Little Spirit).* Juv Op (with Heidemarie Stahl; based on Clara Machado). Pr 1980 Weimar.

LINTZEL, Martin
28 Feb 1901 Magdeburg - 15 July 1955 Halle
Dr. phil.; Professor of history Kiel, later Halle.

1949   *Der göttliche Orpheus (Divine Orpheus).* Com. Pr 19-50 Wismar and Schwerin.

LINZ, Rudi
1982   *Des Kaisers neue Schneider (The Emperor's New Tailors).* Juv Mus Lib (based on Hans Christian Andersen, "The Emperor's New Clothes"; M Henry Kaufmann). Pr 1983 Bernburg.

LIPINSKI, Benno   see Joachim-Dietrich LINK

LOBESAM, Hannchen   see Hedda ZINNER

LOMMER, Horst
19 Nov 1904 Berlin - 17 Oct 1969 Lübeck
Actor; 1929-45 Staatstheater Berlin, then lived in Berlin as independent author; 51 left GDR, lived in Fkft/M and Lübeck. Wrote TV plays.

1937   *Kleine Welt am Narrenseil (Small World Led by the Nose).* Com.

1940   *Das unterschlug Homer (Things Homer Kept from Us).* Com.

1942   *Eine Nacht mit Marie Isabell (A Night with Marie Isabel).* Com.

1945   *Die Arche Noah (Noah's Ark).* Com. Pr 1950 DT.

1946   *Höllenparade (Infernal Parade).* Revue.

1947   *Der General.* Dr. Pr 1947 Zeitz.

1948   *Thersites und Helena.* Dr. Pr 1949 Lpzg.

LORBEER, Inge
After WW II, studied acting Weimar and Erfurt; engaged at various theaters as actress and deputy managing director; 1963-68 studied theater history in Lpzg.
1971   *Alarm im Rosenhaus (Alarm in the Greenhouse)*. Juv. Pr 1972 Annaberg.

LORENZ, Hartmut
1976   *Die Teufelsmühle (The Devil's Mill)*. Pp (based on Jan Drda, "Spiel mit dem Teufel"). Pr 1977 Naumburg.
    Das Schneiderlein (The Little Tailor). Pp (based on Grimm).
    Till Eulenspiegel. Pp.

LÜBKE, Alfred
Managing director, Bautzen Th.
1968   *Die Teegesellschaft (The Tea Party)*. Dr. Pr 1969 Bautzen.

LUCKE, Hans
25 Apr 1927 Dresden –
Service in WW II; 1944 Russian POW; 46 Acting School Dsdn; 54-62 actor in Görlitz, Zittau, Dsdn; 62-73 DT; 73-77 stage director Rostock; since 78 lives as independent author in Zingst. 1958 Lessing Prize. Writes film scripts.
1952   *Fanal (Signal Light)*. Dr. Pr 1953 Dsdn.
1953   *Die letzte Stunde (The Last Hour)*. Dr.
1953   *Taillenweite 68 (Waistline 40)*. Com. Pr 1953 Dsdn.
1954   *Kaution (Security Deposit)*. Dr. Pr 1955 Dsdn.
1955   *Kawulke contra Meyer (Kawulke vs. Meyer)*. Com.
1956   *Glatteis (Slippery Ice)*. Com. Pr 1956 Dsdn.
1957   *Der Keller (The Basement)*. Dr. Pr 1957 Dsdn. Henschel 1958.
1959   *Untersuchungshaft (Detained on Suspicion)*. Dr. Pr 1963 Potsdam.
1962   *Satanische Komödie (Satanic Comedy)*. Com. Pr 1963 VB.
1964   *Haus Pechmühle (The Unlucky Mill House)*. Com.
1968   *Mäßigung ist aller Laster Anfang (Moderation Is the Root of All Evil)*. Com. Pr 1968 DT. Henschel 1968.
    Kameraden (Buddies). Dr.
1974   *Fracht für Coquimbo (Freight for Coquimbo)*. Dr. Pr 1975.
1975   *Besuch von gestern (Yesterday's Visit)*. Dr. Pr 1975 Rostock.
1975   *Die eigene Haut (Your Own Skin)*. Dr. Pr 1976 Rostock.
1981   *Der Abgang (The Exit)*. Dr.
1982   *Stadelmann*. Com. Pr 1983 Weimar. *TdZ* 1983/4. Henschel 1986.
1984   *Lieber Ehm Welk (Dear Ehm Welk)*. Dr (with Konrad Reich). Pr 1985 Rostock.
1984   *Schmierentheater ‹Der doppelte Otto› (Touring Company ‹Double Otto›)*. Com (incidental M Uwe Hilprecht). Pr 1986 Mgdbg. *TdZ* 1985/12. *Stadelmann*, 1986.
1985   *Die Ausbrecher (Breaking Out)*. Com. *Stadelmann*, 1986.

LUDWIG, Carsten
1951 -
Assistant stage director, Dsdn Th.
1982   *Meister Matel (Master Matel)*. Op Lib (based on drama
         by Aziz Nesin; M Jan Trieder). Pr 1983 Dsdn.

MAASS, Heiner
23 Nov 1931 Schönberg –
Studied theater history;   1959-65 dramaturg Schwerin;   65-73
chief dramaturg Mgdbg;   77-79 chief dramaturg Schwerin, since
then dramaturg VB.

1978   *Franziska Linkerhand.* Dr (with Bärbel Jaksch; based
        on 1973 novel fragment by Brigitte Reimann). Pr 1978
        Schwerin. *TdZ* 1978/6.

1979   *Die drei Musketiere (The Three Musketeers).* Mus Lib
        (with Peter M. Schneider; based on novel by Alexander
        Dumas; M Rainer Böhm). Pr 1980 Dsdn/Radebeul.

1980   *Das siebte Kreuz (The Seventh Cross).* Dr (with Bär-
        bel Jaksch; based on novel by Anna Seghers). Pr 1981
        Schwerin. *TdZ* 1981/4.

1980   *Kippenberg.* Dr (with Bärbel Jaksch; based on novel
        by Dieter Noll). Pr 1981 Schwerin.

1981   *Berlin Alexanderplatz (Alexander Square, Berlin).* Dr
        (with Bärbel Jaksch; based on novel by Alexander Döb-
        lin). Pr 1981 VB. *TdZ* 1981/11.

MAASS, Joachim
1969   *Wie Recke, Katze und Maus den Teufel besiegen (How
        Knight, Cat, and Mouse Conquer the Devil).* Juv (with
        Heide Reinhold; based on Byelorussian fairy tale).
        Pr 1972 Th. f. jg. Zuschauer, Mgdbg.

1970   *Kommen wir zur Sache (Let's Get to the Point).* Dr.
        Pr 1970 Mgdbg.

MAHLING, Peter   see Peter MALINK

MAHRHOLZ, Otto
1967   *Der schwarze Pfad (The Black Path).* Dr. Pr 1968 Zwik-
        kau.

MAI, Jürgen
1984   *Das Meisterstück (The Masterpiece).* Dr. Pr 1984 Senf-
        tenberg.

MAKARIUS, Jan
1974   *Der Schatz des alten Kapitän Habakuk (Old Captain Ha-
        bakuk's Treasure).* Juv. Pr 1974 Döbeln.
        Drei weiße Pfeile (Three White Arrows). Pp. Pr Baut-
        zen (in Sorbian).

MALINK, Peter   (also uses spelling Peter MAHLING)
27 July 1931 Lohsa –
Taught in Sorbian adult education program; 1956-60 Instructor
at Sorbian language school; 60-63 editor for Domowina Publishing Co.; 63-68 studied literature. 1962 and 67 Domowina
Prize. Writes prose and radio plays, mostly in Sorbian language.

1956   *Rebell Jan Cuska (Jan Cuska, the Rebel).* Dr (based
        on story by Ben Budar). Pr 1957.

MALINK (cont'd)
1961   *Die Abbitte   (The Apology)*.   Dr (written in Sorbian).
        Pr 1961.
1966   *Der Nachtpatient (The Night Patient)*.   Dr (originally
        written in Sorbian).   Pr 1966 Bautzen.   German Pr 19-
        67 Bautzen.   Bautzen: Domowina, 1967 (in Sorbian).
1972   *Die Antwort   (The Answer)*.   Dr   (written in Sorbian).
        Pr 1973 Bautzen.
1975   *Onkel Schmittka aus Sibirien (Uncle Schmittka from Si-*
        beria).   Com (written in Sorbian). Pr 1976 Bautzen.

MARTENS, Leo
1956   *Die Zaubergans (The Magic Goose)*.   Juv.   Pr 1956 Wei-
        mar.

MARTIN, Christian
1950 Ellefeld -
Worked as electrician; 1968-73 studied pedagogy Lpzg, then became teacher of German and history;   singer with amateur rock
groups; 81-84 studied I.Lit Lpzg; now lives in Ellefeld/KMSt.
Writes poetry, songs, radio plays.
1983   *Der Pferdehändler (The Horse Trader)*.   Com (with Ro-
        land Kästner).   Reading 1984 Lpzg.
        Abseits (Offside).   On.   Pr 1984 Senftenberg.
        Der Fall (The Case).   On.   Pr 1984 Senftenberg.
1983   *Hans und Marie*. Com (incidental M Wolfgang Jahn). Pr
        1984 Schwerin.
        Prinz Moritz von der Wasserburg (Prince Moritz of the
        Water Castle).

MATTHIES, Horst
4 Mar 1939 Radebeul -
Worked as miner, then ten years auxiliary policeman;   studied
I.Lit Lpzg; since 1970 independent author; lives in Hohen Vie-
cheln (Wismar).   1978 Radio Play Prize.   Writes prose and radio plays.
1972   *Plädoyer für Julia   (A Plea for Julia)*.   Dr.   Pr 1973
        Dessau.

MATTHUS, Siegfried
13 Apr 1934 Mallenuppen -
1952-58 studied composition at MHS Berlin with Wagner-Regeny,
58-60 studied at Academy of Arts under Hanns Eisler; since 19-
64 composer-in-residence, Km.Op.   Hanns Eisler Prize, GDR Art
rize, 1972 and 84 National Prize.   Composer and librettist.
1963   *Lazarillo vom Tormes ‹Spanische Tugenden› (Lazarillo*
        of Tormes ‹Spanish Virtues›).   Op (with Horst Seeger;
        based on 1554 Spanish novel).   Pr 1964 KMSt.
1966   *Der letzte Schuß (The Last Shot)*.   Op (based on novel
        by Boris Lavrenyov, "Der Einundzwanzigste").   Pr 1967
        Km.Op.   Lpzg: Dt. Verlag für Musik, 1969.
1972   *Omphale*.   Op (based on play by Peter Hacks).   Pr 1976
        Weimar.   Hacks, *Oper*, Aufbau 1975.   Lpzg: Dt. Verlag
        für Musik, 1977.

MATTHUS (cont'd)

1984   *Die Weise von Liebe und Tod des Cornets Christoph Rilke (The Song of Love and Death of Standard-Bearer Christoph Rilke)*. Op (based on story by Rainer Maria Rilke). Pr 1985 Dsdn. *TdZ* 1985/2.

1985   *Judith*. Op (based on Friedrich Hebbel). Pr 1985 Km. Op.

MATUSCHE, Alfred

8 Oct 1909 Leipzig - 1 Aug 1973 Karl Marx Stadt
Until 1927, studied at Inst. of Technology, Lpzg; then worked for Radio Lpzg; 1933 dismissed, joined anti-Nazi resistance; all manuscripts destroyed by Gestapo; after 45 again Radio Lpzg, later Dsdn; from 69 on lived KMSt. 1973 Lessing Prize. Wrote poetry, radio and TV plays.

1952-53 *Welche von den Frauen? oder Welche Art zu leben lohnt sich? (Which of the Women? or Which Way of Life is Worthwhile?)*. Dr. Pr 1979 Schwedt. *Welche von den Frauen und andere Stücke*, Henschel 1979.

1954   *Die Dorfstraße (The Village Street)*. Dr. Pr 1955 DT. Henschel 1955. *Dramen*, Henschel 1971.

1955-56 *Die Nacht der Linden (The Night of the Linden Trees)*. Dr. Pr 1979 Potsdam. *TdZ* 1979/4. *Welche von den Frauen...*, 1979.

1957   *Nacktes Gras (Naked Grass)*. Dr. Pr 1958 MG. Henschel 1959.

1960   *Die gleiche Strecke (The Same Route)*. Dr. Pr 1961 GDR TV.

1960   *Die feurige Stadt (The Fiery City)*. Dr.

1965   *Der Regenwettermann (The Rainy-Weather Man)*. Dr. Pr 1968 Potsdam. *TdZ* 1965/22. *Sinn & Form* 1968/1. *Sozialistische Dramatik*, Henschel 1968. *Dramen*, 1971.

1966   *Van Gogh*. Dr. Pr 1973 KMSt. *Sinn & Form* 1966/5. Opera version 1977 under title Vincent.

1967   *Das Lied meines Weges (The Song of My Road)*. Dr. Pr 1969 KMSt. Henschel 1969. *Dramen*, 1971.

1969   *Der Widerspenstigen Zähmung (The Taming of the Shrew)*. Com (tr from Shakespeare). Pr 1971 Zwickau.

1970   *Kap der Unruhe (Cap, the Restless)*. Dr. Pr 1970 Potsdam. *Dramen*, 1971.

1971   *Prognose ‹Neue Häuser› (Prognosis ‹New Homes›)*. On. Pr 1971 KMSt. *Welche von den Frauen...*, 1979.

1971   *An beiden Ufern (On Both Shores)*. Dr. Pr 1974 Potsdam. *Sinn & Form* 1971/1. *Welche von den Frauen*, 1979.

1977   *Vincent*. Op (based on Van Gogh; M and Lib Rainer Kunad). Pr 1979 Dsdn.

MAY, Ferdinand

16 Jan 1896 Pfungstadt/Darmstadt - 8 Nov 1977 Leipzig
Wounded in WW I, became pacifist; 1919 actor with traveling theater troupe, then merchant in Wetzlar and Lpzg; 45 director of cabaret "Die Rampe"; 48-51 worked in theater section of Ministry of Adult Education; 51 dramaturg Lpzg; after 58 independent author. 1961 City of Lpzg Prize. Wrote short stories, novels, and cabaret scripts.

MAY (cont'd)
1932   *Sarajewo 1914.* Dr. Pr 1932.
1952   *Der Aufstand des Babeuf (Babeuf's Rebellion).* Dr. Pr
         1953 Halle.
1956   *Gaston macht alles (Gaston Does Everything).* Op Lib
         (M Ernst Röhlmann). Pr 1956 Lpzg.
1957   *Die drei Robinsons (The Three Robinsons).* Mus Lib.
         Pr 1958 Rostock.
1963   *Keimzeit (Time of Germination).* Dr. Pr 1964.

MEDEK, TILO   (also known as Tilo MÜLLER-MEDEK)
22 Jan 1940 Jena –
1959-64 studied musicology in Berlin; also composition student of Wagner-Regeny until 67; since 64 independent composer; now lives in W. Berlin. 1967 Gaudeamus Prize.
1963   *Die betrunkene Sonne (The Drunken Sun).* Juv Mus (with
         Sarah Kirsch). Pr 1969 Brandenburg.
1968   *Einzug (Moving In).* Op (based on I. Babel). Pr 1969
         Potsdam.

MEHLHAUSEN, Kurt
1961   *Standpunkte (Points of View).* Com. Pr 1962 Fkft/O.

MEINCKE, Wilhelm ‹Willi›
1 Apr 1914 Dessau –
1922-33 worked as printer; 1933 emigrated to France, later returned to Germany; 38-46 service in WW II, POW; 46-50 teacher,
then editor; since 55 independent author, first in Berlin,
later in Zittau. 1968 Alex Wedding Prize. Writes short stories, novels, children's books.
         *Der Theatergraf von Remplin (The Stage Count of Remp-
         lin).* Com. Pr 1951 Rostock.

MEINIG, Enni
26 Apr 1921 –
Lives in KMSt. 1961 Culture Prize.
1964   *Der gestohlene Roboter (The Stolen Robot).* Juv. Pr
         1965 Erfurt.

MEISSNER, Hildegard
16 July 1924 –
Journalist, later dramaturg Wittenberg; 1974-80 Chief Dramaturg Stendal; now retired, lives in Mgdbg.
1961   *Frau Holle (Mother Holle).* Juv (based on Grimm). Pr
         1962 Wittenberg.
         *Pannemann, der Ehestifter (Pannemann, the Marriage
         Broker).* Com (based on novel by David Kalisch, "Otto
         Bellmann"). Pr 1976 Stendal.

MENSCHEL, Helmut
14 Feb 1921 Dresden/Radebeul –
1935-39 apprentice electrician; 39-45 service in WW II; 46-48
studied acting Dsdn; actor and later stage director at various theaters.

MENSCHEL (cont'd)

1971　*Klinik Prof. Dr. med. Morton (The Clinic of Prof. Morton, MD)*. Dr.　Pr 1972 Annnaberg.

1973　*‹Teton-Tatanka,› Tochter der Dakota (‹Teton-Tatanka,› Daughter of the Dakotas)*.　Juv.　Pr 1974 Zeitz.

1983　*Der Schatz im Silbersee (The Treasure in Silver Lake)*. Dr (based on novel by Karl May).　Pr 1984 Rathen.

MENZEL, Gerhard Walter
18 Feb 1922 Schkeuditz/ Leipzig - 4 Apr 1980 Leipzig
Book dealer and editor;　after 1945　home study of literature and art;　wrote first literary works;　48-52 dramaturg Radio Lpzg;　after 60 independent author.　1967 City of Lpzg Prize. Wrote short prose, radio plays, and children's books.

1951　*Marek ‹im Westen› (Marek ‹in the West›)*.　Com.　Pr 1952 DT.

MENZEL, Hans-Jochen
1983　*Heinrich, der Wagen bricht (Henry, the Carriage Is Breaking)*.　Pp (with Regina Menzel; based on Kleist). Pr 1983 Neubrandenburg.

MERBST, Martin　　see Martin SELBER

MERCKEL, Rudolf ‹Rolf›
　　Die silberne Flöte (The Silver Flute).　Juv.　Pr 1969 Quedlinburg.
　　Auf alle Fälle Liebe (In Any Case, Love).　Dr.　Pr 969 Quedlinburg.

METHE, Hubertus
1966　*Frau Holle (Mother Holle)*.　Juv (based on Grimm).　Pr 1966 Döbeln.
1967　*Der Froschkönig (The Frog Prince)*.　Juv (based on Grimm).　Pr 1967 Döbeln.
1968　*Die Bremer Stadtmusikanten (The Town Musicians of Bremen)*.　Juv (based on Grimm).　Pr 1968 Döbeln.
　　Vom Peter, der nicht singen konnte (The Story of Peter Who Could Not Sing).　Juv.

MICHELL, Jan　　see Erich GEIGER

MICKEL, Karl
12 Aug 1935 Dresden -
1953-59 studied economics in Berlin;　59-63 editor of journal "Junge Kunst" and instructor of economic history;　71-78 dramaturg BE;　now instructor at School of Drama, Berlin.　1978 Heinrich Mann Prize.　Writes poetry, prose, essays.

1958　*Die Einverstandenen (The Consenters)*.　Dr.
1964　*Requiem für Patrice Lumumba*.　Cantata.　Pr 1964.
1965　*Das zweite Urteil (The Second Verdict)*.　Dr.　*NdL* 19-65/12.
1965-67　*Nausikaa*.　Dr (based on Homer's "Odyssey").　Dr.　Pr 1968 Potsdam.　*Einstein*, Berlin (W): Rotbuch, 1974.

MICKEL (cont'd)
1971   *Wolokolamsker Chaussee (Wolokolamsk Boulevard).* On
        (based on Alexander Beks). Pr 1972 BE. *Sinn & Form*
        1971/6 (scene).
1973   *Einstein.* Op Lib (M Paul Dessau). Pr 1974 St. Op.
        TdZ 1974/4. Berlin (W): Rotbuch, 1974.
1974   *Celestina oder Die Tragikomödie von Calisto und Meli-*
        bea (Celestina or The Tragicomedy of Calisto and Meli-
        bea). Dr (based on de Rojas). Pr 1974 BE. *NdL* 1980/1.
        Briefe an Aja (Letters to Aja). Lib.

MÖBUS, Hans
1974   *He Marie! (Hey, Marie!).* Juv. Pr 1974 Schwerin.

MORGAN, Hans
        Das war im Hafen von Marseille (That Was in the Port
        of Marseilles). Dr. Pr 1952 Mgdbg.

MORGENSTERN, Beate
15 Apr 1946 Cuxhaven –
Studied German literature; now lives in Berlin. Writes prose
and radio plays.
1978   *Pellkartoffel (Potatoes in Their Jackets).* Juv (with
        Sibylle Hentschel; based on radio play). Pr 1981 Th.
        f. jg. Zuschauer, Mgdbg. *TdZ* 1982/11.

MORGNER, Martin
1948 Stollberg –
Graduated high school 1966, then studied economics and theater history; since 75 member of puppet ensemble Gera.
1977   *Die unbekannte Schöne (The Unknown Beauty).* Dr.
1978   *Tante Eugenie und der Mond (Aunt Eugenie and the*
        Moon). Pp. Pr 1979 Gera.
1982-84 *Arno, Katharina und Paul.* Juv. Pr 1986 Th. d. jg. Ge-
        neration, Dsdn.
1983   *Das Feuerzeug (The Tinderbox).* Pp (based on Hans
        Christian Andersen). Pr 1984 Gera.
1983   *Kasper rettet einen Baum (Punch Saves a Tree).* Pp.
        Pr 1985 Gera.

MÜLLER, Armin
25 Oct 1928 Schweidnitz (now Swidnice, Poland) –
War service 1944-45, then journalist Weimar; 57-62 editor for
Radio Weimar. 1953 First Prize, Bucharest Festival, 60 Weimar
Literature Prize, 61 Heinrich Heine Prize, 69 National Prize.
Writes songs, prose, radio and TV plays.
1967   *Die blaue Muschel (The Blue Seashell).* On (based on
        radio play). Pr 1970 Weimar.
1969   *Franziska Lesser.* Dr (based on radio play). Pr 1971
        Weimar. *TdZ* 1971/12. Rev version Pr 1973 Lpzg.
1973   *Sieben Wünsche (Seven Wishes).* Dr. Pr 1974 Weimar.
        TdZ 1974/3.
1974   *Der goldene Vogel (The Golden Bird).* Dr. Pr 1975
        Lpzg. *TdZ* 1975/6.

MÜLLER, Dietmar ‹Dieter›
1943 Chemnitz (now Karl Marx Stadt) –
Puppeteer; 1974-82 actor and dramaturg at Zwickau Th.; now works for puppetry section of GDR TV.

> *Der blaue Vogel (The Blue Bird).* Pp.
> *Der gestiefelte Kater (Puss-in-Boots).* Pp.
> *Mariechen und der Flaschenzwerg (Little Mary and the Dwarf in the Bottle).* Pp (based on Hans Fallada).
> *Judy und Punch.* Pp.

1976 *Des Kaisers neue Kleider (The Emperor's New Clothes).* Pp (based on Hans Christian Andersen). Pr 1977 Zwikkau.

1977 *Aschenputtel (Cinderella).* Pp (based on Grimm). Pr 1977 Dessau.

1978 *Die Schöne und der Papagei (Beauty and the Parrot).* Pp. Pr 1978 Zwickau.

1978 *Kasper treibt den Teufel aus (Punch Drives out the Devil).* Pp (based on Hans Sachs). Pr 1980 Zwickau.

1979 *Der fliegende Pfeil (The Flying Arrow).* Pp. Pr 1980 Eisleben.

1980 *Das Eismeer ruft (The Polar Sea Calls).* Juv. Pr 1980 Pionierth., KMSt.

1980 *Michael Kohlhaas.* Dr (based on Kleist). *TdZ* 1980/11.

1981 *Susanna im Bade oder Kasper rettet die Unschuld (Susannah Takes a Bath or Punch Saves an Innocent Woman).* Com (based on Paul Rebhuhn). Pr 1981 Zwickau. *TdZ* 1981/6.

1983 *Von einem, der auszog, das Gruseln zu lernen (The Lad Who Set Out to Learn Fright).* Pp (based on Grimm). Pr 1984 Gera.

1984 *Die Jüdin von Toledo (The Jewess of Toledo).* Pp (based on Grillparzer). Pr 1985 Dsdn.

1984 *‹Die Prinzessin und› der Schweinehirt (‹The Princess and› the Swineherd).* Pp (based on Hans Christian Andersen; incidental M Volkmar Funke). Pr 1985 Dsdn.

1985 *Die Schöne und das Tier (Beauty and the Beast).* Pp (based on Grimm). Pr 1985 Pp.Th., Berlin.

MÜLLER, Ernst Dietrich
> *Yesterday.* Dr. Pr 1967 Lpzg.

MÜLLER, Gerhard
1939 Saalfeld/Saale –
1959-63 studied journalism at Karl Marx Univ, Lpzg; 63-80 editor for Allgemeiner Deutscher Nachrichtendienst (GDR News Service); since 1980 dramaturg Km.Op. Writes music criticism for newspapers, magazines, and radio.
1981-82 *Candide.* Op Lib (based on Voltaire; M Reiner Bredemeyer). Pr 1983 Halle. *TdZ* 1983/11.

MÜLLER, Harald ‹Harri›
18 May 1934 Memel –
Editor of periodical "Temperamente"; lives in Potsdam.
> *Tilman Riemenschneider.* Dr. Pr 1954 Plauen.

MÜLLER, Heiner
9 Jan 1929 Eppendorf –
1945 drafted into Labor Service; after WW II journalist; 58
dramaturg MG and BE; since 59 independent author, also stage
director and dramaturg VB; 1975 guest professor Univ of Texas
at Austin. 1959 Heinrich Mann Prize (with wife Inge Müller),
64 Erich Weinert Medal, 75 Lessing Prize, 79 Mühlheim Drama
Prize, 85 Georg Büchner Prize.

1951-52 *Die Reise (The Journey)*. Sc (based on Japanese No-
Play by Motekiyo). *Germania Tod in Berlin*, Berlin (W):
Rotbuch, 1977.

1951-56 *Das Laken oder Die unbefleckte Empfängnis (The Sheet
or The Immaculate Conception)*. Sc (later part of Die
Schlacht). Pr 1974 VB (Part of program under collective title "Spektakel 2"). *Sinn & Form* 1966/5.

1951-73 *Die Schlacht (The Slaughter)*. Dr. Pr 1975 VB. *Die
Umsiedlerin*, Berlin (West): Rotbuch, 1975. *Germania
Tod in Berlin*, Henschel 1977. Henschel1981.

1956 *Der Lohndrücker (The Scab)*. Dr (with Inge Müller).
Pr 1958 Lpzg. Lpzg: Hofmeister, 1959. *Zeitgenössi-
sche Dramatik*, Henschel 1960 (with "Die Korrektur").
Sozialistische Dramatik, Henschel 1968. *Geschichten
aus der Produktion I*, Berlin (West): Rotbuch, 1973.
Stücke, Henschel 1975. *Die ersten Schritte*, Halle:
Mitteldt. Verlag, 1986.

1956 *Zehn Tage, die die Welt erschütterten (Ten Days That
Shook the World)*. Dr (with Hagen Müller-Stahl; based
on John Reed). Pr 1957 VB. *Junge Kunst* 1957/1.

1956-61 *Die Umsiedlerin oder Das Leben auf dem Lande (The Re-
settled Woman or Life in the Country)*. Com (based on
a story by Anna Seghers). Pr 1961 HS für Oekonomie,
Berlin. Berlin (W): Rotbuch, 1975. Rev 1964 as Die
Bauern.

1956-61 *Der Traktor (The Tractor)*. Dr (with Inge Müller). Pr
1975 Neustrelitz. *TdZ* 1975/8. *Geschichten aus der Produktion II*, Berlin (W): Rotbuch, 1974. *Die Schlacht*,
1981.

1956-73 *Germania Tod in Berlin (Germany Death in Berlin)*. Dr.
Pr 1978 Kammerspiele, Munich. *Th.h.* 1977, special issue. *Spec* 31, 1979. Berlin (W): Rotbuch, 1977. Henschel 1977. Stuttgart: Klett, 1983.

1957 *Die Korrektur (The Correction)*. Dr (with Inge Müller;
based on radio play). Rev version 1958. Pr 1958 MG.
Neue Dramatik, Reclam 1959. *Zeitgenössische Dramatik*,
1960 (with "Der Lohndrücker"). *Geschichten aus der
Produktion I*, 1973. *Hamlet Machine*, New York: Performing Arts Journal Publications, 1984 (Engl tr Carl Weber).

1957 *Die Brücke fällt aus (The Bridge Is Destroyed)*. Dr.

1958 *Klettwitzer Bericht (Klettwitz Report)*. Dr (with Inge Müller). *Junge Kunst* 1958/8.

1958 *Glücksgott (The Good-Luck Idol)*. Lib (based on fragment by Brecht; M Paul Dessau). *Theaterarbeit*, Berlin (W): Rotbuch, 1975.

MÜLLER, Heiner (cont'd)

1958-65 *Philoktet (Philoctetes)*. Dr. Pr 1968 Munich. *Th.h.* 1965/8. *Sinn & Form* 1965/6. Suhrkamp 1966. *Spec* 12, 1969. *Stücke*, 1975. *Poetisches Drama*, Moscow: Raduga, 1983 (German and Russian). *Philoctetes and the Fall of Troy*, Lincoln: Univ. of Nebraska Press, 1981 (Engl. tr Oscar Mandel).

1963 *Unterwegs (On the Way)*. Dr (with Inge Müller and Günter Jäniche; based on Victor Rosov). Pr 1964 DT.

1964 *Der Bau (The Construction)*. Dr (based on novel by Erik Neutsch, "Spur der Steine"). Pr 1965 DT planned (under title "Spur der Steine"), cancelled. Rev version 1965. Pr 1980 VB. *Sinn und Form* 1965/1-2. *TdZ* 1978/3. *Geschichten aus der Produktion 1*, 1973. *Stücke*, 1975. *Der Auftrag*, Henschel 1981.

1964 *Die Bauern (The Farmers)*. Com (rev of Die Umsiedlerin). Pr 1976 VB. *Stücke*, 1975. *Die Umsiedlerin*, 19-77. *Henschel* 1983.

1964-66 *Herakles 5*. Dr. Pr 1974 Schillerth., West Berlin. Suhrkamp 1966. *Dt. Th. d. Gegenwart 1*, Suhrkamp 1967. *Geschichten aus der Produktion I*, 1973. *Stücke*, 1975. *Der Auftrag*, 1981.

1965-66 *Hamlet*. Dr (tr of Shakespeare). Pr VB.

1966 *Oedypus, Tyrann (Oedipus the Tyrant)*. Dr (based on Sophocles, tr Hölderlin). Pr 1967 DT. *Kursbuch* 19-66/7. Aufbau 1969. Zurich: Benziger, 1971.

1967 *Lanzelot ‹Drachenoper› (Lancelot ‹The Dragon Opera›)*. Op Lib (with Ginka Tscholakowa; based on Yevgenyi Schwarz, "Der Drache"; M Paul Dessau). Pr 1969 St. Op. *TdZ* 1970/3. Berlin/Wiesbaden: Bote und Bock, 19-71. *Theaterarbeit*, 1975.

1967 *Wie es euch gefällt (As You Like It)*. Com (tr of Shakespeare). Pr 1968 Schauspielhaus, Munich. *Kopien: Drei Versuche, Shakespeare zu töten*, Suhrkamp 1983.

1968 *Don Juan oder Der steinerne Gast (Don Juan or The Guest of Stone)*. Com (with Benno Besson; based on Moliere). Pr 1968 DT.

1968 *Prometheus*. Dr (based on Aeschylus). Pr 1969 Zurich. *Spec* 11, 1968. *Geschichten aus der Produktion II*, 19-74.

1968-69 *Der Horatier (The Horatian)*. Dr (based on Livy). Pr 1973 Schillerth., W. Berlin. *Stücke*, 1975. *Mauser*, Berlin (W): Rotbuch, 1978. *Minnesota Review* 1975 (English tr. Marc Silverman, Helen Fehervary and Guntram Weber).

1968-69 *Horizonte (Horizons)*. Dr (with Gerhard Winterlich; rev of his 1967 play). Pr 1969 VB. *Theaterarbeit*, 1975 (first scene).

1969 *Lumumba*. Dr (tr of Aime Cesaire, "Une saison au Congo").

1970 *Der Arzt wider Willen (The Doctor in Spite of Himself)*. Com (with Benno Besson; tr of Moliere, "Le medecin malgre lui"). Pr 1970 VB.

MÜLLER, Heiner (cont'd)

1970   *Weiberkomödie (Comedy of Women)*. Com (based on 1960 radio play by Inge Müller, "Weiberbrigade"). Pr 1970 Mgdbg. *Theaterarbeit*, 1975. *Stücke*, 1975.

1970-71 *Mauser*. Dr (based on theme in novel by Mikhail Sholokhov, "The Silent Don"). Pr 1978 Austin, Texas (in Engl.). Gm Pr 1980 Cologne. *Spec* 27, 1977. Berlin (West): Rotbuch, 1978. *New German Critique* 1976/8 (Engl. tr Helen Fehervary and Marc Silverman).

1971-72 *Macbeth*. Dr (based on Shakespeare). Pr 1972 Brandenburg. *TdZ* 1972/4. *Th.h.* 1972/6. *Stücke*, 1975. Fkft/M: Verlag der Autoren, 1981. *Die Bauern*, 1983.

1971-72 *Die Möwe (The Seagull)*. Dr (with Ginka Tscholakowa; based on Chekhov). Pr 1973 Potsdam.

1972-73 *Zement (Cement)*. Dr (based on Fedor Gladkov). Pr 1973 BE. *TdZ* 1974/6. *Th.h.* 1975/10. *Geschichten aus der Produktion II*, 1974. *Stücke*, 1975. Reclam 1975. *New German Critique* 1979 (Engl. tr Sue-Ellen Case and Helen Fehervary).

1974   *Medeaspiel (Medea Play)*. Sc. *Die Umsiedlerin*, 1975. *Hamlet Machine*, 1984.

1975-76 *Leben Gundlings Friedrich von Preußen Lessings Schlaf Traum Schrei (Gundling's Life Frederick of Prussia Lessing's Sleep Dream Scream)*. Dr. Pr 1979 Fkft/M. *Spec* 26, 1977. Suhrkamp 1977. *Th.h.* 1979/3. *Die Schlacht*, 1981. Fkft/M: Verlag der Autoren, 1982. *Herzstück*, 1983. *Hamlet Machine*, 1984.

1976   *Quadriga*. Dr. Cologne: Prometheus, 1978. *Hamlet Machine*, 1984.

1977   ‹*Der Untergang des Egoisten› Fatzer (‹The Downfall of the Egotist› Fatzer)*. Dr (based on "Fatzer" fragment by Brecht). Pr 1978 Hamburg.

1977   *Hamletmaschine (Hamlet Machine)*. Dr. Pr 1979 Paris. *Th.h.* 1977/12. *Spec* 33, 1980. Cologne: Prometheus, 1978. *Mauser*, 1978. New York: Performing Arts Journal Publications, 1984 (Engl. tr Carl Weber).

1978   *Rosebud*. Dr (with Erich Wonder). Pr 1979 Düsseldorf.

1979   *Der Auftrag (The Mission)*. Dr (based on 1961 story by Anna Seghers, "Das Licht auf dem Galgen"). Pr 1980 VB. *Sinn & Form* 1979/6. *Th.h.* 1980/3. Fkft/M: Verlag der Autoren, 1980. Henschel 1981. Stuttgart: Klett, 1983. *Herzstück*, 1983. *Gambit*, 1983 (Engl. tr Stuart Hood). *Hamlet Machine*, 1984 (tr as "The Task").

1980   *Quartett*. Dr (based on Laclos, "Les liaisons dangereuses"). Pr 1982 Bochum. *Th.h.* 1981/7. Fkft/M: Verlag der Autoren, 1981. *Herzstück*, 1983. *GDR Monitor, Series Literature in Translation*, 1983 (Engl. tr Karin Gartzke and Geoffrey Davis). *Hamlet Machine*, 1984.

1981   *Herzstück (Heart Play)*. Sc. Pr 1981 Bochum. *Th.h.* 1982/1. Berlin (W): Rotbuch, 1983. *Theatre Yale*, 1983/1. *Hamlet Machine*, 1984 (tr as "Heart Piece").

MÜLLER, Heiner (cont'd)
1982   *Verkommenes Ufer   Medeamaterial   Landschaft mit Argo-
          nauten (Despoiled Shore Medea Material Landscape with
          Argonauts)*.   Dr.   Pr   1983 Bochum.   *TdZ* 1983/3 (Medea
          scene).   *Th.h.* 1983/6.   *Herzstück*, 1983.   *Spec* 39, 19-
          84.   *Hamlet Machine*, 1984.
1982-83 *Tarelkins Tod   (Tarelkin's Death)*.   Com   (with Ginka
          Tscholakowa; based on Alexander Sukhovo-Kobylin).
1983   *Wladimir Majakowski   Tragödie   (Vladimir Mayakovsky's
          "Tragedy")*.   Dr (based on tr. by Ginka Tscholakowa).
          Pr 1983 Schillerth., West Berlin.   *Th.h.* 1983/9.
1983   *the CIVIL warS*. Scenes (in play by Robert Wilson). Pr
          1984 Cologne.   Suhrkamp 1984.
1984   *‹Die› Wolokolamsker Chaussee I: Russische   Eröffnung
          (Wolokolamsk Boulevard I: Russian Opening)*. On (based
          on Beck).   Pr   1985   DT   (as prologue to "Die Winter-
          schlacht" by Johannes Becher). *Sinn und Form*, 1985/2.
          Th.h. 1985/7.   *TdZ* 1986/2.
1984   *Bildbeschreibung (Description of a Picture)*.   Dr.   Pr
          1985 Graz.   *Sinn & Form*, 1985/5.   *Th.h.* 1985/12.   Ame-
          rican Pr 1986 planned   (under title *Explosion of a Me-
          mory*; tr Carl Weber).
1984   *Anatomie Titus Fall of Rome Ein Shakespeare Kommentar
          (Anatomy   Titus Fall of Rome   A Shakespeare Commenta-
          ry)*.   Dr (based on Shakespeare).   Pr 1985 Bochum. *Th.
          h.* 1985/3.
1985   *‹Die› Wolokolamsker Chausee II: Wald bei Moskau (Wolo-
          kolamsk Boulevard II: Forest Near Moscow)*.   Dr (based
          on Beck).   Pr 1986 Potsdam.

MÜLLER, Helmut
1922 Nossen –
Grew up in Cottbus and Berlin; finished high school 1939; service in WW II, then POW, member of POW amateur theater group;
after 49 actor and stage director at various theaters; 58
founded cabaret "Wespennest" in Görlitz. Writes radio and TV
plays.
1961   *Ein Amerikaner in Tarent (An American in Tarent)*. Dr.
1962   *Keine Schnittblumen (No   Cut Flowers)*.   Com.   Pr 1962
          Bautzen.
1963   *Yankee Doodle*. Com. Pr 1965 Mgdbg.
1963-64 *Der Fall   Klabautermann   (The Case   of the Bogeyman)*.
          Dr (based on novel by Fallada, "Jeder stirbt für sich
          allein"; first written as radio play).   Pr 1966 Nord-
          hausen.   *TdZ* 1966/21.
1966   *Hurrikan (Hurricane)*.   Dr.   Pr 1967 Nordhausen.
1970   *Der fliegende Pfeil (The Flying Arrow)*.   Juv.   Pr 19-
          71 Nordhausen.
1971   *Der Sohn des Blitzes (Son of Lightning)*.   Juv.   Pr 19-
          72 Nordhausen.
1972   *Der Schatz   von Golden Hill   (The Treasure   of Golden
          Hill)*.   Juv.   Pr 1973 Nordhausen.
1974   *Lederstrumpf (Leather Stocking)*.   Juv (based on James
          Fenimore Cooper).   Pr 1975 Nordhausen.

MÜLLER, Helmut (cont'd)
1978   *Herkules und die Frauen (Hercules and the Women)*. Mus
        Lib (with Gerhard Hartmann; M Manfred Grafe). Pr 19-
        79 Dsdn.
1985   *König Karotte (King Carrot)*. Opt Lib (based on Jac-
        ques Offenbach; M Manfred Grafe). Pr 1986 Nordhausen.

MÜLLER, Inge   (nee Ingeborg SCHWENKNER)
13 Mar 1925 Berlin - 1 June 1966 Berlin
Drafted into Labor Service 1944-45; then worked as secretary,
journalist. 1959 Heinrich Mann Prize (with husband Heiner
Müller), 65 Erich Weinert Medal. Wrote children's books, radio plays.
1956   *Der Lohndrücker (The Scab)*. Dr (with Heiner Müller).
        Pr 1958 Lpzg. Lpzg: Hofmeister, 1959. *Zeitgenössi-
        sche Dramatik*, Henschel 1960 (with "Die Korrektur").
        Sozialistische Dramatik, Henschel 1968. *Geschichten
        aus der Produktion I*, Berlin (West): Rotbuch, 1973.
        Stücke, Henschel 1975. *Die ersten Schritte*, Halle:
        Mitteldt. Verlag, 1986.
1956-61 *Der Traktor (The Tractor)*. Dr (with Heiner Müller).
        Pr 1975 Neustrelitz. *TdZ* 1975/8. *Geschichten aus
        der Produktion II*, Berlin (West): Rotbuch, 1974. *Die
        Schlacht*, Henschel 1981.
1957   *Die Korrektur (The Correction)*. Dr (with Heiner Mül-
        ler; based on radio play). Rev version 1958. Pr 1958
        MG. *Neue Dramatik*, Reclam 1959. *Zeitgenössische Dra-
        matik*, 1960 (with "Der Lohndrücker"). *Geschichten aus
        der Produktion I*, 1973. *Hamlet Machine*, New York: Per-
        forming Arts Journal Publications, 1984 (Engl.tr Carl
        Weber).
1958   *Klettwitzer Bericht (Klettwitz Report)*. Dr (with Hei-
        ner Müller). *Junge Kunst* 1958/8.
1960   *Die Weiberbrigade (The Women's Brigade)*. Radio play
        (dramatized 1970 by Heiner Müller under title "Weiber-
        komödie"; Pr 1970 Mgdbg).
1963   *Unterwegs (On the Way)*. Dr (with Heiner Müller and
        Günter Jäniche; based on Victor Rosov). Pr 1964 DT.

MÜLLER, Jupp (real name Josef MÜLLER)
28 Dec 1921 Weipert (now Vejprty, Czechoslovakia) -
Baker; service in WW II, American POW 1943-46; after 46 coal
miner, later journalist; 60-63 I.Lit Lpzg; since 65 editor.
1959 FDGB Prize. Writes poetry, prose.
1965   *Die kontrollierte Sommerliebe (Controlled Summer
        Love)*. Com.
1969   *Auf Straßen, die wir selber bauten (On Streets Which
        We Built Ourselves)*. Cantata (M Wolfgang Strauß).
        Pr 1970.

MÜLLER-BEECK, Edith   see Edith BERGNER

MÜLLER-GLÖSA, Otto   (Pseud. Jakob SCHIEFHALS)
18 Aug 1892 Glösa - ?
Served in WW I; 1918 joined KPD; worked for various publishers; 45-57 worked for GDR film. Wrote prose, film scripts.
>   *Die Dirne und ihr roter Gast* *(The Whore and Her Red*
>   *Guest)*. On.
>   *Zeuge Kretschmar* *(Kretschmar, the Witness)*. Dr. Pr
>   1951 Mgdbg.
>   *Er hat auch eine Frau (He Also Has a Wife)*. Com. Pr
>   1951 BE.

MÜLLER-MEDEK, Tilo   see Tilo MEDEK

MÜLLER-STAHL, Hagen
1926 -
Dramaturg, theater critic; left GDR 1961; stage director 61-
69 West Berlin, 70-74 Mannheim, then Kassel.
1956   *Zehn Tage, die die Welt erschütterten* *(Ten Days That*
>   *Shook the World)*. Dr (with Heiner Müller; based on
>   John Reed). Pr 1957 VB. *Junge Kunst* 1957/1.

NAWRATH, Marta
1 Sep 1906 Gleiwitz (now Gliwice, Poland) –
Worked as secretary; moved to Naumburg 1929; journalist until
1933; also tour guide; after 45 worked for theaters in Dessau
and Halle. Writes poetry, songs, prose.
1954   *Die Mutprobe (The Test of Courage)*. Dr. Lpzg: Hof-
        meister, 1959.
1968   *Ein ehernes Denkmal - lebendige Herzen (A Brazen Me-
        morial - Living Hearts)*. Dramatic Cantata.

NEEF, Wilhelm
28 Jan 1916 Cologne –
Studied in Aachen and Bonn; composer, conductor, stage director at various theaters; 1953-55 St. Op; since 55 independent
author in Kleinmachnow/Potsdam.
1958   *Madame Dubarry*. Opt Lib (new adaptation; based on
        Zell and Genee; M Karl Millöcker). Pr 1959 Rostock.
        Orpheus in der Unterwelt (Orpheus in Hades). Opt Lib
        (new adaptation; based on Meilhac and Halevy; M Jac-
        ques Offenbach).
        Die Fledermaus (The Bat). Opt Lib (new adaptation;
        based on Haffner and Genee; M Johann Strauß).
        *Das Spitzentuch der Königin (The Queen's Lace Ker-
        chief)*. Opt Lib; new adaptation; based on Haffner and
        Genee; M Johann Strauß).
1961   *Das schweigende Dorf (The Silent Village)*. Opt (based
        on story by Willi Bredel). Pr 1961 Plauen.
1962   *Die Millionen der Yvette (Yvette's Millions)*. Mus.
        Pr 1963 Schwerin.
        Die Stumme von Portici (The Mute Woman of Portici).
        Op Lib (new adaptation; based on Eugene Scribe; M Da-
        niel Francois Aubert).
        Die Weber von Lyon (The Weavers of Lyons). Op Lib
        (new adaptation; based on Jacques Gaucheron; M Joseph
        Kosma).
        *Die Heuchlerin aus Liebe (The Woman Who Cheated for
        Love)*. Op Lib (new adaptation; based on Marco Coltel-
        lini; M Mozart).
        Shakespeareana (Shakespeare Episodes). Bl. Pr 1968
        Halle.
1973   *Wieviel Erde braucht der Mensch? (How Much Earth Does
        a Person Need?)*. Bl. Pr 1974 St.Op.
1983   *Regina*. Op Lib (new adaptation; M Albert Lortzing).
        Pr 1984 Wittenberg.

NEHER, Caspar
11 Apr 1897 Augsburg – 30 June 1962 Vienna
1918-22 studied in Munich, then Berlin, Essen, and Fkft/M; became set designer; 46-49 worked in Zurich Th., Salzburg Festival, then with Brecht in BE; also W. Berlin and Cologne.
1931   *Die Bürgschaft (The Hostage)*. Op Lib (M Kurt Weill).
        Vienna: Universal, 1932.

NEHER (cont'd)

1934 *Der Günstling (The Favorite).* Op Lib (based on Georg Büchner; M Rudolf Wagner-Regeny). Pr 1935 Dsdn. Vienna: Universal, 1935. Rev 1952 as Der Günstling oder Die letzten Tage des großen Herrn Fabiano.

1938 *Die Bürger von Calais (The Citizens of Calais).* Op Lib (based on Georg Kaiser; M Rudolf Wagner-Regeny). Pr 1939 St.Op. Vienna: Universal, 1938.

1940 *Johanna Balk.* Op Lib (M Rudolf Wagner-Regeny). Pr 1941 Vienna. Vienna: Universal, 1941.

1940-50 *Persische Späße ‹Persische Episode› (Persian Jests ‹Persian Episode›).* Op Lib (M Rudolf Wagner-Regeny). Pr 1963 Rostock.

1952 *Der Günstling oder Die letzten Tage des großen Herrn Fabiano (The Favorite or The Last Days of the Great Mr. Fabiano).* Op Lib (rev of Der Günstling; M Rudolf Wagner-Regeny). Pr 1953 Dsdn. Reclam 1960.

NELL, Peter (real name Kurt HEINZE)
10 Oct 1907 Berlin - 27 Nov 1957 Berlin
Worked as salesman; 1927 joined KPD; 31-32 correspondent in Soviet Union; after 33 active in anti-Nazi resistance; service in WW II, heavily wounded; after 45 editor Berlin and Potsdam; from 55 on, Head of Literature Section, Ministry of Culture. Wrote poetry, prose, essays.

1949 *Die Eysenhardts: Der Weg einer Frau (The Eysenhardts: A Woman's Progress).* Dr. Pr 1950 Potsdam. Halle: Mitteldt. Verlag, 1950.

NESTLER, Joachim ‹Jochen›
3 May 1936 Wittgendorf -
Graduated high school 1954; became librarian Zwickau; 56-60 studied at Film HS Potsdam; then screen writer for DEFA. 1968 Erich Weinert Medal.

1966 *Seemannsliebe (Sailor's Love).* Mus Lib (with Manfred Freitag; M Günter Hauk). Pr 1967 MG. *TdZ* 1967/15. Henschel 1968.

1971 *Tandem oder Moralisches Rezept für doppelte Eheführung (Tandem or Moral Recipe for Bigamy).* Com (with Manfred Freitag). Pr 1971 Brandenburg.

NEUBERT, Kurt R‹udolf› (Pseud. RUDOLPHI)
Wrote novels, short stories, radio, TV, and film scripts.
2 x klingeln (Ring Twice). Com. Pr 1947 Gera.

NEUHAUS, Lutz W‹olfgang›
27 Mar 1929 Glauchau - 24 Aug 1966 Berlin
Drafted 1945, deserted; after end of war, worked as miner; 47 began writing . Wrote stories, film and TV scripts.

1947 *Illusion.* Dr. Pr 1948 Mgdbg.
  Brot der Armen (The Bread of the Poor). Dr.

1957 *Mittelstürmer Brumme (Center Forward Brumme).* Dr.

NEUMANN, Gerhard
16 Oct 1928 Rostock -
Th. manager Quedlinburg, Eisleben. Writes poetry, stories, essays.

1954   *Die Premiere fällt aus (The Premiere Is Cancelled).* Com (with Hans Albert Pederzani; based on novel). Pr 1954 Eisenach.

1961   *Hochverrat (High Treason).* Dr. Pr 1962 Halberstadt. *Siebtens: Stiehl ein bißchen weniger (Seventh: Steal a Little Less).* Com (with Joachim Knauth; based on Dario Fo). *Der Bürger als Ehrenmann (The Bourgeois as Gentleman).* Com (with Rainer Kirsch; based on Moliere, "Le bourgeois gentilhomme").

NEUMANN, Jürg-Michael   see Jürg-Michael KOERBL

NEUMANN, Karl
30 July 1916 Ellenburg -
Worked as painter; service in WW II; Russian POW 1945-46; became art teacher and author. 1969 Alex Wedding Prize. Writes children's books.

1958   *Frank.* Juv (based on novel). Pr 1961 Th. d. jg. Garde, Halle.

NEUTSCH, Erik
21 June 1931 Schönebeck -
1950-53 studied journalism Lpzg; 53-60 editor, journal "Freiheit" in Halle; since then independent author. Member AdK; 1961 and 62 FDGB Prize, 64 National Prize, 71 Heinrich Mann Prize, 73 Händel Prize. Writes stories and novels.

1963-4   *Spur der Steine (A Trail of Stones).* Novel (dramatized by Heiner Müller under title Der Bau). Pr 1980 VB. See Heiner Müller for bibliographic data.

1968   *Fingerübungen (Finger Exercises).* Sc. Pr 1969 Halle (part of program under collective title Anregung 1). Later became part of Haut oder Hemd.

1970   *Haut oder Hemd (Skin or Shirt).* Dr. Pr 1970 Halle, rev version Pr 1971 Halle. *TdZ 1971/4. Da sah ich den Menschen*, Berlin: Tribüne, 1983.

1971   *‹Der Prozeß der› Karin Lenz (‹The Trial of› Karin Lenz).* Op Lib (M Günter Kochau). Pr 1971 St.Op. *TdZ 1971/11.*

NICOLAUS, Alfred
1980   *Die Liebe der Babet (Babette's Love).* Mus. Pr 1981 Greifswald.

NITSCHKE, Manfred
1926 Leipzig -
Studied composition. Worked as arranger and composer for GDR Radio.

1963-64 *Küssen verboten (No Kissing).* Mus (with Heinz Hall and Hans Peter). Pr 1964 Rostock. *TdZ 1964/20.*

NITSCHKE (cont'd)
1965   *Millionär wider Willen   (The Reluctant Millionaire)*.
        Mus (with Heinz Hall). Pr 1965 Rostock.
1968   *Ein Strom, der Liebe heißt (A River Called Love)*. Mus
        (with Heinz Hall). Pr 1969 Rostock.
1971   *Sommersonnabendsonntag   (Summer   Weekend)*. Mus (with
        Heinz Hall). Pr 1972 Rostock.
1974   *Auf glattem Parkett (On Slippery Grounds)*. Mus (with
        Heinz Hall). Pr 1974 Plauen.

NOACK, Christian
1937 Glauchau –
Studied physics in Lpzg, graduated 1969; worked at computer
center of Humboldt Univ, Berlin; since 82 author and director of amateur puppet group at Humboldt Univ.
        Fräulein Paulmanns Heirat (Miss Paulmann's Marriage).
        Juv (based on E. T. A. Hoffmann).
1971   *Sechse kommen durch die ganze Welt (The Six Servants)*
        Juv (based on Grimm). Pr 1972 Th. f. jg. Zuschauer,
        Mgdbg.
1973   *Fuente ovejuna*. Juv (based on Lope de Vega). Pr 19-
        73 Zittau.
1974   *Abenteuer des Theseus (The Adventures of Theseus)*.
        Juv.
1975   *Der Streit zwischen Kaiser und Bäcker (The Quarrel
        between the Emperor and the Baker)*. Juv.
1977-82 *Der kleine Prinz (The Little Prince)*. Pp (based on
        St. Exupery). Pr 1983 Halle.
1980   *Die Argonautensage (The Legend of the Argonauts)*. Juv.
        TdZ 1980/11.
1981   *Arenia, hurra!* Pp. *TdZ* 1981/6.
1983   *Einer macht den Hansel (He Who Plays the Fool)*. Com
        (based on Feydeau, "Le dindon").
1984   *Gilgamesch und Enkidu*. Pp (based on an ancient le-
        gend).

NOACK, Siegfried
1966   *Schwarzer Freitag (Black Friday)*. Dr.

NOWOTNY, Joachim
16 June 1933 Rietschen –
Worked as carpenter, then studied German literature Karl Marx
Univ. Lpzg 1954-58; worked as editor; since 67 Lecturer for
prose, I. Lit Lpzg. 1970 and 71 City of Lpzg Prize, 71 Alex
Wedding Prize. Writes children's books, radio plays, short
stories, novels.
1970   *Kleine Gärten - große Leute (Small Gardens - Big
        People)*. Com (with Peter Gosse, Christoph Hamm, Hans
        Pfeiffer, Helmut Richter). Pr 1971 Lpzg.
1978   *Ein seltener Fall von Liebe (A Rare Case of Love)*.
        Com (based on story and radio play). Pr 1984 Lpzg.

NÜRNBERG, Ilse   (married name Ilse BÖTTCHER)
1921 -
Actress; married to Wolfgang Böttcher.

1952   *Ehe eine Ehe eine Ehe wird (Before a Marriage Becomes a Marriage)*. Mus Lib (with Wolfgang Böttcher; M Benno Lipinski). Pr 1953 Lpzg.

1954   *Zum Glück hat sie Pech (Luckily She's Unlucky)*. Mus Lib (with Wolfgang Böttcher; M Conny Odd). Pr 1955 Rostock.

1956   *Der verlorene Schlaf (The Lost Sleep)*. Mus Lib (with Wolfgang Böttcher; based on Friedrich Dietz; M Olaf Koch).

1958   *Don Juans Höllenfahrt (Don Juan's Descent into Hell)*. Mus Lib (with Wolfgang Böttcher; M Conny Odd).

1966   *Irene und die Kapitäne (Irene and the Captains)*. Mus Lib (with Wolfgang Böttcher; M Conny Odd). Pr 1967 Dsdn. *TdZ* 1967/10.

1969-70 *Von einem, der auszog, das Gruseln zu lernen (The Lad Who Set Out to Learn Fright)*. Juv Op Lib (with Wolfgang Böttcher; based on Grimm; M Joachim-Dietrich Link). Pr 1970 Gera.

1971   *Frau Mohr hat ihre Schuldigkeit getan (Mrs. Mohr Has Done Her Duty)*. Mus Lib (with Wolfgang Böttcher; M Benno Lipinski). Pr 1972 Schwerin.

OEHME, Hartmut
Actor.
1973   *Krabat.* Dr. Pr 1973 Bautzen (in Sorbian language).
1975   *Der Meister (The Master).* Dr. Pr 1975 Bautzen (in Sorbian language).

OEHME, Ralph
1954 -
After high school, became tractor driver; studied theater history Lpzg; stage director and teacher at Th. HS Lpzg.
1981-83 *Krischans Ende (Krischan's End).* Op Lib (M Thomas Heyn). Pr 1986 Stralsund.
1984   *"Ich ist ein anderer. Rimbaud" ("Me Is Someone Else. Rimbaud").* Dr for chamber ensemble (M Thomas Heyn).

OSSOWSKI, Leonie
15 Aug 1925 Röhrsdorf -
Now lives in Mannheim. Writes novels, film scripts, radio and TV plays, film scripts.
1958   *Stern ohne Himmel (A Star without Heaven).* Dr (based on Jo von Tiedemann). Pr 1961 Greifswald.

OSTAREK, Hans
1953 Weißenberg -
1971-76   studied music Berlin; 76 conductor, Th. d. Freundschaft, Berlin; now musical director. Composer and librettist.
        Ganz Ohr (All Ears). Juv Mus (with Steffen Klaus).
1985   *Die Abenteuer des Don Quijote, gespielt von seinen Freunden (The Adventures of Don Quijote, Performed by His Friends).* Juv Mus. *TdZ* 1986/3.

OTTE, Volkmar
Director of pantomime ensemble, DT.
1976   *Don Quichote in Murzeledo.* Pant (with Burkhart Seidemann). Pr 1976 DT.
1977   *Vom Kalaf und Prinzessin Turandot (Calaf and Princess Turandot).* Pant (with Burkhart Seidemann). Pr 1977 DT.
        Der andere Paul (The Other Paul). Pant.
1979   *Die fremde Haut (The Strange Skin).* Pant (with Burkhart Seidemann). Pr 1979 DT.
        Wer hat Angst vorm schwarzen Mann? (Who's Afraid of the Bogeyman?) Pant. Pr DT.
1984   *Das Spiel vom tapferen Schneiderlein (The Play about the Brave Little Tailor).* Juv (based on Grimm; with Eva-Marie Otte). Pr 1985 Th. d. jg. Generation, Dsdn.

OTTO, Herbert
15 Mar 1925 Breslau (now Wroclaw, Poland) –
Service in WW II, Russian POW; returned home 1949; worked as
editor and dramaturg; traveled to Orient 57, to Cuba 60; now
lives in suburb of Berlin. 1956 and 62 Fontane Prize, 71 Heinrich Mann Prize, 78 National Prize. Writes novels and short
stories.
1966   *Die Zeit der Störche (The Season of the Storks).* Dr
         (based on novel). Pr 1970.

OTTO, Marie
         König Drosselbart (King Thrushbeard). Juv (with Armin Gerd Kuckhoff; based on Grimm). Pr 1947 Th. am
         Schiffbauerdamm, Berlin.

PAARMANN, Heinz
1949 *Insel im Weltmeer (Island in the Ocean).* Dr. Pr 19-50 Anklam.

PAFFRATH, Elifius
1942 -
Studied theater history Lpzg, then worked as dramaturg for radio as well as Halle and Eisleben Th.; 1976-78 I. Lit. Lpzg; since 80 independent author. Writes radio plays.
1971 *Vater sein dagegen sehr (It's Hard to Be a Father).* Com. Pr 1972 Eisleben.
1983 *Teufelskarl (That Devil Charles).* Juv (based on radio play). Pr 1985 Th. d. Freundschaft, Berlin. *TdZ* 1985/3.

PALISANDER, Alfred see Gerhard JÄCKEL

PASCH, Albert
1973 *Das Spiel vom argen Schalk Till Eulenspiegel (The Play about the Mischievous Rogue Till Eulenspiegel).* Juv (with Wolfgang Rinecker). Pr 1974 Meiningen.
1977 *Münchhausen.* Com (with Wolfgang Rinecker). Pr 1978 Meiningen.
Schneeweißchen und Rosenrot (Snow-White and Rose-Red). Juv Mus Lib (based on Grimm; M Ulrich Hermann).

PASTOWSKI, Klaus Manfred
29 Apr 1921 Königsberg -
1955-59 studied Th. HS Lpzg; 59-63 dramaturg Annaberg; then active in various cultural institutions.
1959 *Der Weg zum Wir (The Road towards Us).* Dr (with Martin Viertel). Pr 1960 Workers' Theater, Wismut.
1960-61 *Die schwarze Kugel ‹Der schwarze Engel› (The Black Bullet ‹The Black Angel›).* Juv. Pr 1961 Annaberg.
1962 *Karl Stülpner.* Dr. Pr 1963 Annaberg.
1971-72 *Indianer am Mississippi (Indians at the Mississippi).* Juv (based on James Fenimore Cooper). Pr 1972 Annaberg.
1972 *Karrieristen (Careerists).* Com (with Maria Pastowski; based on novel by Ivan Vasov). Pr 1973 Annaberg.
1978 *Schiller in Bauerbach.* Dr. Pr 1979 Workers' and Peasants' Th., Bauerbach.
1982 *Der letzte Mohikaner (The Last of the Mohicans).* Juv (with Klaus Königsberger; based on James Fenimore Cooper). Pr 1983 Eisenach.

PÄTSCH, Stefan see Konrad REICH

PAUL-CZECH, Ilse see Ilse CZECH-KUCKHOFF

PEDERZANI, Hans Albert   (Pseud. A. G. PETERMANN)
20 Sep 1923 Berlin –
After high schol, became actor and assistant director Schillerth., Berlin and DT; 1943 drafted, English POW; 46-49 actor in Fkft/O. and Mgdbg; 49-50 dramaturg Stendal, 50-51 managing director Bernburg, 51-53 director DEFA; since 56 independent author in Berlin. 1968 National Prize. Writes poetry, radio and TV plays, film scripts.

1947   *Der Puppenschuster (The Doll Shoemaker).* Juv. Pr 19-50 Chemnitz (now KMSt).

1954   *Die Premiere fällt aus (The Premiere Is Cancelled).* Com (with Gerhard Neumann; based on novel). Pr 1954 Eisenach.

1960   *Die Jagd nach dem Stiefel (The Hunt for the Boot).* Juv (based on story by Max Zimmerling). Pr 1961 Th. d. Freundschaft, Berlin.

1962   *Unser kleiner Trompeter (Our Little Trumpeter).* Juv Mus Lib (based on novella and drama by Otto Gotsche; M Jean Kurt Forest). Pr 1963 Th. d. Freundschaft, Berlin. *TdZ* 1963/22. *Neue sozialistische Dramatik*, Henschel 1968.

1968   *Der eigene Kopf (One's Own Head).* Juv (based on Karl Grünberg, "Flucht aus dem Eden"). Pr 1968 Th. d. Freundschaft, Berlin.

PESCHKE, Michael
          Abfahrtszeiten (Times of Departure). Dr. *Temperamente* 1983/1.

PETER, Hans
1962   *Geschichten meiner Frau (Stories of My Wife).* Com (with Hans Henkels and Ralph Wiener). Pr 1962 Rostock.

1963-64   *Küssen verboten (No Kissing).* Mus Lib (with Heinz Hall; M Manfred Nitschke). Pr 1964 Rostock. *TdZ* 19-64/20.

1979   *Erneuerte Ehe (Renewed Marriage).* Com. Pr 1980 Rostock.

1981   *Alle Mütter waren Töchter (All Mothers Were Daughters).* Com. Pr 1982 Rostock.

1985   *Wie oft soll man heiraten? (How Often Should You Get Married?)* Com. Pr 1986 Rostock.

PETER, Jörg   see Fritz DABRITZ

PETERMANN, A. G.   see Hans Albert PEDERZANI

PEUST, Dieter
1970   *Der kleine Prinz (The Little Prince).* Juv (based on St. Exupery). Pr 1970 Mgdbg.

1980   *Die Geschichte vom Pfefferkuchenmann Knusperle (The Story of Crispy, the Gingerbread Man).* Pp. Pr 1980 Wittenberg.

PFAFF, Siegfried
21 Jan 1931 Kreuzberg (now Kluczbork, Poland) -
1949-52 teacher in Chemnitz (now KMSt); 52-57 studied philosophy and German literature in Lpzg and Berlin; 57-60 asst.
stage director and dramaturg VB; since 60 radio dramaturg. 19-
68 FDGB Prize, 70 Literature Prize. Writes radio plays.
1967   *Regina B. - Ein Tag in ihrem Leben (Regina B. - A Day
        in Her Life).* Dr (based on radio play). Pr 1968 Ge-
        ra. *TdZ* 1970/2. Rev 1968. Pr 1969 Greifswald. *Neue
        Stücke*, Henschel 1971.

PFEIFFER, Hans
22 Feb 1925 Schweidnitz (now Swidnice, Poland) -
After school, service in WW II; 1946-52 teacher; 52-56 studied philosophy and German literature in Lpzg, then became Instructor there, later Lecturer I.Lit. Lpzg. 1965 and 71 City
of Lpzg Prize, 80 National Prize. Writes stories, essays, radio and TV plays.
1946   *Kopf ab - zum Gebet (Heads Off - Ready for Prayer).*
        Revue.
1947   *Faust im Inferno.* Dr.
1955   *Nachtlogis (Lodgings for a Night).* Dr. Pr 1955 Alten-
        burg.
1956   *Laternenfest (Party with Lanterns).* Dr. Pr 1957 Dsdn.
        Zeitgenössische Dramatik, Henschel 1958. Henschel 19-
        61. Rev 1962 as Op (M Julius Kowalski; Pr 1963 Bra-
        tislava).
1957   *Ein Abschied (A Farewell).* Dr. Kassel and Basel: Bä-
        renreiter, 1958.
1958   *Hamlet in Heidelberg.* Dr.
1959   *Zwei Ärzte (Two Doctors).* Dr. Pr 1959 Lpzg.
1959   *Das Restaurant in Shanghai.* On.
1960   *Das schwedische Zündholz (The Safety Match).* Com
        (based on Chekhov; originally radio play). Pr 1961
        Lpzg. Lpzg: Hofmeister, 1962.
1960   *Die dritte Schicht (The Third Shift).* Dr. Pr 1960
        Eisleben.
1961   *Schuld sind die anderen (The Others are at Fault).*
        Dr. Pr 1961 Lpzg.
1965   *Begegnung mit Herkules (Encounter with Hercules).* Com.
        Pr 1966 Lpzg. *NdL* 1966/6.
1966   *Wem die Glocke schlägt (For Whom the Bell Tolls).* Dr.
1967   *Woldja, Alexei und ich (Voldya, Alexey and I).* Dr (co-
        author).
1970   *Münchhausen auf Artemis (Munchhausen on Artemis).* Juv
        (with Günter Kaltofen). Pr 1971 Lpzg.
1970   *Kleine Gärten - große Leute (Small Gardens - Big
        People).* Com (with Peter Gosse, Christoph Hamm, Joa-
        chim Nowotny, and Helmut Richter). Pr 1971 Lpzg.
1971   *Thomas Müntzer.* Dr (based on novel). Pr 1975 Qued-
        linburg. *TdZ* 1975/7.
1976   *Salut an alle. Marx (Regards to Everyone, Marx).* Dr
        (with Günter Kaltofen). Pr 1976 Halle. *TdZ* 1976/7.

PFEIFFER (cont'd)
1977   *Heines letzte Liebe (Heine's Last Love).* Dr (with Gün-
         ter Kaltofen). Pr 1977 TiP.

PFÜTZNER, Klaus
1929 –
After school, worked in chemical factory; 1952-63 studied at
Th. HS Lpzg; since 64 dramaturg DT; also journalist.
         Der ältere Sohn (The Older Son). Com (based on Ale-
         xander Vampilov; tr Valentina Schalagina).
1983   *Das Mädchen Irgendwohin (The Girl Somewhere).* Dr
         (with Jan Martinec). Pr 1984 Rostock. *TdZ* 1984/6.

PHILIPP, Horst
11 Feb 1938 Berlin –
1959-62 studied library science; 63-68 studied theater history at Karl Marx Univ and Th. HS Lpzg; then worked as cultural
editor for various newspapers; since 81 with "Sächsisches Ta-
geblatt".
1973   *Die weiße Schlange (The White Serpent).* Juv. Pr 19-
         73 Freiberg.
1974   *Das Märchen von den zwei Jägern (The Tale of the Two
         Hunters).* Juv. Pr 1974 Plauen.

PIJET, Georg Waldemar
14 Feb 1907 Berlin –
After school, worked in bank; 1924 unemployed, 25 joined KPD;
member of workers' theater group; 33 emigrated to Denmark, later returned and joined anti-Nazi underground; 44-45 war service; journalist, editor for "Neues Deutschland" and for GDR
Radio. 1960 Johannes Becher Medal. Writes poems, children's
books, short stories, radio and TV plays.
1927   *Kreuzer unter Rot (Cruiser under the Red Flag).* Dr
         (based on Eisenstein film, "Potemkin"). Pr 1927.
         Lpzg: Arbeitertheaterverlag Jahn, 1927.
1928   *D-Zug CK3 (Express Train CK3).* Dr.
1928   *Schlacht im Turm (Battle in the Tower).* Dr. Pr 1928.
         Lpzg: Arbeitertheaterverlag Jahn, 1928.
1929   *Die Kumpels (The Miners).* Dr. Lpzg: Arbeitertheater-
         verlag Jahn, 1929.
1929   *Das Mandat (The Mandate).* Com. Lpzg: Arbeiterthea-
         terverlag Jahn, 1929.
1929   *Die Zermalmten (The Downtrodden).* Dr. Lpzg: Arbeiter-
         theaterverlag Jahn, 1929.
1930   *Verrat in der Nacht (Betrayal at Night).* Dr. Pr 1931.
1931   *Treibjagd (The Hunt).* Juv (based on radio play). Pr
         1952.
1934   *Der Herr von der Generaldirektion (The Man from the
         Head Office).* Com. Pr 1934.
1947   *Tauwetter (The Thaw).* Com.
1951   *Die glückliche Stadt (The Happy City).* Opt Lib (M
         Jean Kurt Forest).
1952   *Das leuchtende Ziel (The Shining Goal).* Opt Lib (M
         Jean Kurt Forest).

PIJET (cont'd)

1955   *Der Vogelscheuchenmann (The Scarecrow Man)*. Juv. Lpzg:
Hofmeister, 1956.

1956   *Die Berggeister des Hallasan (The Mountain Spirits of
Hallasan)*. Com (based on radio and TV play, "Die Gei-
ster des Hallasan"). Pr 1958 Th. d. jg. Welt, Lpzg.

1957   *Der stumme Zeuge (The Silent Witness)*. Com (based on
radio play). Pr 1960 Lpzg. Lpzg: Hofmeister, 1960.

1965   *Der Verdacht (The Suspicion)*. Dr.

1967   *Tilla und der Burgvogt (Tilla and the Castle Steward)*.
Juv Mus (with Hans-Hermann Krug; M Hans Auenmüller).
Pr 1976 Halberstadt.

PILLEP, Peter

Das Waldhaus (The House in the Forest). Pp (based on
Edith Bergner).
*Schnurps Ferienabenteuer (Schnurp's Vacation Adven-
ture)*. Pp. Pr 1976 KMSt.
*Der ‹vergessene› Weihnachtsauftrag (The ‹Forgotten›
Christmas Order)*. Pp. Pr 1977 Wittenberg.
Die Weihnachtsüberraschung (The Christmas Surprise).
Pp. Pr 1978 KMSt.
*Teddys größter Weihnachtswunsch (Teddy's Greatest
Christmas Wish)*. Pp.

PITSCHMANN, Siegfried
21 Jan 1930 Grünberg (now Zielona Gora, Poland) –
Moved to Mühlhausen in 1945; worked as watchmaker, 57-59 ma-
chinist, then began writing; since 65 lives in Rostock. 1961
Radio Play Prize, 62 FDGB Prize (with Brigitte Reimann).
Writes prose, radio and TV plays, film scripts.

1959   *Ein Mann steht vor der Tür (A Man Stands in Front of
the Door)*. Dr (with Brigitte Reimann; based on radio
play). Pr 1961. Radio version in *Die Reihe*, Aufbau
1960.

1960   *Sieben Scheffel Salz (Seven Bushels of Salt)*. Com
(with Brigitte Reimann; based on radio play). Pr 19-
67 Dsdn. Radio version in *Hörspieljahrbuch 1*, Henschel 1961.

1974   *Er und sie (He and She)*. Com. Pr 1975 Rostock.

PLENZDORF, Ulrich
26 Oct 1934 Berlin –
Studied Marxism and Leninism, Lpzg; 1955-58 stagehand DEFA;
58-59 GDR Army; 59-63 studied at Film HS Potsdam; 75 writer-
in-residence, Oberlin College; now independent author in Berlin. 1971 Heinrich Greif Prize, FDGB Prize, 73 Heinrich Mann
Prize, 78 Ingeborg Bachmann Prize. Writes prose and film sce-
narios.

1972   *Die neuen Leiden des jungen W. (The New Sorrows of
Young W.)*. Dr (based on film script and novel). Pr
1972 Halle. *Sinn & Form* 1972/2. *Spec* 20, 1974. Suhrkamp 1973. Henschel 1974. "The New Pain of the Young
W." (Engl. tr Christopher Silver), Pr 1977 Bates Col-

PLENZDORF (cont'd)

lege, Lewiston, ME. *The New Sufferings of Young W.* (Engl. tr Kenneth P. Wilson), New York: Ungar, 1979.

1974 *Buridans Esel (Buridan's Donkey).* Com (based on novel by Günter de Bruyn). Pr 1975 Lpzg. Henschel 1986.

1979 *Legende vom Glück ohne Ende (The Legend of Happiness without End).* Dr (based on film script and novel). Pr 1983 Schwedt. Henschel 1986 (with *Buridans Esel*).

PODEHL, Peter
Actor.

1948 *Kommen und Gehen (Coming and Going).* Dr. Pr 1948 Weimar.

POLONSKI, Georg
23 Mar 1920 Antonin –
Actor. Writes poetry, short stories, novels, TV plays.

1974 *Warten wir den Montag ab (Let's Wait until Monday).* Juv. Pr 1975 Th. d. Freundschaft, Berlin.
Der falsche Schwiegersohn (The False Son-in-Law). Com.
Frechdachs Willibald (Willibald the Rascal). Juv.
Weihnachtslegende (Christmas Legend). Dr.

PONS, Peter

1970 *Feuer im Dorf (Fire in the Village).* Dr. Lpzg: Hofmeister, 1971.

PÖRSCHMANN, Jürgen

1970 *Zeit der Störche (The Season of the Storks).* Dr. Pr 1971 Nordhausen.

PREIL, Hans-Joachim
Singer and librettist.

Doppelt gebacken (Baked Twice). Com.

1970 *Die Zwickmühle (The Dilemma).* Mus Lib (M Jochen Allihn). Pr 1971 Rostock.

1980 *Hände hoch, sonst knallt's! (Hands Up or I Shoot!)* Mus Lib (M Rudi Werion). Pr 1981 Zeitz.
Ja, so ein Mann bin ich (Yes, That's the Kind of Man I Am). Com.

PREISSLER, Helmut
16 Dec 1925 Cottbus –
Construction worker; served in WW II, then POW 1945-47; 48-55 teacher Cottbus; 55-57 I.Lit Lpzg, then dramaturg Kleist Th., Fkft/O. 1960 Erich Weinert Medal, 61 FDGB Prize. Writes poetry.

1960 *Blast das Feuer an (Blow on the Fire).* Dr (with Werner Bauer).

1968 *Kinder werden Leute (Children Become People).* Revue (M Gunther Reinecker). Pr 1969 Fkft/O.

1978 *Der König soll geigen (The King Is Supposed to Play the Violin).* Juv Op Lib (M Gunther Reinecker). Pr 1979 Fkft/O.

PREUSS, Gunter
15 Sep 1940 Lpzg -
After various occupations, studied art in Berlin 1958-60; 70-
73 I. Lit Lpzg. 1979 Erich Weinert Medal. Writes children's
books, novels, short stories, radio plays, film scripts.
1976   *Muzelkopp (Muddlehead)*. Juv. Pr 1976 Lpzg.
1979   *Ameisengeschichten (Ant Stories)*. Juv. Pr 1980 Pio-
        nierth., KMSt.

PROBST, Anneliese
23 Mar 1926 Düsseldorf -
Editor; began writing 1950; now lives in Halle. Writes radio
plays, film scripts, children's books.
1953   *Der steinerne Mühlmann (The Stone Millhand)*. Juv
        (based on film script). Pr 1956 Th. d. jg. Garde, Hal-
        le. Henschel 1954.
1964   *Der Zauberring (The Magic Ring)*. Juv. Pr 1964 Wei-
        mar.

PRODÖHL, Günter
21 May 1920 Berlin -
1936 became merchant's apprentice; 49-54 journalist, since 54
independent author; now lives in Potsdam. 1962 Heinrich Greif
Prize. Writes detective stories, radio and TV plays, ilm
scripts.
1960   *Kippentütchen (Paper Cones)*. Dr. Pr 1961 Halber-
        stadt.
1963   *Affäre Corinth (The Corinth Affair)*. Dr. Pr 1963 Ei-
        senach.

RADVANYI, Netty Reiling see Anna SEGHERS

RAHN, Karlheinz
30 Mar 1920 Brunshaupten –
1937-39 studied at School of Advertising, Berlin; served in WW II, then British POW; 49-52 asst. director and dramaturg Th. am Schiffbauerdamm, Berlin; 53-61 TV dramaturg; since 61 independent author. Writes prose, radio and TV plays.

1968   *Mordsache Stagnelius (The Stagnelius Murder Case)*. Dr. Pr 1968 Brandenburg.
1969   *Robin Hood*. Dr. Pr 1970 Dsdn/Radebeul.
1972   *‹Juro› Janosik – ein Held der Berge (‹Yuro› Yanosik – A Hero of the Mountains)*. Dr. Pr 1973 Annaberg.
1973   *Der verlegene Magistrat (The Embarrassed Magistrate)*. Op Lib (based on anecdote by Kleist; M Kurt Dietmar Richter). Pr 1978 Cottbus.
1982   *Der Aufruhr des Michael Kohlhaas (The Rebellion of Michael Kohlhaas)*. Op Lib (based on novella by Kleist; M Kurt Dietmar Richter).

RAINER, Wolfgang
    Die Bremer Stadtmusikanten (The Town Musicians of Bremen). Juv Op Lib (based on Grimm). Pr 1966 Bernburg.
    Potto, der faule Affe (Potto, the Lazy Monkey). Juv Mus Lib (with Kurt Frank-Zwarg). Pr 1967 Bernburg.
    Mascha und der Bär (Masha and the Bear). Juv Mus Lib (based on Russian fairy tale; M Siegfried Tiefensee). Pr 1968 Bernburg.
    Till Eulenspiegel in Bernburg. Juv Bl Lib. Pr 1972 Bernburg.
1974   *Der starke Hans ‹und seine Brüder› (Strong Jack ‹and His Brothers›)*. Juv. Pr 1975 Bernburg.
1979   *Tischlein, deck dich! (The Table, the Ass, and the Stick)*. Juv (based on Grimm). Pr 1979 Bernburg.
1984   *Von Märchen zu Märchen (From Fairy Tale to Fairy Tale)*. Juv. Pr 1985 Bernburg.

RAITHEL, Hugo
6 Apr 1932 Schwarzenbach –
Attended MHS Cologne 1951-52, Munich 52-54; 55-57 choir conductor Bautzen; 57-61 solo rehearsal pianist, Km.Op; since 61 music director Bautzen. Composer.
1983   *Hans Nasehoch (Jack Nose-in-the-Air)*. Juv Op (based on fairy tale by Serge Mikhalkov). Pr 1983 Bautzen.

RAUCHFUSS, Hildegard Maria
22 Feb 1918 Breslau (now Wroclaw, Poland) –
After high school, took voice instruction; then became bank employee and writer; now lives in Lpzg. 1963 Lpzg Prize, 73 Johannes Becher Medal, 75 National Order of Merit. Writes poetry, songs, stories, radio and TV plays.
1977   *Falsch verbunden (Wrong Number)*. On (based on TV play). Pr 1984 Lpzg.

REICH, Konrad   (Pseud. Stefan PÄTSCH)
29 June 1928 Magdeburg –
Worked in book store; attended evening courses Univ Lpzg, later studied German literature Rostock; since 1959 editor Hinstorff Verlag.   1970 Culture Prize Rostock.   Writes essays and
TV films.
1972   *Versuch mit Upsilon ‹Einesteils der Liebe wegen› (Ex-
          periment with Y ‹On the One Hand, Because of Love›)*.
          Com   (based on story by Sigbjörn Hölmebakk).   Pr 1972
          Rostock.
1984   *Lieber Ehm Welk (Dear Ehm Welk)*. Dr   (with Hans
          Lucke).   Pr 1985 Rostock.

REICHWALD, Fritz ‹Fred›
15 Mar 1921 Berlin – 17 Jan 1963 Berlin
Jewish parents killed in concentration camp; emigrated to England, Australia, India; returned to Germany 1947; 55-56 studied I.Lit Lpzg. 1959 National Prize. Wrote TV scripts.
1951   *Dachziegel oder Bomben (Roof Tiles or Bombs)*.   Dr.
          Halle: Mitteldt. Verlag, 1954.
1956   *Das Haberfeldtreiben (Judgment by the People)*.   Dr
          (based on TV play).   Pr 1957 Eisleben.
1957   *Das Wagnis der Maria Diehl (Maria Diehl's Bold Ven-
          ture)*. Dr (based on TV play).   Pr 1959 Anklam.   Auf-
          bau 1959.
1957   *Verdacht auf Dieter (Dieter Under Suspicion)*.   Juv.
          Lpzg: Hofmeister, 1957.   Henschel 1962.
1959   *Der Hektarjäger (The Acreage Hunter)*.   Dr   (based on
          TV play).   *Das Wagnis der Maria Diehl*, 1959.
1960   *Erzieher im Examen (The Examination of the Educator)*.
          Dr (based on TV play).   Pr 1960 Potsdam.   Aufbau 1961.

REIF, Guido
31 Mar 1902 Mährisch-Schönburg – 6 Dec 1953 Dresden
Worked for Radio Dresden.   Wrote novels, short stories, radio
plays.
1947   *Der Rebell (The Rebel)*.   Dr.   Pr 1948 Bautzen.
1949   *Deutsche Tragödie (German Tragedy)*. Dr. Pr 1949 Dsdn.

REILING, Netty   see Anna SEGHERS

REIMANN, Brigitte
21 July 1933 Burg/Magdeburg – 20 Feb 1973 Berlin
Worked as teacher and in various other occupations;   then became author.   1962 FDGB Prize (with Siegfried Pitschmann), 65
Heinrich Mann Prize.   Wrote stories, radio plays.
1959   *Ein Mann steht vor der Tür (A Man Stands in Front of
          the Door)*.   Dr (with Siegfried Pitschmann; based on
          radio play).   Pr 1961.   Radio version in *Die Reihe*,
          Aufbau 1960.
1960   *Sieben Scheffel Salz (Seven Bushels of Salt)*.   Com
          (with Siegfried Pitschmann; based on radio play).   Pr
          1967 Dsdn.   Radio version in *Hörspieljahrbuch 1*, Hen-
          schel 1961.

REIMANN (cont'd)
1978   *Franziska Linkerhand*. Dr (based on 1973 novel frag-
        ment; dramatized posthumously by Bärbel Jaksch and
        Heiner Maaß). Pr 1978 Schwerin. *TdZ* 1978/6.

REIME, Paul G.
        Der Wundervogel (The Magic Bird). Op Lib (based on
        Chinese legend; M Guido Masanetz). Pr 1955 Dsdn/Ra-
        debeul.

REINHOLD, Heide
        Das blaue Pferdchen (The Little Blue Horse). Juv
        (based on Maria Clara Machado).
1969   *Wie Recke, Katze und Maus den Teufel besiegen (How
        Knight, Cat, and Mouse Conquer the Devil)*. Juv (with
        Joachim Maaß; based on Byelorussian fairy tale). Pr
        1972 Th. f. jg. Zuschauer, Mgdbg.

REISSINGER, Horst
1971   *Peter der Froschkönig (Peter, the Frog King)*. Juv.
        Pr 1971 Zeitz.
1974   *Aschenputtel (Cinderella)*. Juv (based on Grimm). Pr
        1974 Wittenberg.

RENTZSCH, Gerhard
24 Apr 1926 Leipzig –
1941-43 studied engineering Lpzg; service in WW II, 45-46 British POW; became teacher, then studied I.Lit Lpzg; 52 radio
dramaturg, 57-66 chief dramaturg Radio Berlin. 1965 Lessing
Prize. Writes essays, radio and TV plays.
1960   *Altweibersommer (Indian Summer)*. Dr (based on radio
        play). Pr 1967 Dsdn. Radio version in *Hörspieljahr-
        buch 1*, Henschel 1961.

RET, Joachim
26 Dec 1912 Chemnitz (now Karl Marx Stadt) – 20 Feb 1983 Berlin
1928-31 commercial high school in Chemnitz; 32-40 worked as
traveling salesman; 40-45 war service, then Russian POW; 1948
returned home; 54-56 studied German literature Lpzg and Berlin; then editor. Wrote stories, radio and TV scripts.
1960   *Die Zange (The Pliers)*. Dr. Pr 1960.

RICHTER, Egon
12 Dec 1932 Bansin/Usedom –
Attended high school in Anklam; studied German literature at
Humboldt Univ., Berlin 1951-53; 55-56 reporter for journal
"Sonntag"; journalist and editor. Johannes R. Becher Medal,
Heinrich Heine Prize. Writes stories and novels.
1983   *Der lange Weg nach Afrika (The Long Road to Africa)*.
        Com (based on story "Der Lügner und die Bombe"). Pr
        1984 Rostock.

RICHTER, Hans Michael
20 Nov 1923 -
Chief dramaturg and stage director Weimar and DT; now Deputy
General Manager, Lpzg Th.
1965   *Guyana Johnny*. Op Lib (based on Nancy Bush, "The Su-
         gar Reapers"; M Alan Bush). Pr 1966 Lpzg.
1979   *Drei Perücken (Three Wigs)*. Mus Lib (based on Johann
         Nestroy; M Jens Uwe Günther). Pr 1979 Lpzg.
1982   *Kafkas Schloß (Kafka's Castle)*. Dr (based on novel
         by Franz Kafka). Pr 1983 Lpzg.

RICHTER, Helmut
30 Nov 1933 Freudenthal (now Bruntal, Czechoslovakia) -
1945 moved to Saxony, worked on farm; 1950 Lpzg, became apprentice machinist; 56-58 studied physics; 58-61 engineer; 61-
64 studied literature, became journalist and author; since 70
conducts poetry seminar, I. Lit. Lpzg. Writes poetry, prose,
radio and TV plays.
1967   *Gute Zeit für Liebe (A Good Time for Love)*. Mus Lib.
         Pr 1967 Mgdbg.
1970   *Kleine Gärten - große Leute (Small Gardens - Big
         People)*. Com (with Peter Gosse, Christoph Hamm, Joa-
         chim Nowotny, Hans Pfeiffer). Pr 1971 Lpzg.
1974   *Kommst du mit nach Madras? (Are You Coming along to
         Madras?)* Com. Pr 1974 Lpzg.

RICHTER, Kurt Dietmar
Composer and librettist.
         Hans Clauert Eulenspiegel.
         Adam und Eva.
1963   *Pazifik 1960 (Pacific 1960)*. Op. Pr 1964 Döbeln.
1966   *Sie haben aber Glück! (Aren't You Lucky!)* Mus. Pr
         1966 Döbeln.
1969   *Sekundenoper (Instant Opera)*. Op. Pr 1970 Greifswald.
1983   *Marx spielte gern Schach (Marx Liked to Play Chess)*.
         Chamber Op (with Nils Werner). Pr 1985 Stralsund.

RICHTER, Manfred
16 Oct 1929 Dresden -
After various occupations, studied at Academy of Music and
Theater, Dsdn, 1950; then attended DEFA Film School, Berlin
School of Drama, 56-59 I.Lit Lpzg; dramaturg Weimar and Dessau; 63-66 script writer DEFA, since then independent author;
lives in Dsdn. Writes stories, criticism, radio and film
scripts.
1954   *Lotos und der Knecht Mao Te (Lotos and the Hired Man
         Mao Te)*. Juv. Pr 1955 Th. d. Freundschaft, Berlin.
1955   *Das Zauberfaß (The Magic Barrel)*. Juv (based on Chi-
         nese motifs). Pr 1955 Th. d. Freundschaft, Berlin.
         Lpzg: Hofmeister, 1957.
1957   *Die Familie der guten Leute (The Good People's Fami-
         ly)*. Dr. Pr 1958.
1958   *Kommando von links (Command from the Left)*. Dr. Pr
         1958 Weimar.

RICHTER, Manfred (cont'd)

1959   *Die Insel Gottes (The Isle of God).*   Dr.   Pr 1959 Rostock. *Zeitgenössische Dramatik*, Henschel 1962.

1960   *Ehrengericht oder Der Tag ist noch nicht zu Ende (Court of Honor or The Day Is Not Yet Over).*   Dr.   Pr 1961 Weimar.

1961   *‹Das› Rübchen (‹The› Little Turnip).*   Juv   (based on Pavel Malyarevsky).   Pr 1965 Senftenberg.

1962   *Was vom Himmel kommen soll (What Is Supposed to Come from Heaven).*   Juv Mus Lib (M H. Irrgang).

RICHTER, Peter

1972   *Rumpelstilzchen (Rumpelstiltskin).*   Juv   (based on Grimm).   Pr 1972 Parchim.

1973   *Hänsel und Gretel.*   Juv   (based on Grimm).   Pr 1973 Parchim.

1974   *König Drosselbart (King Thrushbeard).*   Juv (based on Grimm).   Pr 1974 Parchim.

1976   *Vom Fischer und seiner Frau (The Fisherman and His Wife).*   Juv (based on Grimm).   Pr 1977 Parchim.

RICHTER, Siegfried

1971   *Schneeweißchen und Rosenrot (Snow-White and Rose-Red).* Juv (based on Grimm).   Pr 1971 Freiberg.

RICHTER-ROSTALSKI, Gisela
16 Jan 1927 Leipzig –
Studied acting School of Drama Lpzg; then member of ensemble Lpzg and DT; since 1970 independent author. Writes radio and TV plays, film scripts.

1976   *Ich gehe nach Hause (I Am Going Home).*   Juv.   Pr 1977 Th. d. jg. Garde, Halle.

RINECKER, Wolfgang
23 Mar 1931 Bürden – 20 Dec 1982 Meiningen
1949 graduated high school, went to FRG, Switzerland, France; returned to GDR 50; until 60 various occupations; 60-62 studied history, classical languages, and theology Jena; after 62 independent author in Meiningen. Wrote short stories and novels.

1973   *Das Spiel vom argen Schalk Till Eulenspiegel (The Play about the Mischievous Rogue Till Eulenspiegel).* Juv (with Albert Pasch).   Pr 1974 Meiningen.

1977   *Münchhausen.*   Com (with Albert Pasch).   Pr 1978 Meiningen.

ROEHRICHT, Karl Hermann
12 Oct 1928 Leipzig –
Insurance agent; service in WW II, American POW; 1946-50 construction worker, carpenter, puppeteer; 51 studied painting Academy of Arts, W. Berlin; traveled to Italy, France, Spain; 60 returned to GDR, painter and author; lives in Berlin. 1970 Honorable Mention, Drama Contest; 79 Art Prize. Writes ballads, short stories, radio plays.

ROEHRICHT (cont'd)

1972   *Monologe I ‹Meine Privatgalerie› (Monologues I ‹My Private Gallery›)*. Dr (with Günther Rücker; based on radio play). Pr 1974 DT. *Meine Privatgalerie*, Henschel 1975.

1974   *Familie Birnchen (Family Pearlet)*. Com. Pr 1975 MG.

1979   *Friedas letzter Vormittag oder Der Tod einer Kleinbürgerin (Frieda's Last Morning or The Death of a Petty Bourgeois Woman)*. Com. Pr 1979 Schwerin.

ROSE, Andreas

1967   *Die Kinder des Kapitän Grant (Captain Grant's Children)*. Juv (with Ewald Autengruber; based on Jules Verne). Pr 1968 Th. d. jg. Garde, Halle.

ROSENLÖCHER, Thomas

29 Aug 1947 –

Served in GDR Army, then went back to school, graduated 1970; studied business management; 76-79 I.Lit Lpzg; dramaturg Th. d. jg. Generation, Dsdn; since 82 independent author in Dsdn. 1982 Poetry Prize.

1980   *Die Bremer Stadtmusikanten (The Town Musicians of Bremen)*. Juv (based on Grimm). Pr 1981 Th. d. jg. Generation, Dsdn.

1982   *Blitzdonnerschock (Thunderation!)* Juv. Pr 1982 Th. d. jg. Generation, Dsdn.

RÖTTGER, Heinz

6 Nov 1909 Herford – 26 Aug 1977 Dessau

1928-34 studied at Academy of Music, Munich; 34-45 rehearsal conductor Augsburg; 48-51 musical director Stralsund, 51-54 Rostock, 54-77 Dessau. 1961 Händel Prize, 62 Peace Prize. Composer and librettist.

1946   *Bellmann*. Op.

1959   *Der Heiratsantrag (The Marriage Proposal)*. Op (based on Chekhov). Pr 1961 Mgdbg.

1961   *Die Frauen von Troja (The Women of Troy)*. Op (with Eva Johnn). Pr 1964 Dessau.

1963   *Der Kreis (The Circle)*. Op. Pr 1964 Dessau.

1965   *Der Weg nach Palermo (The Road to Palermo)*. Op (with E. Weeber-Fried). Pr 1967 Dessau

1976   *Spanisches Capriccio (Spanish Capriccio)*. Op (with Elke Schneider; based on Tirso de Molina). Pr 1976 Dessau.

RUDOLPHI   see Kurt R. NEUBERT

RÜCKER, Günther   (Pseud. Johann GÜNTHER)

2 Feb 1924 Reichenberg (now Liberec, Czechoslovakia) –

Served in WW II 1942-45, then POW; 47-49 studied directing at Th. HS Lpzg; 49-51 radio and film director Lpzg; since 51 lives in Berlin. 1956, 71, and 80 National Prize; 66 Heinrich Greif Prize and Erich Weinert Medal; 72 AdK; 1980 Grand Prix Film Festival Karlovy Vary. Writes stories, radio and film scripts.

RÜCKER (cont'd)
1955   *Pierrot und Colombine ‹Harlekin und Colombine›*. On
        (based on radio play; incidental M Klaus Zoephel). Pr
        1956 Güstrow.
1961   *Der Platz am Fenster (The Window Seat)*. Dr (based on
        radio play). Pr 1963 Mgdbg. Radio version *Hörspiele
        2*, Henschel 1962.
1968   *Der Herr Schmidt. Ein deutsches Spektakel mit Poli-
        zei und Musik (Mr. Schmidt. A German Spectacle with
        Police and Music)*. Com. Pr 1969 DT. *TdZ 1969/2.
        Neue Stücke*, Henschel 1971. *Sieben Takte Tango*, Re-
        clam 1979.
1969   *Der Nachbar des Herrn Pansa (Mr. Panza's Neighbor)*.
        Com (based on Anatoly Lunacharsky, "Der befreite Don
        Quixote"). Pr 1969 DT.
1972   *Monologe I ‹Meine Privatgalerie› (Monologues I ‹My
        Private Gallery›)*. Dr (with Karl Hermann Roehricht;
        based on radio play). Pr 1974 DT. *Meine Privatgale-
        rie*, Henschel 1975.
1974   *Schalmeienstunde (The Hour of the Shepherd's Pipe)*.
        On (based on radio play). Pr 1974 VB (Part of pro-
        gram under collective title "Spektakel 2").

RÜEDI, Hans   see Friedrich WOLF

RÜLICKE-WEILER, Käthe
Brecht collaborator at DT.
1952   *Bonn im Spiegel (Bonn in the Mirror)*. Com (with Klaus
        Hubalek). Pr 1953 BE.

SABO, Wolf
1984   *Verteidigung (Defense)*. Dr. Pr 1984 Quedlinburg.

SAEGER, Uwe
1948 Ueckermünde –
1966-70 studied pedagogy in Greifswald, 70-76 school teacher;
since then independent author; lives in Ueckermünde. Writes
novels, short stories, radio and TV plays, film scripts.
    Nöhr. Dr (based on novel).
    Warten auf Schnee (Waiting for Snow). Dr (based on
    short story).
1977   *Das Vorkommnis (The Happening)*. Dr. Pr 1978 DT. *TdZ*
    1978/4.
1978   *Flugversuch (Attempted Flight)*.   Dr (based on film;
    incidental M Thomas Bürkholz). Reading 1980 Lpzg. Pr
    1983 Lpzg. *TdZ* 1983/7.
1978   *Im Glashaus (In the Glass House)*. Dr (based on TV
    play). Pr 1983 Neustrelitz.
1979   *Schuldspiel (Game of Guilt)*. Dr. Rev 1983 as Außer-
    halb von Schuld.
1983   *Außerhalb von Schuld (Beyond Guilt)*. Dr (rev of
    Schuldspiel). Pr 1984 Lpzg. *TdZ* 1985/1.

SAKOWSKI, Helmut
1 June 1924 Jüterbog –
1941-43 apprentice forester, then service in WW II, POW until
46;   47-49 studied Institute for Forestry, then worked in Ministry of Agriculture and Forestry; since 1961 independent author; lives in Neustrelitz. Member, Central Committee of SED,
AdK; National Prize 1959, 65, 68, and 72; 63 Lessing Prize,
64 Fritz Reuter Prize, 69 FDGB Prize. Writes prose, radio and
TV scripts.
1957   *Die Entscheidung der Lene Mattke (Lene Mattke's Deci-
    sion)*. Dr (based on radio and TV play). Pr 1959 Hal-
    berstadt. Henschel 1965. *Wege übers Land*, Henschel
    1984.
1959   *Die Säge im Langenmoor (The Sawmill in Langenmoor)*.
    Dr (with Hans Müncheberg). Aufbau 1960.
1960   *Weiberzwist und Liebeslist (Women's Quarrels and
    Love's Cunning)*. Com (based on TV play). Pr 1961 Mad-
    geburg.
1960-62 *Steine im Weg (Stones in the Path)*. Dr (based on TV
    play). Pr 1963 MG. *TdZ* 1963/10. Henschel 1965. *So-
    zialistische Dramatik*, Henschel 1968. *Wege übers Land*,
    984.
1964   *Sommer in Heidkau (A Summer in Heidkau)*. Dr (based
    on TV play). Pr 1965 Neustrelitz. *TdZ* 1964/24. Rev
    1965 as Letzter Sommer in Heidkau.
1965   *Letzter Sommer in Heidkau (Last Summer in Heidkau)*.
    Dr (rev of Sommer in Heidkau). Pr 1966 Putbus. Hen-
    schel 1967. *Wege übers Land*, 1984.

SAKOWSKI (cont'd)

1968   *Wege übers Land (Cross-Country Roads)*. Dr (based on TV play). Pr 1969 Lpzg. Halle: Mitteldeutscher Verlag, 1969. Henschel 1984.

1970   *Die Schule der Polzins (The School of the Polzins)*. On. Pr 1970 Halle (part of program under collective title "Anregung II").

1977   *Die Verschworenen (The Conspirators)*. Dr (based on TV play). Pr 1977 Neustrelitz.

1983   *Daniel Druskat.* Dr (based on TV script; dramatized by Joseph-Adolf Weindich). Pr 1984 Neustrelitz.

SALCHOW, Werner
16 Nov 1902 Berlin - 21 Mar 1964 Muchau/Anklam
Studied law 1921-25, then worked as administrative attorney for Weimar government; 33 dismissed from state service; after 45 held various state and cultural positions.

1954   *Die verschwundene Brieftasche (The Missing Wallet)*. Com.

1955   *Der Teufel im Haus (The Devil in the House)*. Dr. Pr 1956 Neustrelitz.

1958   *Ein Liebestrunk ‹Himbeersaft und Liebe› (A Love Potion ‹Raspberry Syrup and Love›)*. Com. Pr 1958 Anklam.

1959   *Schritt der Millionen (Stride of Millions)*. Dr.

1960   *Lenchen Demuth.* Dr.

1962   *Nachts wenn die Katzen grau sind (At Night, When All Cats Are Grey)*. Com. Pr 1962 Anklam.

1963   *Die Hähne von Flotow (The Roosters of Flotow)*. Com. Pr 1964 Anklam.

SALOMON, Horst
6 May 1929 Pillkollen (now Debrowelsk, USSR) - 20 June 1972 Gera
Attended high school in Allenstein (now Olsztyn, Poland); 1949-50 FDJ functionary in Thuringia; 51-58 worked as miner; 58-61 studied I. Lit. Lpzg, then miner again; after 65 independent author in Gera. Member AdK; 1960 Erich Weinert Medal, 64 National Prize, 66 City of Gera Prize.

1960   *Vortrieb (Propulsion)*. Dr. Pr 1961 Workers' Th, Wismut. *Junge Kunst* 1961/7-8.

1962   *Der Hund des Gärtners (The Gardener's Dog)*. Com (based on Lope de Vega). Pr 1969 Nordhausen.

1963-64 *Katzengold (Fool's Gold)*. Dr. Pr 1964 Gera. *TdZ* 1964/16. *Zeitgenössische Dramatik*, Henschel 1965.

1966   *Der ‹Ein› Lorbaß (The ‹A› Ne'er-Do-Well)*. Com. Pr 1967 Gera. *TdZ* 1967/7. *Zeitgenössische Dramatik*, Henschel 1968. *Neue Stücke*, Henschel 1971.

1968   *Juana ‹von Joachim›*. Op Lib. Pr 1968 Gera.

1969   *Genosse Vater (Comrade Father)*. Dr. Pr 1969 Gera.

1970   *Hausbesuche (House Visits)*. On. Pr 1970 Halle (part of program under collective title "Anregung II").

SAUER, Günther
1918 –
1946   *Signal Stalingrad.* Dr. Pr 1946 Mgdbg.
1946   *Der Staatsstreich (The Coup d'Etat).* Com. Pr 1947
        Kamenz.

SCHÄFER, Paul Kanut
16 Apr 1922 Dresden –
After high school, drafted 1941; at end of war, became tutor;
48–51 editor of journal "Junge Welt"; then various occupations; 57–59 studied I.Lit Lpzg; since then independent author; lives in Berlin. Writes children's books, short stories, novels.
1958   *Die Brüder Seebald (The Seebald Brothers).* Dr. Pr
        1959 Plauen.
1984   *1:0 für Onkel (1:0 in Uncle's Favor).* Juv. Pr 1985
        Plauen.

SCHÄFER-ROSE, Helmut
1960   *Beethoven.* Dr. Pr 1961 Meißen.

SCHALLER, Rudolf
16 Aug 1891 Halle – 25 Mar 1984 Schwerin
1912–14 studied German literature, history, philosophy, and
theater history in Kiel; 14–19 service in WW I, then journalist, editor, and theater critic in Munich, Schwerin, Rostock;
since 1941 translator. 1956 Translation Prize, Ministry of
Culture, 64 F. C. Weiskopf Prize, 70 Dr. h.c. Münster. Wrote
prose.
1924   *Nordische Hochzeit (Nordic Wedding).* Dr. Pr 1924.
        Berlin: Wolf Heyer, 1932.
        Antigone. Dr (tr of Sophocles). Pr 1949.
        Kain (Cain). Dr (tr of Byron). Pr 1967.
        Der Kaffeehauspolitiker (The Coffee-House Politician).
        Com (tr of Henry Fielding). Pr 1956.
        Shakespeare translations, in *Shakespeares Werke* (four
        vols.), Aufbau 1960–67:
        Macbeth. Dr. Pr 1952.
        *Die lustigen Weiber von Windsor (The Merry Wives of
        Windsor).* Com. Pr 1952.
        König Lear (King Lear). Dr. Pr 1955.
        *Hamlet, Prinz von Dänemark (Hamlet, Prince of Den-
        mark).* Dr. Pr 1957.
        Maß für Maß (Measure for Measure). Com. Pr 1968.
        Romeo und Julia. Dr. Pr 1959.
        Othello. Dr. Pr 1959.
        Die Komödie der Irrungen (A Comedy of Errors). Com.
        Pr 1960.
        *Die Zähmung der Widerspenstigen (The Taming of the
        Shrew).* Com. Pr 1961.
        Viel Lärm um Nichts (Much Ado about Nothing). Com.
        Pr 1962.
        König Richard der Dritte (King Richard III.). Dr. Pr
        1964.

SCHALLER, Rudolf (cont'd)
>   *Julius Caesar*. Dr. Pr 1965.
>   *Der Sturm (The Tempest)*. Com. Pr 1967.
>   *Ein Sommernachtstraum (A Midsummer Night's Dream)*. Com. Pr 1967.
>   *König Heinrich der Vierte (King Henry IV.)*. Dr. Pr 1970.
>   *König Richard der Zweite (King Richard II.)*. Dr. Pr 1970.

SCHALLER, Wolfgang
20 Apr 1940 Breslau (now Wroclaw, Poland) –
Teacher; 1964-67 I.Lit Lpzg; cabaret author; since 1970 dramaturg cabaret "Herkuleskeule," Dsdn. 1981 FDGB Prize.
1970   *Des Königs allerneuste Kleider (The King's Brand-New Clothes)*. Juv (based on Hans Christian Andersen, "The Emperor's New Clothes"). Pr 1970 Zwickau. Henschel 1983.
1976   *Ein kleines bißchen Stück (A Little Bit of a Play)*. Com (based on Dsdn cabaret pieces). Pr 1980 Zwickau.
1979   *Bürger schützt eure Anlagen oder Wem die Mütze paßt (Citizens Protect Your Parks or If the Cap Fits)*. Com (with Peter Ensikat). Pr 1982 Stralsund. Henschel 1983.

SCHAUB, Eugen
1963   *Das Brigadekind (The Child of the Brigade)*. Com (with Martin Elbers). Pr 1963 Halle.

SCHEER, Maximilian   (Real name Maximilian Walter SCHLIEPER-SCHEER)
22 Apr 1896 Haan/Rh. – 3 Feb 1978 Berlin
Studied literature and theater history in Cologne, then journalist and critic; 1933 emigrated to France; interned 39, escaped via Portugal to US, worked as press agent; returned to Germany 47, became editor-in-chief of journal "Ost und West"; 49-52 section head of Radio Berlin; then independent author. 1962 National Prize. Wrote stories, radio and TV scripts.
1952   *Das Brandenburger Tor (The Brandenburg Gate)*. Dr. Pr 1953 MG.
1953   *Die Rosenbergs*. Dr.
1954   *Hotelboy Ed Martin ‹Die Wahl› (Bellhop Ed Martin ‹The Choice›)*. Dr (based on Albert Maltz and G. Sklar; first written as radio play). Pr 1954 DT.
1960   *Hassan und der Scheich (Hassan and the Sheik)*. Dr. Aufbau 1960.
1966   *Die Prinzessin von Sansibar (The Princess of Zanzibar)*. Dr. Engl. excerpts in *Cross Section*, Lpzg, 19-70 (tr Marjorie Meyer).

SCHEINERT, Andreas
Dramaturg Mgdbg.
1975   *Die Schildbürger (The Burghers of Schilda)*. Com. Pr 1975 Schwerin.

SCHELL, H.   see Horst SEEGER

SCHIEFHALS, Jakob   see Otto MÜLLER-GLÖSA

SCHILL, Rolf
1933 Tarutino, Bessarabia (now USSR) -
Studied piano, composition, and conducting at MHS Stuttgart;
since 1970 orchestra conductor, Hans Otto Th., Potsdam; wrote
music for some 50 stage works, also some libretti.
1976   *Madame Favart ‹Schauspieler müßte man sein›* (Madame
        Favart ‹*You Ought to Be an Actor*›). Mus (new adapta-
        tion; based on Jacques Offenbach). Pr 1977 Potsdam.
1978   *Julius und Romea.* Mus.

SCHILLING, Tom
23 Jan 1928 Esperstedt/Halle -
Director of dance ensemble and choreographer, 1946-52 Lpzg,
53-56 Weimar, 56-64 Dsdn, since 65 Km. Op; Prof. Th.HS Lpzg.
1982 National Prize.
        Schwarze Vögel (Black Birds). Bl Lib (with Bernd Köl-
        linger; M Georg Katzer). Pr Km. Op.
        Wahlverwandtschaften (Elective Affinities). Bl Lib
        (with Bernd Köllinger; based on Goethe; M Franz Schu-
        bert).

SCHIRMER, Bernd
23 Feb 1940 Leipzig -
After high school, served two years in GDR Army; 1960-64 studied English and German literature Karl Marx Univ, Lpzg; dramaturg, GDR radio; 1969-72 taught German Univ. of Algiers,
then returned to Berlin, worked as dramaturg GDR TV. Hans
Machwitza Prize; 1981 and 84 Radio Play Prize. Writes short
stories, novels, radio, TV and film scripts.
1979   *Ein Stuhl bleibt leer (One Chair Stays Empty).* Juv
        (based on radio play). Pr 1979 Th. d. jg. Welt, Lpzg.
        Ceremoniel pour un combat. Dr (tr of Claude Prin).
        Kammertheater (Chamber Theater). Dr (tr of Michael
        Vinaver, "Theatre de chambre").

SCHLEEF, Einar
17 Jan 1944 Sangerhausen -
Now lives in W. Berlin. Writes radio plays.
1975   *Der Fischer und seine Frau (The Fisherman and His
        Wife).* Juv (based on Grimm). Pr 1976 Dsdn.

SCHLEIF, Klaus
1973   *So scharf wird nie ein Mann (No Man Ever Gets That
        Sharp).* Dr. Pr 1973 Erfurt.

SCHLEINITZ, Karl Heinz
11 July 1921 Brieskow -
Merchant's apprentice, then service in WW II; after 1945 several occupations; 52 editor of "Neue Rundschau" and "Neues
Deutschland"; since 61 independent author in Berlin. 1961

SCHLEINITZ (cont'd)
FDGB Prize. Writes essays, children's books, short stories,
TV plays.
> *Ein Sommer und so weiter (A Summer and So Forth)*. Com.
> Pr 1970 Dsdn.
> *Mein Fräulein Frau (Miss Wife of Mine)*. Com. Pr 1972
> Rostock.

SCHLESINGER, Klaus
9 Jan 1937 Berlin -
After school, worked in chemistry laboratory; later studied
chemistry and worked in industrial research lab; 1963-66 journalist, then independent author; 79 expelled from GDR Writers
Assoc.; since 80 lives in W. Berlin. 1956 Juvenile Radio Play
Prize. Writes essays, novels, short stories, film scripts,
radio plays.
1978   *Der Niedergang des Kleinhandels   (The Decline of the
Retail Trade)*. Com. Pr 1979 Halle.

SCHLIEPER-SCHEER, Maximilian Walter   see Maximilian SCHEER

SCHLOSSAREK, Erich
22 Apr 1928 Spremberg -
Attended commercial high school; 1944 drafted; 46-50 teacher;
50-54 studied Teachers' College, Potsdam; 54 left for FRG,
worked at various jobs; returned to GDR 55, became teacher in
Potsdam; since 65 instructor for film and TV, Film HS Potsdam. Writes cabaret texts, radio and TV plays.
1964   ‹*Roland und*› *Regine*. Op Lib (M Joachim Werzlau). Pr
1966 Potsdam.
Sommer in Sans Souci (A Summer in Sans Souci). Cantata (M Hans Naumilkat). Pr 1968.
Der Prüfungsaufsatz (The Examination Question). Juv.
Pr 1970. *Forum* 1970/9.
*Eine Stelle hinterm Komma (One Place after the Deci-
mal Point)*. Com. Pr 1970.
1980   *Ossel kommt (Ossie's Coming)*. Juv. Pr 1981.
1981   *Frech wie Oskar (Fresh Like Oscar)*. Juv (with Peter
Ensikat and Heinz Kahlau). Pr 1982 Fkft/O.

SCHLOTT, Ulrich
> *König Drosselbart (King Thrushbeard)*. Pp (based on
> Grimm). Pr Wismar.
> *Hase und Igel (The Hare and the Hedgehog)*. Pp.
> *Die Sonnenfinsternis (The Solar Eclipse)*. Pp (based
> on Monterroso). Pr Wismar.
> *Der Hahn (The Rooster)*. Pp. Pr Wismar.
> *Kasper baut ein Haus (Punch Builds a House)*. Pp (with
> Martin Klingel). Pr Wismar.
1983   *Maskerade (Masquerade)*. Juv. Pr 1984 Schwerin.

SCHLOTTERBECK, Anna
2 May 1902 Munich - 24 July 1972 Groß-Glienicke
1933 emigrated to Switzerland; 48 settled in GDR, first Dsdn,
then Potsdam. 1958 Fontane Prize (with husband Friedrich).

SCHLOTTERBECK, Anna (cont'd)
Wrote prose, radio plays (many with husband).
1957   *SMS Prinzregent Luitpold (HMS Prince Regent Luit-pold)*. Dr (with Friedrich Schlotterbeck; based on ra-dio play). Pr 1958 Potsdam. Berlin: Verlag d. Mini-steriums f. Natl. Verteidigung, 1959.
1961   *Frührot (Aurora)*. Dr (with Friedrich Schlotterbeck; based on radio play "An der Fernverkehrsstraße 106"). Henschel 1964.

SCHLOTTERBECK, Friedrich
6 Jan 1909 Reutlingen - Apr 1979 Potsdam
Worked as carpenter,then unemployed; 33 joined anti-Nazi re-sistance; 34-43 prison and concentration camp; 44 escaped to Switzerland; 45 President, Red Cross Württemberg; 48 settled in GDR, first Dsdn, then Potsdam. 1958 Fontane Prize (with wife Anna). Wrote prose, radio plays (many with wife).
1957   *SMS Prinzregent Luitpold (HMS Prince Regent Luit-pold)*. Dr (with Anna Schlotterbeck; based on radio play). Pr 1958 Potsdam. Berlin: Verlag d. Ministe-riums f. Natl. Verteidigung, 1959.
1961   *Frührot (Aurora)*. Dr (with Anna Schlotterbeck; based on radio play "An der Fernverkehrsstraße 106"). Hen-schel 1964.

SCHMIDT, Eberhard
1952   *Bolero*. Opt Lib (with Otto Schneidereit).   Pr 1952 Met.
1981   *Die wundersame Schusterfrau (The Shoemaker's Amazing Wife)*. Op Lib (based on Garcia Lorca; M Udo Zimmer-mann). Pr 1982 Schwetzingen.

SCHMIDT, Eduard   see Eduard CLAUDIUS

SCHMIDT, Friedrich   see Friedrich SCHMIDT-BEHRENS

SCHMIDT, Gerhard
Prose author.
1962   *Und weil wir uns lieben (Because We Love Each Other)*. Dr.

SCHMIDT, Hans-Dieter
8 Mar 1926 Wurzen -
Service in WW II, POW; after return, teacher; then studied medicine, later acting and directing at Drama School Halle; 1948 began career as actor and stage director in Lpzg, Pots-dam, Erfurt, and Berlin; 58-77 managing director Th. d. jg. Welt, Lpzg; since 82 managing director Pp Th Halle. 1966 Na-tional Prize and City of Lpzg Prize, 71 Erich Weinert Medal.
        Mein Bruder spielt Klarinette (My Brother Plays the Clarinet). Juv Mus Lib (based on Anatoly Aleksin; M Oskar Felzmann).
1957   *Onkel Toms Hütte (Uncle Tom's Cabin)*. Juv (with Ale-xandra Brustein; based on Harriet Beecher-Stowe).
1958   *Allez hopp! (Alley Oop!)* Juv. Pr 1964 Weimar.

SCHMIDT, Hans-Dieter (cont'd)

1959   *Cipollino (Little Onion)*. Juv Mus Lib (based on Giovanni Rodari, "Zwiebelchen"; M Siegfried Tiefensee). Pr 1959 Weimar.

1960   *Katz und Kätzchen (Cat and Kitten)*. Juv Op Lib (based on Samuil Marshak, "Das Katzenhaus"; M Siegfried Tiefensee.)

1960   *3 x klingeln (Ring Three Times)*. Com. Pr 1960 Döbeln.

1961   *Quartett mit Schlagern (Quartet with Hit Songs)*. Juv Mus Lib (with Gisela Schwarz-Marell; based on her TV play; M Hans Sandig). Pr 1961 Th. d. jg. Welt, Lpzg.

1961   *Die Ehrgeizigen (The Ambitious Ones)*. Juv (with Günther Görlich; based on his novel). Pr 1962 Th. d. Freundschaft, Berlin. Rev 1970 as Den Wolken ein Stück näher.

1961   *Jungfrau, Stier und Waage (Virgo, Taurus, and Libra)*. Com. Pr 1962 Meiningen.

1962   *Schluß mit Blindekuh (Stop with Blind Man's Buff)*. Com. Pr 1962 Lpzg.

1962   *Wettlauf zwischen Hase und Igel (The Race Between the Hare and the Hedgehog)*. Juv (based on Ota Hofmann). Pr 1962 Th. d. jg. Welt, Lpzg.

1962   *Mohr und die Raben von London (Mohr and The Ravens of London)*. Dr (with Vilmos and Ilse Korn; based on novel and film). Pr 1973 Th. d. jg. Welt, Lpzg.

1963   *Lorenz kontra Lausejungen (Lorenz vs. the Rascals)*. Juv. Pr 1963 Th. d. jg. Welt, Lpzg.

1963   *Egon und das achte Weltwunder (Egon and The Eighth Wonder of the World)*. Juv (with Günther Görlich; based on novel by Joachim Wohlgemuth). Pr 1965 Th. d. jg. Welt, Lpzg.

1964   *‹Das Märchen von der alten› Die alte Straßenbahn Therese (‹The Tale of› The Old Streetcar Named Theresa)*. Juv (with Heinz Kahlau; based on Ota Hofmann and Jan Gerstel). Pr 1964 Th. d. jg. Welt, Lpzg. *TdZ* 1966, special issue.

1965   *‹Die› Messedetektive (Detectives at the Fair)*. Juv. Pr 1965 Th. d. jg. Welt, Lpzg.

1966   *Gabor-Gabor*. Juv (based on Ludwig Aschkenazy). Pr 1966 Th. d. jg. Welt, Lpzg.

1966   *Kännchen voll (A Little Potful)*. Juv. Pr 1967 Th. d. jg. Welt, Lpzg.

1967   *Football Story*. Juv (with Barbara Winkler). Pr 1968 Th. d. jg. Welt, Lpzg.

1968   *Tinko*. Juv (based on novel by Erwin Strittmatter). Pr 1969 Th. d. jg. Welt, Lpzg. *TdZ* 1970/7.

1969   *Der kleine Muck (Little Muck)*. Juv (based on story by Hauff). Pr 1970 Th. d. jg. Welt, Lpzg.

1970   *Den Wolken ein Stück näher (A Little Closer to the Clouds)*. Juv (rev of Die Ehrgeizigen; with Günther Görlich). Pr 1971 Th. d. jg. Welt, Lpzg. Berlin: Kinderbuchverlag, 1971.

1971   *Pause für Wanzka (Recess for Wanzka)*. Juv (based on novel by Alfred Wellm). Pr 1971 Th. d. jg. Welt Lpzg.

SCHMIDT, Hans-Dieter (cont'd)

1971   *Der neue Struwelpeter (The New Shaggy-Pete).* Juv Op
        Lib (based on H. G. Stengel; M Siegfried Tiefensee).
        Pr 1972 Th. d. jg. Welt, Lpzg.

1973   *Die Prinzessin auf der Erbse (The Princess and the
        Pea).* Juv Op Lib (based on Hans Christian Andersen; M
        Günter Schimm). Pr 1974 Th. d. jg. Welt, Lpzg.

1974   *Robby Kruse.* Juv Mus Lib (based on Daniel Defoe, "Ro-
        binson Crusoe"; M Hans Sandig). Pr 1975 Th. d. jg.
        Welt, Lpzg.

1974   *Eins und eins ist nicht immer gleich zwei (One Plus
        One Does Not Always Make Two).* Juv. Pr 1974 Th. d.
        jg. Welt, Lpzg.

1976   *Plädoyer für die über Vierzig (A Plea for Those Over
        Forty).* Juv. Pr 1976 Th. d. jg. Welt, Lpzg.

1978   *Die fröhliche Gasse (The Cheerful Street).* Juv (based
        on Kima Kadreva). Pr 1978 Th. d. jg. Garde, Halle.

SCHMIDT, Jürgen
Dramaturg at Neustrelitz and DT; now artistic director of GDR
record company "Deutsche Schallplatten."

1956   *Dienstgruppe 729 (Unit 729).* Dr. Pr 1957 DT.

SCHMIDT, Konrad
27 May 1926 Döbeln –
Attended high school in Meißen; 1944-45 served in WW II, then
British POW; 46 completed school, 47-49 studied painting and
sculpture at Academy of Fine Arts, Dsdn; began writing, independent author since 52; frequent travel to Balkan and Near
East; now lives in Berlin. Writes essays, short stories, TV
plays.

1963   *Der unterschlagene Ehemann (The Hidden Husband).* Com
        (with Kurt Zimmermann). Pr 1964 Rostock.

SCHMIDT, Wilfried
Actor in Bautzen and Th. d. jg. Generation, Dsdn; also musician.

1976   *Kenen Sie Kahlow? (Do You Know Kahlow?)* Revue (with
        Heinz Kahlow). Pr 1977 Mgdbg.

SCHMIDT-BEHRENS, Friedrich (also known as Friedrich SCHMIDT)
        Warum starb Dr. Ellens? (Why Did Dr. Ellens Die?).
        Dr.

1959   *Verdammtes Gift (Damned Poison).* Dr.

1962   *Die Prinzessin auf der Erbse (The Princess and the
        Pea).* Juv (based on Hans Christian Andersen). Pr
        1963 Rudolstadt. Rev 1974 as Juv Op.
        Der weiße Dakota (The White Dakota). Juv. Pr 1964
        Th. d. jg. Welt, Lpzg.
        Häuptling Büffelherz (Chief Buffalo-Heart). Juv. Pr
        1966 Rudolstadt.
        Der Tod Tatanka Yotankas (Tatanka Yotanka's Death).
        Juv. Pr 1967 Rudolstadt.

SCHMIDT-BEHHRENS (cont'd)
>*Indianer, Farmer und Banditen* (*Indians, Farmers, and Bandits*). Juv. Pr 1970 Gera.
>*Das große Bündnis* (*The Great Alliance*). Juv. Pr 1970 Gera.

1974 *Die Prinzessin auf der Erbse* (*The Princess and the Pea*). Juv Op Lib (rev of 1962 Juv; M Joachim-Dietrich Link). Pr 1974 Gera.

SCHNEIDER, Elke
7 May 1940 Bitterfeld -
1960-63 studied theater history Lpzg; dramaturg for drama, musical, and cabaret; since 80 Pp. Th. Mgdbg.; 84 managing director.

1975 *Spanisches Capriccio* (*Spanish Capriccio*). Op Lib (based on Tirso de Molina; M Heinz Röttger). Pr 1976 Dessau.

1979 *Timbu Limbu und die Schneemüller* (*Timbu Limbu and the Snow Millers*). Pp. Pr 1979 Mgdbg.

1980 *Abrakadabra*. Pp (with Bernd Götz). Pr 1981 Mgdbg.

1981 *Der Froschkönig* (*The Frog Prince*). Pp. Pr 1982 Mgdbg.

1982 *Das Buckauer Hofspektakel* (*The Uproar at the Court of Buckau*). Pp. Pr 1983 Mgdbg.

SCHNEIDER, Frank
1982 *Die Verwandlung* (*Metamorphosis*). Op Lib (based on story by Franz Kafka; M Paul-Heinz Dittrich). Pr 1983 Metz.

SCHNEIDER, Hansjörg
15 Mar 1927 Langburkersdorf -
Worked in saw mill; served in Navy 1941-46, then laborer; 49-53 FDJ functionary; 53-55 studied law and political science Potsdam; law degree 59, then state's attorney Cottbus; since 62 independent author. Writes detective stories, TV and radio plays.

1963 *Seilfahrt* (*Cablecar Ride*). Dr (based on short story). Pr 1963 Senftenberg.

1984 *Damals in Prag* (*That Time in Prague*). Mus Lib (with Brigitte Wulkow; M Jochen Allihn). Pr 1985 Erfurt.

SCHNEIDER, Peter M.
19 Oct 1936 Sachsenhausen -
Studied engineering; took voice lessons, became opera singer; writes radio and film scripts; lives in Rostock.

1966 *Der Tod des Archimedes* (*The Death of Archimedes*). Dr. Pr 1967 Döbeln.

1976 *Seemann, Tod und Teufel* (*Sailor, Death, and Devil*). Revue (M Helmut Hanke). Pr 1977 Stralsund.

1979 *Die drei Musketiere* (*The Three Musketeers*). Mus Lib (with Heiner Maaß; based on novel by Alexander Dumas; M Rainer Böhm). Pr 1980 Dsdn/Radebeul.

1981 *Die blaue Nachtigall* (*The Blue Nightingale*). Mus Lib (M Paul Krawinkel). Pr 1981 Greifswald.

1982 *Das Fell* (*The Pelt*). Dr. Pr 1983 Rostock.

SCHNEIDER, Peter M. (cont'd)
1983   *Es war einmal ein König Drosselbart (Once Upon a Time
        There Was a King Thrushbeard).* Juv Mus Lib (based on
        Grimm; M Reinhard Möller). Pr 1984 Rostock.
1983   *Reise nach dem Süden (Journey to the South).* Dr
        (based on West German newspaper articles by Peter
        Schütt). Reading 1984 Rostock. Rev 1984 as Mutter-
        milchpumpe.
1984   *Muttermilchpumpe oder Bilder aus dem anderen Amerika
        (Breast Milk Pump or Scenes from the Other America).*
        Dr (rev of Reise nach den Süden). Pr 1985 Schwerin.
1985   *Das Märchen vom schwarzen Riesen (The Fairytale of
        the Black Giant).* Juv Mus Lib (M Reinhard Möller).
        Pr 1985 Rostock.

SCHNEIDER, Rolf
17 Apr 1932 Chemnitz (now Karl Marx Stadt) –
1951-55 studied German literature at Halle; 55-58 editor with
Aufbau Verlag, Berlin; since then independent author; also
worked as dramaturg in Bonn; lives in Berlin. Member PEN GDR
and FRG; 1962 Lessing Prize, 66 FRG Radio Prize, 72 FDGB
Prize; 79 expelled from GDR Authors' Ass'n. Writes poetry,
radio and TV plays.
1958   ‹Der› Dieb und ‹der› König (‹The› Thief and ‹the›
        King). Com (based on E. E. Kisch "Der König und sein
        Dieb"; first radio play, then TV play). Pr 1966 Gera.
        Sinn & Form 1968/5. Fkft/M: Fischer, 1969. *Stücke*,
        Henschel 1970.
1961   *Godefroys.* Dr. Pr 1962 Mgdbg.
1961   *Prozeß Richard Waverley (The Richard Waverley Trial).*
        Dr (based on radio play). Pr 1963 DT. *TdZ* 1964/2.
        Stücke, 1970.
1962   *Der Mann aus England (The Man from England).* Dr
        (based on radio and TV play, "Entlassung"). Pr 1962
        VB. *TdZ* 1963/16. *Stücke*, 1970. 1963 rev as Op (M
        Rainer Kunad). Pr 1965 Dsdn/Radebeul under title "Old
        Fritz."
1963   *Ankunft in Weilstedt (Arrival in Weilstedt).* Juv
        (based on radio play). Pr 1964 Th. d. jg. Welt, Lpzg.
1964-65 *Die Geschichte vom Moischele (Moishele's Story).* Dr
        fragment. *TdZ* 1965/10. *Stücke*, 1970.
1966   *prozeß in nürnberg (Trial in Nuremberg).* Dr. Pr 1967
        DT. *TdZ* 1967/24. Fkft/M: Fischer, 1968. *Stücke*, 19-
        70.
1968   *Einzug ins Schloß (Moving into the Castle).* Com. Pr
        1971 DT. *NdL* 1968/1. Henschel 1972.
1968   *Krankenbesuch (Visiting the Sick).* On. Pr 1969 Mag-
        deburg.
1969   *Haltestelle (Bus Stop).* On. Pr 1969 Magdeburg.
1971   *Octavius und Kleopatra (Octavian and Cleopatra).* On.
        Pr 1972 Schwerin. Fkft/M: Fischer, 1972.
1971   *Die Heiligung Johannas (The Sanctification of Joan).*
        On. Pr 1972 Schwerin. *Octavius...*, 1972.

SCHNEIDER, Rolf (cont'd)

1974 *Die beiden Nachtwandler oder Das Notwendige und das Ü-berflüssige (The Two Somnambulists or The Necessary and the Superfluous).* Com (based on Nestroy). Pr 19-75 Magdeburg.

1975 *Der Kaiser und der Wolf (The Emperor and The Wolf).* Dr. Pr 1976 Magdeburg.

1976 *Der alte Mann mit der jungen Frau (The Old Man with the Young Wife).* Com (based on Nestroy). Pr 1976 Magdeburg.

1980 *Die Mainzer Republik (The Mainz Republic).* Dr. *Sinn & Form* 1981/5 (scenes).

SCHNEIDEREIT, Otto
4 Jan 1915 Berlin - 1978 Leipzig
After 1935, actor and singer; 40-45 service in WW Il, POW; then again actor, stage director, and dramaturg at various theaters; also worked with radio and TV; after 59 independent author. Wrote novels, film and TV scripts.

1944 *Hotel Spanischer Kaiser (Hotel Spanish Emperor).* On. Pr 1945.

1945 *Liebeslied (Love Song).* Mus Lib. Pr 1945.

1945 *Zwei Ohrfeigen (Two Slaps).* Com. Pr 1945.

1946 *Alarm im Werk (Alarm in the Factory).* Dr. Pr 1946.

1946 *Der Schatz (The Treasure).* Com (based on Lessing). Pr 1946.

1947 *Das tapfere Schneiderlein (The Brave Little Tailor).* Juv (based on Grimm). Pr 1948.

1949 *So wie neulich (Just Like the Other Day).* Cabaret (with H. Jobst and H. G. Stengel). Pr 1950. Rev 1951 as Wer lacht, lebt länger.

1951 *Wer lacht, lebt länger (He Who Laughs Lives Longer).* Cabaret (rev of So wie neulich). Pr 1951.

1951 *Der Zigeunerbaron (The Gypsy Baron).* Opt Lib (new a-daptation; based on Ignaz Schnitzer; M Johann Strauß). Pr 1952 Dsdn.

1952 *Bolero.* Opt Lib (with Eberhard Schmidt). Pr 1952 Met.

1954 *Wiener Blut (Vienna Blood).* Opt Lib (new adaptation; based on Victor Leon and Leo Stein; M Johann Strauß).

1954 *Wer braucht Geld? (Who Needs Money?).* Mus Lib (M Guido Masanetz). Pr 1956 Met. Rev 1961 as In Frisco ist der Teufel los.

1955 *Die Fledermaus (The Bat).* Opt Lib (new adaptation; based on Karl Haffner and Richard Genee; M Johann Strauß).

1956 *Frau Luna (Mrs. Luna).* Opt Lib (new adaptation; based on Heinrich Bolten Baeckers; M Paul Lincke). Pr 1957 Met.

1961 *In Frisco ist der Teufel los (All Hell Is Loose in Frisco).* Mus Lib (rev of Wer braucht Geld?; with Maurycy Janowski; M Guido Masanetz). Pr 1962 Met.

1962 *Fatinitza.* Opt Lib (new adaptation; based on F. Zell and Richard Genee; M Franz von Suppe, arranged by Herbert Kawan). Pr 1962 Gera.

SCHNEIDEREIT (cont'd)
1967 *Die Großherzogin von Gerolstein (The Grand Duchess of Gerolstein)*. Opt Lib (new adaptation; based on Henri Meilhac and Ludovic Halevy; M Jacques Offenbach). Pr 1968 Lpzg.
1972 *Die Geisha*. Opt Lib (with Karl Farkas; based on Owen Hall; M Sidney Jones). Pr 1973 Raimundth., Vienna.
Die Flößer der Bistritza (The Bistritza Raftsmen). Opt Lib (M Filaret Barbu).

SCHÖBEL, Helfried
1982 *Das Gemälde (The Painting)*. Dr (based on novel by Daniil Granin). Pr 1984 Weimar.

SCHÖBEL, Hildegard
Dramaturg, Th. d. jg. Generation, Dsdn.
1962 *Pioniere an Bord (Pioneers on Board)*. Juv. Pr 1962 Th. d. jg. Generation, Dsdn.
1969 *Annette*. Com. Pr 1969 Dsdn.
1973 *2 x Katharina (Two Times Catherine)*. Com. Pr 1974 Dsdn.
1981 *Kellerklub (Basement Club)*. Juv. Pr 1981 Neustrelitz.

SCHÖBEL, Manuel
27 June 1960 Dresden –
Son of Hildegard Schöbel. After high school, served in GDR Army, then became dramaturg Th. d. jg. Generation, Dsdn. 1980 began studying theater history, Humboldt Univ, Berlin. Writes poetry.
1980 *Maxis neue Freunde (Maxie's New Friends)*. Juv.
1981 *Maria, die Siebenschläferin (Lazybones Mary)*. Juv. Pr 1982 Th. d. jg. Generation, Dsdn.
1982 *Das wenigstens will ich selber tun (I'd Rather Do It Myself)*. Juv. Reading 1983 Halle.
1984 *Aus dem Leben eines Tauglichen (Tales from the Life of a Draftee)*. Juv. Pr 1985 Th. d. jg. Generation, Dsdn.
1985 *Prinz Tausendfuß (Prince Thousandfoot)*. Juv.

SCHÖNBERG, Klaus
1927 –
Member of Hitler Youth, then served in WW II, POW; after war, studied medicine in Kiel; then became actor and stage director at various theaters; since 1977 Potsdam.
1982-83 *Minotaurus oder Die glückselige Insel der Erfindungen (The Minotaur or The Happy Island of Inventions)*. Dr. Reading 1983 Potsdam. Rev version *TdZ* 1985/6.

SCHONROCK, Hans
8 July 1902 Hamburg – 7 Sep 1982 Boizenburg/Elbe
Worked as farmer. 1958 Fritz Reuter Prize. Wrote prose, poetry, TV and film scripts.
1957 *Mecklenburg*. Dr. Pr 1958.
1959 *Saatzeit (Sowing Season)*. Dr (based on TV play). Pr 1961.

SCHOTT, Manfred
1970 *Lolotte oder Keiner nimmt den Kaiser ernst (Lolo or Nobody Takes the Emperor Seriously).* Mus Lib. Pr 19-71 Dsdn.

SCHRADER, Julie
1976 *Ach, es war nur die Laterne (Alas, It Was Only The Lantern).* Com. Pr 1976 Schwerin.

SCHRADER, Karl see Paul KÖRNER-SCHRADER

SCHRADER, Richard
1950 *Krethi und Plethi ‹Des Kaisers neue Kleider› (Tom, Dick and Harry ‹The Emperor's New Clothes›).* Juv Mus Lib (based on Hans Christian Andersen; M Gerhard E. Rischka). Pr 1951 Görlitz.
1951 *Rumpelstilzchen (Rumpelstiltskin).* Juv (based on Grimm). Pr 1954 Nordhausen.

SCHREIBER, Helmut
 Die Nachtigall (The Nightingale). Bl Lib (based on Hans Christian Andersen; M Otto Reinhold). Pr 1958 Dsdn.

SCHREITER, Helfried
12 June 1935 Lomnitz/Dresden -
After school, served in GDR Army until 1960; 60-64 studied Th. HS Lpzg; since then independent author; lives in Berlin. 1968 FDGB Prize, 71 Heinrich Greif Prize. Writes poetry, prose, film scripts, radio and TV plays.
1971 *Ich spiele dir die Welt durch (I'll Play through the Whole World For You).* Dr. Pr 1971 Gera. TdZ 1971/7.
1973 *Companeros.* Dr (based on radio play). Pr 1974 Freiberg.
1977 *Aufruhr der Engel (The Angels' Rebellion).* Com (based on Anatole France). Pr 1978 Weimar.

SCHREYER, Wolfgang
20 Nov 1927 Magdeburg -
Served in WW II; POW until 1946; 48-51 worked as pharmacist; now independent author in Mgdbg; member PEN. 1956 Heinrich Mann Prize. Writes novels, film scripts, radio and TV plays.
1966 *Ein Fremder im Paradies (A Stranger in Paradise).* Com (based on novel).
1970 *Tod des Chefs (The Death of the Boss).* Dr. Pr 1972 Mgdbg.
1973 *Die Liebe zur Opposition oder Bomben auf den Palast (Love for the Opposition or Bombs on the Palace).* Dr. Pr 1974 Rostock.
1974 *Die Lawine oder Russisches Roulette (The Avalanche or Russian Roulette).* Dr.

SCHRÖDER, Carl
Managing director of Bautzen Pp. Th.
>*Pinocchios Abenteuer* *(The Adventures of Pinocchio).* Pp.
>*Prinz Wegda (Prince Begone).* Pp.
>*Das Puppenspiel von Dr. Faustus* *(The Puppet Play of Dr. Faustus).* Pp.

SCHUBERT, Dieter
15 May 1929 Görlitz –
Went to high school in Berlin; 1945 participated in last days of WW II; worked as forest ranger, then finished school; various occupations, including amateur boxer; 49 journalist, 56-68 editor; since then independent author in Berlin. 1968 Hans Marchwitza Prize. Writes stories, essays, children's books.
1976   *Der Olle Henry (Ol' Henry).* Dr. Pr 1977 Potsdam.

SCHUBERT, Helga
7 Jan 1940 Berlin –
After school worked as a mechanic; 1958-63 studied psychology in Berlin, then worked as clinical psychologist; 73-77 studied clinical psychology Humboldt Univ, Berlin; lives in Berlin. Writes poetry, prose, radio and TV plays.
1975   *Eine unmögliche Geschichte (An Impossible Story).* Dr (based on radio play). Pr 1977 Rudolstadt.
1984   *David.* On. Pr 1984 TiP (part of program under collective title "Männermonologe").
1984   *Goliath.* On. Pr 1984 TiP (part of program under collective title "Männermonologe").
1985   *Verbotene Umklammerung (Forbidden Embrace).* Dr. Pr 1985 Gera.

SCHUCHART, R‹einhardt› Ottmar
>*Wie werd ich dich, mein Junge, pflegen? (How Will I Take Care of You, My Boy?).* Dr. Pr 1985 Stralsund.

SCHUDER, Rosemarie
24 July 1928 Jena –
After high school, became journalist; 1957-59 study trips to Italy; married to author Rudolf Hirsch; lives in Berlin. 1958 Heinrich Mann Prize, 59 National Prize. Writes novels, short stories.
1978   *Welt und Traum des Hieronymus Bosch* *(World and Dream of Hieronymus Bosch).* Dr. Pr 1979 TiP.

SCHULZ, Anneliese (nee Tischler)
16 Apr 1934 Oppach –
Lives in Berlin. Writes prose, children's books, radio and TV plays.
1984   *Der Frosch und die Grasmücke (The Frog and the Hedge-Sparrow).* Pp (based on radio play). Pr 1984 Dsdn.

SCHULZE, GERNOT
   Des Teufels goldene Haare <Der dumme Teufel Stanis-
   las> (The Devil's Golden Hairs <Stanislas, the Stupid
   Devil>). Juv (based on Grimm). Pr 1967 Putbus.

SCHUMACHER, Ernst
12 Sep 1921 Urspring/Bavaria –
Service in WW II, then studied philosophy, literature, and
history, first in Munich, later in Lpzg; journalist, theater
critic; now Prof. of Theater, Humboldt Univ, Berlin. President, GDR PEN; since 1972 member AdK. Writes poetry, essays.
1961   *Jerry und der Gamsbart (Jerry and the Chamois Goat's*
       Beard).
1974   *Die Versuchung des Forschers oder Visionen aus der*
       Realität (The Temptation of the Scientist or Visions
       from Reality). Dr. Pr 1975 Rostock.
1977   *Poem des Nichtvergessens (The Poem of Not Forgetting)*
       Op Lib (M Bernd Wefelmeyer). Pr 1977 St.Op.

SCHUSTER, Uwe
1933 Gleiwitz –
Attended school in Mgdbg; worked on farms and in industry;
studied German literature Humboldt Univ., Berlin; became a
school teacher in Mecklenburg, started amateur theater; later
actor and dramatzg at various theaters.
       Der Diener zweier Herren (The Servant of Two Masters)
       Com (tr from Goldoni).
       Krach in Chiozza (A Ruckus in Chiozza). Com (tr from
       Goldoni).
       Die Verliebten (The Lovers). Com (tr from Goldoni).
       Feuervogel und Rotfüchslein (Fire Bird and Little Red
       Fox). Juv (based on Jan Tilek).
1974   *Karl Damerow ist tot oder Das Testament eines Fuchses*
       (Karl Damerow Is Dead or The Testament of a Fox). Com.
       Com. Pr 1977 Meiningen. *TdZ 1976/2.*

SCHÜTZ, Helga
2 Oct 1937 Falkenstein (now Zlotoryja, Poland) –
Graduated high school Dsdn 1944; worked as gardener; 55-58
studied Film HS Potsdam/Babelsberg; 58-62 DEFA dramaturg; now
lives in Berlin. 1969 Heinrich Greif Prize, 73 Heinrich Mann
Prize, 74 Fontane Prize. Writes prose, TV plays, film scripts.
1974   *Julia oder Die Erziehung zum Chorgesang (Julia or The*
       Training for Choral Singing). Dr (based on novel).
       Aufbau 1980.

SCHÜTZ, Stefan
19 Apr 1944 Memel –
Son of actors; 1963-66 attended Drama School Berlin; 66-71 actor Neustrelitz, Halle, then asst. stage director BE, DT; 82
moved to FRG; dramaturg Wuppertal. 1979 Gerhart Hauptmann
Prize.
1970-77 *Gloster (Gloucester).* Dr (based on Shakespeare, "Ri-
       chard III."). Pr 1981 Munich. *Laokoon,* Berlin (W.):
       Rotbuch, 1980.

SCHÜTZ, Stefan (cont'd)

1971   *Majakowski*. Dr. Pr 1979 London (Engl.); Gm. Pr 19-82 Osnabrück. *Th.h.* 1980/2 (scene). *Stasch*, Berlin (W.): Rotbuch, 1978.

1971   *Seneca*. Com.

1972-74 *Odysseus' Heimkehr (The Homecoming of Ulysses)*. Dr. Pr 1981 Wuppertal. Fkft/M: Verlag der Autoren, 19-74. Henschel 1977. Berlin (W.): Rotbuch, 1979.

1973   *Fabrik im Walde ‹Weder der Teufel los noch Stille› (Factory in the Forest ‹Neither All Hell is Loose Nor Silence›)*. Dr (based on novel by Anna Karayeva). Pr 1975 Potsdam. *TdZ* 1975/12. *Odysseus' Heimkehr*, 1977.

1973   *Golemanow oder Wie man Minister wird (Golemanov or How to Become a Minister of State)*. Com (based on Stefan Kostov).

1974-76 *Die Amazonen ‹Antiope und Theseus› (The Amazons ‹Antiope and Theseus›)*. Dr. Pr 1978 Basel. *TdZ* 1978/2. Fkft/M: Verlag der Autoren, 1976. *Spec* 28, 1978. *Heloisa und Abaelard*, Berlin (W.): Rotbuch, 1979.

1974-77 *Der Hahn (The Rooster)*. Dr. Pr 1980 Heidelberg. In *Stasch*, Berlin (W.): Rotbuch, 1978.

1975-76 *Heloisa und Abaelard*. Dr. Pr 1978 Potsdam. Berlin: (W.): Rotbuch, 1979. *Odysseus' Heimkehr*, 1977.

1975-76 *Kohlhaas*. Dr (based on Heinrich Kleist, "Michael Kohlhaas"). Pr 1978 Th. d. Karl Marx Univ, Lpzg. *Th.h.* 1978/11. *Odysseus' Heimkehr*, 1977. *Laokoon*, Berlin (W.): Rotbuch, 1980.

1977   *Stasch*. Dr. Pr 1982 Osnabrück. *Deutsche Biografien - Stücke*, Suhrkamp 1978. Berlin (W.): Rotbuch, 19-78. *Semiotext* 1982/2 (Engl. tr Dagmar Stern).

1978   *Vom freien Leben träumt Jan Hus (Jan Hus Dreams of a Free Life)*. Dr. Pr 1979 Constance, Switzerland.

1979   *Laokoon*. Dr. Berlin (W.): Rotbuch, 1980.

1980   *Die Schweine (The Pigs)*. Com. Fkft/M: Fischer, 1981 (with *Sappa*).

1980   *Lysistrata*. Com.

1981   *Sappa (Sappho)*. Dr. Pr 1982 Wuppertal. *Die Schweine*, 1981.

1981   *Kleistfragment (Kleist Fragment)*. Scene. *Jahresring* 1981-82.

1983   *Die Seidels ‹Groß und Klein› (The Seidels ‹Big and Small›)*. Dr. Fkft/M: Fischer, 1984.

1983   *‹Spectacle› Cressida*. Dr. Fkft/M: Fischer, 1984.

SCHWAEN, Kurt
21 June 1909 Kattowitz (now Katowice, Poland) -
1929-33 studied music and German literature Berlin and Breslau (now Wroclaw, Poland); 32 joined KPD; after 33 taught piano; active in anti-Nazi underground; imprisoned 36-39; 43-45 served in WW II; 45-45 music teacher, since then independent composer and librettist. 1961 member AdK, 77 National Prize.

1957   *Die Abenteuer des tapferen Schneiderleins (The Adventures of the Brave Little Tailor)*. Juv Op (with Egon Günther; based on Grimm). Pr 1962 Th. d. jg. Garde, Halle.

SCHWAEN (cont'd)

1959   *Leonce und Lena*. Op (based on Büchner). Pr 1961 St. Op.

1962   *Die Morgengabe (The Dowry)*. Op (with Gerhard Branstner). Pr 1963 Fkft/O.

1967   *Ballade vom Glück (The Ballad of Happiness)*. Op (with Edith Dörwaldt-Kühl). Pr 1967 Staatsoper, Dsdn.

1969   *Pinocchios Abenteuer (The Adventures of Pinocchio)*. Juv Op (with Claus and Wera Küchenmeister; based on Carlo Collodi). Pr 1970 Zwickau. *TdZ* 1970/1.

1973   *Alle helfen Häppi (Everyone Helps Happy)*. Juv Op. Pr 1974 Fkft/O.

1976   *Blümchen und die Schurken (Little Flower and the Scoundrels)*. Juv Op. Pr 1977 Zwickau.

1979   *Der eifersüchtige Alte (The Jealous Old Man)*. On Op. Pr 1980 St.Op.

1979   *Kalifah der Fischer von Bagdad (Calipha the Fisherman of Baghdad)*. On Op. Pr 1980 St.Op.

1982   *Das Spiel vom Dr. Faust (The Play of Dr. Faust)*. Op. Pr 1983 Brandenburg.

1983   *Der ABC Stern (The Alphabet Star)*. Juv Op (with Wera and Claus Küchenmeister; based on their children's book). Pr 1984 Lpzg.

1985   *Craqueville oder Die unschuldige Sünderin (Craqueville or The Innocent Sinner)*. Op (with Wera and Claus Küchenmeister). Pr 1986 Brandenburg.

SCHWARZ-MARELL, Gisela
2 Oct 1927 Berlin -
Writes for radio and TV.

1955   *Die großen Drei (The Big Three)*. Juv.

1956   *Ehe in 3 Tagen (Marriage in 3 Days)*. Com.

1957   *Mit Zitronen gehandelt (Trading with Lemons)*. Com.

1959   *Hampelmann Schönbunter (The Multicolored Jumpingjack)*. Juv Op Lib (with Manfred Grafe).

1960   *Das tapfere Schneiderlein (The Brave Little Tailor)*. Juv (based on Grimm). Pr 1960 Th. d. Freundschaft, Berlin.

1961   *Quartett mit Schlagern (Quartet with Hit Songs)*. Juv Mus Lib (with Hans-Dieter Schmidt; based on TV play; M Hans Sandig). Pr 1961 Th. d. jg. Welt, Lpzg.

SCHWEICKERT, W‹alter› K‹arl›
26 Aug 1908 Freiburg i. Br. -
Started writing political articles in 1920's; 30 moved to Lpzg, 32 founded leftist cabaret "Die Zeitlupe"; 33-49 various jobs; since 50 independent author. Writes novels, short stories, radio and TV plays, film scripts, children's books.

1960   *Ein gemütlicher Abend (A Pleasant Evening)*. On.

1960   *Der Bus fährt um 20 Uhr (The Bus Leaves at 8 pm)*. On.

1960   *Strafsache Pfeifer (Criminal Case Pfeifer)*. On.

1960   *Uhr im Ohr (A Clock in the Ear)*. On.

1960   *Das Pferd auf dem Dach (The Horse on the Roof)*. On.

1960   *Erich währt am längsten (Eric Lasts Longest)*. Com with W. Beck). Pr 1960.

SCHWEICKERT (cont'd)

1963 *Tatort Lehrerzimmer (Scene of Crime: Teachers' Room)*. Juv (based on 1960 novel; dramatized by Rainer Lange and Manfred Streubel). Pr 1964 Th. d. Freundschaft, Berlin. *TdZ* 1964/8.

1963 *Das Heizkissen (The Heating Pad)*. Cabaret Sc.

1966 *Drei anonyme Briefe (Three Anonymous Letters)*. On.

SCHWENKNER, Ingeborg see Inge MÜLLER

SEEGER, Bernhard
6 Oct 1927 Roßlau/Elbe -
Attended teachers' college, then served in WW II; became Russian POW; after war, taught school for seven years; then became reporter and author; now lives in Stücken. 1956 Fontane Prize, 60 Erich Weinert Medal, 62 Heinrich Heine Prize and FDGB Prize, 63 and 67 National Prize; 69 member AdK. Writes poetry, radio and TV plays.

1958 *Unser Leben im Lied (Our Life in Song)*. Cantata.

1961 *Unterm Wind der Jahre (Under the Wind of the Years)*. Dr (based on radio play). Pr 1964 Schwerin. *TdZ* 1964/22. Aufbau 1968.

1963 *Fünfzig Nelken (Fifty Carnations)*. Dr (based on radio and TV play, "Die Erben des Manifests"). Pr 1969 Parchim. Aufbau 1968.

SEEGER, Horst (Pseud. H. SCHELL)
6 Nov 1926 Erkner/Berlin -
Served in WW II, then finished school; 1946-50 taught German history; 50-54 studied musicology in Berlin, Dr. phil. 58; music critic; 59-60 editor-in-chief of journal "Musik und Gesellschaft"; 60-73 head dramaturg Km.Op, since then managing director Dsdn Op.; translator and librettist. 1972 Lessing Prize.

1960 *Rigoletto*. Op Lib (new adaptation; M Verdi). Pr 1961 Km.Op.

1961 *Falstaff*. Op Lib (new adaptation; M Verdi). Pr 1962 Km.Op.

1963 *Ritter Blaubart (Bluebeard the Knight)*. Opt Lib (new adaptation; M Jacques Offenbach). Pr 1963 Km.Op.

1963 *Lazarillo vom Tormes ‹Spanische Tugenden› (Lazarillo of Tormes ‹Spanish Virtues›)*. Op Lib (based on 1554 Spanish novel, "Das Leben des Lazarillo vom Tormes"; M Siegfried Matthus). Pr 1964 KMSt.

1965 *Don Giovanni*. Op Lib (new adaptation; M Mozart). Pr 1966 Km.Op.

1966 *Oberon*. Op Lib (new adaptation; M Weber). Pr 1966 Km.Op.

1967 *Pique Dame (Queen of Spades)*. Op Lib (new adaptation; M Tchaikovsky). Pr 1967 Km.Op.

1968 *Der Doppelgänger (The Double)*. Mus Lib (M Fritz Geißler). Pr 1969 Km.Op.

1972 *Weiße Nächte (White Nights)*. Op Lib (based on story by Dostoevsky; M Jurij Buzko). Pr 1973 Km.Op.

SEELIG, Käthe
1962   *Der Weg zu Dir (Finding You)*. Dr. Pr 1962 Meiningen.
1977   *Detektiv Sonnenstrahl (Detective Sunbeam)*. Pp. Pr 1977 Halle.

SEGHERS, Anna   (real name Netty Radvanyi, nee Reiling)
19 Nov 1900 Mainz - 1 June 1983 Berlin
1919-24 studied history and art history Univ Cologne and Heidelberg, Dr. phil. 24; 28 joined KPD; 33 arrested, escaped to
France; 40 emigrated to Mexico; 47 returned to Berlin.   Since
their founding, member AdK and President GDR Authors' Association.   1947 Büchner Prize,   51 Lenin Peace Prize;   51, 59 and
71 National Prize, 59 Dr. h.c. Jena, 69 FDGB Prize. Wrote novels, short stories, essays, radio plays.
1952   *Der Prozeß der Jeanne d'Arc zu Rouen 1431   (The Trial
        of Joan of Arc at Rouen 1431)*. Dr (based on 1931 ra-
        dio play, dramatized by Bertolt Brecht).   Pr 1952 BE.
        TdZ 1946/6 (radio play).   Reclam 1965 (radio play).
1979   *Der Auftrag (The Mission)*.   Dr (based on 1961 story,
        "Das Licht auf dem Galgen", dramatized by Heiner Mül-
        ler). Pr 1980 VB. *Sinn & Form* 1979/6. *Th.h.* 1980/3.
        Fkft/M: Verlag der Autoren, 1980. Henschel 1981.
        Stuttgart: Klett, 1983.   *Gambit*, 1983 (Engl. tr. Stu-
        art Hood).   *Hamlet Machine*, New York: Performing Arts
        Journal Publications, 1984 (Engl. tr as "The Task" by
        Carl Weber).
1980   *Das siebte Kreuz (The Seventh Cross)*.   Dr (based on
        1942 novel; dramatized by Bärbel Jaksch and Heiner
        Maaß). Pr 1981 Schwerin. *TdZ* 1981/4.

SEIDEL, Georg
1945 Dessau -
Tool-and-die maker; since 1968 stage hand and electrician Dessau Th., Potsdam, now DT.
1980   *Kondensmilchpanorama (Condensed Milk Panorama)*.   Dr.
        Pr 1980 Schwerin.   *TdZ* 1981/2. *Neue DDR Dramatik*, Hen-
        schel 1981.
1981   *Mehr Licht (More Light)*.   Dr.
1982   *Jochen Schanotta*. Dr. Pr 1985 BE.
1983   *Friedensfeier (Celebration of Peace)*.   Dr.

SEIDEL, Klaus
1978   *Die drei Musketiere (The Three Musketeers)*. Dr (based
        on novel by Alexander Dumas). Pr 1979 Quedlinburg.

SEIDEMANN, Burkhart
Member of pantomime ensemble, DT.
1976   *Don Quichote in Murzeledo*.   Pant (with Volkmar Otte).
        Pr 1976 DT.
1977   *Vom Kalaf und Prinzessin Turandot (Calaf and Princess
        Turandot)*. Pant (with Volkmar Otte). Pr 1977 DT.
1979   *Die fremde Haut (The Strange Skin)*. Pant (with Volk-
        mar Otte). Pr 1979 DT.
1981   *Blaubart (Bluebeard)*. Pant. Pr 1981 DT.

SEIDEMANN (cont'd)
1982   *Die Höllenfahrt des Doktor Faust (Doctor Faust's Descent into Hell)*. Pant (with Peter Baumgart). Pr 19-
82 DT.
1985   *Orfeus*. Pp. Pr 1985 DT.

SEIFERT, Herbert
        Hans Ohnefurcht (Fearless Jack). Juv. Pr 1954 Cott-
bus.

SEITZ, Robert
        Orpheus und der Bürgermeister (Orpheus and the Mayor)
Op Lib (M Paul Dessau).

SELBER, Martin   (Real name Martin Merbst)
27 Feb 1924 Dresden -
Worked as apprentice bookkeeper; service in WW II; Russian
POW; farmer, musician, actor; began writing 1948; since 54
independent author. 1960 Moritz Arndt Medal. Writes prose,
children's books.
1949   *Das Werk (The Work)*. Dr. Halle: Mitteldeutscher Verlag, 1949.
1955   *Das Trommelmädchen (The Drummer Girl)*. Dr. Pr 1959.
Lpzg: Hofmeister, 1955.
1966   *Old-Germans-Story*. Com. Pr 1966 Mgdbg.
1967   *Schiffbruch vor Feuerland (Shipwreck before Tierra
del Fuego)*. Juv. Pr 1967 Straßfurt.

SELBMANN, Fritz
29 Sep 1899 Lauterbach - 26 Jan 1975 Berlin
Worked as miner; service in WW I, member of Soldiers' Council
1918;   22 joined KPD, arrested several times; 32-33 Reichstag
Delegate;   33-45 interned in concentration camp;   46 Minister
for Economics, Saxony; 49-55 Minister for Industry, 55-58 Deputy President, Council of Ministers; after 58 independent author. 1970 Heinrich Mann Prize. Wrote essays, novels, short
stories.
1961   *Die Heimkehr des Joachim Ott   (Joachim Ott's Homecoming)*. Dr (based on novel).
1962   *Ein Mann und sein Schicksal (A Man and His Fate)*. Dr
(based on short story, radio and TV play). Pr 1963
Weimar.

SEYLER, F. Willy   see Martin BLANKENFELD

SEYPPEL, Joachim ‹Hans›
3 Nov 1919 Berlin -
1939-43 studied German literature and philosophy Berlin, Lau-
sanne, Rostock;   became actor;   served in WW II, then Russian
POW;   after return, lecturer and author in Berlin;   49-50 and
51-60 Professor of German in US; 61-73 West Berlin, editor of
"Die Diagonale";   73-79 GDR, then returned to FRG;   now lives
in Hamburg. Translator, writes essays, novels, short stories.
1947   *Wo wir sterblich sind (Where We Are Mortal)*. Dr.
1971   *Amen Corner*. Dr (tr from James Baldwin).

SEYPPEL (cont'd)

1978   *Die Unperson oder Schwitzbad und Tod Majakowskis (The Non-Person or Mayakovsky's Steambath and Death).* Dr. Pr 1979 Münster. Cologne: Europäische Verlagsanstalt, 1979.

SIMON, Jens   see Gerd FOCKE

SOLGA, Norbert

1977   *Die Geschichte vom tapferen Schneiderlein (The Tale of the Brave Little Tailor).* Juv Bl Lib (based on Grimm; M Siegfried Tiefensee). Pr 1978 Erfurt.

1980   *Der Zauberer von Smaragdenstadt (The Wizard of Emerald City).* Juv Op Lib (based on Baum, "The Wizard of Oz"; M Siegfried Tiefensee). Pr 1981 Halberstadt.

1983   *Was wird denn hier gespielt oder Maus und Kater im Theater (What Is Playing Here or Cat and Mouse in the Theater).* Juv Mus Lib (M Siegfried Tiefensee). Pr 1984 Th. d. jg. Welt, Lpzg.

SONNENBERG, Günter

1962   *Der eisgraue Müller (The Icy-Grey Miller).* Juv. Pr 1963 Potsdam.

SPICKERMANN, Adolf

1967   *Schüsse, Küsse (Shots and Kisses).* Com. Pr 1968 Halle.

1967   *Kontraste (Contrasts).* Mus Lib (with Henn Haas). Pr 1968 Halle.

STÄCKER, Hans-Dieter

1938 –

Worked as electrician; later puppeteer, actor, and stage director at various theaters; since 1966 manager Pp. Th., Zwickau. Kurt Barthel Medal.

  Alle Mäuse lieben den Käse (All Mice Love Cheese). Pp. Pr Zwickau.

  Wie der kleine Elefant zu seinem Rüssel kam (How the Little Elephant Got His Trunk). Pp (based on Rudyard Kipling). Pr Zwickau.

1976   *Das alte Puppenspiel vom Dr. Faustus ‹Dr. Fausts Höllenfahrt oder Hans Wurst, Faust und andere› (The Old Puppetplay of Dr. Faustus ‹Dr. Faust's Descent into Hell or Punch, Faust, and Others›).* Pp. Pr 1977 Zwickau.

1977   *Die gestohlenen Pfannkuchen (The Stolen Pancakes).* Pp (based on Nils Werner). Pr 1978 Zwickau.

1979   *Jahrmarktsspäße (Fun at the Fair).* Pp. Pr 1979 Zwickau.

1982   *Geschichten aus der Kiste (Stories out of the Trunk).* Pp. Pr 1983 Zwickau.

1984   *Rumpelstilzchen (Rumpelstiltskin).* Pp (based on Grimm). Pr 1984 Zwickau.

STAHL, Heidemarie   (also known as Heidemarie FÖRSTER-STAHL)
9 Feb 1941 Wörkau (now Czechoslovakia) –
1960-64 studied musicology and th. history; then stage director and dramaturg Gera, KMSt., Weimar; now lives in Großhoch-
berg.

	Samson. Op Lib (M Sandor Szokolay).
1979	*Pluft, das Geisterlein (Pluft, the Little Spirit)*. Juv Op Lib (based on Clara Machado; M Joachim-Diet-rich Link). Pr 1980 Weimar.
1983	*Die Wette des Serapion (Serapion's Wager)*. Op Lib (based on novella by Karl Wilhelm Contessa; M Karl Dietrich). Pr 1984 Gera.
1984	*Oedipus*. Op Lib (M George Enescu). Pr 1985 Weimar.
1985	*Es war einmal ein Pumphut (Once upon a Time There Was a Borrowed Hat)*. Pp. Pr 1986 Naumburg.

STAUDER, Josef   (Pseud. Jakob JOSTAU)
1897 – ?
Managing director, Th. d. jg. Welt, Lpzg.

1950	*2 : 1 für Irmgard (2 : 1 in Favor of Irmgard)*. Com. Pr 1951 Dsdn/Radebeul.
1951	*Wer seine Frau lieb hat (If You Love Your Wife)*. Mus Lib (M Joachim-Dietrich Link). Pr 1952 Lpzg. Hen-schel 1956.
1952	*Der Weg ins Leben (The Road to Life)*. Dr. Pr 1952 Lpzg.

STAVE, John   (Pseud. Thomas ZABEL, Hans FASSDAUBE)
7 Feb 1929 Berlin –
1951-64 editor of satiric periodical "Frischer Wind" (renamed
"Eulenspiegel" after 54); since 62 independent author. Writes
humorous short stories.

1976	*Oskar Kasuskes letzter Gang (Oscar Kasuske's Last Er-rand)*. Dr. Pr 1977 Mgdbg.

STEINECKERT, Gisela
13 May 1931 Berlin –
Social worker in day-care center, later reporter and cultural
editor. 1962 Heinrich Greif Prize, FDGB Prize. Writes prose,
poetry, radio, TV, and film scripts.

1972	*Die letzte Seite im Tagebuch (The Last Page in the Di-ary)*. Juv (based on radio play). Pr 1985 Th. d. jg. Welt, Lpzg.
1984	*Grünspan auf Messing (Patina on Brass)*. On. Pr 1984 TiP (part of program under collective title "Männer-monologe").

STEPHAN, Klaus
27 Oct 1927 Treptow –
Writes novels, essays, radio and TV plays.

	Tendako. Dr.
1979	*Josef und Josefine*. Juv. Pr 1980 Anklam.
1982	*Das Wunder des Mädchens mit den drei Tauben und der Prinz (The Miracle of the Girl with the Three Doves and the Prince)*. Juv. Pr 1983 Brandenburg.

STERNFELDE, Karl
1962 *Aladdin und die Wunderlampe (Aladdin and the Magic Lamp)*. Juv. Pr 1962 Wismar.

STOCKHAUS, Heinz
Good-by Nicky. Dr (with Dieter Tolk). Pr 1969 Parchim.
‹Entscheidung› Zwischen Gestern und Morgen (‹Decision› Between Yesterday and Tomorrow). Dr. Pr 1972 Parchim.
Nur die Liebe... (Only Love...). Dr. Pr 1974 Parchim.
Heute um Mitternacht wirst du Witwe (Today at Midnight You'll Become a Widow). Mus Lib (based on Jan Makarius; M Hans J. Rogoll). Pr 1978 Parchim.
Die tolle Lisette (Crazy Lizzy). Mus Lib (M Hans J. Rogoll). Pr 1981 Parchim.
Die Mansarde (The Attic). Com. Pr 1981 Parchim.

STOLLE, Kurt Werner
1946 *Mensch an der Wende (Humanity at the Turning Point)*. Dr. Pr 1948 Schwerin.

STOLPER, Armin
23 Mar 1934 Breslau (now Wroclaw, Poland) –
Attended high school Görlitz; 1952-53 studied German literature and philosophy Jena; 53-59 dramaturg Senftenberg, MG, VB and Halle; 72-76 chief dramaturg DT; since then independent author; lives in Berlin. 1969 Erich Weinert Medal, 70 Lessing Prize, 72 FDGB Prize. Writes essays, poetry, prose, TV and radio plays.
1963 *Das Geständnis (The Confession)*. Dr (based on story by Galina Nikolayeva). Pr 1963 Wartenberg. *TdZ* 19-63/10.
1964 *Zwei Physiker (Two Physicists)*. Dr (based on novel by Daniil Granin, "Zwischen den Gewittern"). Pr 1964 DT planned, cancelled. Rev Pr 1965 Gera. *TdZ* 1965/24.
1966 *Ruzante*. Com (based on Angelo Beolco; incidental M Reiner Bredemeyer). Pr 1967 Halle. *Stücke*, Henschel 1974.
1967 *Amphytrion*. Com. Pr 1967 Halle. *TdZ* 1968/12. *Stücke*, 1974.
1967 *Vietnamesische Schulstunde (Vietnamese Lesson)*. Cantata (M Bernd Wefelmeyer). *Sinn & Form* 1968.
1969 *Zeitgenossen (Contemporaries)*. Dr (based on novel and film by Gabrilovitch and Raisman). Pr 1969 Halle. *TdZ* 1969/11. Henschel 1970. *Neue Stücke*, Henschel 1971. *Stücke*, 1974. Rev 1979 as Dienstreisende.
1970 *Der Zeitfaktor (The Time Factor)*. On. Pr 1970 Halle (part of program under collective title of "Anregung I").
1970 *Finale*. Scene. Pr 1970 Halle (part of program under collective title of "Anregung II").
1971 *Himmelfahrt zur Erde (Ascension to Earth)*. Dr (based on story by Sergey Anatov, "Der zerrissene Rubel"). Pr 1971 Halle. *TdZ* 1971/6. *Stücke*, 1974.

STOLPER (cont'd)

1972 *Klara und der Gänserich (Clara and the Gander)*. Com. Pr 1973 Halle. *TdZ* 1973/10. *Stücke*, 1974. Rev Pr 1977 Fkft/O. *Lausitzer Trilogie*, Henschel 1980.

1975 *Der Schuster und der Hahn (The Shoemaker and the Rooster)*. Com. Pr 1976 Weimar. *TdZ* 1976/1. *Lausitzer Trilogie*, 1980.

1976 *Aufzeichnungen eines Toten (Notes of a Dead Man)*. Dr (based on novel by Mikhail Bulgakov, "Theaterroman"). Pr 1976 Weimar. *Concerto Dramatico*, Henschel 1979.

1977 *Das Naturkind (The Child of Nature)*. Com (based on Voltaire, "L'ingenue"). Pr 1978 Senftenberg. *TdZ* 1978/8. *Concerto Dramatico*, 1979.

1977 *Die Vogelscheuche oder Die Heimkehr des verlorenen Sohnes (The Scarecrow or The Return of the Prodigal Son)*. Dr. Reading 1979 Dsdn. Pr 1981 Potsdam. *TdZ* 1980/6. *Lausitzer Trilogie*, 1980.

1978 *Concerto Dramatico*. Dr (based on Goethe). Pr 1978 Eisleben. Henschel 1979.

1978 *Hintereinanderweg (One After the Other)*. Four On: *Der Tod des Narren (The Fool's Death); Die nachgeholte Hochzeitsreise (The Belated Honeymoon); Wie du mir, so ich dir (I Do Unto You As You Do Unto Me); Der Schornsteinfeger und seine Frau (The Chimney Sweep and His Wife)*. Pr 1978. First two in *Poesie trägt einen weiten Mantel*, Henschel 1982.

1979 *Dienstreisende (Traveling on Official Business)*. Dr (rev of Zeitgenossen). Pr 1979 Stralsund, 2nd rev Pr 1982 Potsdam. *TdZ* 1982/9.

1979 *Konferenz mit Knarrpanti (A Conference with Knarrpanti)*. Com. *Die Karriere des Seiltänzers*, Rostock: Hinstorff, 1979.

1982 *Das Gemälde (The Painting)*. Dr (based on novel by Daniil Granin). Reading 1983 Potsdam. Pr 1984 Meiningen. *TdZ* 1984/5.

1984 *Die Ballade vom ‹sturen Planer Dieter Konczak und vom› aufsässigen Eisenbahner ‹Horst Hilpert› (The Ballad of ‹the Obstinate Planner Dieter Konczak and› the Recalcitrant Railroad Worker ‹Horst Hilpert›*. Com (incidental M Henry Krtschil). Pr 1986 Bautzen. *TdZ* 1986/5.

STOLZENBACH, Beatrice (also STOLZENBACH-MACHLER, Beatrice)

1951 *Dornröschen (Sleeping Beauty)*. Juv (based on Grimm). Pr 1952 Th. d. jg. Welt, Lpzg.

1952 *Zwerg Nase (Nose, the Dwarf)*. Juv (based on Hauff). Pr 1953 Th. d. jg. Garde, Halle.

1984 *Der märkische Eulenspiegel (Eulenspiegel of Brandenburg)*. Pp.

STOPF, Manfred

Hugo mit der Pauke (Hugo with the Kettledrum). Pp.

1979 *Hilfe, Freunde, die Vorstellung fällt aus (Help, Friends, the Performance is Cancelled)*. Pp. Pr 1977 KMSt.

STRAHL, Rudi
14 Sep 1931 Stettin (now Szczecin, Poland) –
After high school, various occupations (farmer, locksmith,
porcelain painter, motorcycle racer); then served for eight
years as officer in GDR army; studied at I.Lit Lpzg; editor,
satiric periodical "Eulenspiegel"; since 1961 independent author; lives in suburb of Berlin. Member GDR PEN; 1974 Lessing
Prize, 76 TV Prize, 77 FDGB Prize and Goethe Prize, 80 National Prize. Writes poetry, short stories, children's books,
TV and film scripts.

1968   *In Sachen Adam und Eva (The Case of Adam and Eve).*
         Com. Pr 1969 Halle. Henschel 1970. *Stücke*, Henschel
         1976. *Lustspiele, Einakter und szenische Miniaturen*,
         Henschel 1984.

1969   *Nochmal ein Ding drehen (Pulling Another Caper).* Com.
         Pr 1970 Mgdbg. Eulenspiegel 1972.

1970   *Wie die ersten Menschen (Like the First Humans).* Com.
         Pr 1971 Anklam. *Stücke*, 1976. Rev Pr 1979 Cottbus.
         Lustspiele..., 1984.

1971   *Die Trauerrede (The Funeral Oration).* Scene. Pr 19-
         71 Stralsund (under collective title of "Neun Minia-
         turen"). *Von Augenblick zu Augenblick*, Eulenspiegel
         1976. *Lustspiele...*, 1984.

1971   *‹Ein› ‹Der› Todestag (Anniversary of a Death).* Scene.
         Pr 1971 Stralsund (under collective title of "Neun
         Miniaturen"). *Stücke*, 1976. *Lustspiele...*, 1984.

1972   *Keine Leute, keine Leute (No People, No People).* Com.
         Pr 1973 Gera. *Stücke*, 1976.

1973   *Adam und Eva und kein Ende (Adam and Eve and No End).*
         Com. Pr 1973 Halle. *NdL* 1974/5. Eulenspiegel 1975.

1974   *Kein Ende auf Raten (No End in Installments).* Scene.
         Pr 1977 Wittenberg. *Von Augenblick...*, 1976. *Lust-*
         spiele..., 1984.

1974   *Ein Wiedersehen (A Reunion).* Scene. Pr 1977 Witten-
         berg. *Von Augenblick...*, 1976. *Der Schlips des Hel-*
         den, Henschel 1981. *Lustspiele...*, 1984.

1974   *Spätere Heirat nicht ausgeschlossen (Later Marriage*
         Not Impossible). Scene. Pr 1977 Wittenberg. *Von Au-*
         genblick..., 1976. *Lustspiele...*, 1984. *Menschen, Mas-*
         ken, Mimen, Henschel 1984.

1974   *Er, Sie, Es (He, She, It).* Scene. Pr 1977 Rudol-
         stadt (under collective title of "Die Trauerrede und
         anderes"). *Von Augenblick...*, 1976. *Lustspiele...*,
         1984.

1974   *Der Anruf (The Phone Call).* Scene. Pr 1977 Rudol-
         stadt (under collective title of "Die Trauerrede und
         anderes"). *Von Augenblick...*, 1976. *Lustspiele...*, 19-
         84.

1974   *Die Hose (The Trousers).* Scene. Pr 1977 Rudolstadt
         (under collective title of "Die Trauerrede und ande-
         res"). *Von Augenblick...*, 1976. *Lustspiele...*, 1984.

1974   *Der Sündenbock (The Scapegoat).* Scene. Pr 1978 Mei-
         ningen. *Von Augenblick...*, 1976. *Lustspiele...*, 1984.

STRAHL (cont'd)

1975   *Ein irrer Duft von frischem Heu (A Maddening Scent of Fresh Hay)*. Com. Pr 1975 MG. *Stücke*, 1976. *Lustspiele...*, 1984. Rev as Op Lib (M Wilhelm Neef). Pr 1981 Erfurt.

1976   *Arno Prinz von Wolkenstein oder Kader entscheiden alles (Arno Prince of Wolkenstein or Personnel Decides Everything)*. Com. Pr 1977 MG. Eulenspiegel 1979. *Lustspiele...*, 1984.

1978   *Der Schlips des Helden (The Hero's Tie)*. Scene. Pr 1984 Mgdbg. Henschel 1981. *Lustspiele...*, 1984.

1978   *Die Flüsterparty (The Whisper Party)*. Com. Pr 1978 MG planned, cancelled. *MG Programmheft* 1978/22 (one scene).

1979   *Er ist wieder da (He's Back Again)*. Com. Pr 1980 MG. *Der Schlips...*, 1981. *Lustspiele...*, 1984. Rev 1982 as Barby.

1980   *Und plötzlich: Ein Clown (And Suddenly: A Clown)*. Sc. Pr 1982 Brandenburg (under collective title of "Miniaturen"). Henschel 1982. *Lustspiele...*, 19-84. *Menschen...*, 1984.

1980   *Die Lust zum Gesang (The Pleasure of Singing)*. Sc. Pr 1984 Mgdbg. *Lustspiele...*, 1984. *Menschen...*, 1984.

1980   *Ein Zimmer mit Frühstück - für Musiker (A Room with Breakfast - for Musicians)*. Scene. Pr 1984 Mgdbg. *Lustspiele...*, 1984. *Menschen...*, 1984.

1980   *Sehr jung, sehr blond und das gewisse Etwas (Very Young, Very Blond, and a Certain Something)*. Scene (based on TV play). Pr 1985 Fkft/O. *Der Schlips...*, 1981. *Lustspiele...*, 1984.

1980   *Ein gewisser Katulla (A Certain Mr. Katulla)*. Scene. Pr 1984 Wittenberg. *Der Schlips...*, 1981.

1981   *Alles im Lot, alles im Eimer (Everything under Control, Everything Ok)*. On. Pr 1982 Döbeln (under collective title of "Gestrahltes"). *Der Schlips...*, 19-81. *Lustspiele...*, 1984.

1981   *Die Grimasse (The Grimace)*. Scene. Pr 1984 Mgdbg. *Lustspiele...*, 1984. *Menschen...*, 1984.

1981   *Vor aller Augen (In Plain Sight)*. Com. Pr 1982 Lpzg. TdZ 1982/8. Eulenspiegel 1983. *Lustspiele...*, 1984.

1981   *Schöne Ferien (Lovely Vacation)*. Com (based on TV play). Pr 1982 Döbeln (under collective title of "Gestrahltes"). *Lustspiele...*, 1984.

1982   *Barby*. Com (with Peter Hacks; rev of Er ist wieder da). Pr 1983 Halle. *NdL* 1983/6. Hacks, *Stücke nach Stücken 2*, Aufbau 1985.

1983   *Das Blaue vom Himmel (Pie in the Sky)*. Dr. Pr 1984 VB planned, cancelled. *TdZ* 1984/2. Pr 1986 Osnabrück.

1984   *Der Stein des Anstoßes (The Bone of Contention)*. Com. Pr 1985 Das Ei, Berlin. *TdZ* 1985/10.

STRANKA, Walter
20 Jan 1920 Kaaden (now Kadan, Czechoslovakia) –
Worked as glove maker; 1938 joined Communist Party; after 45
studied sociology Halle, Jena, Lpzg; since 47 independent author; lives in Weimar. 1958 Erich Weinert Medal, 59 Heinrich
Heine Prize. Writes poetry, TV scripts.

>Das Goldkind (The Darling Child). Juv. Pr 1968 Stral-
>sund.
>Die Brüder (The Brothers). Dr. Pr 1974.

STREUBEL, Manfred
5 Nov 1932 Leipzig –
After school, worked first for newspaper "Junge Welt", then
for DEFA newsreels and documentaries; 1953-57 studied German
literature Berlin, became editor for publisher Volk und Welt;
1972 I.Lit Lpzg, since then independent author in Dsdn. 1962
and 70 Erich Weinert Medal, 70 Heinrich Heine Prize. Writes
poetry, children's books, radio plays.

1963 Tatort Lehrerzimmer ‹Tatort Klassenzimmer› (Scene of
      Crime: Teachers' Room ‹Scene of Crime: Classroom›).
      Juv (with Rainer R. Lange; based on 1960 novel by W.
      K. Schweickert). Pr 1964 Th. d. Freundschaft, Berlin.
      TdZ 1964/8.
1963 Das jüngste Gericht von Rasselbach (The Last Judgment
      at Rasselbach). Juv. Pr 1964 Th. d. jg. Generation,
      Dsdn.
1965 Unser Drache Kasimir (Our Dragon Kasimir). Juv (based
      on radio play). Pr 1966 Th. d. jg. Welt, Lpzg. Rev
      1975 as Juv Mus Lib (M Bernd Wefelmeyer). Pr 1975
      Th. d. jg. Garde, Halle.
1968 Icke und die Hexe Yu (Me and Yu, the Witch). Juv Mus
      Lib (based on radio play; M Tilo Medek). Pr 1971
      Dsdn. TdZ 1971/5.
1969 Kinderkantate (Children's Cantata). Cantata (M G. Erd-
      mann). Pr 1969.
1973 Ratcliff rechnet ab (Ratcliff Settles All Accounts).
      Com. Pr 1974 Rostock.
1980 Da kam ein junger Königssohn (And Then a Young Prince
      Came). Juv Mus Lib (based on radio play; M Uwe Hilp-
      recht). Pr 1980 Th. d. jg. Generation, Dsdn.
1983 Testfahrt nach Thule (Test Run to Thule). Mus Lib.
      Pr 1984 Rostock.
      Stadt ohne Liebe (City Without Love). Juv (based on
      Lev Ustinov).

STRITTMATTER, Erwin
14 Aug 1912 Spremberg –
Became baker's apprentice, then worked as waiter, zookeeper,
and chauffeur; 1934 arrested for antifascist activity; served
in WW II, deserted; after 45 again baker, then farmer; joined
SED in 47; later became newspaper correspondent and editor,
now lives in Dollgow as independent author. Member AdK since
1959; Vice-President of GDR Authors' Assoc; 53, 55, 64, and
76 National Prize, 61 Lessing Prize, 66 Fontane Prize, 82 Order of Merit. Writes novels, short stories, children's books.

STRITTMATTER (cont'd)
1951-52 ‹Die neue Straße von› Katzgraben (‹The New Street of›
         Katzgraben). Com (incidental M Hanns Eisler). Pr
         1953 BE. TdZ 1970/9 (Act I, Scene 4). Aufbau 1954.
         Stücke, Henschel 1957. Lpzg: Hofmeister, 1961. Auf-
         bau 1967 (with Holländerbraut). Die ersten Schritte,
         Halle: Mitteldt. Verlag, 1986.
1958   Katzgraben 1958. Com. Pr 1958 DT. Aufbau 1960.
1959   Die Holländerbraut (The Dutch Bride). Dr. Pr 1960 DT.
         Aufbau 1961. Sozialistische Dramatik, Henschel 1968.
         Aufbau 1967 (with Katzgraben).
1968   Tinko. Juv (based on 1954 novel, dramatized by Hans-
         Dieter Schmidt). Pr 1969 Th. d. jg. Welt, Lpzg. TdZ
         1970/7.
         Kramkalender (Odds-and-Ends Calendar). Dramatic Col-
         lage (based on Brecht). Pr 1974 DT.

STRUDTHOFF, Inge‹borg›   see Inge‹borg› KRENGEL-STRUDTHOFF

STURM, Herbert
1980   Das Gespenst von Canterville (The Canterville Ghost).
         Mus Lib (based on Oscar Wilde; M Friedrich-Wilhelm
         Tiller). Pr 1981 Gera.

STÜRZEBECHER, Charlotte
1903 - ?
After WW II, worked on farm; 1959 became member of worker-
writer group (with husband Friedrich); 62 began association
with Eisleben Th. Wrote short stories.
         Brinkmanns Tochter (Brinkmann's Daughter). Dr.
1963   Der Bus hält an der Brücke (The Bus Stops at the
         Bridge). Dr (with Friedrich Stürzebecher). Pr 1964
         Eisleben. TdZ 1964/6.

STÜRZEBECHER, Friedrich
1901 - ?
After WW II, worked on farm; 1959 became member of worker-
writer group (with wife Charlotte); 62 began association with
Eisleben Th.
         Unruhe im Dorf (Unrest in the Village). Dr.
1963   Der Bus hält an der Brücke (The Bus Stops at the
         Bridge). Dr (with Charlotte Stürzebecher). Pr 1964
         Eisleben. TdZ 1964/6.

SÜSS, Anna
1952   Aschenbrödel (Cinderella). Juv (with Susanne Dancker
         and Herbert Bendey; based on Grimm). Pr 1952 Th. am
         Schiffbauerdamm, Berlin. Berlin: Jg. Welt, 1952.
1954   Hans, der Wettermacher (Jack the Rainmaker). Juv.

SWAROWSKY, Hans

Orpheus und Euridice. Op Lib (new adaptation; M Christoph Glück).

Die Pilger von Mekka (The Pilgrims of Mecca). Op Lib (new adaptation, based on "La rencontre imprevue"; M Christoph Glück).

SWITZ, Dusan   see Jurij **BREZAN**

TASCHE, Elke
20 Nov 1927 Wuppertal –
Studied theater history; after 1960 worked with amateur theaters; since 71 dramaturg VB. Writes radio plays.

1974   *Die stumme Schönheit (The Mute Beauty)*. On (based on Elias Schlegel, "Der Witzling"). *Einakter*, Lpzg: Zentralhaus für Kulturarbeit der DDR, 1974.

1979   *Gespräche im Salon (Conversations in the Parlor)*. Dr.

1979   *Nun könntest du auch etwas tun (Now You Could Do Something Too)*. On (based on radio play by Hansgeorg Meyer). *Neumann: 2 x klingeln*, Lpzg: Zentralhaus für Kulturarbeit der DDR, no date.

1979   *Der Kriminalfall (The Criminal Case)*. On (based on radio play by Gerhard Jäckel). *Neumann: 2 x klingeln*.

1979   *Der blinde Passagier (The Stowaway)*. On (based on radio play by P. Brock). *Neumann: 2 x klingeln*.

1980   *Ich bin nicht Isaak (I am Not Isaac)*. Juv.

1983   *Hänsel und Gretel – kein Märchen (Hansel and Gretl – Not a Fairy Tale)*. Juv (based on Grimm).

1985   *Mariken von Niwegen*. Dr (based on Dutch mystery play).

THIEME, Rolf
1976   *Animationen (Animations)*. Pp. Pr 1977 Halle.

1978   *Die beiden Geschenke (The Two Gifts)*. Pp (with Lena Foellbach). Pr 1978 Halle.

THILMANN, Johannes Paul
11 Jan 1906 Dresden – 1973 Dresden
1965   *Peter Schlemihl*. Bl Lib (based on story by Adalbert von Chamisso). Pr 1966 Brandenburg.

THON, Manfred
1955   *Die Insurrektion*. Dr.

TIEFENSEE, Siegfried
20 Oct 1922 Rastenburg –
Received music instruction as child, started composing at age 14; served in WW II, POW until 1946; studied music pedagogy at Quedlinburg Conservatory, later at MHS Halle; theater orchestra conductor Stendal, Gera, since 58 Lpzg. Wrote music for more than 250 plays, among them about 100 juvenile plays, operas, and ballets.

   Der Tuchkauf zu Tratting (The Cloth Purchase at Tratting). Bl (based on legend). Pr 1958 Annaberg.

1959   *Cipollino (Little Onion)*. Juv Mus (with Hans-Dieter Schmidt; based on Giovanni Rodari, "Zwiebelchen"). Pr 1959 Weimar.

1960   *Katz und Kätzchen (Cat and Kitten)*. Juv Op (with Hans-Dieter Schmidt; based on Samuil Marshak, "Das Katzenhaus").

1965   *Adrian und das rote Auto (Adrian and the Red Car)*. Juv Op. Pr 1966 Th. d. jg. Welt, Lpzg.

TIEFENSEE (cont'd)
        Mascha und der Bär (Masha and the Bear). Juv Mus
        (with Wolfgang Rainer; based on Russian fairy tale).
        Pr 1968 Bernburg.
1971   *Der neue Struwelpeter (The New Shaggy-Pete)*. Juv Op
        (with Hans-Dieter Schmidt; based on H. G. Stengel).
        Pr 1972 Th. d. jg. Welt, Lpzg.
1973   *Vom Äffchen, das eine Brille trug ‹Der Brunnen unterm
        Mangobaum› (The Little Monkey Who Wore Glasses ‹The
        Well under the Mango Tree›)*. Juv Op (based on African
        fairy tale). Pr 1973 Erfurt.
        Der Prinz von Portugal (The Prince of Portugal). Juv
        Op.
        Rotkäppchen (Little Red Riding Hood). Juv Op (based
        on Grimm, as adapted by Yevgenyi Schwarz).
1980   *Der Zauberer von Smaragdenstadt (The Wizard of Emer-
        ald City)*. Juv Op (with Norbert Solga; based on Baum,
        "The Wizard of Oz"). Pr 1981 Halberstadt.
1983   *Was wird denn hier gespielt oder Maus und Kater im
        Theater (What is Playing Here or Cat and Mouse in the
        Theater)*. Juv Mus (with Norbert Solga). Pr 1984 Th.
        d. jg. Welt, Lpzg.

TISCHLER, Anneliese   see Anneliese SCHULZ

TITTEL, Gerhard
1965   *Der Bauer und sein König (The Peasant and His King)*.
        Dr. Pr 1966 Cottbus.

TRADOWSKY, Walter
        Das tapfere Schneiderlein (The Brave Little Tailor).
        Juv (based on Grimm). Pr 1950 Dsdn.

TRIMM, Thomas   see Ehm WELK

TROCHE, Peter
1942 Berlin –
Worked as insurance agent, construction laborer, auxiliary policeman; amateur actor; after 1969 professional actor in Görlitz, Zittau, Senftenberg. Writes poetry, prose, radio plays.
1978-79 *Barackenliebe (Barracks Love)*. Dr. Reading 1982 Lpzg.
        TdZ 1982/10.
        Sonniges Wetter (Sunny Weather). Two On.
        Der Aufenthaltsraum (The Dayroom). Dr.
1984   *Die Haltestelle (The Bus Stop)*. On. Pr 1984 Senften-
        berg.

TROLLE, Lothar
1944 –
Studied theater history and philosophy; now independent author, lives in Berlin.
1966   *Papa Mama*. On. Pr 1979 Krefeld. Suhrkamp 1968.
1968   *König Lear (King Lear)*. Dr (based on Shakespeare).
1969   *Der letzte Einzelbauer (The Last Independent Farmer)*.
        Dr.

TROLLE (cont'd)

1970   ‹Das ‹beispielhafte› Spiel vom› Leben und Tod des Peter Göring: Biografie eines glücklichen Bürgers (‹The
‹Exemplary› Play about› Life and Death of Peter Göring: Biography of a Happy Citizen). Dr (with Thomas
Brasch). Pr 1971 student production Berlin. Henschel
1971.

1970-74 Greikemeier--Tod, Auferstehung, Leben eines Genossen-
schaftsbauern (Greikemeier--Death, Resurrection, Life
of a Collective Farmer). Part I of dramatic trilogy.
Pr 1978.

1975 Weltuntergang Berlin (End of the World Berlin). Trilogy, Part II. Pr 1979 student production, West Berlin.

1978 Bibelgeschichten ‹Geschichten nach der Bibel› (Bible
Stories ‹Stories Based on the Bible›). Scenes. Th.h.
1979/3. Reading 1982 Lpzg.

1979 Waldeslust (Forest Delight). Trilogy, Part III.

1980 Hammel und Bammel als Verkehrspolizisten (Mutt and
Jeff as Traffic Cops). Com. Pr 1980 Heidelberg.

1983 ‹34› Sätze über eine Frau (‹34› Statements about a
Woman). On. Pr 1985 Gera.

1984 Kasperltrilogie (Punch Trilogy). Three On: Die Stim-
me seines Herrn (His Master's Voice); Kasperl erhält
eine Lektion (Punch Receives a Lesson); Kasperl findet eine Frau (Punch Finds a Wife).

TROMMER, Rudolf
1981   Puffi. Juv. Pr 1982 Nordhausen.

TSCHESNO-HELL, Michael
17 Feb 1902 Wilna (now Vilnjus, Poland) - 24 Feb 1980 Leipzig
1922 joined KPD; worked for Communist Press; 33-45 emigration
to France, Holland, Switzerland; after return, founded publishing company "Volk und Welt." 1954, 57 and 66 National
Prize, 69 City of Lpzg Prize, 72 FDGB Prize; member AdK since
69. Translator, editor, wrote film scripts.
1956   Der Hauptmann von Köln (The Captain from Cologne).
Com (with Slatan Dudow; based on film). Pr 1959 Lpzg.
Henschel 1956.

TSCHOLAKOWA, Ginka
Native of Bulgaria, studied in Berlin; now married to Heiner
Müller. Translator.
1967   Lanzelot ‹Drachenoper› (Lancelot ‹The Dragon Opera›).
Op Lib (with Heiner Müller; based on Yevgenyi Schwarz
"Der Drache"; M Paul Dessau). Pr 1969 St. Op. TdZ
1970/3. Theaterarbeit, Berlin (W): Rotbuch, 1975.

1971-72 Die Möwe (The Seagull). Dr (with Heiner Müller; based
on Chekhov). Pr 1973 Potsdam.

1977 Das fliegende Pferd (The Flying Horse). Juv (based on
Bengalese legend).

1982-83 Tarelkins Tod (Tarelkins's Death). Com (with Heiner
Müller; based on Alexander Sukhovo-Kobylin).

TSCHOLAKOWA (cont'd)

1983   *Wladimir Majakowski Tragödie (Vladimir Mayakovsky's "Tragedy")*. Dr (adaptation with Heiner Müller). Pr 1983 Schillerth., West Berlin. *Th.h.* 1983/9.

TUMMELEY, Werner   see Werner BERNHARDY

UX, Catherine   see Elisabeth HAUPTMANN

VEKEN, Karl
22 July 1904 Essen - 21 July 1971 Karl Marx Stadt
Studied economics and music, then became teacher in Berlin;
1927 joined SPD, 29 KPD; worked as journalist; 34-36 imprisoned for high treason; 37 fled to Czechoslovakia and France;
rearrested, 41-45 concentration camp; after WW II became high
school principal. 1955 Literature Prize. Wrote prose, children's books, radio plays.
1951   *Baller contra Baller (Baller vs. Baller).* Com. Pr
        1951 DT. *Gegenwartsdramatik*, Lpzg: Hofmeister, 1954.

VENUS, Frieder
Actor.
1977   *Traumtanz (Dream Dance).* Dr. Pr 1978 Eisenach.

VIERTEL, Martin
2 Oct 1925 Lugau -
Served in WW II, then POW; 1948-56 various occupations, including journalist; 56-59 I.Lit Lpzg; 59-62 managing director, Workers' Theater, Wismut. 1969 FDGB Prize, Erich Weinert Medal, 70 Heinrich Mann Prize. Writes novels, short stories, children's books.
1959   *Der Weg zum Wir (The Road towards Us).* Dr (with Klaus
        Manfred Pastowski). Pr 1960 Workers' Theater, Wis-
        mut.
1973   *Robert Bottenschuh.* Dr. Pr 1974 Workers' Theater,
        Wismut.

VOGEL, Roderich
1978   *Wieder übern Regenbogen (Over the Rainbow Again).* Juv
        Mus Lib (based on Alexander Wolkow; M Klaus Hofmann).
        Pr 1978 Wittenberg.

VOGT, Helmut
1 Sep 1901 Berlin - 28 May 1953 Borna
Wrote novels and short prose.
1923   *Mitternacht (Midnight).* Dr.
1924   *Prometheus.* Dr.
1932   *Etappe Preußen (Base Prussia).* Dr.
1938   *Die Lampe der Felicitas (Felicity's Lamp).* Com.
1939   *Das Andenken aus Lancaster (The Memento from Lancas-
        ter).* Dr.
1946   *Der Scharlatan (The Charlatan).* Com.
1947-48 *Oberst Hagenachs Gäste (Colonel Hagenach's Guests).*
        Com.
1949   *Jede Nacht geht zu Ende (Every Night Comes to an End)*
        Dr. Pr 1950 Chemnitz (now KMSt).
1949   *Herr Glitsch wird es schaffen (Mr. Glitsch Will Man-
        age).* Com. Pr 1950 Neustrelitz.
1950   *Zwischenfall auf Norderney (Incident on Norderney).*
        Dr. Pr 1951 Meißen.

VOGT (cont'd)
1951   *Das Fräulein aus Potsdam (The Young Lady from Pots-
        dam).* Com (incidental M Otto Wahrenburg). Pr 1951
        Görlitz.
1953   *Hundetage (Dog Days).* Dr. Pr 1954 Meißen.

VÖLKEL, Ulrich
30 Oct 1940 Platien –
After high school, served in GDR Army; assistant in Putbus
Th; cultural functionary Schwerin; 1963-65 studied at I.Lit
Lpzg, then worked in Schwerin and Rostock Th; since 71 independent author. 1968 Fritz Reuter Prize. Writes songs, poetry, prose, children's books.
1969   *Spektakel in Seltensow (A Ruckus in Seltensow).* Com.
        Pr 1969 Rostock.
1973   *Das ideale Ehepaar (The Ideal Married Couple).* Com.
        Pr 1974 Bautzen.

VÖLLGER, Wilfried
Writes short stories, children's books. Lives in Halle.
1977   *Der blaue Teppich (The Blue Carpet).* Pp (M Hans Jür-
        gen Wenzel). Pr 1978 Halle.
1978   *Die fliegenden Pferde von Habis Bat (The Flying Hor-
        ses of Habis Bat).* Pp (with Wolf Bulter). Pr 1978
        Dessau.

VOLLSDORFF, Erwin
        Bi de Düwelswieden (At the Devil's Pasture). Dr (in
        Low German). Pr 1952 Rostock.
        *Den Letzten beißen die Hunde (Last One Is a Rotten
        Egg).* Juv. Lpzg: Hofmeister, 1955.
        Heine und der Tannenbaum (Heine and the Fir Tree).
        Juv. Lpzg: Zentralhaus für Volkskunst, 1955.
        Glück über den kurzen Weg (Luck in the Short Run).
        On. Lpzg: Zentralhaus für Volkskunst, 1956.

VOSS, Helmut
4 May 1932 Ludwigslust (now Slupsk, Poland) –
After school, worked in factory and as carpenter; now lives
near Lpzg. Writes for Protestant lay theater groups.
1964   *Doktor Martinus.* Dr. *Verkündigungsspiele der Gemein-
        de,* Berlin: Evangelischer Verlag, 1964.
1965   *Der ungehorsame Prophet (The Disobedient Prophet).*
        Dr. *Verkündigungsspiele der Gemeinde,* Berlin: Evange-
        lischer Verlag, 1965.

WAGNER, Bernd
30 May 1948 Wurzen –
Teacher; lives in Berlin. Writes prose, poetry, children's books.
1970   *Das Hemd eines Glücklichen (A Happy Man's Shirt)*. Juv (based on story by Anatole France). Pr 1971 Th. d. Freundschaft, Berlin. *TdZ* 1971/9.

WAGNER-REGENY, Rudolf
28 Aug 1903 Szaszregen (Hungary) – 18 Sept 1983 Berlin
1919-23 studied in Lpzg and Berlin; 23-25 rehearsal conductor Volksoper, Berlin; independent composer until 45, then Prof. MHS Rostock; 50-68 Prof. of composition, MHS Berlin. Member AdK Berlin East and West, Bavarian Academy of Fine Arts; 1955 National Prize.
1923   *Sganarelle oder Der Schein trügt (Sganarelle or Appearances Are Deceiving)*. Op (based on Moliere). Pr 1929 Essen.
1927   *Moschopulos*. Op (based on Franz Pocci). Pr 1928 Gera.
1928   *Der nackte König (The Naked King)*. Op (based on Hans Christian Andersen, "The Emperor's New Clothes"). Pr 1930 Gera.
1929   *Esau und Jakob*. Oratorio. Pr 1930 Gera.
1934   *Der Günstling (The Favorite)*. Op (with Caspar Neher; based on Georg Büchner). Pr 1935 Dsdn. Vienna: Universal, 1935. Revised 1952 as Der Günstling oder Die letzten Tage des großen Herrn Fabiano.
1936   *Der zerbrochene Krug (The Broken Jug)*. Bl (based on Heinrich Kleist). Pr 1937 Berlin.
1938   *Die Bürger von Calais (The Citizens of Calais)*. Op (with Caspar Neher; based on Georg Kaiser). Pr 1939 St.Op. Vienna: Universal, 1938.
1940   *Johanna Balk*. Op (with Caspar Neher). Pr 1941 Vienna. Vienna: Universal, 1941.
1940-50 *Persische Späße ‹Persische Episode› (Persian Jests ‹Persian Episode›)*. Op (with Caspar Neher; based on "1001 Nights"). Pr 1963 Rostock.
1952   *Der Günstling oder Die letzten Tage des großen Herrn Fabiano (The Favorite or The Last Days of the Great Mr. Fabiano)*. Op (rev of Der Günstling; with Caspar Neher). Pr 1953 Dsdn. Reclam 1960.
1957-58 *Prometheus*. Oratorio (based on Aeschylos). Pr 1959 Kassel.
1958-60 *Das Bergwerk zu Falun (The Mine at Falun)*. Op (based on novella by Hugo von Hofmannsthal). Pr 1961 Salzburg.

WALLENDORFF, Siegfried
1982   *Das kalte Herz (The Cold Heart)*. Juv (based on Wilhelm Hauff). Pr 1982 Neustrelitz.

WALLROTH, Werner W.
Die Geldheirat (Marrying for Money).   Com (based on Scribe). Pr 1970 Mgdbg.

WALLSTEIN, Bärbel
Studied sociology and German literature; now works for Brecht Center, Berlin.
1980   *Männerwirtschaft (Male Household).* Com (incidental M Hans Henkels). Pr 1981 Wittenberg.

WALTHER, Joachim
6 Oct 1943 Chemnitz (now Karl Marx Stadt) –
1962-63 worked as stage hand and mechanic; 63-67 studied art history, pedagogy, and German literature Univ. Berlin; after 68 worked as teacher and editor in Berlin; now lives in Kladrun. Writes prose, film scripts, and radio plays.
1975   *Ich bin nun mal kein Yogi (I'm Just Not a Yogi).* Mus (based on story and film; M Jens-Uwe Günther).   Pr 1978 Weimar.

WANDER, FRED
5 Jan 1917 Vienna –
Left school at age 14, traveled through Europe taking various jobs; 1939 arrested and interned in France, deported to Germany, interned in concentration camp; after 45 joined Austrian Communist Party; worked as reporter; studied directing at Reinhardt Seminar; married Maxie Wander; 55 I. Lit Lpzg; after 58 lived in GDR as independent author; now back in Vienna. 1966 Fontane Prize, 72 Heinrich Mann Prize. Writes children's books, short stories.
1976   *Josua läßt grüßen (Regards from Joshua).* Dr. Pr 19-77 Weimar. *TdZ* 1977/1. Aufbau 1979.
1977   *Der Bungalow.* Dr (based on TV play).   Pr 1978 Senftenberg. Aufbau 1979 (with *Josua...*).
1979   *Das taubengraue Haus (The Dove-Grey House).* Com. Pr 1980 Weimar. *TdZ* 1980/3.
1980   *Das Erdbeben von Bukarest (The Bucharest Earthquake).* Dr.
1982   *Patrique, Patrique oder Der Salamander.* Com. Pr 19-83 Weimar.

WANDER, Maxie
3 Jan 1933 Vienna – 20 Nov 1977 Berlin
Left school to work in factory and office; married Fred Wander, moved with him to GDR in 1958; worked as secretary, photographer, journalist. Wrote radio plays, children's books, short stories.
1977   *Guten Morgen, du Schöne (Good Morning, My Lovely).* Dr (based on tape-recorded interviews). Pr 1978 DT. Berlin: Der Morgen, 1977. Darmstadt: Luchterhand, 1978. Aufbau 1980. Engl. tr *Connexions*, 1982.

WANGENHEIM, Friedel von
Son of Gustav and Inge von Wangenheim.
> *Ein erfundenes Fressen (An Invented Godsend).* Com. Pr 1980 Tip.
> *Neptuns Damen (Neptune's Ladies).* Com. Pr 1983 Met.

WANGENHEIM, Gustav von (Pseud. Hans HUSS)
18 Feb 1895 Wiesbaden - 5 Aug 1975 Berlin
After school, first worked on farm, then became actor; studied under Max Reinhardt; served in WW I, then actor again; 19-22 joined KPD; after 28 author and stage director for workers' theater; 33-45 exile in USSR, worked as film director; after return, became managing director of DT and independent author. 1957 Ernst Moritz Arndt Medal, 59 Erich Weinert Medal, 66 National Prize. Wrote poetry, prose, film scripts.

1917   *Der Mann Fjodor (That Man Feodor).* Dr. Pr 1921.
1918   *Der Lausbub Fritz (Fritz, the Rascal).* Com. Pr 1918.
1923   *Chor der Arbeiter (Workers' Chorus).* Choral work. Berlin: Vereinigung Int'l Verlagsanstalten, 1924.
1924   *7000.* Choral work.
1924   *Massenpantomime gegen den Krieg (Mass Pantomime Against the War).* Pantomime.
1928   *Erinnert Euch (Remember).* Choral work.
1929   *Chorwerk über den 8-Stundentag (Choral Work about the 8-Hour Day).*
1930   *Die Mausefalle (The Mousetrap).* Com. Pr 1931 Berlin. Rev 1947 as Die Maus in der Falle.
1931   *Da ‹Hier› liegt der Hund begraben (There's the Rub!).* Com. Pr 1932.
1932   *Wer ist der Dümmste? (Who Is the Dumbest?).* Com. Pr 1933.
1933   *Das Urteil (The Verdict).* Dr. Pr 1934.
1934   *Helden im Keller (Heroes in the Basement).* Dr. Pr 19-34.
1936   *Agenten (Agents).* Dr.
1937-38 *Volksfreunde (Friends of the People).* Com.
1938   *Der Friedensstörer (The Disturber of the Peace).* Dr. Pr 1938 Moscow.
1946   *Die fromme Marta (Pious Martha).* Dr (based on Tirso de Molina). Pr 1950 Altenburg.
1947   *Die Maus in der Falle (The Mouse in the Trap).* Com (rev of Die Mausefalle). Pr 1948 Weimar. Henschel 1947.
1949   *Du bist der Richtige (You're Just the One).* Com. Pr 1950 Th. d. Freundschaft, Berlin. Berlin: Neues Leben, 1950.
1950   *Auch in Amerika (Even in America).* Dr. Pr 1950 DT.
1951   *Jetzt sind wir schon weiter ‹Wir sind schon weiter› (‹By Now› We've Already Made Some Progress).* Juv. Pr 1951 Th. d. Freundschaft, Berlin.
1952   *An beiden Ufern der Spree (On Both Shores of the Spree).* Revue. Pr 1952 Met.
1953   *Toleranz (Tolerance).* Dr.

WANGENHEIM,Gustav von (cont'd)

1958   *Studentenkomödie ‹Mit der Zeit werden wir schon fertig› (Student Comedy ‹We'll Deal with the Times, All Right›).* Com. Pr 1959 Rostock. Berlin: Neues Leben, 1958.

1959   *Die vertauschten Brüder (The Interchanged Brothers).* Com. Pr 1959 Rostock.

1960   *Hier muß ein Mann ins Haus (A Man is Needed in this House).* Com (based on Lope de Vega).

WANGENHEIM, Inge von   (nee Franke)
1 July 1912 Berlin -
After school, became actress in Piscator troupe; 1930 joined KPD; 33 emigrated to USSR by way of France; married Gustav von Wangenheim; worked as editor of journal "Freies Deutschland"; after 45 journalist, actress, and director for stage and TV; now independent author in Weimar. 1966 FDGB Prize, 68 Heinrich Heine Prize. Writes novels, short stories, essays.

1961   *Professor Hudebraach.* Dr (based on novel). Pr 1964 Erfurt.

1982   *Genosse Jemand und die Klassik (Comrade Somebody and the Classics).* Com.

WASCHINSKY, Peter

    Schneewittchen (Snow White). Pp (based on Grimm). Pr Neubrandenburg.

    Regenwürmer ‹Legenden aus dem alten Vietnam› (Earthworms ‹Legends from Old Vietnam›). Juv. Pr Neubrandenburg.

    Kasparette (Miss Punch). Pp. Pr Neubrandenburg.

WATERSTRADT, Berta
9 Aug 1907 Kattowitz (now Katowice, Poland) -
Worked as typist; 1925 moved to Berlin; 31 joined KPD; 33 arrested, went to England; 34 returned to Germany, imprisoned for anti-fascist activity; 44-45 forced labor in armament industry; after 45 worked for GDR Radio, then independent author in Berlin. 1949 National Prize, 55 Clara Zetlin Medal. Writes radio plays, film scripts, short stories.

1958   *Ehesache Lorenz (The Lorenz Marriage Case).* Com. Pr 1958 Prague.

1963   *Einen Tick hat schließlich jeder (After All, Everyone Is a Little Peculiar).* Com. Pr 1964 Rostock.

1967   *Die Männer sind alle Verbrecher (All Men Are Criminals).* Com. Pr 1967.

WEFELMEYER, Bernd
16 Mar 1940 Berlin -
1960-66 MHS Berlin; 64-68 studied composition with Ruth Zechlin and Rudolf Wagner-Regeny; 68-73 music director GDR Radio, then music director VB. Writes music for stage, radio, and TV, as well as own libretti.

1972   *Tambari.* Juv Op.

1973   *Party.* Bl.

WEFELMEYER (cont'd)

1973   *Das Durchgangszimmer (The Connecting Room)*. Mus (with Heinz Kahlau; based on story by Renate Holland-Moritz). Pr 1973 Halle.

1974   *Die Weihnachtsgans Auguste (A Christmas Goose Called Augusta)*. Juv Op (with Rolf Rohde; based on story by Friedrich Wolf). Pr 1974 Brandenburg.

1975   *Unser Drache Kasimir (Our Dragon Kasimir)*. Juv Mus (with Manfred Streubel; based on his play). Pr 1975 Th. d. jg. Garde, Halle.

1984   *Dreiklang (Three-Part Harmony)*. Juv Mus (with Peter Ensikat). Pr 1983 Th. d. Freundschaft, Berlin.

WEGERDT, Friedrich (Fritz)

1952   *Der Zeuge wird zum Richter (The Witness Becomes the Judge)*. Dr. Pr 1953 Th. am Schiffbauerdamm, Berlin.

WEICKER, Regina

4 June 1945 Zöblitz –

Worked as sales clerk and bookkeeper. Since 1974 independent author in KMSt.

1973   *Die Ausgezeichneten (The Distinguished Ones)*. Dr. Pr 1974 VB (part of program under collective title of "Spektakel 2"). *TdZ* 1974/12.

1980   *König Eduards Moral (King Edward's Moral)*. Dr. Pr 1980 Workers' Theater, Sömmerda.

WEIDE, Martina

1965   *Die heute 17 sind (Those Who Are 17 Today)*. Juv. Pr 1966 Th. d. jg. Welt, Lpzg.

WEIDERMANN, Werner

Dramaturg, Th. d. Freundschaft, Berlin

1977   *Schneewittchen (Snow White)*. Juv (based on Grimm). Pr 1977 Stendal.

WEINDICH, Günter

Manager and stage director, Zeitz Th.

1968   *Generalprobe (Dress Rehearsal)*. Com. Pr 1968 Zeitz.

1970   *Die unsichtbare Front (The Invisible Front)*. Dr. Pr 1971 Zeitz.

1974   *Weil wir keine Kinder sind (Because We're Not Children)*. Dr. Pr 1974 Zeitz.

1977   *Der letzte Gast (The Last Guest)*. Dr. Pr 1977 Zeitz.

1985   *Das Pawlow Haus (The Pavlov House)*. Dr. Pr 1985 Zeitz.

WEINDICH, Josef-Adolf

1983   *Daniel Druskat*. Dr (based on TV script by Helmut Sakowski). Pr 1984 Neustrelitz.

WEINHOLD, Siegfried
16 Oct 1934 Drebach -
Various occupations, including stagehand KMSt; 1967-70 I.Lit
Lpzg; since 71 independent author in Merseburg. Writes children's books, prose, radio plays.
1968   *Lockruf des Abenteuers   (The Lure of Adventure)*. Dr
        (based on novel). Pr 1969 Zwickau.

WEISS, Rudolf
5 Apr 1920 Eisenach - 17 Dec 1974 Eisenach
1937-40 worked for savings bank; service in WW II, severely
wounded; after 45 bookkeeper; 55 I.Lit Lpzg, then independent
author in Eisenach. Wrote radio plays, children's books, adventure and crime novels.
        Zum Sterben geboren (Born to Die). Dr. Pr 1949 Guben.

WEISSIG, Bernd
Composer and librettist.
1983   *So long, Cello*. Rock Mus. Pr 1984 Potsdam.

WELK, Ehm   (Pseud. Thomas TRIMM)
29 Aug 1884 Biesenbrow - 19 Dec 1966 Bad Doberan/Rostock
After middle school, worked for Stettin newspaper; became seaman for a few years, then journalist and editor; 1934 arrested and placed in concentration camp; 45 founded adult education system, became director of Schwerin school; after 50 independent author. Member AdK; 1954 National Prize, 56 Dr. h.
c. Greifswald, 64 honorary Professor. Wrote poetry, short stories, novels, film scripts.
1920   *Gewitter über Gotland (Thunderstorm over Gotland)*. Dr.
        Pr 1927 VB. Rostock: Hinstorff, 1964.
1926   *Kreuzabnahme   (Descent from the Cross)*. Dr. Pr 1927
        Mannheim. Rostock: Hinstorff, 1964.
1931   *‹Michael› Knobbe oder Das Loch im Gesicht (‹Michael›
        Knobbe or The Hole in the Face)*. Com. Rev 1960 as
        Der Geist von Potsmar.
1932   *Schwarzbrot (Dark Bread)*. Dr. Rev 1961. *Stücke*, Hen-
        schel 1964.
1960   *Der Geist von Potsmar (The Ghost of Potsmar)*. Dr (rev
        of ‹Michael› Knobbe...). *Stücke*, 1964.

WENDLAND, Heide   (real name Annemarie HEROLD, nee HUNGER)
15 Dec 1924 Dresden -
Sales clerk; after 1945 became teacher, later editor; married
to author Gottfried Herold; lives in Dsdn. Writes short stories, children's books, TV plays.
1963   *Der Liebe ist kein Wind zu kalt (No Wind Is Too Cold
        for Love)*. Com (with Gottfried Herold; based on his
        story "Der rothaarige Widerspruch"). Pr 1964 Bautzen.

WENDLER, Horst-Ulrich
5 Mar 1926 Berlin -
Served in WW II, POW until 1946; then teacher until 48; 49-51
dramaturg at various theaters; 52-53 studied I.Lit Lpzg; 54-
59 director of cabaret "Brennessel," Brandenburg; 60-64 dra-

WENDLER, Horst-Ulrich (cont'd)

maturg VB; since then independent author in Berlin; married to Ursula Damm-Wendler. 1953 Drama Prize, 54 Juvenile Book Prize. Writes radio and TV plays, children's books.

1949   *Der kleine und der große Klaus (Little Claus and Big Claus).* Juv (based on Hans Christian Andersen). Pr 1962 Rostock.

1950   *Das Spiel von der verlorenen Zeit (The Play about Lost Time).* Juv (based on Yevgenyi Schwarz). Pr 19-53 Th. d. jg. Welt, Lpzg. Lpzg: Hofmeister, 1953.

1950   *Jeppe oder Der Lohn der Dummheit (Jeppe or The Reward of Stupidity).* Com (based on Ludvig Holberg). Pr 19-50 Th. d. jg. Welt, Lpzg. Rev 1952 as ‹Das große Abenteuer des› Jeppe vom Berge.

1952   *Der Fall Merzbach ‹Wenn wir zusammenstehen› (The Merzbach Case ‹If We Stand Together›).* Dr. Pr 1953 Erfurt.

1952   *‹Das große Abenteuer des› Jeppe vom Berge (‹The Great Adventure of› Jeppe from the Mountain).* Com (rev of Jeppe oder Der Lohn der Dummheit). Pr 1965 Schwerin.

1953   *Thomas Müntzer in Mühlhausen.* Dr. Pr 1953 Eisleben.

1953-55 *Von Leichtgläubigen und Denkfaulen (Of Credulous and Mentally Lazy People).* 3 On (based on Hans Sachs).

1954   *Das Märchen vom Mond (The Tale of the Moon).* Juv. Lpzg: Hofmeister, 1954. Henschel 1964.

1954-55 *Von Gaunern und Narren (Of Scoundrels and Fools).* 3 On (based on Hans Sachs).

1955   *Von List, Torheit und Betrug (Of Cunning, Folly, and Deceit).* 2 On (based on Hans Sachs).

1956   *Von Zank und Streit und bösen Zungen (Of Quarrels and Squabbles and Wicked Tongues).* 2 On (based on Hans Sachs).

1956   *Vom Peter, der auszog, das Fürchten zu lernen (Peter Who Set Out to Learn Fear).* Juv (based on Grimm). Pr 1961 Zwickau.

1956   *Des Teufels drei goldene Haare (The Devil's Three Golden Hairs).* Juv (based on Grimm; incidental M Franz P. Müller-Sybel).

1956   *Die Hussiten vor Bernau (The Hussites before Bernau).* Dr. Berlin: Rat der Stadt, 1956.

1957   *Das Gefecht in der Schlafkammer (The Battle in the Bedchamber).* Com.

1957   *Der getaufte Star (The Christened Starling).* Com.

1957   *Wer zuletzt lacht... (He Who Laughs Last...).* On (based on anonymous French farce, "Maitre Pathelin"). Pr 1962 Halle. Lpzg: Verlag für Volkskunst, 1957. Lpzg: Hofmeister, 1958. Rev 1968 as Op, Maitre Pathelin oder Die Hammelkomödie.

1958   *Der Weg zurück (The Road Back).* Dr.

1958   *Wiedersehn am Wochenende (Weekend Reunion).* Com (with Ursula Damm-Wendler).

1960   *Die Reise nach Afrika (The Journey to Africa).* Com. Pr 1961 Rostock.

1962   *Schloß Gripsholm (Gripsholm Castle).* Com (based on Kurt Tucholsky). Pr 1963 Rostock.

WENDLER, Horst-Ulrich (cont'd)

1963   *Die Fehde des Michael Kohlhaas (The Feud of Michael Kohlhaas).* Dr (with Ursula Damm Wendler; based on novella by Heinrich Kleist). Pr 1963 Quedlinburg.

1964   *Verflixter Alltag (Darned Everyday Routine).* Mus Lib (with Ursula Damm-Wendler; M Jochen Allihn). Pr 1965 Rostock.

1965   *Der Flaschenteufel (The Devil in the Bottle).* Mus Lib (based on Robert Louis Stevenson). Pr 1965 Th. d. jg. Garde, Halle.

1965   *Die drei Musketiere (The Three Musketeers).* Mus Lib (with Ursula Damm-Wendler; based on Alexander Dumas). Pr 1966 Quedlinburg. Part II 1969 as Die vier Musketiere.

1966   *Zwerg Nase (Nose the Dwarf).* Juv (based on Wilhelm Hauff). Pr 1966 Rostock.

1966   *Jakob und sein Herr (Jacob and His Master).* Dr (based on Diderot). Pr 1967 Wittenberg.

1967   *Rheinsberg.* Com (based on Tucholsky). Pr 1967 Rostock.

1967   *Das neue Kapitel (The New Chapter).* Dr (with Horst Enders). TdZ 1967/21.

1968   *Maitre Pathelin oder Die Hammelkomödie (Master Pathelin or The Mutton Comedy).* Op Lib (rev of Wer zuletzt lacht...; M Rainer Kunad). Pr 1969 Dsdn. Lpzg: Peters, 1968.

1968   *Für fünf Groschen Urlaub (Vacation for Five Cents).* Mus Lib (with Ursula Damm-Wendler). Pr 1969 Met.

1969   *Meine fremde Frau (My Mife, the Stranger).* Dr. Pr 1969 Rostock.

1969   *Die vier Musketiere (The Four Musketeers).* Dr (with Ursula Damm-Wendler; based on Alexander Dumas). Part II of Die drei Musketiere. Pr 1970 Rudolstadt.

1970   *Die Musterfamilie oder Wie halten Sie's zu Hause? (The Model Family or How Do You Do It at Home?).* Com. Pr 1970 Rostock.

1973   *Letzter Ausweg Heirat (Last Alternative Marriage).* Mus Lib (with Ursula Damm-Wendler). Pr 1974 Dsdn.

1975   *Tschüß bis Freitag (See You Friday!).* Mus Lib (with Ursula Damm-Wendler). Pr 1976 Parchim.

1978   *Ein Vormittag im Hause Körner (A Morning in the Körner Household).* Com (based on Friedrich Schiller and Theodor Körner, "Der Vetter aus Bremen"). Pr 1980 Weimar.

1983   *Lenz oder Die Empfindsamen (Lenz or The Sensitive People).* Dr. Pr 1986 Weimar.

WENDLER, Otto Bernhard
10 Dec 1895 Frankenberg - 7 Jan 1958 Burg/Magdeburg
Served in WW I; 1919 became teacher; 33 fired by Nazis; 45 school principal, then official in Cultural Section, Mgdbg. Wrote novels, short stories, film scripts, radio plays.

1924   *Theater eines Gesichts (Theater of a Vision).* Dr. Pr 1925.

1926   *Der Sprung über den Leierkasten (The Leap Over the Hurdy-Gurdy).* Com.

WENDLER, Otto Bernhard (cont'd)

1927   *Der Stilze Rumpel (The Stiltskin Rumple).* Pp (based on Grimm). Berlin: E. Bloch, 1928.

1928   *Spuk um Mitternacht (Apparition at Midnight).* Com. Lpzg: A. Strauch, 1928.

1928   *Sieben auf einen Streich (Seven at One Blow).* Pp (based on Grimm, "The Brave Little Tailor"). Lpzg: A. Strauch, 1928.

1928   *Knüppel aus dem Schnupftabak (Cudgel out of Snuff).* Pp (M Helmut Weiss). Berlin: E. Bloch, 1928.

1929   *Liebe, Mord und Alkohol (Love, Murder, and Alcohol).* Dr. Pr 1929 Tribüne, Berlin.

1932   *Ein Schauspieler geht durch die Politik (An Actor Goes through Politics).* Dr.

1935   *Der Bärenhäuter (The Man in the Bear Skin).* Juv (based on Grimm). Pr 1948 Berlin. Berlin: E. Bloch, 1935.

1942   *Pygmalia.* Com. Pr 1942 Lpzg.

1950   *Die Glut in der Asche (The Glow in the Embers).* Dr.

1957   *Kapriolen ‹Aphrodite› (Capers ‹Aphrodite›).* Com. Pr 1957 Görlitz.

WENDT, Albert
1948 Borsdorf/Leipzig –
1966 various occupations, such as skilled worker, farm technician, wrestler; correspondence study of literature at Univ Lpzg; 73-74 stage hand Lpzg; since 75 independent author in Berlin. 1980 GDR Radio Play Prize. Writes children's books, radio and TV plays.

1972   *Das Hochhaus ‹Das Geburtstagsgeschenk› (The Skyscraper ‹The Birthday Present›).* Com. Pr 1972 Workers' Theater, Rackwitz.

1976   *Nachtfrost (Night Frost).* On. Pr 1976 Lpzg. *Die Dachdecker und andere Stücke,* Henschel 1984.

1976   *‹Die› Weihnachtsmänner (‹The› Santa Clauses).* On. Pr 1976 Lpzg. *Die Dachdecker...,* 1984.

1976   *Die Grille (The Whim).* On. Pr 1976 Lpzg. *Die Dachdecker...,* 1984.

1977   *Schritte (Steps).* Dr. Pr 1980 Friedrichspalast, Berlin. *Die Dachdecker...,* 1984.

1978   *Die wilden Wege ‹Wilde Wege› (‹The› Wild Ways).* Com (based on radio play, "Der Fahrer und die Köchin"). Pr 1979 Brandenburg.

1978   *Die Dachdecker (The Roofers).* Dr. Pr 1979 Lpzg. *TdZ* 1979/5. *Neue DDR Dramatik,* Henschel 1981. *Die Dachdecker...,* 1984.

1979   *Die fremde Fuhre (The Strange Load).* On (based on radio play).

1980   *Die Teefrau (The Tea Lady).* Dr. Pr 1981 Karl Marx Univ, Lpzg. *Die Dachdecker...,* 1984.

1980   *Das Hexenhaus (The Witch's House).* Juv (based on radio play). Pr 1981 Workers' Theater Maxim Gorki, Berlin. *Die Dachdecker...,* 1984.

WENDT (cont'd)

1981   *Der Stolperhahn (The Stumbling Rooster).* Juv (based on radio play). Pr 1982 Th. d. jg. Generation, Dsdn. *Die Dachdecker...,* 1984. Rev 1983 as Pp under title Eierhuhn und Stolperhahn.

1981   *Der Dorftrottel (The Village Idiot).* Com.

1982   *Mein dicker Mantel (My Thick Coat).* On (based on radio play). Pr 1984 Senftenberg. Radio version in *Dame vor Spiegel,* Henschel 1983. *Heduda...,* 1985.

1982   *Der Sauwetterwind (The Beastly Wind).* Juv (based on radio play). Pr 1982 Th. d. jg. Welt, Lpzg. *Die Dachdecker...,* 1984.

1983   *Das verbummelte Leben (The Squandered Life).*

1983   *Eierhuhn und Stolperhahn (Laying Hen and Stumbling Rooster).* Pp (rev of Der Stolperhahn). Pr 1984 Halle.

1984   *Prinzessin Zartfuß und die sieben Elefanten (Princess Tenderfoot and the Seven Elephants).* On (based on radio play). Pr 1984 VB. *TdZ* 1985/8.

1984   *Der Vogelkopp (The Bird Brain).* On (based on radio play). Pr 1985 Th. d. Freundschaft, Berlin. Pp version Pr 1985 Mgdbg. *TdZ* 1985/8.

1984   *Die fahrende Pappel (The Traveling Poplar).* Com.

1985   *Heduda auf dem Pflaumenbaum (Hey-you-there on the Plumtree).* Com (based on radio play). Pr 1985 Gera. Henschel 1985.

1985   *Das Blechboot (The Tin Boat).* Com (based on radio play). *Heduda...,* 1985.

WENK, Rudolf   see Rudi CZERWENKA

WENZEL, Hans Jürgen
1939 –
Studied violin in Potsdam and Rostock, conducting and composition in Berlin; musical director Th. d. jg. Garde, Halle. Composer and librettist.

1964   *Belli, Maxe und Gespenster (Belli, Max, and Ghosts).* Juv Mus (with Piet Drescher). Pr 1965 Th. d. jg. Garde, Halle.

1977   *Der blaue Teppich (The Blue Carpet).* Pp (with Wilfried Völlger). Pr 1978 Halle.

1981   *Denkmal Standort (Monument Site).* Cantata. Pr 1982 Halle.

WERDA, Johannes
        Netze an Bord (Nets on Board). Dr (with Bodo Krautz). Pr 1953 Stralsund.

WERNER, Johannes   see Jan WORNAR

WERZLAU, Joachim
5 July 1913 Leipzig –
Worked in piano factory, then studied music; became pianist, accordion player and ballet accompanist; since 1952 independent composer; lives in Berlin. President of GDR Assoc. of Composers and Musicians.

WERZLAU (cont'd)
1964   *‹Roland und› Regine.* Op (with Erich Schlossarek). Pr
        1966 Potsdam.
1973   *Meister Röckle (Master Jacket).* Juv Op (with Günther
        Deicke; based on Ilse and Vilmos Korn, "Meister Hans
        Röckle und Meister Flammfuß"). Pr 1976 St.Op. Lpzg:
        Edition Peters, 1978.

WESTPHAL, Horst
Locksmith's apprentice, then auto mechanic; 1946 member FDJ
amateur theater group; actor at various theaters.
1982   *Schießt nicht auf weiße Schwäne (Don't Shoot at White
        Swans).* Dr (based on 1973 novel by Boris Vassilyev;
        tr Wolfgang Köppe). Pr 1983 Senftenberg.

WIEDE, Anna E‹lisabeth›   (married name Anna Elisabeth HACKS)
20 Feb 1928 Berlin –
Worked as editor in Munich; moved to GDR in 1955; married to
Peter Hacks. 1957 Prize for Children's and Juvenile Literature. Writes translations, children's books.
        Ein idealer Gatte (An Ideal Husband). Com (tr of Os-
        car Wilde).
        Eine Frau ohne Bedeutung (A Woman of No Importance).
        Com (tr of Oscar Wilde).
        *Keine Hochzeit ohne Ernst ‹Bunbury› (No Wedding with-
        out Ernest ‹Bunbury›).* Com (tr of Oscar Wilde, "The
        Importance of Being Earnest").
        Lady Windermeres Fächer (Lady Windermere's Fan). Com
        (tr of Oscar Wilde).
1956   *Der Held der westlichen Welt (The Hero of the Western
        World).* Com (with Peter Hacks; based on J. M. Synge,
        "Playboy of the Western World"). Pr 1956 BE. Reclam
        1961.
1957   *Das Untier von Samarkand (The Monster of Samarkand).*
        Juv (with Eugen Eschner and Peter Hacks). Pr 1957 Th.
        d. Freundschaft, Berlin. *Märchendramen,* Henschel 19-
        80.
1957   *Die Ratten von Hameln (The Rats of Hamelin).* Juv
        (based on legend of the Pied Piper). Pr 1979 Greifs-
        wald. *NdL* 1958/4.
1958   *Der Osteresel (The Easter Donkey).* Juv. Lpzg: Hof-
        meister, 1959. *Die Sonnenuhr,* Henschel 1962.
1958   *Die Sonnenuhr (The Sun Dial).* Juv. Henschel 1962.
1965   *Der Mann, der bei Schirocco kam (The Man Who Came
        with the Desert Wind).* Com (with Peter Hacks, under
        pseud. Ernst Eylt). Pr 1967 Altenburg.
1968   *Ein Freund der Wahrheit (A Friend of Truth).* Com (tr
        of William Wicherley, "The Plain Dealer"). Pr 1970.

WIELAND, Gerhard   see Berta LASK

WIELAND, Günter
28 July 1925 Wüsterwaltersdorf –
Studied theater history; now lives in Bad Frankenhausen;
writes radio plays.

WIELAND, Günter (cont'd)
1950   *Liebe auf den zweiten Blick (Love at Second Sight).*
        Com. Pr 1951 Meißen.
1953   *Tödliche Tinte (Deadly Ink).* Com.
1953   *Untermieter (Sub-tenant).* Mus Lib.
1956   *Die Mädchenkarawane (The Caravan of Girls).* Com.
1962   *Camillos Doppelhochzeit (Camillo's Double Wedding).*
        Com. Pr 1963 Meißen.

WIENER, C‹laus› U‹lrich›
1 Jan 1933 Brandenburg –
Attended Interpreter's Institute; then worked as editor 1952–
53 Verlag Volk & Wissen, 53–55 Verlag Volk & Welt, 57–60 Eulenspiegelverlag; also theater critic; since 64 independent
author. Writes for cabaret, film, and radio.
1962   *Einer geht baden (Someone Goes Bathing).* Com. Pr 19–
        63 Rostock.
1963   *Die Robinsoninsel (Robinson's Island).* Com.
1968   *Kleinekortes große Zeiten   (Little Korte's Great
        Times).* Com. Pr 1969 Rostock.
1968   *Verlieb dich nicht in eine Heilige (Don't Fall in
        Love with a Saint).* Mus Lib (M Siegfried Schäfer). Pr
        1969 Dsdn. *TdZ* 1969/3.
1969   *Scharf nachwaschen (Rewash Thoroughly).* Com. Pr 1969
        Rostock.
1975   *Die verschwundene Partitur (The Lost Score).* Mus Lib.
        Pr 1976 Halle.

WIENER, Ralph   (Pseud. for Felix ECKE)
15 May 1924 Baden/Vienna –
Editor of satiric periodical "Eulenspiegel." Writes short stories, cabaret texts.
1962   *Geschichten meiner Frau (Stories of My Wife).* Com
        (with Hans Peter and Hans Henkels). Pr 1962 Rostock.
1963   *Fragen Sie Sibylle (Ask Sibyl).* Com. Pr 1964 Prenz
        lau.
1974   *Ein himmlischer Abend (A Heavenly Evening).* Com. Pr
        1974 Rudolstadt.

WILDE, Erika
1949   *Tischlein, deck dich (The Table, the Ass, and the
        Stick).* Juv (based on Grimm). Pr 1950 Th. am Schiff
        bauerdamm, Berlin.
1950   *Der Weiberheld (The Ladykiller).* Com with M (based
        on Plautus, "Miles Gloriosus"). Pr 1952 Lpzg.
1959   *Das Wunderknäuel (The Magic Skein).* Juv.

WILLERS, Rosel
1961   *Gelegenheit macht Liebe (Opportunity Makes Lovers).*
        Com. Pr 1962 Dessau.

WINDISCH, Helmut
1975   *Zeit der Störche (The Season of the Storks).* Dr (with
        Ulf Keyn). Pr 1976 Neustrelitz.

WINKLER, Barbara
    Annette und die wilden Räuber (Annette and the Wild Robbers). Pp.
1967   *Football Story.* Juv (with Hans-Dieter Schmidt). Pr 1968 Th. d. jg. Welt, Lpzg.

WINTER, Klaus
1975   *Frohes Wochenende (Happy Weekend).* Mus Lib (with Klaus Eidam; M Rolf Zimmermann). Pr 1976 Halle.
1977   *Der Zauberring (The Magic Ring).* Juv Mus Lib (M Jürgen Ecke). Pr 1977 Halle.
1981   *Des Königs Datsche oder Nackenstützen für Badewannen (The King's Dacha or Neck Braces for Bathtubs).* Mus Lib (with Klaus Eidam; M Martin Hattwig). Pr 1982 Halle.

WINTERLICH, Gerhard
4 Dec 1926 Neustädtel –
Prose author. 1969 FDGB Prize.
1967   *Horizonte (Horizons).* Dr. Pr 1968 Workers' Theater, Schwedt. Rev 1968–69 (with Heiner Müller). Pr 1969 VB. Müller, *Theaterarbeit*, Berlin (W): Rotbuch, 1975 (first scene).

WITT, Wolfram
1983   *Lieber Flegel (Dear Lout).* Pp (based on Gottfried Keller). Pr 1984 Fkft/O.
1984   *Der kleine Häwemann (Little Häwemann).* Pp (based on Theodor Storm). Pr 1984 Fkft/O.

WITTE, Joachim
30 May 1921 –
Lives in Berlin. 1977 Gerhard Eisler Medal, 78 FDGB Prize. Writes juvenile radio plays.
1975   *Mit dem Kopf durch die Wand (Knocking One's Head Against the Wall).* Com. Pr 1975 Rostock.

WOGATZKI, Benito
31 Aug 1932 Berlin –
Worked as a weaver; then studied journalism in Potsdam and Lpzg; worked as journalist for eight years; now independent author; lives in Berlin. Member AdK; 1967 Lessing Prize; 67, 68, and 82 National Prize; 69 FDGB Prize. Writes short stories, radio and TV plays.
1969   *Der Klassenauftrag (The Class Assignment).* Scene. Pr 1970 Halle (part of program under collective title of "Anregung II").
1976   *Viola vor dem Tor (Viola in Front of the Gate).* Com. Pr 1978 TiP.

WOHLGEMUTH, Joachim
27 June 1923 Prenzlau –
Studied philosophy Potsdam and Lpzg, then became cultural official; since 1960 independent author. 1962 Erich Weinert

WOHLGEMUTH (cont'd)
Medal, 62 and 67 Fritz Reuter Prize, 63 FDGB Prize. Writes prose and radio plays.

1962   *Egon oder Die Ankunft im Alltag (Egon or The Arrival in the Daily Routine)*. Com (based on novel "Egon und das achte Weltwunder"). Pr 1964.

1978   *Der Vater bin ich (I Am the Father)*. Com. Pr 1979 Neustrelitz.

WOLF, Friedrich   (Pseuds. Christian Baetz, Hans Rüedi, Dr. Isegrimm)
23 Dec 1886 Neuwiedl/Rhein - 5 Oct 1953 Lehnitz/Berlin
Studied art in Munich, then medicine in Tübingen, Bonn, and Berlin; Dr. med. 1913, then worked as ship's doctor; 1918 imprisoned for refusing military service; after WW I, member of Workers' and Soldiers' Council, Dsdn, then general practitioner; 28 joined KPD; 33 emigration via Austria, Switzerland, and France to USSR; co-founder National Committee "Free Germany"; 45 returned to Berlin, worked for radio and theater; 50-51 GDR Ambassador to Poland; then independent author. Member AdK; 1949 and 50 National Prize. Wrote essays, poetry, prose, radio plays, film scripts.

1916   *Mohammed*. Dr. Pr 1924 Fkft/M. Stuttgart: Chronos, 1924. *Ausgewählte Werke*, vol. 1: *Dramen 1*, Aufbau 19-50. *Gesammelte Werke*, vol. 1: *Dramen 1*, Aufbau 1960.

1917   *Der Löwe Gottes (The Lion of God)*. Dr. Pr 1921.

1918   *Das bist du (That's You)*. Dr. Pr 1919 Dsdn. *Ausgewählte Werke*, vol. 1, 1950. *Gesammelte Werke*, vol. 1, 1960. *Dramen*, Reclam and Fkft/M: Röderberg, 1978.

1919   *Der Unbedingte (The Unconditional Man)*. Dr. Pr 1921 Stettin. *Gesammelte Werke*, vol. 1, 1960.

1921   *Die schwarze Sonne (The Black Sun)*. Com. Pr 1924 Oldenburg. Berlin: Rowohlt, 1921. *Ausgewählte Werke*, vol. 1, 1950. *Gesammelte Werke*, vol. 1, 1960.

1921   *Tamar*. Dr. Pr 1922 Fkft/M. *Ausgewählte Werke*, vol. 1, 1960. *Gesammelte Werke*, vol. 1, 1960.

1922   *Elemente (Elements)*. Three On. Stuttgart: Chronos, 1922.

1922   *Die Schrankkomödie (The Closet Comedy)*. Com. Pr 19-57 Lpzg. *Ausgewählte Werke*, vol. 9: *Dramen 5*, Aufbau 1955. *Gesammelte Werke*, vol. 1, 1960.

1923   *Der Arme Konrad (Poor Conrad)*. Dr. Pr 1924 Stuttgart. Stuttgart: Chronos, 1924. Stuttgart: Dt. Verlagsanstalt, 1930. Berlin: Volk und Wissen, 1950. Halle: Mitteldeutscher Verlag, 1950. Reclam 1953. Aufbau 1959. *Gesammelte Werke*, vol. 2: *Dramen 2*, Aufbau 19-60. Stuttgart: Reclam, 1975. *1525: Dramen zum dt. Bauernkrieg*, Aufbau 1975. *Dramen*, 1978. Rev 1959 as Op (M Jean Kurt Forest).

1925   *Der Mann im Dunkeln (The Man in the Dark)*. Dr. Pr 1927. Stuttgart: Chronos, 1925.

1926   *Koritke*. Dr. Pr 1927 Stuttgart (Performance title: "Die Zeche zahlt Koritke"). *Ausgewählte Werke*, vol. 9, 1955. *Gesammelte Werke*, vol. 2, 1960.

WOLF, Friedrich (cont'd)

1927   *Kolonne Hund (The Dog Column)*. Dr. Pr 1927 Hamburg. Stuttgart: Dt. Verlagsanstalt, 1927. *Ausgewählte Werke*, vol. 2: *Dramen 2*, Aufbau 1950. *Gesammelte Werke*, vol. 2, 1960.

1928   *Und das Licht leuchtet in der Finsternis (And the Light Shines in the Darkness)*. Dr (with August Scholz; based on Tolstoy). Pr 1928 Erfurt. *Gesammelte Werke*, vol. 2, 1960.

1929   *Zyankali ‹Paragraph 218› (Cyanide ‹Paragraph 218›)*. Dr. Pr 1929 Lessingth., Berlin. Berlin: Internat'l Arbeiterverlag, 1929. *Ausgewählte Werke*, vol. 2, 19-50. *Gesammelte Werke*, vol. 2, 1960. *Dramen*, 1978. *Cyankali*, Stuttgart: Klett, 1983.

1929   *"Krassin" rettet "Italia" ("Krassin" Saves "Italia")*. Juv. Pr 1961 Th. d. jg. Welt, Lpzg. Stuttgart: Dt. Verlagsanstalt, 1930. *Ausgewählte Werke*, vol. 10: *Hörspiele und Laienspiele*, Aufbau 1955. Lpzg: Hofmeister, 1959. *Gesammelte Werke*, vol 7: *Hörspiele, Laienspiele, Szenen*, Aufbau 1960.

1930   *John D. erobert die Welt (John D. Conquers the World)* Dr. Lpzg: Hofmeister, 1959. *Ausgewählte Werke*, vol. 10, 1955. *Gesammelte Werke*, vol. 7, 1960.

1930   *Die Matrosen von Cattaro (The Sailors of Cattaro)*. Dr. Pr 1930 VB. *Ausgewählte Werke*, vol. 2, 1950. Lpzg: Insel, 1958. *Gesammelte Werke*, vol. 3: *Dramen 3*, Aufbau 1960. Reclam 1960. Aufbau 1961.

1930   *Tai Yang erwacht (Tai Yang Awakens)*. Dr. Pr 1931 Thalia Th., Berlin. *Ausgewählte Werke*, vol. 2, 1950. *Gesammelte Werke*, vol. 3, 1960. Rev as Op (with Walter Pollatschek; M Jean Kurt Forest), Pr 1960 St.Op.

1931   *Die Jungens von Mons (The Boys from Mons)*. Dr. Pr 19-31 Berlin. *Ausgewählte Werke*, vol. 2, 1950. *Gesammelte Werke*, vol. 3, 1960.

1932   *Wie stehn die Fronten? (How Are the Fronts Going?)*. Dr. Pr 1932 Stuttgart. *Gesammelte Werke*, vol. 7: *Dramen 7*, Aufbau 1960.

1932   *Von New York bis Schanghai (From New York to Shanghai)*. Revue. Pr 1932 Stuttgart. Engels (USSR): Dt. Staatsverlag, 1936. *Ausgewählte Werke*, vol.10, 1955. *Gesammelte Werke*, vol. 7, 1960.

1933   *Bauer Baetz (Farmer Baetz)*. Dr (incidental M Hanns Eisler). Pr 1933 Stuttgart. *Ausgewählte Werke*, vol. 10, 1955. *Gesammelte Werke*, vol. 7, 1960.

1933-34 *Professor Mamlock*. Dr. Pr 1934 Zurich. *Ausgewählte Werke*, vol. 3: *Dramen 3*, Aufbau, 1950. Berlin: Volk & Wissen, 1952. Reclam 1960. *Gesammelte Werke*, vol. 3, 1960. Aufbau, 1960. *Stücke gegen den Faschismus*, Henschel 1970 and Fkft/M: Röderberg, 1972. Stuttgart: Reclam, 1980.

1934   *Der Kampf um die Schafsquelle ‹Laurentia oder Die Schafsquelle› (The Struggle for the Sheep Spring ‹Laurentia or The Sheep Spring)*. Dr (based on Lope de Vega, "Fuente Ovejuna"). Pr 1934 Dt. Th., Engels, USSR. *Gesammelte Werke*, vol. 3, 1960.

WOLF, Friedrich (cont'd)

1934-35 *Floridsdorf*. Dr. Pr 1935 Moscow (in Russian); Gm. Pr 1953 Dsdn. Zurich: Oprecht & Helbling, 1935. *Ausgewählte Werke*, vol. 3, 1950. *Gesammelte Werke*, vol. 4: *Dramen 4*, Aufbau 1960.

1935 *Optimistische Tragödie (Optimistic Tragedy)*. Dr (tr of Vsevolod Vishnevsky).

1936 *Das trojanische Pferd (The Trojan Horse)*. Dr. Pr 19-37 Moscow. Lpzg: Hofmeister, 1955. *Ausgewählte Werke*, vol. 9, 1955. *Gesammelte Werke*, vol. 4, 1960.

1936 *Peter kehrt heim ‹Bajonette und Brot› (Peter Returns Home ‹Bayonets and Bread›)*. Dr. Pr 1937 Dt. Th., Engels, USSR. *Gesammelte Werke*, vol. 4, 1960.

1937 *Wir sind mit euch: Drei Szenen aus Spanien (We Are With You: Three Scenes from Spain)*. Dr. *Ausgewählte Werke*, vol. 10, 1955. *Gesammelte Werke*, vol. 7, 1960.

1938-39 *Das Schiff auf der Donau (The Ship on the Danube)*. Dr (with Leo Mittler). Pr 1955 MG. *Zeitgenössische Dramatik*, Henschel 1960. *Ausgewählte Werke*, vol. 9, 19-55. *Gesammelte Werke*, vol. 4, 1960.

1940-41 *Beaumarchais oder Die Geburt des "Figaro" (Beaumarchais or The Birth of "Figaro")*. Dr. Pr 1946 DT. Aufbau 1945. Berlin: Volk & Wissen, 1949. Lpzg: Insel, 1954. *Ausgewählte Werke*, vol. 3, 1950. *Gesammelte Werke*, vol. 5: *Dramen 5*, Aufbau 1960.

1942-43 *Patrioten (Patriots)*. Dr. Pr 1946 Coburg. *Drei Dramen*, Aufbau 1946. *Ausgewählte Werke*, vol. 3, 1950. *Gesammelte Werke*, vol. 5, 1960.

1944 *Dr. ‹Lilli› Wanner*. Dr. Pr 1946 Chemnitz (now KMSt). *Drei Dramen*, 1946. *Ausgewählte Werke*, vol. 4: *Dramen 4*, Aufbau 1950. *Gesammelte Werke*, vol. 5, 1960.

1945 *Was der Mensch säet... (What Man Soweth...)*. Dr. Pr 1946 Eisleben. *Drei Dramen*, 1946. *Ausgewählte Werke*, vol. 4, 1950. *Gesammelte Werke*, vol. 5, 1960.

1946 *Die letzte Probe (The Last Test)*. Dr (original title "Vera"). Pr 1946 Dsdn. *Ausgewählte Werke*, vol. 4, 19-50. *Gesammelte Werke*, vol. 6: *Dramen 6*, Aufbau 1960.

1946-47 *Wie Tiere des Waldes (Like The Animals in The Woods)*. Dr. Pr 1948 Lpzg. *Ausgewählte Werke*, vol. 4, 1950. *Gesammelte Werke*, vol. 6, 1960. Rev 1963 as Op (M Jean Kurt Forest).

1947 *Ich war, ich bin, ich werde sein (I Was, I Am, and I Shall Be)*. Dr. Pr 1955 Lpzg.

1947 *Die Nachtschwalbe (The Night Swallow)*. Op Lib (M Boris Blacher). Pr 1948.

1949-50 *Bürgermeister Anna ‹Anna und der Männerstreik› (Mayor Anna ‹Anna and the Men's Strike›)*. Com (original title: "Die Bürgermeisterin"; based on film). Pr 19-50 Dsdn. *Ausgewählte Werke*, vol. 4, 1950. *Gesammelte Werke*, vol. 6, 1960. *Die ersten Schritte*, Halle: Mitteldt. Verlag, 1986.

1950 *Lilo Herrmann*. Cantata. Pr 1953 Lpzg.

1950 *So fing es an (That's How It Began)*. Two Scenes. Halle: Mitteldt. Verlag, 1950.

WOLF, Friedrich (cont'd)
1952-53 *Thomas Mün‹t›zer, der Mann mit der Regenbogenfahne (Thomas Mün‹t›zer, the Man with the Rainbow Flag)*. Dr. Pr 1953 DT. Aufbau 1953. *Ausgewählte Werke*, vol. 9, 1955. Reclam 1960. *Gesammelte Werke*, vol. 6, 1960. *1525: Dramen zum dt. Bauernkrieg*, Aufbau 1975.
1974 *Die Weihnachtsgans Auguste (A Christmas Goose Called Augusta)*. Juv Op (based on his story; dramatized by Rolf Rohde; M Bernd Wefelmeyer). Pr 1974 Brandenburg. Rev 1977 as Pp by Karin Dörner. Pr 1977 Halle. Prose text Aufbau 1965.
Tiergeschichten ‹Die Geschichte vom Hahn Hallo, dem Hund Schnapp, und wie der weise Rabe Streit schlichtete› (Animal Stories ‹The Story of the Rooster Hallo, the Dog Snap, and How the Wise Raven Settled a Dispute›). Juv.

WOLF, Gerhard
16 Oct 1928 Bad Frankenhausen -
Service in WW II, American POW; 1945-47 school teacher; 48-52 studied German literature and history at Jena and Berlin; 52-57 worked for GDR Radio; since then independent author; lives in Berlin; married to Christa Wolf. Since 1972 member GDR PEN; 74 Heinrich Mann Prize. Writes essays, stories, criticism, film scripts.
1974 *Litauische Claviere (Lithuanian Pianos)*. Op Lib (based on 1965 novel by Johannes Bobrowski; M Rainer Kunad). Pr 1976 Dsdn. *TdZ* 1975/9. Henschel 1975.
1982 *Till Eulenspiegel*. Dr (with Christa Wolf; based on film). Pr 1983 Lpzg. Aufbau 1985 (film script).

WOLF, Klaus Martin
4 July 1935 Burg -
1952-53 officer in Maritime Police; followed by various occupations; 57-58 I.Lit Lpzg; then dramaturg, editor of journal "Volksstimme," independent author; now lives in Mgdbg. Writes poetry, prose, TV scripts, cabaret texts.
1960 *Gebt Frieden (Give Peace)*. Oratorio (M H. Siewecke).
1969 *Das Lagefeuer (The Campfire)*. Dr. Pr 1969 Potsdam. *TdZ* 1969/10.
1969 *König Karl oder Das fünfte Rad am Wagen (King Charles or The Fifth Wheel on the Wagon)*. Com (based on TV play). Pr 1971 Dsdn/Radebeul.
1970 *Theater über Theater (Theater about Theater)*. Two Scenes. *NdL* 1970/6.
1970 *Platz zum Denken, Leben, Lieben (Room to Think, Live, and Love)*. Dr. Pr 1970 Mgdbg.

WOLFF, Bernd
12 Sep 1939 Magdeburg -
1957-60 studied at Institute of Pedagogy, Erfurt; 60-67 teacher; since 69 independent author in Blankenburg. Writes poetry, children's books.

WOLFF (cont'd)

1978   *Der Bärenhäuter (The Man with the Bear Skin).* Juv Op Lib (based on Grimm; M Hans Auenmüller). Pr 1978 Halberstadt.

1983   *Komödianten‹welt› (‹The World of› Actors).* Mus Lib (M Hans Auenmüller). Pr 1984 Halberstadt.

WORNAR, Jan   (also known as Johannes **WERNER**)

7 Dec 1934 Horka –

Studied Karl Marx Univ, Lpzg; since then, teacher at Sorbian High School in Bautzen. 1970 Literature Prize of the Domowina. Writes short stories, radio plays.

1969   *Die gestohlene Sonne (The Stolen Sun).* Juv (in Sorbian language).

1970   *Die Zimmerleute (The Lodgers).* Juv (in Sorbian language).

Z

ZABEL, Thomas   see John STAVE

ZECHLIN, Ruth   (nee Oschatz)
22 June 1926 Großhartmannsdorf -
1943-49 studied MHS Lpzg;   now Prof. MHS Berlin, composer and librettist.   1962   Berlin   Goethe Prize,   75 and 82   National Prize.
1956   *Lidice*. Cantata (with Franz Fühmann).   Pr 1958 Berlin.
1961   *Wenn der Wacholder blüht (When the Juniper Blooms)*. Oratorio (with Günther Deicke).   Pr 1961.
1962   *Reineke Fuchs (Reynard, the Fox)*. Op (with Günther Deicke).   Pr 1968 Th. d. Freundschaft, Berlin. *NdL* 1968/8.

ZEHLEN, Petra
1922 -
1949   *Dramaturgie und Liebe ‹Theaterkrise› (Dramaturgy and Love ‹Theater Crisis›)*. Com. Pr 1950 Halle.
        Liebe klein geschrieben (Love Written in Lower Case). Com.

ZIMMER, Rita
1968   *Fisch zu viert (Fish for Four)*. Com (with Wolfgang Kohlhaase; based on radio and TV play). Pr 1970 Th. d. jg. Generation, Dsdn.

ZIMMERMANN, Ingo
17 Dec 1940 Dresden -
1959-66 studied theology at Lpzg; 66-67 journalist, then lecturer in theology, Lpzg. Librettist.
1967-68 *Die weiße Rose (The White Rose)*. Op Lib (based on Sophie and Hans Scholl; M Udo Zimmermann). Pr 1968 Schwerin.
1970   *Die zweite Entscheidung (The Second Decision)*. Op Lib (M Udo Zimmermann). Pr 1970 Mgdbg. *TdZ* 1970/5.
1972   *Lewins Mühle (Levin's Mill)*. Op Lib (based on novel by Johannes Bobrowski; M Udo Zimmermann). Pr 1973 Dsdn. *TdZ* 1972/5. Lpzg: Dt. Verlag für Musik, 1973.
1982   *Amphytrion*. Op Lib (M Rainer Kunad). Pr 1984 St.Op.

ZIMMERMANN, Kurt
11 Mar 1927 -
Studied theater history; worked as editor and dramaturg for cabaret "Die Distel"; since 1960 independent author in Berlin. Writes novels, TV and radio plays, cabaret texts.
1963   *Der unterschlagene Ehemann (The Hidden Husband)*. Com (with Konrad Schmidt). Pr 1964 Rostock.

ZIMMERMANN, Rolf
Composer and librettist.
        Alles für Figaro (Everything for Figaro). Mus. Pr 1972 Dsdn.

ZIMMERMANN, Udo
6 Oct 1943 Dresden –
1962-68 studied MHS Dsdn; 70-74 music dramaturg Dsdn Op; 74-82 director of Studio Neue Musik, St. Op; since 78 Prof. of Composition, MHS Dsdn. Member AdK, Hamburg Akademie der Künste; 1972 Hanns Eisler Prize, 1975 National Prize.

1981   *Die wundersame Schusterfrau (The Shoemaker's Amazing Wife)*. Op (with Eberhard Schmidt; based on Garcia Lorca). Pr 1982 Schwetzingen.

1984-85 *Weiße Rose (White Rose)*. Chamber Op (based on texts by Wolfgang Willaschek). Pr 1986 Hamburg. *TdZ* 1986/4.

ZINNER, Hedda   (married name Hedda ERPENBECK; pseud. Elisabeth FRANK, Hannchen LOBESAM)
20 May 1905 Vienna –
1923-25 attended Th. Academy, Vienna; actress in Vienna, Baden-Baden, Stuttgart, Breslau, Berlin; married Fritz Erpenbeck; 30 joined KPD; 33 emigrated via Vienna and Prague to Soviet Union, wrote for Moscow Radio; 45 returned to Berlin; since then independent author. 1954 National Prize, 60 Goethe Prize, 61 Lessing Prize, 73 Feuchtwanger Prize, 75 Literature Prize, 80 Karl Marx Medal, 82 FDGB Prize. Translator, writes novels, short stories, radio and TV plays.

1940-41 *Cafehaus Payer (Coffeehouse Payer)*. Dr. Pr 1945 Rostock. *Stücke*, Henschel 1972.

1950-51 *General Landt*. Dr (first written as a radio play; based on novel by Martha Dodd, "Sowing the Wind"). Pr 1957 Weimar. *Stücke*, 1972.

1951   *Spiel ins Leben (Game into Life)*. Juv. Pr 1951 Th. d. Freundschaft, Berlin.

1952   *Der Mann mit dem Vogel (The Man with the Bird)*. Com. Pr 1952 Lpzg.

1953   *Der Teufelskreis (The Infernal Circle)*. Dr. Pr 1953 Th. am Schiffbauerdamm, Berlin. Henschel 1953. Reclam 1960. *Zeitgenössische Dramatik*, Henschel 1961. *Stücke*, 1972.

1955   ‹*Die*› *Lützower (‹The› Men of Lützow)*. Dr. Pr 1955 DT. Rev 1956. *Zeitgenössische Dramatik*, Henschel 19-58. Henschel 1961.

1957   *Das Urteil (The Verdict)*. Revue. Pr 1958.

1958   *Plautus im Nonnenkloster (Plautus in the Nunnery)*. Op Lib (based on Conrad Ferdinand Meyer; M Max Butting). Pr 1959.

1959   *Auf jeden Fall verdächtig (Under Suspicion in Any Case)*. Dr. Pr 1959 Erfurt.

1959   *Die Fischer von Niezow (The Fishermen of Niezow)*. Opt Lib (M Jean Kurt Forest).

1959   *Was wäre, wenn? (What Would Happen, If?)*. Com. Pr 1959 VB. *Zeitgenössische Dramatik*, Henschel 1959.

1960   *Leistungskontrolle (Production Control)*. Juv. Pr 19-60 Th. d. Freundschaft, Berlin.

1961   *Ravensbrücker Ballade (The Ballad of Ravensbrück)*. Dr. Pr 1961 VB. *Zeitgenössische Dramatik*, Henschel 1961. *Stücke*, 1972.

ZINNER (con'd)
1963   *Ein Amerikaner in Berlin (An American in Berlin).* Mus
        Lib (M Andre Asriel). Pr 1963 VB.
1967   *Elisabeth Trave.* Dr.

ZOCH, Georg
        Eine Uhr schlug dreimal (A Clock Struck Three Times).
        Dr. Pr 1951 Bernburg.   '

ZUCHARDT, Karl
10 Feb 1887 Leipzig - 12 Nov 1968 Dresden
Studied literature, history, economics, philosophy at Berlin,
Freiburg, and Lpzg; Dr. phil. 1910; taught school for several
years, then traveled through Syria and Spain; since 40 independent author in Dsdn. 1961 City of Dsdn Prize. Wrote historical novels, short stories.
1936   *Erbschaft aus Amerika (Inheritance from America).* Com.
        Pr 1936 Dsdn. Lpzg: Dietzmann, 1936.
1937   *Frisch verloren, halb gewonnen (Well Lost Is Half
        Won).* Com. Pr 1939 Mannheim. Lpzg: Dietzmann, 1937.
1938   *Die Prinzipalin (Lady Boss).* Com. Pr 1938 VB. Lpzg:
        Dietzmann, 1938.
1940   *Held im Zwielicht (Hero in Twilight).*   Dr. Pr 1940
        Dsdn. Essen: Essener Verlag, 1942.
1941   *Am nächsten Morgen (The Next Morning).* Com. Pr 1942
        Halle.   .
1942   *Cäsars Traum (Caesar's Dream).* Com. Pr 1942 Cologne.
        Memmingen: Dietrich, 1948.
1942   *Start in die Unsterblichkeit (A Start into Immortali-
        ty).* Dr.
1946   *Herrenmensch (Superman).* Com.
        Kaiser und Komödiant (Emperor and Actor). Dr.
1960   *Stirb du Narr (Die, You Fool).* Dr (based on novel).

ZUCHARDT, Renate
1961   *Ohne Dich war es Nacht (Without You It Was Night).* Dr
        (based on newspaper articles and diary by Joe Parker).
        Pr 1961 Dsdn/Radebeul.
1963   *Irrungen-Wirrungen (Error and Confusion).* Dr (based
        on novel by Theodor Fontane). Pr 1964 Brandenburg.

ZWEIG, Arnold
10 Nov 1887 Groß-Glogau (now Glogow, Poland) - 26 Nov 1968
Berlin
Attended school in Kattowitz until 1906, began writing; 07-19
studied German and English literature, Romance languages, history, philosophy, and art history at Breslau, Munich, Berlin,
Göttingen, Rostock, Tübingen, interrupted 14-18 by military
service; 23 editor, "Jüdische Rundschau" and contributor to
"Weltbühne"; 33 emigration via Prague, Switzerland, France to
Palestine; several trips to USA; 48 returned to Berlin. 1950-
53 President AdK, also President GDR PEN; 50 National Prize,
58 Lenin Peace Prize. Wrote novels, short stories, essays.

ZWEIG (cont'd)

1909-12 *Abigail und Nabal.* Dr in verse. *Die Gäste,* 1909. Rev prose version 1919. *Dramen,* Aufbau 1963.

1910 *Das neue Kanaan (New Canaan).* Dr. Berlin: Hyperion, 1914.

1913 *Ritualmord in Ungarn (Ritual Murder in Hungary).* Dr. Pr 1918. Berlin: Hyperion, 1914. Rev 1918 as Die Sendung Samaels.

1914-25 *Die Umkehr ‹des Abtrünnigen› (The Return ‹of the Renegade›).* Dr. Pr 1929 Neues Th., Fkft/M. Berlin: G. Kiepenheuer, 1927.

1917-18 *Die Lucilla.* Com. Pr 1963. *Dramen,* 1963.

1918 *Die Sendung Samaels (Samael's Mission).* Dr (rev of Ritualmord in Ungarn). Pr 1920 DT. Lpzg: Kurt Wolff, 1918. *Dramen,* 1963.

1921-29 *Das Spiel vom ‹Der Streit um den› Sergeanten Grischa (The Play of ‹The Quarrel about› Sergeant Grisha).* Dr (based on novel; original title "Der Bjuschew"). Pr 1930 Th. am Nollendorfplatz, Berlin. *Soldatenspiele,* Aufbau 1956. *Dramen,* 1963.

1922 *Laubheu und keine Bleibe (Dry Hay and No Shelter).* Com. *Dramen,* 1963.

1930 *Die Aufrichtung der Menorah (The Erection of the Menorah).* Pantomime. Berlin: Aldus, 1930.

1934 *Bonaparte ‹Napoleon› in Jaffa.* Dr. Pr 1955 VB. *Soldatenspiele,* 1956. *Dramen,* 1963.

1936 *Das Spiel vom kleinen Propheten Jona (The Play of the Little Prophet Jonah).* Juv.
Berge von Schaum (Mountains of Foam). Com.
Das Spiel vom Herrn und vom Jockel (The Play of the Master and the Servant). Com. Pr 1963 Th. d. jg. Welt, Lpzg.

1946 *Austreibung 1744 ‹Das Weihnachtswunder› (Expulsion 1744 ‹The Christmas Miracle›).* Dr. *Soldatenspiele,* 1956. *Dramen,* 1963.

TITLE INDEX

German play titles of are listed in alphabetical sequence, beginning with the first word following a definite or indefinite article. Alphabetization is on a word-by-word basis (e.g. *Der Bauer und sein König* before *Die Bauern*). German umlaut *ä,ö*, and *ü* are alphabetized as a, o, and u respectively. German *ß* is alphabetized as ss. German numerals are alphabetized as if they were written out. Double titles (e.g. *Die Acharner oder Der private Frieden)* are listed under both entries. Alternate title forms are listed within brackets (e.g. *Doktor ‹Lilli› Warner*). Authors are listed by last name first. Coauthors are not identified in the index. When there are different plays with the same title (e.g. *Aladdin und die Wunderlampe),* the title is repeated for each author. On the other hand, if several plays by different authors were performed under a single collective title *(e.g. Männermonologe),* authors are listed in alphabetical order, separated by semi-colons.

A

Die Abbitte	Malink, Peter
Der ABC-Stern	Küchenmeister, Claus
Ein Abend in Mantua	Knauth, Joachim
Abenteuer am Mississippi	Heym, Georg
Die Abenteuer der drei Musketiere	Kunkel, Erhard
Die Abenteuer der Johanna von Döbeln	Baierl, Helmut
Die Abenteuer der Mona Lisa	Bauer, Andreas
Die Abenteuer der Musketiere	Damm-Wendler, Ursula
Die Abenteuer des braven Soldaten Schwejk	Kunkel, Erhard
Die Abenteuer des Don Quijote, gespielt von seinen Freunden	Ostarek, Hans
Die Abenteuer des tapferen Schneiderleins	Günther, Egon
Abenteuer des Theseus	Noack, Christian
Aber wenn der Schleier fällt	Korn, Vilmos
Abfahrtszeiten	Peschke, Michael
Der Abgang	Lucke, Hans
Abigail und Nabal	Zweig, Arnold
Der Abiturmann	Leonhardt, Arne
Abraham Lincoln	Gilbricht, Walter
Abrakadabra	Schneider, Elke
Ein Abschied	Pfeiffer, Hans
Abseits	Martin, Christian
Ach du liebe Liebe	Liebenberg, Günter
Ach, es war nur die Laterne	Schrader, Julie
Die Acharner	Bartsch, Kurt
Adam und Eva	Hacks, Peter
Adam und Eva	Richter, Kurt Dietmar
Adam und Eva und kein Ende	Strahl, Rudi
Adieu Olivia	Kahlow, Heinz
Adrian und das rote Auto	Tiefensee, Siegfried
Affäre Corinth	Prodöhl, Günter

Affentheater	Felkel, Günter
Agenten	Wangenheim, Gustav von
Aktion Polarkuß	Hirsch, Rudolf
Aladdin und die Wunderlampe	Hall, Heinz
Aladdin und die Wunderlampe	Kaltofen, Günter
Aladdin und die Wunderlampe	Sternfelde, Karl
Alarm im Rosenhaus	Lorbeer, Inge
Alarm im Werk	Schneidereit, Otto
Alarm in Pont l'Evequce	Janowski, Maurycy
Der Alchimist	Lange, Hartmut
Ali Baba und die vierzig Räuber	Hubert, Gerhard
Alibi vor Mitternacht	Koch, Günter
Alle helfen Häppi	Schwaen, Kurt
Alle Mäuse lieben den Käse	Stäcker, Hans-Dieter
Alle Mütter waren Töchter	Peter, Hans
Alles für Figaro	Zimmermann, Rolf
Alles im Haus	Drewniok, Heinz
Alles im Lot, alles im Eimer	Strahl, Rudi
Alles oder etwas	Koerbl, Jürg-Michael
Alles um die Liebe	Arnold, Hans Dieter
Allez hopp!	Schmidt, Hans-Dieter
Das alltägliche Wunder	Hartmann, Gerhard
Alte Männer am Meer	Koerbl, Jürg-Michael
Der alte Mann mit der jungen Frau	Schneider, Rolf
Das alte Puppenspiel vom Dr. Faustus	Stäcker, Hans-Dieter
Die alte Straßenbahn Therese	Schmidt, Hans-Dieter
Der alte und der neue Faust	Gressmann, Uwe
Der ältere Sohn	Pfützner, Klaus
Altweibersommer	Rentzsch, Gerhard
Alwin der Letzte	Gruchmann-Reuter, Margret
Am Ende der Nacht	Hauser, Harald
Am nächsten Morgen	Zuchardt, Karl
Amazonen	Schütz, Stefan
Ambrosio tötet die Zeit	Koerbl, Jürg-Michael
Ameisengeschichten	Preuß, Gunter
Amen Corner	Seyppel, Joachim
Das Amerika Abraham Lincolns	Gilbricht, Walter
Ein Amerikaner in Berlin	Zinner, Hedda
Ein Amerikaner in Tarent	Müller, Helmut
Amphitruo	Hoffmann, Walter
Amphytrion	Hacks, Peter
Amphytrion	Stolper, Armin
Amphytrion	Zimmermann, Ingo
Das Amulett	Freyer, Paul Herbert
An beiden Ufern	Matusche, Alfred
An beiden Ufern der Spree	Wangenheim, Gustav von
Anatomie Titus Fall of Rome Ein Shakespeare Kommentar	Müller, Heiner
Das Andenken aus Lancaster	Vogt, Helmut
Der andere Don Quichote	Bortfeldt, Kurt
Das andere Gesicht	Heiduczek, Werner
Der andere Paul	Otte, Volkmar
Die Angsthasen	Körner-Schrader, Paul
Aniko	Bejach, Peter

Animationen	Thieme, Rolf
Ankerplatz	Enders, Horst
Die Ankunft im Alltag	Wohlgemuth, Joachim
Ankunft in Weilstedt	Schneider, Rolf
Anna	Holdsch, Hans
Anna und der Männerstreik	Wolf, Friedrich
Annemarie	Brosch, Alwin
Annette	Schöbel, Hildegard
Annette und die wilden Räuber	Winkler, Barbara
Anonyme Briefe	Leonhard, Rudolf
Anregung	Drewniok, Heinz
Anregung I ‹Eins›	Fensch, Eberhard;
	Gosse, Peter;
	Neutsch, Erik
Anregung II ‹Zwei›	Sakowski, Helmut;
	Salomon, Horst;
	Stolper, Armin;
	Wogatzki, Benito
Der Anruf	Strahl, Rudi
Anständige Menschen	Kucksholm, Heinz
Anstoß für Claudia	Albig, Hans Georg
Antigone	Schaller, Rudolf
Die Antigone des Sophokles	Brecht, Bertolt
Die Antigone des Sophokles	Goertz, Heinrich
Antiope und Theseus	Schütz, Stefan
Die Antwort	Malink, Peter
Aphrodite	Wendler, Otto Bernhard
Apollino	Schmidt, Hans-Dieter
AR 2 ruft Ikarus	Krupkat, Günter
Arbeiter, Bauern und Soldaten	Becher, Johannes R.
Arbeiter und Bauern	Braun, Volker
Die Arche Noah	Lommer, Horst
Arenia, Hurra!	Noack, Christian
Aretino	Knauth, Joachim
Die argentinische Nacht: Eine Hundetragödie	Brasch, Thomas
Die Argonautensage	Noack, Christian
Der Arme Konrad	Wolf, Friedrich
Armer Ritter	Hacks, Peter
Arno, Katharina und Paul	Morgner, Martin
Arno, Prinz von Wolkenstein	Strahl, Rudi
Arturo Ui	Brecht, Bertolt
Der Arzt wider Willen	Müller, Heiner
Asche im Mund	Groß, Jürgen
Aschenbrödel	Bendey, Herbert
Aschenputtel	Bortfeldt, Kurt
Aschenputtel	Braun, Klaus Dieter
Aschenputtel	Müller, Dietmar
Aschenputtel	Reissinger, Horst
Der Aschenstocherer	Hawemann, Horst
Auch in Amerika	Wangenheim, Gustav von
Auf alle Fälle Liebe	Merckel, Rudolf
Auf dem Feldherrnhügel	Kleineidam, Horst
Auf dem Hinterhof, vier Treppen links	Lask, Berta

Auf dem zweiten Hof, fünf Treppen	Lask, Berta
Auf der Durchreise nach Petersburg	Lange, Hartmut
Auf der Suche nach einer bunten Kuh	Baierl, Helmut
Auf glattem Parkett	Hall, Heinz
Auf jeden Fall verdächtig	Zinner, Hedda
Auf Straßen, die wir selber bauten	Müller, Jupp
Auf und ab	Drewniok, Heinz
Auf verlorenem Posten	Freyer, Paul Herbert
Der Aufenthaltsraum	Troche, Peter
Aufführung verboten	Bankel, Walter
Aufgesang	Gozell, Rolf
Der aufhaltsame Aufstieg des Arturo Ui	Brecht, Bertolt
Aufregung um Teigmenger	Kühne, Hans J.
Die Aufrichtung der Menorah	Zweig, Arnold
Aufruhr der Engel	Schreiter, Helfried
Der Aufruhr des Michael Kohlhaas	Rahn, Karlheinz
Der Aufstand	Felkel, Günter
Der Aufstand des Babeuf	May, Ferdinand
Der Aufstieg des Alois Piontek	Kipphardt, Heinar
Aufstieg und Fall der Stadt Mahagonny	Brecht, Bertolt
Der Aufstieg von Edith Eiserbeck	Gozell, Rolf
Der Auftrag	Müller, Heiner
Aufzeichnungen eines Toten	Stolper, Armin
Augenblick im Tunnel	Gröschke, Gerhard
Ein Augenblick ist mein gewesen	Habeck-Adamek, Anne
August Cäsar	Hoffmann, Max K.
Auguste, die Weihnachtsgans	Dörner, Karin
Augustus Potter	Herrmann, Klaus
Die Aula	Kant, Hermann
Aulus und sein Papagei	Griesbach, Rudi
Aus dem Leben eines Tauglichen	Schöbel, Manuel
Die Ausbrecher	Lucke, Hans
Die Ausgezeichneten	Weicker, Regina
Die Ausnahme und die Regel	Brecht, Bertolt
Außerhalb von Schuld	Seeger, Uwe
Austreibung 1744	Zweig, Arnold
Ein Auto zum Heiraten	Koerbl, Jürg-Michael
Auweia und Ratzbatz	Kahlau, Heinz
Axel	Brüning, Elfriede
Die Axt	Berg, Jochen
Die Axt im Haus	Gratzik, Paul

B

Baal	Brecht, Bertolt
Babettes grüner Schmetterling	Hanell, Robert
Das Badener Lehrstück vom Einverständnis	Brecht, Bertolt
Badenweiler Abgesang	Knauth, Joachim
Der Bajazzo	Herz, Joachim
Bajonette und Brot	Wolf, Friedrich
Ballade vom Glück	Dorwaldt-Kühl, Edith

Die Ballade vom Kipper Paul Bauch	Braun, Volker
Die Ballade vom ‹sturen Planer Dieter Konczak und vom› aufsässigen Eisenbahner ‹Horst Hilpert›	Stolper, Armin
Baller contra Baller	Veken, Karl
Die Banditen	Eidam, Klaus
Der Bär	Freiheit, Peter
Barackenliebe	Troche, Peter
Baran	Bauer, Friedhold
Baran in Reinsdorf	Bauer, Friedhold
Baran und die Leute im Dorf	Bauer, Friedhold
Barbara	Hauser, Harald
Barby	Hacks, Peter
Der Bärenhäuter	Wendler, Otto Bernhard
Der Bärenhäuter	Wolff, Bernd
Barfuß nach Langenhanshagen	Kleineidam, Horst
Barrikade	Gerlach, Harald
Bartleby	Kipphardt, Heinar
Die Bataille am Bluewater Creek	Hacks, Peter
Der Bau	Müller, Heiner
Der Bauch	Bartsch, Kurt
Bauer Baetz	Wolf, Friedrich
Der Bauer und sein König	Tittel, Gerhard
Die Bauern	Müller, Heiner
Der Bauerngeneral	Kunzelmann, Gerhard Heinz
Die Baumaschine	Kuhnert, Reinhard Frieder
Beaumarchais	Wolf, Friedrich
Beethoven	Schäfer-Rose, Helmut
Befragung Anna O.	Bahr, Peter
Der Befreier	Herrmann, Klaus
Befreiung	Gentz, Friedrich
Die Befreiung	Lask, Berta
Begegnung 1957	Keller, Herbert
Begegnung bei Nacht	Krupkat, Günter
Begegnung mit Herkules	Pfeiffer, Hans
Die Behlings	Koeppel, Jochen
Bei Mirandolina	Geiger, Erich
Die beiden Geschenke	Foellbach, Lena
Die beiden Nachtwandler	Schneider, Rolf
Das beispielhafte ‹Spiel vom› Leben und Tod des Peter Göring	Brasch, Thomas
Belastungsprobe	Felkel, Günter
Bellebelle	Knauth, Joachim
Belli, Maxe und Gespenster	Drescher, Piet
Bellmann	Rücker, Günther
Berge von Schaum	Zweig, Arnold
Die Berggeister des Hallasan	Pijet, Georg Waldemar
Das Bergwerk zu Falun	Wagner-Regeny, Rudolf
Bericht vom Sterben des Musikers Jack Tiergarten	Brasch, Thomas
Berlin Alexanderplatz	Jaksch, Bärbel
Berlin, wie es weint und lacht	Degenhardt, Jürgen
Bernardo Albas Haus	Köllinger, Bernd
Die Bernsteinbrigade	Blach, Erich

Besuch aus dem Nebel	Bonhoff, Otto
Ein Besuch für die Vergangenheit	Hornawsky, Gerd
Besuch in Muchowiec	Drewniok, Heinz
Besuch von gestern	Lucke, Hans
Die betrunkene Sonne	Kirsch, Sarah
Der Bettler	Brecht, Bertolt
Der Bettler von Damaskus	Hanell, Robert
Die Bewährung	Blume, Horst
Bewährungsfrist	Grubert, Peter
Bi de Düwelswieden	Vollsdorff, Erwin
Die Bibel	Brecht, Bertolt
Bibelgeschichten	Trolle, Lothar
Biedermänner	Bormann, Arnold
Das Biest des Monsieur Racine	Lang, Alexander
Bijou	Eckert, Holger
Bikini	Denger, Alfred
Bildbeschreibung	Müller, Heiner
Bilder aus dem anderen Amerika	Schneider, Peter M.
Bilder der Liebe	Kunad, Rainer
Bill Brook	Kunad, Rainer
Bindegarn	Faust, Bernhard
Die Binsen	Hacks, Peter
Blast das Feuer an	Bauer, Werner
Blaubart	Seidemann, Burkhart
Die blaue Akte	Hacks, Peter
Das blaue Licht	Drescher, Piet
Die blaue Muschel	Müller, Armin
Die blaue Nachtigall	Schneider, Peter M.
Das blaue Pferdchen	Reinhold, Heide
Der blaue Teppich	Völlger, Wilfried
Der blaue Vogel	Müller, Dietmar
Das Blaue vom Himmel	Strahl, Rudi
Das Blechboot	Wendt, Albert
Der blinde Passagier	Tasche, Elke
Blinder Eifer	Groß, Jürgen
Blitzdonnnerschock	Rosenlöcher, Thomas
Blümchen und die Schurken	Schwaen, Kurt
Die Blumen von Hiroshima	Forest, Jean Kurt
Das Blumenmädchen von Kanton	Arnold, Hans Dieter
La Boheme	Herz, Joachim
Bolero	Schneidereit, Otto
Bomben auf den Palast	Schreyer, Wolfgang
Bonaparte in Jaffa	Zweig, Arnold
Bonn im Spiegel	Rülicke-Weiler, Käthe
Boris Godunov	Erb, Elke
Boulevard Durand	Keisch, Henryk
Das Brandenburger Tor	Scheer, Maximilian
Die braven Börgers von Kreihenbarg	Heinrichs, Eckart
Die Bremer Stadtmusikanten	Auenmüller, Hans
Die Bremer Stadtmusikanten	Eckert, Holger
Die Bremer Stadtmusikanten	Ensikat, Peter
Die Bremer Stadtmusikanten	Helfricht, Klaus
Die Bremer Stadtmusikanten	Kaltofen, Günter
Die Bremer Stadtmusikanten	Methe, Hubertus
Die Bremer Stadtmusikanten	Rainer, Wolfgang

Die Bremer Stadtmusikanten	Rosenlöcher, Thomas
Brennende Ruhr	Grünberg, Karl
Bretter, die die Welt bedeuten	Bez, Helmut
Briefe an Aja	Mickel, Karl
Das Brigadekind	Elbers, Martin
Brinkmanns Tochter	Stürzebecher, Charlotte
Brittanicus	Hein, Christoph
Brokat aus Frankreich	Freyer, Paul Herbert
Brot der Armen	Neuhaus, Lutz W.
Der Brotladen	Brecht, Bertolt
Die Brücke fällt aus	Müller, Heiner
Die Brüder	Stranka, Walter
Bruder Aljoscha	Erb, Elke
Bruder Eichmann	Kipphardt, Heinar
Die Brüder Seebald	Schäfer, Paul Kanut
Brüderchen und Schwesterchen	Bodeit, Gerhard
Der Brunnen unterm Mangobaum	Tiefensee, Siegfried
Bruno der Erste	Groß, Jürgen
Bruno der Unsichtbare	Kirsch, Rainer
Büchner	Harnisch, Klaus
Büchner	Herrmann, Klaus
Das Buckauer Hofspektakel	Schneider, Elke
Das bucklige Pferdchen	Endler, Adolf
Der Bungalow	Wander, Fred
Das buntgescheckte Kalb	Bostroem, Annemarie
Der Bürger als Ehrenmann	Kirsch, Rainer
Bürger schützt eure Anlagen	Ensikat, Peter
Die Bürger von Calais	Neher, Caspar
Bürgermeister Anna	Wolf, Friedrich
Die Bürgschaft	Neher, Caspar
Buridans Esel	Plenzdorf, Ulrich
Der Bus fährt um 20 Uhr	Schweickert, W. K.
Der Bus hält an der Brücke	Stürzebecher, Charlotte
Büsching	Brecht, Bertolt

C

Cafehaus Payer	Zinner, Hedda
Calamity Jane	Bez, Helmut
Camillos Doppelhochzeit	Wieland, Günter
Die Campagne	Knauth, Joachim
Candide	Müller, Gerhard
Carmagnole	Knaup, Andreas
Casanova	Bez, Helmut
Casanova auf Schloß Dux	Gassauer, Karl
Cäsars Traum	Zuchardt, Karl
Cecil	Hanell, Robert
Celestina	Mickel, Karl
Ceremoniel pour un combat	Schirmer, Bernd
Das Chagrinleder	Deicke, Günther
Die Chance des Mannes	Görlich, Günther
Der Chargierkran	Bormann, Arnold
Charlotte Hoyer	Hacks, Peter
Charlotte Stieglitz	Hacks, Peter
Chatyn	Groß, Jürgen

Chor der Arbeiter	Wangenheim, Gustav von
Chorkwerk über den 8-Stundentag	Wangenheim, Gustav von
Cipollino	Schmidt, Hans-Dieter
the CIVIL warS	Müller, Heiner
Colonel Foster ist schuldig	Hauptmann, Elisabeth
Columbus	Hacks, Peter
Companeros	Schreiter, Helfried
Concerto Dramatico	Stolper, Armin
Conchos Land	Knietzsch, Karl Christian
Connie und der Löwe	Eidam, Klaus
Copernicus	Hartmann, Gerhard
Coriolan	Brecht, Bertolt
Cosima von Bülow	Hacks, Peter
Craqueville	Küchenmeister, Claus
Cressida	Schütz, Stefan
Cromwell	Hein, Christoph
Cyankali	Wolf, Friedrich
Cyrano aus Bergerac	Kirsch, Rainer

D

D-Zug CK3	Pijet, Georg Waldemar
Da kam ein junger Königssohn	Streubel, Manfred
Da liegt der Hund begraben	Wangenheim, Gustav von
Da schaut der Ochs zum Fenster raus	Körner-Schrader, Paul
Der Dachboden	Goertz, Heinrich
Die Dachdecker	Wendt, Albert
Dachziegel oder Bomben	Reichwald, Fritz
Damals 18/19	Küchenmeister, Claus
Damals in Prag	Schneider, Hansjörg
Damals vor 15 Jahren	Kerndl, Rainer
Die Dame aus Indien	Arnold, Hans Dieter
Der Damm	Lang, Ottomar
Der Dämpfer	Freyer, Paul Herbert
Daniel Druskat	Weindich, Josef-Adolf
Dann wollen wir einmal wieder	Dinkelmann, Kurt
Dansen	Brecht, Bertolt
Dantons Tod	Kuba
Das bist du	Wolf, Friedrich
Das geht auf keine Kuhhaut	Gruchmann-Reuter, Margret
Das ist Diebstahl	Bortfeldt, Kurt
Das ist unser Jahr	Günther, Jens-Uwe
Das unterschlug Homer	Lommer, Horst
Das war im Hafen von Marseille	Morgan, Hans
Das wenigstens will ich selber tun	Schöbel, Manuel
Däumlings Abenteuer	Däbritz, Fritz
Dave	Berg, Jochen
David	Schubert, Helga
David der Glöckner	Baierl, Helmut
David und Batsheba	Kuhn, Fritz
Das Decameronical	Kahlow, Heinz
Demeter	Braun, Volker
Denkmal	Groß, Jürgen
Denkmal Standort	Wenzel, Hans Jürgen

Detektiv Sonnenstrahl	Seelig, Käthe
Detektiv Tom	Gerlach, Wolfgang Rainer
Deutsche Tragödie	Reif, Guido
Ein deutsches Herz	Findeisen, Kurt Arnold
Ein deutsches Schicksal	Branstner, Gerhard
Die heute 17 sind	Weide, Martina
‹Der› Dieb und ‹der› König	Schneider, Rolf
Die Diebin und die Lügnerin	Groß, Jürgen
Der Diener zweier Herren	Schuster, Uwe
Der Diener zweier Herrn	Böttcher, Wolfgang
Dienstgruppe 729	Schmidt, Jürgen
Dienstreisegeschichten	Helm, Heinz
Dienstreisende	Stolper, Armin
Diese Eh' döggt nix	Heinrichs, Eckart
Dimitroff	Grabner, Hasso
Dir zuliebe	Bortfeldt, Kurt
Die Dirne und ihr roter Gast	Müller-Glösa, Otto
Disko mit Oskar	Dechant, Lutz
Ein Diskurs über das Holzhacken	Lange, Hartmut
Dissonanzen	Enders, Horst
Dmitri	Braun, Volker
Dobberkau ist da	Bez, Helmut
Doch der Vierzehnte	Gerisch, Klaus
Doch unterm Rock der Teufel	Djacenko, Boris
Doktor Fausts Höllenfahrt	Stäcker, Hans-Dieter
Doktor ‹Lilli› Wanner	Wolf, Friedrich
Doktor Martinus	Voss, Helmut
Doktor Wanner	Wolf, Friedrich
Don Giovanni	Seeger, Horst
Don Juan	Brasch, Peter
Don Juan	Brecht, Bertolt
Don Juan	Honigmann, Barbara
Don Juan	Müller, Heiner
Don Juans Höllenfahrt	Böttcher, Wolfgang
Don Quichote in Murzeledo	Otte, Volkmar
Don Quijote	Bohne, Monika
Dona Juanita	Günther, Jens-Uwe
Das Donnerwetter	Goertz, Heinrich
Der Doppelgänger	Seeger, Horst
Der Doppelmord in der Rue Morgue	Koerbl, Jürg-Michael
Doppelt gebacken	Preil, Hans-Joachim
Der doppelte Otto	Lucke, Hans
Der doppelte Schatten	Feustel, Gotthard
Doppeltes Spiel	Kerndl, Rainer
Die Dorfstraße	Matusche, Alfred
Der Dorftrottel	Wendt, Albert
Dorian Gray	Hanell, Robert
Dornröschen	Bergner, Edith
Dornröschen	Beygang, Hans-Joachim
Dornröschen	Borowski, S. A.
Dornröschen	Ensikat, Peter
Dornröschen	Stolzenbach, Beatrice
Dr. Fausts Höllenfahrt	Stäcker, Hans-Dieter
Dr. ‹Lilli› Wanner	Wolf, Friedrich
Der Drache	Lange, Hartmut

Drachen steigen gegen den Wind	Denger, Alfred
Drachenoper	Müller, Heiner
Dramaturgie und Liebe	Zehlen, Petra
Draufgänger	Flegel, Walter
Drei anonyme Briefe	Schweickert, W. K.
Die drei Irrtümer des Sebastian Fünfling	Baierl, Helmut
3 x ‹Drei Mal› klingeln	Schmidt, Hans-Dieter
Die drei Musketiere	Damm-Wendler, Ursula
Die drei Musketiere	Maaß, Heiner
Die drei Musketiere	Seidel, Klaus
Drei Perücken	Richter, Hans Michael
Die drei Robinsons	May, Ferdinand
Die drei Schwestern	Foellbach, Lena
Drei weiße Pfeile	Makarius, Jan
Die Dreigroschenoper	Brecht, Bertolt
Dreiklang	Ensikat, Peter
Der dreizehnte	Baierl, Helmut
Die dritte Schicht	Pfeiffer, Hans
Dschungel	Djacenko, Boris
Du bist der Richtige	Wangenheim, Gustav von
Du meine Tante	Branstner, Gerhard
Du sollst dir kein Bildnis machen	Czech-Kuckhoff, Ilse
The Duchess of Malfi	Brecht, Bertolt
Das Duell	Hornawsky, Gerd
Der dumme Teufel Stanislas	Schulze, Gernot
Das Durchgangszimmer	Kahlau, Heinz
D-Zug CK3	Pijet, Georg Waldemar

E

Ebbe und Sündflut	Denger, Alfred
Das Eden Hotel	Baierl, Helmut
Eduard un de lütten Sünd'n	Korf, Rudolf
Der Egoist	Freitag, Franz
Egon	Wohlgemuth, Joachim
Egon ist da	Drewniok, Heinz
Egon und das achte Weltwunder	Schmidt, Hans-Dieter
Ehe eine Ehe eine Ehe wird	Böttcher, Wolfgang
Ehe in 3 Tagen	Schwarz-Marell, Gisela
Ehe ungenügend	Allihn, Jochen
Das Ehekollektiv	Lange, Friedrich
Ehekrach und heiße Noten	Freitag, Franz
Ein ehernes Denkmal - lebendige Herzen	Nawrath, Marta
Ehesache Lorenz	Waterstradt, Berta
Ehrengericht	Richter, Manfred
Die Ehrgeizigen	Görlich, Günther
Eierhuhn und Stolperhahn	Wendt, Albert
Der eifersüchtige Alte	Schwaen, Kurt
Die eigene Haut	Lucke, Hans
Der eigene Kopf	Pederzani, Hans Albert
Der Einbruch	Lebrecht, Georg
Einer geht baden	Wiener, C. U.
Einer macht den Hansel	Gersch, Christel

Die erste Reiterarmee	Hauptmann, Elisabeth
Die ersten Schritte	Kubsch, Hermann Werner
Erstens kommt es anders	Corrinth, Curt
Erwischt	Körner-Schrader, Paul
Erzieher im Examen	Reichwald, Fritz
Die Erziehung zum Chorgesang	Schütz, Helga
Es ist eine alte Geschichte	Bormann, Arnold
Es war...	Bejach, Peter
Es war eine Mutter	Ebert, Günther
Es war einmal ein König Drosselbart	Schneider, Peter M.
Es war einmal ein Pumphut	Stahl, Heidemarie
Es wird, wie es bleibt	Koerbl, Jürg-Michael
Esau und Jakob	Wagner-Regeny, Rudolf
Esel schrein im Dunkel	Kipphardt, Heinar
Die Eselskomödie	Ebel, Karl-Albert
Esther	Deicke, Günther
Etappe Preußen	Vogt, Helmut
Eulenspiegel	Brasch, Thomas
Eva und der Moralist	Baierl, Helmut
Die Eysenhardts: Der Weg einer Frau	Nell, Peter

F

Fabrik im Walde	Schütz, Stefan
Die fahrende Pappel	Wendt, Albert
Der Fahrer und die Köchin	Wendt, Albert
Le Faiseur	Hammel, Claus
Der Fakir	Gerlach, Harald
Der Fall	Martin, Christian
Der Fall Denziger	Krupkat, Günter
Der Fall des Professors Zorillo	Brasch, Thomas
Ein Fall für Sherlock Holmes	Degenhardt, Jürgen
Der Fall Klabautermann	Müller, Helmut
Der Fall Merzbach	Wendler, Horst-Ulrich
Der Fall Schandauer	Eidam, Klaus
Falsch verbunden	Rauchfuß, Hildegard Maria
Der falsche Schwiegersohn	Polonski, Georg
Falstaff	Seeger, Horst
Familie	Koerbl, Jürg-Michael
Familie Birnchen	Roehricht, Karl Hermann
Die Familie der guten Leute	Richter, Manfred
Familie Morgenwind	Borde-Klein, Ingeborg
Familiensonntag	Freyer, Paul Herbert
Fanal	Lucke, Hans
La Farola	Burger, Hanus
Fatinitza	Schneidereit, Otto
Fatzer	Brecht, Bertolt
Fatzer	Müller, Heiner
Faule Eier	Kypke, Peter Günter
Faust	Gressmann, Uwe
Faust im Inferno	Pfeiffer, Hans
Die Fehde des Michael Kohlhaas	Wendler, Horst-Ulrichl
Der Feigling	Dudow, Slatan
Feliks D.	Hammel, Claus

Das Fell	Schneider, Peter M.
Ferien am Schneeberg	Bejach, Peter
Ferien auf dem Lande	Kubsch, Hermann Werner
Eine Ferienfahrt ist fein	Böhme, Susanne
Das Fest der Waldgeister	Burger, Hanus
Die Feststellung	Baierl, Helmut
Feuer im Dorf	Pons, Peter
Die feuerrote Blume	Auenmüller, Hans
Die feuerrote Blume	Djacenko, Boris
Feuervogel und Rotfüchslein	Schuster, Uwe
Die feurige Stadt	Matusche, Alfred
Das Feuerzeug	Frenzel, Klaus
Das Feuerzeug	Herzka, Peter-Maria
Das Feuerzeug	Kirsch, Rainer
Das Feuerzeug	Morgner, Martin
Fiesta	Hanell, Robert
Finale	Stolper, Armin
Fingerübungen	Neutsch, Erik
Fisch zu viert	Kohlhaase, Wolfgang
Die Fische	Hacks, Peter
Der Fischer und seine Frau	Schleef, Einar
Die Fischer von Niezow	Zinner, Hedda
Fischerkinder	Hammel, Claus
Der Fischzug	Brecht, Bertolt
Der Flaschenteufel	Wendler, Horst-Ulrich
Die Fledermaus	Neef, Wilhelm
Die Fledermaus	Schneidereit, Otto
Der fliegende Arzt	Hein, Christoph
Der fliegende Pfeil	Müller, Dietmar
Der fliegende Pfeil	Müller, Helmut
Das fliegende Pferd	Tscholakowa, Ginka
Der fliegende Teppich	Eidam, Klaus
Die fliegenden Pferde von Habis Bat	Völlger, Wilfried
Fliegenfängergeschichte	Dancker, Susanne
Floridsdorf	Wolf, Friedrich
Die Flößer der Bistritza	Schneidereit, Otto
Flüchtlingsgespräche	Brecht, Bertolt
Der Flug der Lindberghs	Brecht, Bertolt
Flugversuch	Saeger, Uwe
Die Flüsterparty	Strahl, Rudi
Die Fontäne	Jakobs, Karl-Heinz
Football Story	Schmidt, Hans-Dieter
Fracht für Coquimbo	Lucke, Hans
Fragen Sie Sibylle	Wiener, Ralph
Francis Bacon	Gentz, Friedrich
Frank	Neumann, Karl
Franziska Lesser	Müller, Armin
Franziska Linkerhand	Jaksch, Bärbel
Die Frau da draußen und der Mann	Gröschke, Gerhard
Die Frau des Jahres	Degenhardt, Jürgen
Frau Fischer Ilsebill	Lange, Katrin
Frau Flinz	Baierl, Helmut
Frau Holle	Borde-Klein, Ingeborg
Frau Holle	Däbritz, Fritz

Frau Holle	Hahn, Gustav
Frau Holle	Heinrichs, Eckart
Frau Holle	Kaltofen, Günter
Frau Holle	Kirsch, Rainer
Frau Holle	Küchenmeister, Claus
Frau Holle	Meissner, Hildegard
Frau Holle	Methe, Hubertus
Frau Jenny Treibl	Hammel, Claus
Frau Luna	Schneidereit, Otto
Eine Frau mit Vergangenheit	Eckert, Holger
Frau Mohr hat ihre Schuldigkeit getan	Böttcher, Wolfgang
Eine Frau ohne Bedeutung	Wiede, Anna E.
Eine Frau verliert die Maske	Herzog, Alfred
Frau von Kauenhofen	Lange, Hartmut
Frauen sind Männersache	Ender, Roland
Die Frauen von Troja	Röttger, Heinz
Das Fräulein aus Potsdam	Vogt, Helmut
Fräulein Mama	Kramer, Heinz
Fräulein Paulmanns Heirat	Noack, Christian
Fräulein Reisebüro	Bauer, Andreas
Das Fräulein wird Minister	Eidam, Klaus
Frech wie Oskar	Ensikat, Peter
Frechdachs Willibald	Polonski, Georg
Fredegunde	Hacks, Peter
Der Freier als Jagdhund	Korn, Nina
Fremde Federn	Geiger, Erich
Die fremde Fuhre	Wendt, Albert
Die fremde Haut	Otte, Volkmar
Fremder im Paradies	Schreyer, Wolfgang
Ein Freund der Wahrheit	Wiede, Anna E.
Freunde	Braun, Volker
Der freundliche Drache	Borde-Klein, Ingeborg
Friedas letzter Vormittag	Roehricht, Karl Hermann
Der Frieden	Hacks, Peter
Friedensfeier	Seidel, Georg
Der Friedensstörer	Wangenheim, Gustav von
Friedrich und Montezuma	Hartmann, Gerhard
Frisch verloren, halb gewonnen	Zuchardt, Karl
Fritze mit der Zipfelmütze	Brosch, Alwin
Frl. Reisebüro	Bauer, Andreas
Frohes Wochenende	Eidam, Klaus
Die fröhliche Gasse	Schmidt, Hans-Dieter
Der fröhliche Sünder	Gerster, Ottmar
Die fromme Marta	Wangenheim, Gustav von
Fronten	Focke, Gerd
Der Frosch und die Grasmücke	Schulz, Anneliese
Der Froschkönig	Günther, Horst
Der Froschkönig	Kaltofen, Günter
Der Froschkönig	Schneider, Elke
Die Froschzarin	Haas, Henn
Froufrou	Bez, Helmut
Frühlingsgewitter	Kosk, Jan
Frühlingskapriolen	Eschner, Eugen
Frühlingswalzer	Böttcher, Wolfgang

Frührot	Schlotterbeck, Anna
Der Fuchs	Hauptmann, Elisabeth
Die Füchse	Fabian, Gerhard
Fuente ovejuna	Noack, Christian
Führer & Co.	Leonhard, Rudolf
Das Führerbild	Becher, Johannes R.
Fünf Spiele	Günther, Egon
Fünfmal die Drei	Focke, Gerd
Das fünfte Rad am Wagen	Wolf, Klaus Martin
Fünfzig Nelken	Seeger, Bernhard
Für fünf Groschen Urlaub	Damm-Wendler, Ursula
Furcht und Elend des dritten Reiches	Brecht, Bertolt
Futuronauten	Kunert, Günter

G

Gabor-Gabor	Schmidt, Hans-Dieter
Galilei	Brecht, Bertolt
Die Gallwespe	Gilbricht, Walter
Die Galoschenoper	Kahlau, Heinz
Gangster lieben keine Blumen	Janowski, Maurycy
Ganz Ohr	Ostarek, Hans
Gardeschütze Mattrosow	Fabian, Gerhard
Garga	Brecht, Bertolt
Der Gast	Krengel-Strudthoff, Inge
Der Gast aus Paris	Böttcher, Wolfgang
Der Gast aus Saadulla	Heiduczek, Werner
Gaston macht alles	May, Ferdinand
Gatt	Hamm, Christoph
Gaunerballade	Focke, Gerd
Gavroche	Ensikat, Peter
Gebt Frieden	Wolf, Klaus Martin
Die Geburt des "Figaro"	Wolf, Friedrich
Geburtstagsgäste	Groß, Jürgen
Das Geburtstagsgeschenk	Wendt, Albert
Gefährliches Schweigen	Focke, Gerd
Das Gefecht in der Schlafkammer	Wendler, Horst-Ulrich
Gefrühstückt wird um acht	Focke, Gerd
Das Geheimnis des Kupferbergs	Borowski, S. A.
Gehobene Unterhaltung	Eidam, Klaus
Die Geier der Helen Turner	Collin, Christian
Geiger, Gauner und Geschäfte	Geiger, Erich
Geiseln	Leonhard, Rudolf
Die Geisha	Schneidereit, Otto
Der Geist von Cranitz	Köhler, Erich
Der Geist von Potsmar	Welk, Ehm
Der Geizige	Gersch, Christel
Das gekaufte Mädchen	Günther, Egon
Das gelbe Fenster, der gelbe Stein	Hammel, Claus
Geld wie Heu	Eidam, Klaus
Die Geldheirat	Wallroth, Werner W.
Gelegenheit macht Liebe	Willers, Rosel
Das Gemälde	Schöbel, Helfried
Das Gemälde	Stolper, Armin

Die gestohlene Weihnachtsuhr	Bischoff, Karl-Heinrich
Die gestohlenen Pfannkuchen	Stäcker, Hans-Dieter
Gestrahltes	Strahl, Rudi
Der getaufte Star	Wendler, Horst-Ulrich
Die Gewehre der Frau Carrar	Brecht, Bertolt
Gewissen und Gewalt	Jungnickel, Rudolf
Ein gewisser Herr Wolf	Hoerning, Walter
Ein gewisser Katulla	Strahl, Rudi
Gewitter über Gotland	Welk, Ehm
Der gewöhnliche Skandal	Groß, Jürgen
Giftgasnebel über Sowjetrußland	Lask, Berta
Gilgamesch und Enkidu	Noack, Christian
Gladiolen, ein Tintenfaß und eine bunte Kuh	Baierl, Helmut
Gladiolen zum Geburtstag	Baierl, Helmut
Das gläserne Glöckchen	Foellbach, Lena
Das Glas Wasser	Böttcher, Wolfgang
Glatteis	Lucke, Hans
Die gleiche Strecke	Matusche, Alfred
Die Glocken von Straßburg	Brosch, Alwin
Gloster	Schütz, Stefan
Glück über den kurzen Weg	Vollsdorff, Erwin
Glücklich, aber verheiratet	Ender, Roland
Die glückliche Insel	Dröge, Ernst Wolf
Die glückliche Stadt	Pijet, Georg Waldemar
Die glückselige Insel der Erfindungen	Schönberg, Klaus
Glücksgott	Müller, Heiner
Glückwunsch, Paul	Gustmann, Egbert
Die Glut in der Asche	Wendler, Otto Bernhard
Die Gnadenlosen	Kuhn, Fritz
Die Gnomenwette	Hanell, Robert
Godefroys	Schneider, Rolf
Golden fließt der Stahl	Grünberg, Karl
Die goldene Gans	Bergner, Edith
Die goldene Gans	Kaltofen, Günter
Die goldene Gans	Kirchner, Annerose
Goldene Hände	Görlich, Günther
Der goldene Kessel	Bormann, Arnold
Das goldene Korn	Borde-Klein, Ingeborg
Die goldene Kuh	Korb, Irene
Der goldene Vogel	Müller, Armin
Die Goldgräber	Bartsch, Kurt
Das Goldkind	Stranka, Walter
Goldsucher in den Rocky Mountains	Günther, Lutz
Golemanow	Schütz, Stefan
Golf bei Sniders	Collin, Christian
Goliath	Schubert, Helga
Die Gondolieri	Degenhardt, Jürgen
Good-by Nicky	Stockhaus, Heinz
Gösta Berling	Brecht, Bertolt
Die Götterwitwe	Herrmann, Klaus
Der göttliche Orpheus	Lintzel, Martin
Grabbes Grab	Latchinian, Sewan
Grabgeflüster	Bläss, Helmut

Hamlet	Müller, Heiner
Hamlet aus Wittenberg	Albrecht, Paul
Hamlet in Heidelberg	Pfeiffer, Hans
Hamlet, Prinz von Dänemark	Schaller, Rudolf
Hamletmaschine	Müller, Heiner
Hammel und Bammel als Verkehrspolizisten	Trolle, Lothar
Die Hammelkomödie	Wendler, Horst-Ulrich
Hammer oder Amboß	Berthold, Siegfried
Hampelmann Schönbunter	Grafe, Manfred
Handbetrieb	Gratzik, Paul
Hände hoch, Mr. Copper	Böttcher, Wolfgang
Hände hoch, sonst knallt's	Preil, Hans-Joachim
Hannibal	Brecht, Bertolt
Hans Bockums Höllenfahrt	Djacenko, Boris
Hans Clauert Eulenspiegel	Richter, Kurt Dietmar
Hans, der Wettermacher	Süss, Anna
Hans Faust	Braun, Volker
Hans im Glück	Auenmüller, Hans
Hans im Glück	Becher, Johannes R.
Hans im Glück	Kaltofen, Günter
Hans Nasehoch	Raithel, Hugo
Hans Ohnefurcht	Seifert, Herbert
Hans Pfriem	Küchenmeister, Claus
Hans und der Teppich	Brosch, Alwin
Hans und der Zirkus	Brosch, Alwin
Hans und Marie	Martin, Christian
Hans Wurst, Faust und andere	Stäcker, Hans-Dieter
Hänsel und Gretel	Bodeit, Gerhard
Hänsel und Gretel	Brosch, Alwin
Hänsel und Gretel	Dorowa, Almut
Hänsel und Gretel	Frenzel, Klaus
Hänsel und Gretel	Herzka, Peter Maria
Hänsel und Gretel	Richter, Peter
Hänsel und Gretel - kein Märchen	Tasche, Elke
Happy End	Brecht, Bertolt
Harlekin und Colombine	Drewniok, Heinz
Harlekin und Colombine	Rücker, Günther
Häschen Schnurks	Hauser, Harald
Der Hase und der Igel	Leidner, Susanne
Hase und Igel	Ensikat, Peter
Hase und Igel	Schlott, Ulrich
Hassan und der Scheich	Scheer, Maximilian
Ein Hauch von Romantik	Kuba
Häuptling Büffelherz	Schmidt-Behrens, Friedrich
Der Hauptmann von Köln	Dudow, Slatan
Das Haus am Strom	Krengel-Strudthoff, Inge
Das Haus im Schatten	Enders, Horst
Haus Pechmühle	Lucke, Hans
Hausbesuche	Salomon, Horst
Ein Häuschen mit Butler	Làtzsch, Monika
Hausfrau gesucht	Hastedt, Regina
Der Hausgeist	Damm-Wendler, Ursula
Der Hausmeister	Freyer, Paul Herbert
Haut oder Hemd	Neutsch, Erik

Die Havarie	Lange, Katrin
He Marie!	Möbus, Hans
Heduda auf dem Pflaumenbaum	Wendt, Albert
Die heilige Johanna der Schlachthöfe	Brecht, Bertolt
Die heiligen drei Affen	Czech-Kuckhoff, Ilse
Die Heiligung Johannas	Schneider, Rolf
Heimdalls Erneuerung	Gentz, Friedrich
Heimkehr aus Luzon	Lindner, Otto
Die Heimkehr des Joachim Ott	Selbmann, Fritz
Die Heimkehr des verlorenen Sohnes	Jakobs, Karl-Heinz
Die Heimkehr des verlorenen Sohnes	Stolper, Armin
Die Heimkehr des verlorenen Vaters	Collin, Christian
Heine und der Tannenbaum	Vollsdorff, Erwin
Heines letzte Liebe	Kaltofen, Günter
Heinrich VIII. ‹der Achte›	Knauth, Joachim
Heinrich, der Wagen bricht	Menzel, Hans-Jochen
Heinrich Heine: Dichter unbekannt	Beck, Rolf
Heinrich Schlaghands Höllenfahrt	Kirsch, Rainer
Heinrich von Kleist‹s Tod›	Jungnickel, Rudolf
Die Heinzelmännchen	Ehrhardt, Rolf
Die Heirat	Erb, Elke
Der Heiratsantrag	Freiheit, Peter
Der Heiratsantrag	Röttger, Heinz
Die Heiratsanzeige	Brüning, Elfriede
Heiße Eisen	Koeppel, Jochen
Heißer Stern	Koerbl, Jürg-Michael
Das Heizkissen	Schweickert, W. K.
Der Hektarjäger	Reichwald, Fritz
Der Held der westlichen Welt	Hacks, Peter
Held im Zwielicht	Zuchardt, Karl
Held Ulysses	Gerlach, Harald
Der Held und sein Gefolge	Hacks, Peter
Der Held und sein Kapital	Hacks, Peter
Helden im Keller	Wangenheim, Gustav von
Der Heldentod	Kuhnert, Reinhard Frieder
Heloisa und Abaelard	Schütz, Stefan
Das Hemd eines Glücklichen	Wagner, Bernd
Der Henker von Braunau	Brennecke, Bert
Herakles	Lange, Hartmut
Herakles 5	Müller, Heiner
Der Herbstgarten	Anderson, Edith
Herbstgewitter	Damm-Wendler, Ursula
Herkules und die Frauen	Grafe, Manfred
Hermann oder Einesteils Vernunft	Gröschke, Gerhard
Der Herr aus England	Lindner, Otto
Herr Geiler	Brasch, Thomas
Herr Glitsch wird es schaffen	Vogt, Helmut
Der Herr Haysaemon	Hein, Christoph
Herr Märchen spielt Märchen	Borde-Klein, Ingeborg
Herr Plim	Groß, Jürgen
Herr Puntila und sein Knecht Matti	Brecht, Bertolt
Der Herr Schmidt	Rücker, Günther
Der Herr von der Generaldirektion	Pijet, Georg Waldemar
Die Herren des Strandes	Gerlach, Friedrich

Herrenmensch	Zuchardt, Karl
Herrnburger Bericht	Brecht, Bertolt
Herzstück	Müller, Heiner
Die Heuchlerin aus Liebe	Neef, Wilhelm
Heute um Mitternacht wirst du Witwe	Stockhaus, Heinz
Die Hexe Bimbambulla	Eckert, Holger
Die Hexe von Passau	Gerster, Ottmar
Das Hexenhaus	Wendt, Albert
Hier ist ein Neger zu lynchen	Hammel, Claus
Hier liegt der Hund begraben	Holdsch, Hans
Hier liegt der Hund begraben	Wangenheim, Gustav von
Hier muß ein Mann ins Haus	Wangenheim, Gustav von
Hier wird Geld verdient	Bremer, Claus
Hilfe, Freunde, die Vorstellung fällt aus	Stopf, Manfred
Hilfe, ich bin der Kaspar	Frenzel, Klaus
Himbeersaft und Liebe	Salchow, Werner
Der Himmel fällt aus den Wolken	Branstner, Gerhard
Himmeldonnerwetter	Eidam, Klaus
Himmelfahrt zur Erde	Stolper, Armin
Ein himmlischer Abend	Wiener, Ralph
Die Hinrichtung	Heym, Stefan
Hinter dem Regenbogen	Kleineidam, Horst
Hintereinanderweg	Stolper, Armin
Hinze und Kunze	Braun, Volker
Hirsch Heinrich	Feustel, Gotthard
Hirse für die Achte	Hauptmann, Elisabeth
Die Hitze	Körner, Thomas
Das Hochhaus	Wendt, Albert
Hochverrat	Brüning, Elfriede
Hochverrat	Neumann, Gerhard
Hochverratsaffäre	Keisch, Henryk
Hochwasser	Gröschke, Gerhard
Die Hochzeit	Brecht, Bertolt
Die Hochzeit des Figaro	Eidam, Klaus
Hochzeit einer Nonne	Collin, Christian
Hochzeit in Luxemburg	Hoffmann, Eugen Ferdinand
Die Hochzeit in Tomsk	Kleineidam, Horst
Die Hochzeitsreise	Eisenlohr, Friedrich
Ein hoffnungsloser Fall	Bonn, Karl Heinrich
Der Hofmeister	Brecht, Bertolt
Hoftheater	Eidam, Klaus
Hoheit die Liebe	Brosch, Alwin
Die Holländerbraut	Strittmatter, Erwin
Die Höllenfahrt des Doktor Faust	Baumgart, Peter
Höllenparade	Lommer, Horst
Die Holz-Eisenbahn	Honigmann, Barbara
Hommage a Marx	Hammel, Claus
Der Horatier	Müller, Heiner
Die Horatier und die Curatier	Brecht, Bertolt
Horizonte	Müller, Heiner
Die Hose	Strahl, Rudi
Hotel Spanischer Kaiser	Schneidereit, Otto

Hotelboy Ed Martin	Scheer, Maximilian
HUAC - Der Fall Eisler	Bunge, Hans
Hugo mit der Pauke	Stopf, Manfred
Humboldt und Bolivar	Hammel, Claus
Der Hund des Gärtners	Salomon, Horst
Der Hund des Generals	Kipphardt, Heinar
Die 100 ‹hundert› Tage	Groß, Jürgen
Hundetage	Vogt, Helmut
Eine Hundetragödie	Brasch, Thomas
Der Hundsprozeß - Zwischenspiel - ‹Stalin als› Herakles	Lange, Hartmut
Hunger	Denger, Alfred
Hurrikan	Müller, Helmut
Husarenstreiche	Grohmann, Gottfried
Die Hussiten vor Bernau	Wendler, Horst-Ulrich

I

Ich bin einem Mädchen begegnet	Kerndl, Rainer
Ich bin nicht Isaak	Tasche, Elke
Ich bin nicht meine Tante	Krause, Hans
Ich bin nun mal kein Yogi	Walther, Joachim
Ich gehe nach Hause	Richter-Rostalski, Gisela
"Ich ist ein anderer. Rimbaud"	Oehme, Ralph
Ich sehn' den Tag herbei	Kuba
Ich spiele dir die Welt durch	Schreiter, Helfried
Ich war, ich bin, ich werde sein	Wolf, Friedrich
Icke bin doch Icke	Dechant, Lutz
Icke und die Hexe Yu	Streubel, Manfred
Das ideale Ehepaar	Völkel, Ulrich
Ein idealer Gatte	Wiede, Anna E.
Der Idiot	Gerlach, Harald
Das Idol von Mordassow	Bauer, Friedhold
Die Igeltreppe	Kirsch, Sarah
Ihr seid ein Grünhorn, Sir!	Baierl, Helmut
Ihre große Liebe	Bonn, Karl Heinrich
Ikaros	Becher, Johannes R.
Illusion	Neuhaus, Lutz
Im Dickicht ‹der Städte›	Brecht, Bertolt
Im Garten	Koerbl, Jürg-Michael
Im Glashaus	Saeger, Uwe
Im Himmel und auf Erden	Herrmann, Klaus
Im himmlischen Garten	Hauser, Harald
Im Schatten des Kaisers	Jungnickel, Rudolf
Im Schatten des Turmes	Hauser, Harald
Im Taurerland	Berg, Jochen
Im Trocknen	Kuhnert, Reinhard Frieder
Immanuel Kleist	Koerbl, Jürg-Michael
Immer obenauf	Bauer, Werner
Impressum	Kant, Hermann
In der Sache J. Robert Oppenheimer	Kipphardt, Heinar
In Frisco ist der Teufel los	Janowski, Maurycy
In Jehudas Stadt	Lask, Berta
In Sachen Adam und Eva	Strahl, Rudi
Indianer am Mississippi	Pastowski, Klaus M.

Indianer, Farmer und Banditen	Schmidt-Behrens, Friedrich
Der Ingwertopf	Brecht, Bertolt
Die Insel Gottes	Richter, Manfred
Insel im Weltmeer	Paarmann, Heinz
Ein Inspektor kommt	Krengel-Strudthoff, Inge
Das Institut des Herrn Maillard	Goertz, Heinrich
Der Instrukteur soll heiraten	Janowski, Maurycy
Die Insurrektion	Thon, Manfred
Interview der verlorenen Söhne	Kuhn, Fritz
Inuk jagt die Sonne	Grubert, Peter
Iphigeneia	Berg, Jochen
Die irdene Lampe	Bostroem, Annemarie
Irene und die Kapitäne	Böttcher, Wolfgang
Ein irrer Duft von frischem Heu	Strahl, Rudi
Irrungen - Wirrungen	Zuchardt, Renate

J

Ja, die Familie	Allihn, Jochen
Ja, diese Biedermänner	Bormann, Arnold
Ja, so ein Mann bin ich	Preil, Hans-Joachim
Jacke wie Hose	Karge, Manfred
Jäckels Traum	Kuhnert, Reinhard Frieder
Jacques und sein Herr	Gersch, Christel
Jagar Bagala	Koch, Jurij
Die Jagd nach dem Stiefel	Pederzani, Hans Albert
Die Jäger	Drewniok, Heinz
Des Jägers Wunderhorn	Branstner, Gerhard
Das Jahr und Katrin	Gerisch, Klaus
Jahresringe	Foellbach, Lena
Das Jahrmarktsfest zu Plundersweilen	Hacks, Peter
Jahrmarktsspäße	Stäcker, Hans-Dieter
Jakob und sein Herr	Wendler, Horst-Ulrich
Jan Suschka	Krautz, Bodo
Jana und der kleine Stern	Heiduczek, Werner
Janosik - ein Held der Berge	Rahn, Karlheinz
Jarash: Ein Tag im September	Kerndl, Rainer
Der Jasager und Der Neinsager	Brecht, Bertolt
Jede Nacht geht zu Ende	Vogt, Helmut
Jedes Jahr im Mai	Bejach, Peter
Jeff und Andy	Hartmann, Gerhard
Jenseits von Gut und Böse	Lange, Hartmut
Jeppe	Wendler, Horst-Ulrich
Jeppe vom Berge	Lange, Hartmut
Jeppe vom Berge	Wendler, Horst-Ulrich
Jerry und der Gamsbart	Schumacher, Ernst
Jetzt sind wir schon weiter	Wangenheim, Gustav von
Jetzt und in der Stunde meines Todes	Günther, Egon
Jochen Schanotta	Seidel, Georg
Joel Brand: Die Geschichte eines Geschäfts	Kipphardt, Heinar
Johann der Knecht	Lask, Berta
Johann Faustus	Eisler, Hanns

Johanna Balk	Neher, Caspar
Johanna von Döbeln	Baierl, Helmut
John Blake	Groß, Jürgen
John D. erobert die Welt	Hein, Christoph
John D. erobert die Welt	Wolf, Friedrich
Jones' Familie	Kahlau, Heinz
Josef und Josefine	Stephan, Klaus
Josua läßt grüßen	Wander, Fred
Juana	Link, Joachim-Dietrich
Juana ‹von Joachim›	Salomon, Horst
Die Jüdin von Toledo	Müller, Dietmar
Judith	Matthus, Siegfried
Judy und Punch	Müller, Dietmar
Jugend	Bürger, Ernst
Julia	Schütz, Helga
Julie findet Freunde	Heiduczek, Werner
Julius Caesar	Schaller, Rudolf
Julius und Romea	Schill, Rolf
Die Jungen von Nyk	Lindner, Otto
Die Jungens von Mons	Wolf, Friedrich
Jungfrau, Stier und Waage	Schmidt, Hans-Dieter
Die Jungfrau von Orleans	Koerbl, Jürg-Michael
Die Junggesellensteuer	Dornik, Miklaws
Die Jungs	Drewniok, Heinz
Das jüngste Gericht von Rasselbach	Streubel, Manfred
Juro Janosik - ein Held der Berge	Rahn, Karlheinz
Jutta	Bez, Helmut

K

Kabelwerk Oberspree	Grubert, Peter
Kader entscheiden alles	Strahl, Rudi
Der Kaffeehauspolitiker	Schaller, Rudolf
Kafkas Schloß	Richter, Hans Michael
Kain	Schaller, Rudolf
Der Kaiser und der Wolf	Schneider, Rolf
Kaiser und Komödiant	Zuchardt, Karl
Des Kaisers neue Kleider	Braun, Klaus Dieter
Des Kaisers neue Kleider	Müller, Dietmar
Des Kaisers neue Kleider	Schrader, Richard
Des Kaisers neue Schneider	Linz, Rudi
Kälberserenade	Bauer, Werner
Kalif Storch	Eckert, Holger
Kalifah der Fischer von Bagdad	Schwaen, Kurt
Kalifornische Ballade	Eisler, Hanns
Das kalte Herz	Gerlach, Harald
Das kalte Herz	Kaltofen, Günter
Das kalte Herz	Wallendorff, Siegfried
Kameraden	Lucke, Hans
Kammertheater	Schirmer, Bernd
Die Kampagne	Knauth, Joachim
Kampf im Westen	Baierl, Helmut
Der Kampf um die Schafsquelle	Wolf, Friedrich
Der Kampf um Erdöl	Felkel, Günter
Kampf um Gott	Herzog, Alfred

Kampfregel	Günther, Egon
Kännchen voll	Schmidt, Hans-Dieter
Die Kantine	Branstner, Gerhard
Kap der Unruhe	Matusche, Alfred
Kapitän Pudelmütze	Foellbach, Lena
Die kapitolinische Venus	Brock, Rudolf Peter
Kapriolen	Wendler, Otto Bernhard
Karambolage	Janowski, Maurycy
Karaseck	Kleineidam, Horst
Karaseck	Link, Joachim-Dietrich
Karibische Nacht	Krupkat, Günter
Karin Lenz	Neutsch, Erik
Karl Damerow ist tot	Schuster, Uwe
Karl Marx	Freyer, Paul Herbert
Karl Stülpner	Beygang, Hans-Joachim
Karl Stülpner	Eger, Steffen
Karl Stülpner	Kahlow, Heinz
Karl Stülpner	Pastowski, Klaus M.
Karl und Kasimir	Drewniok, Heinz
Der Karneval von Nikolsburg	Herzog, Alfred
Die Karriere	Collin, Christian
Karriere	Kent, Alexander
Karrieristen	Pastowski, Klaus M.
Kasimir der Kinderdieb	Hacks, Peter
Kaspar und das Wahrheitstuch	Foellbach, Lena
Kasparette	Waschinsky, Peter
Kasper baut ein Haus	Schlott, Ulrich
Kasper rettet die Unschuld	Müller, Dietmar
Kasper rettet einen Baum	Morgner, Martin
Kasper treibt den Teufel aus	Müller, Dietmar
Kasper und die Farben	Beckert, Dieter
Kasper und die kluge Bauerntochter	Hellwig, Gerd Gunthar
Kasper und Iwanuschka	Feustel, Gotthard
Kasper und Nixi	Däbritz, Fritz
Kasperl erhält eine Lektion	Trolle, Lothar
Kasperl findet eine Frau	Trolle, Lothar
Kasperltrilogie	Trolle, Lothar
Käte Kerri	Fink, Walter
Katz und Kätzchen	Schmidt, Hans-Dieter
Die Katze	Hawemann, Horst
Katze aus dem Sack	Groß, Jürgen
Katze und Maus in Gesellschaft	Bergner, Edith
Katzengold	Salomon, Horst
Katzgraben	Strittmatter, Erwin
Katzgraben 1958	Strittmatter, Erwin
Der kaukasische Kreidekreis	Brecht, Bertolt
Kaution	Lucke, Hans
Kawulke contra Meyer	Lucke, Hans
Keep Smiling	Bez, Helmut
Keimzeit	May, Ferdinand
Kein Ende auf Raten	Strahl, Rudi
Kein Hüsing	Korf, Rudolf
Kein Mensch lebt zweimal	Keyn, Ulf
Keine Hochzeit ohne Ernst	Wiede, Anna E.
Keine Leute, keine Leute	Strahl, Rudi

Keine Schnittblumen	Müller, Helmut
Keiner nimmt den Kaiser ernst	Schott, Manfred
Der Keller	Lucke, Hans
Kellerklub	Schöbel, Hildegard
Kennen Sie Kahlow?	Kahlow, Heinz
Kennen Sie Pieferding?	Bergner, Edith
Die Kette fällt	Bostroem, Annemarie
Der Ketzer aus Nola	Engelmann, Heinz
Der Ketzerkönig	Knauth, Joachim
Kikeriki	Baierl, Helmut
Die Kinder	Hacks, Peter
Kinder auf Zeit	Bortfeldt, Kurt
Die Kinder des Kapitän Grant	Autengruber, Ewald
Die Kinder von Damutz	Bez, Helmut
Kinder werden Leute	Preissler, Helmut
Ein Kindergeburtstag	Jäckel, Gerhard
Kinderkantate	Streubel, Manfred
Die Kindermörderin	Hacks, Peter
Kippenberg	Bigott, Gabriele
Kippenberg	Jaksch, Bärbel
Kippentütchen	Prodöhl, Günter
Die Kipper	Braun, Volker
Kipper Paul Bauch	Braun, Volker
Kirschenpflücken	Baierl, Helmut
Klara und der Gänserich	Stolper, Armin
Der Klassenauftrag	Wogatzki, Benito
Klaus Störtebeker	Kuba
Kleider machen Leute	Griesbach, Rudi
Die Kleinbürgerhochzeit	Brecht, Bertolt
Kleine Ente Namenlos	Feustel, Gotthard
Kleine Gärten - große Leute	Gosse, Peter
Das kleine Gespenst	Köhler, Erich
Der kleine Häwemann	Witt, Wolfram
Die kleine Hexe, die nicht böse sein konnte	Grubert, Peter
Die kleine Liebelei	Branstner, Gerhard
Das kleine Mahagonny	Brecht, Bertolt
Der kleine Muck	Krug, Hans-Hermann
Der kleine Muck	Schmidt, Hans-Dieter
Der kleine Prinz	Noack, Christian
Der kleine Prinz	Peust, Dieter
Der kleine und der große Klaus	Wendler, Horst-Ulrich
Kleine Welt am Narrenseil	Lommer, Horst
Kleinekortes große Zeiten	Wiener, C. U.
Ein kleines bißchen Stück	Schaller, Wolfgang
Kleinstadtgeschichten	Bez, Helmut
Kleistfragment	Schütz, Stefan
Klettwitzer Bericht	Müller, Heiner
Klinik Prof. Dr. med. Morton	Menschel, Helmut
Der kluge Achmed	Bormann, Arnold
Die kluge Bauerntochter	Hellwig, Gerd Gunthart
Die kluge Prinzessin	Bauer, Andreas
Die kluge Susanne	Kahlau, Heinz
Klytemnestra	Berg, Jochen
Der Kniebist	Gratzik, Paul

Knirps und das Zirkuspferd	Janowski, Maurycy
Knobbe	Welk, Ehm
Knüppel aus dem Schnupftabak	Wendler, Otto Bernhard
Kohlhaas	Schütz, Stefan
Kokori	Hawemann, Horst
Kolonne Hund	Wolf, Friedrich
Kolumbus	Griesbach, Rudi
Der Komet	Brennecke, Bert
Kommando von links	Richter, Manfred
Kommen und Gehen	Podehl, Peter
Kommen wir zur Sache	Maaß, Joachim
Kommst du mit nach Madras?	Richter, Helmut
Komödianten‹welt›	Wolff, Bernd
Die Komödie der Irrungen	Schaller, Rudolf
Komplicen	Lindner, Otto
Kondensmilchpanorama	Seidel, Georg
Konferenz mit Knarrpanti	Stolper, Armin
Der Kongreß der Weißwäscher	Brecht, Bertolt
Der König des Böhmerwalds	Krüger, Wolfgang
König Drosselbart	Bergner, Edith
König Drosselbart	Brosch, Alwin
König Drosselbart	Czechowski, Heinz
König Drosselbart	Kuckhoff, Armin Gerd
König Drosselbart	Richter, Peter
König Drosselbart	Schlott, Ulrich
König Drosselbart und das Mädchen Prinzessin	Hawemann, Horst
König Eduards Moral	Weicker, Regina
König für einen Tag	Kupsch, Joachim
König Heinrich IV. ‹der Vierte›	Hacks, Peter
König Heinrich der Vierte	Schaller, Rudolf
König Johann	Lange, Hartmut
König Jorg	Eschner, Eugen
König Karl	Wolf, Klaus Martin
König Karotte	Grafe, Manfred
König Lear	Schaller, Rudolf
König Lear	Trolle, Lothar
König Richard der Dritte	Schaller, Rudolf
König Richard der Zweite	Schaller, Rudolf
Der König soll geigen	Preissler, Helmut
König von Moskau	Bauer, Friedhold
König von Preußen	Liebig, Dieter
Der König von Trinador	Corrinth, Curt
Des Königs allerneuste Kleider	Schaller, Wolfgang
Des Königs Datsche	Eidam, Klaus
Kontraste	Haas, Henn
Die kontrollierte Sommerliebe	Müller, Jupp
Kopf ab - zum Gebet	Pfeiffer, Hans
Kopf ist das Beste	Hawemann, Horst
Koritke	Wolf, Friedrich
Kornblumen	Freyer, Paul Herbert
Die Korrektur	Müller, Heiner
Krabat	Oehme, Hartmut
Krach in Chiozza	Schuster, Uwe
Krach um Goliath	Lange, Friedrich

Krach um Leutnant Blumenthal	Herzog, Alfred
Krali Marko	Endler, Adolf
Kramkalender	Strittmatter, Erwin
Krankenbesuch	Schneider, Rolf
"Krassin" rettet "Italia"	Wolf, Friedrich
Das Kräutlein Wahrheit	Link, Joachim-Dietrich
Kredit bei Nibelungen	Kuhn, Fritz
Der Kreis	Röttger, Heinz
Krethi und Plethi	Schrader, Richard
Kreuzabnahme	Welk, Ehm
Kreuzer unter Rot	Pijet, Georg Waldemar
Der Kriminalfall	Tasche, Elke
Krischans Ende	Oehme, Ralph
Die Kristallkugel	Eschner, Eugen
Ein Krug mit Oliven	Kahlau, Heinz
Kühnheit zahlt sich aus	Küchenmeister, Claus
Die Kumpels	Pijet, Georg Waldemar
Die Kündigung	Bauer, Werner
Der künstliche Mond geht auf	Kuhn, Fritz
Kurier der schwarzen Jäger	Grohmann, Gottfried
Der Kuß der Juanita	Bejach, Peter
Küssen verboten	Hall, Heinz

L

Das Lächeln der Freiheit	Liebig, Dieter
Lachen Sie einfach mit	Ender, Roland
Die Lachtaube	Baierl, Helmut
Lady Windermeres Fächer	Wiede, Anna E.
Das Lagefeuer	Wolf, Klaus Martin
Das Laken	Müller, Heiner
Die Lampe	Köhler, Erich
Die Lampe der Felicitas	Vogt, Helmut
Das Land Bum-Bum	Kirsch, Rainer
Landvermesser	Koch, Jurij
Die lange Ankunft des Alois Fingerlein	Kerndl, Rainer
Der lange Matz	Brennecke, Bert
Eine lange Nacht	Hoffmann, Walter
Der lange Weg nach Afrika	Richter, Egon
Der lange Weg zu Lenin	Baierl, Helmut
Langusten	Denger, Alfred
Lanzelot	Müller, Heiner
Laokoon	Schütz, Stefan
Lasalle ‹fragt Herrn Herbert nach Sonja›	Hein, Christoph
Lassen wir uns ein bißchen scheiden	Liebenberg, Günter
Laßt mich doch singen	Bejach, Peter
Die Lästerschule	Eidam, Klaus
Laternenfest	Pfeiffer, Hans
Laubheu und keine Bleibe	Zweig, Arnold
Laurentia	Wolf, Friedrich
Der Lausbub Fritz	Wangenheim, Gustav von
Lautlose Vögel	Günther, Jens-Uwe

Die Lawine	Schreyer, Wolfgang
Lazarillo vom Tormes	Matthus, Siegfried
Leben - aber wie?	Heiduczek, Werner
Das Leben auf dem Lande	Müller, Heiner
Das Leben des Galilei	Brecht, Bertolt
Das Leben des Konfutse	Brecht, Bertolt
Das Leben des Ovid	Lange, Hartmut
Leben Eduard des Zweiten von England	Brecht, Bertolt
Leben Gundlings Friedrich von Preußen Lessings Schlaf Traum Schrei	Müller, Heiner
Das Leben ist kein Traum	Goertz, Heinrich
Leben lassen	Gosse, Peter
Leben und Tod des Herrn Marski	Lange, Hartmut
Leben und Tod des Peter Göring	Brasch, Thomas
Lederstrumpf	Müller, Helmut
Legende vom Glück ohne Ende	Plenzdorf, Ulrich
Die Legende von Klaus Störtebeker	Kuba
Legenden aus dem alten Vietnam	Waschinsky, Peter
Ein lehrreicher Lehrvertrag	Grünberg, Karl
Die Leichenschändung	Corrinth, Curt
Leicht bewölkt, vorwiegend heiter	Kuhn, Fritz
Der leichtgläubige Thomas	Dudow, Slatan
Leistungskontrolle	Zinner, Hedda
Lenchen Demuth	Salchow, Werner
Lenins Tod	Braun, Volker
Lenz	Wendler, Horst-Ulrich
Leo und Rosa	Baierl, Helmut
Leonce und Lena	Hertel, Thomas
Leonce und Lena	Körner, Thomas
Leonce und Lena	Schwaen, Kurt
Die Lerche, Tagverkünderin	Lange, Katrin
Letizia	Gilbricht, Walter
Der letzte Einzelbauer	Trolle, Lothar
Der letzte Gast	Weindich, Günter
Der letzte Häuptling	Eidam, Klaus
Der letzte Mohikaner	Pastowski, Klaus M.
Die letzte Probe	Wolf, Friedrich
Die letzte Prüfung	Koch, Jurij
Der letzte Schuß	Matthus, Siegfried
Die letzte Seite im Tagebuch	Steineckert, Gisela
Die letzte Stunde	Brennecke, Bert
Die letzte Stunde	Lucke, Hans
Das letzte Wochenende	Bonn, Karl Heinrich
Den Letzten beißen die Hunde	Vollsdorff, Erwin
Die letzten Stunden der Reichs-kanzlei	Lange, Hartmut
Die letzten Tage des großen Herrn Fabiano	Neher, Caspar
Letzter Ausweg Heirat	Damm-Wendler, Ursula
Letzter Sommer in Heidkau	Sakowski, Helmut
Das leuchtende Ziel	Pijet, Georg Waldemar
Leuna ‹1921›	Lask, Berta
Lewins Mühle	Zimmermann, Ingo

Licht auf den Feldern	Blume, Horst
Die Lichter von Rustawi	Bodeit, Gerhard
Lidice	Fühmann, Franz
Liebe auf den zweiten Blick	Wieland, Günter
Die Liebe der Babet	Nicolaus, Alfred
Liebe für Ingeborg	Bormann, Arnold
Der liebe Gott hat Ausgang	Koch, Ellen
Der Liebe ist kein Wind zu kalt	Herold, Gottfried
Liebe ist nicht immer blind	Gentz, Friedrich
Liebe klein geschrieben	Zehlen, Petra
Liebe, Mord und Alkohol	Wendler, Otto Bernhard
Die Liebe zur Opposition	Schreyer, Wolfgang
Lieben Sie Tschaikowski?	Groß, Jürgen
Die Liebenden vom Tisch 10	Brasch, Thomas
Lieber Ehm Welk	Lucke, Hans
Lieber Flegel	Witt, Wolfram
Lieber Georg	Brasch, Thomas
Liebeslied	Schneidereit, Otto
Das Liebespaar von Kiang-nan	Baierl, Helmut
Ein Liebestrunk	Salchow, Werner
Liebhabereien	Bez, Helmut
Das Lied meines Weges	Matusche, Alfred
Lilith	Eschner, Eugen
Lilo Herrmann	Wolf, Friedrich
Die linke Wand	Bieler, Manfred
Lisa	Gratzik, Paul
Litauische Claviere	Wolf, Gerhard
Little Girl	Koerbl, Jürg-Michael
Das Loch im Gesicht	Welk, Ehm
Lockruf des Abenteuers	Weinhold, Siegfried
Der Lohn der Dummheit	Wendler, Horst Ulrich
Der Lohndrücker	Müller, Heiner
Lokomotive im Spargelbeet	Hammel, Claus
Lolotte	Schott, Manfred
Der ‹Ein› Lorbaß	Salomon, Horst
Lord Arthurs pflichtbewußtes Verbrechen	Hornawsky, Gerd
Lorenz kontra Lausejungen	Schmidt, Hans-Dieter
Lorenzaccio	Gersch, Christel
Löser	Fischborn, Gottfried
Die Lösung	Kuhnert, Reinhard Frieder
Lotos und der Knecht Mao Te	Richter, Manfred
Lovely Rita	Brasch, Thomas
Der Löwe Gottes	Wolf, Friedrich
Lucie geh	Brasch, Thomas
Die Lucilla	Zweig, Arnold
Lucius Sulla	Geiger, Erich
Der Lügner	Eidam, Klaus
Lumumba	Müller, Heiner
Die Lust zum Gesang	Strahl, Rudi
Der lustige Musikant	Kirsch, Rainer
Die lustigen Weiber von Windsor	Schaller, Rudolf
‹Die› Lützower	Zinner, Hedda
Lux in tenebris	Brecht, Bertolt
Lysistrata	Böttcher, Wolfgang

Lysistrata	Knauth, Joachim
Lysistrata	Schütz, Stefan

M

M. M. greift ein	Herrmann, Klaus
Macbeth	Müller, Heiner
Macbeth	Schaller, Rudolf
Macette	Günther, Jens-Uwe
Die Macht des Schicksals	Herz, Joachim
Madame Cyprienne	Kramer, Heinz
Madame Dubarry	Neef, Wilhelm
Madame Favart	Schill, Rolf
Madame Lieselotte	Gerster, Ottmar
Das Mädchen auf dem Traktor	Kubsch, Hermann Werner
Das Mädchen aus Caen	Jungnickel, Rudolf
Das Mädchen Irgendwohin	Pfützner, Klaus
Das Mädchen Ming Ming	Korb, Irene
Das Mädchen Sabine	Brehmer, Joachim
Die Mädchenkarawane	Wieland, Günter
Das Mädel von der Grenze	Herzog, Alfred
Die magische Nacht	Köllinger, Bernd
Mahagonny	Brecht, Bertolt
Die Mainzer Republik	Schneider, Rolf
Maitre Pathelin	Kunad, Rainer
Majakowski	Schütz, Stefan
Malwa	Gratzik, Paul
Man liest kein fremdes Tagebuch	Janowski, Maurycy
Man sollte nicht schwindeln	Bejach, Peter
Manana Manana	Collin, Christian
Das Mandat	Pijet, Georg Waldemar
La Mandragola	Koerbl, Jürg-Michael
Der Mann als Hund	Brasch, Thomas
Der Mann aus England	Schneider, Rolf
Der Mann, der bei Schirocco kam	Hacks, Peter
Der Mann, der Dr. Watson war	Bez, Helmut
Der Mann des Jahres	Lätzsch, Monika
Der Mann Fjodor	Wangenheim, Gustav von
Der Mann im Dunkeln	Wolf, Friedrich
Mann ist Mann	Brecht, Bertolt
Der Mann mit dem Vogel	Zinner, Hedda
Ein Mann mit Herz	Czech-Kuckhoff, Ilse
Der Mann ohne Heimat	Herzog, Alfred
Ein Mann steht vor der Tür	Pitschmann, Siegfried
Mann und Frau im Essigkrug	Greef, Hertha
Ein Mann und sein Schicksal	Selbmann, Fritz
Mann und Vaterland	Corrinth, Curt
Ein Mann zum Heiraten	Eidam, Klaus
Die Männer sind alle Verbrecher	Waterstradt, Berta
Die Männer von Schilling-Reede	Koebel-Tusk, Eberhard
Männerbekanntschaften	Lambrecht, Christine
Männermonologe	Bigott, Gabriele; Königsdorf, Helga; Schubert, Helga; Steineckert, Gisela

Männerwirtschaft	Wallstein, Bärbel
Mannesjahre	Brezan, Jurij
Die Mansarde	Stockhaus, Heinz
Der Mantel	Hartmann, Gerhard
Märchen aus der Truhe	Lange, Hanns
Märchen aus Märchen	Kaltofen, Günter
Das Märchen vom Bären Mischa	Kunkel, Erhard
Das Märchen vom Kaiser und vom Hirten	Czechowski, Heinz
Das Märchen vom Mond	Wendler, Horst-Ulrich
Das Märchen vom salzigen Quell	Foellbach, Lena
Das Märchen vom schwarzen Riesen	Schneider, Peter M.
Das Märchen von den zwei Jägern	Philipp, Horst
Das Märchen von der alten Straßenbahn Therese	Kahlau, Heinz
Das Märchen von einem, der auszog, das Fürchten zu lernen	Gratzik, Paul
Marek ‹im Westen›	Menzel, Gerhard Walter
Margarete in Aix	Hacks, Peter
Maria, die Siebenschläferin	Schöbel, Manuel
Maria Theresia Schulze	Haufe, Jochen
Maria Tudor	Eidam, Klaus
Marie Charlotte Corday	Gilbricht, Walter
Marie Hedder	Fabian, Gerhard
Marie und der Nußknacker	Kollhoff, Helga
Marie und ein Hans im Glück	Knaup, Andreas
Marie vom Hinterhof	Denger, Alfred
Mariechen und der Flaschenzwerg	Müller, Dietmar
Maries Baby	Hacks, Peter
Marike Weiden	Griesbach, Rudi
Mariken von Niwegen	Tasche, Elke
Marja Jancowa	Brezan, Jurij
Mark Aurel	Heiduczek, Werner
Der märkische Eulenspiegel	Stolzenbach, Beatrice
Marski	Lange, Hartmut
Die Martinsgans	Albrecht, Paul
Die Marulas	Heiduczek, Werner
Marx spielte gern Schach	Richter, Kurt Dietmar
März: Ein Künstlerleben	Kipphardt, Heinar
Mascha und der Bär	Rainer, Wolfgang
Ein Maskenball	Herz, Joachim
Maskerade	Czechowski, Heinz
Maskerade	Schlott, Ulrich
Maskerade von Liebe	Bormann, Arnold
Maß für Maß	Schaller, Rudolf
Massenpantomime gegen den Krieg	Wangenheim, Gustav von
Mäßigung ist aller Laster Anfang	Lucke, Hans
Die Maßnahme	Brecht, Bertolt
Match	Groß, Jürgen
Mathematik und ein Tintenfaß	Baierl, Helmut
Die Matrosen von Cattaro	Wolf, Friedrich
Der Maulheld	Knauth, Joachim
Die Maus in der Falle	Wangenheim, Gustav von
Maus und Kater im Theater	Solga, Norbert
Die Mausefalle	Wangenheim, Gustav von

Mauser	Müller, Heiner
Max und Moritz	Burger, Hanus
Maxi	Heiduczek, Werner
Maxis neue Freunde	Schöbel, Manuel
Mecklenburg	Schönrock, Hans
Medeaspiel	Müller, Heiner
Mehr Licht	Seidel, Georg
Mein Bruder spielt Klarinette	Schmidt, Hans-Dieter
Mein dicker Mantel	Wendt, Albert
Mein Fräulein Frau	Schleinitz, Karl Heinz
Mein Freund Bunbury	Bez, Helmut
Mein Freund, meine Frau	Bormann, Arnold
Mein spöttisches Glück	Erb, Elke
Meine Florentinerin	Lange, Friedrich
Meine Frau ist keine Frau für mich	Eckert, Holger
Meine fremde Frau	Wendler, Horst-Ulrich
Meine Geschichte mit Aniko	Bejach, Peter
Meine junge alte Stadt	Kuba
Meine Privatgalerie	Roehricht, Karl Hermann
Der Meister	Oehme, Hartmut
Meister Hans Röckle und Meister Flammfuß	Korn, Ilse
Meister Matel	Ludwig, Carsten
Meister Röckle	Deicke, Günther
Der Meister und Margarita	Czechowski, Heinz
Das Meisterstück	Mai, Jürgen
Memoiren eines Aktivisten	Freitag, Franz
Mensch an der Wende	Stolle, Kurt Werner
Ein Mensch ist kein Schmetterling	Brehmer, Joachim
Der Mensch lebt nicht vom Brot allein	Blach, Erich
Mensch Marx	Hammel, Claus
Menschen an der Grenze	Djacenko, Boris
Menschen ohne Heimat	Herzog, Alfred
Menschenskind, Nikolka!	Fabian, Gerhard
Mercedes	Brasch, Thomas
Die merkwürdigen Umstände der Marquise von O.	Günther, Egon
‹Die› Messedetektive	Schmidt, Hans-Dieter
Messeschlager Gisela	Bez, Helmut
Der Messingkauf	Brecht, Bertolt
Michael Knobbe	Welk, Ehm
Michael Kohlhaas	Gilbricht, Walter
Michael Kohlhaas	Müller, Dietmar
Mildernde Umstände: keine	Fischborn, Gottfried
Eine Million für ein Lächeln	Enders, Horst
Millionär wider Willen	Hall, Heinz
Die Millionen der Yvette	Neef, Wilhelm
Der Millionenschmidt	Kleineidam, Horst
Miniaturen	Strahl, Rudi
Mink	Braun, Volker
Minotaurus	Schönberg, Klaus
Mirandolina	Eidam, Klaus
Mit dem Kopf durch die Wand	Witte, Joachim

Mit der Zeit werden wir schon fertig	Wangenheim, Gustav von
Mit 60 ‹sechzig› fängt das Leben an	Eidam, Klaus
Mit Zitronen gehandelt	Schwarz-Marell, Gisela
Mittelstürmer Brumme	Neuhaus, Lutz W.
Mitternacht	Lask, Berta
Mitternacht	Vogt, Helmut
Mohammed	Wolf, Friedrich
Mohr und die Raben von London	Korn, Ilse
Molochs Wohnungsnot	Grünberg, Karl
Monk	Brennecke, Wolf D.
Monologe I	Roehricht, Karl Hermann
Montague und Capulet	Bischoff, Karl-Heinrich
Die Moorbande	Beseler, Horst
Moralisches Rezept für doppelte Eheführung	Freitag, Manfred
Mord an der Grenze	Guddat, Rolf
Mordprozeß Consolini	Glowalla, Klaus
Mordsache Brisson	Koch, Günter
Mordsache Mergel	Jäckel, Gerhard
Mordsache Stagnelius	Rahn, Karlheinz
Morgen kommt der Schornsteinfeger	Hammel, Claus
Die Morgengabe	Branstner, Gerhard
Moritz Tassow	Hacks, Peter
Moschopulos	Wagner-Regeny, Rudolf
Motzek	Groß, Jürgen
Die Möwe	Müller, Heiner
Der Möwenschrei	Gerster, Ottmar
Mühle im Schwarzwald	Arnold, Hans Dieter
Die Mühle im Schwarzwald	Brosch, Alwin
Der Müller von Sans-Souci	Hacks, Peter
Münchhausen	Eidam, Klaus
Münchhausen	Kirsch, Rainer
Münchhausen	Pasch, Albert
Münchhausen auf Artemis	Kaltofen, Günter
Münzers Tod	Korn, Vilmos
Muschebubu	Hornbogen, Chris
Musen	Hacks, Peter
Musik aus der Kiste	Jäckel, Gerhard
Musik ist mein Glück	Degenhardt, Jürgen
Das musikalische Nashorn	Hacks, Peter
Muß das sein?	Gruchmann-Reuter, Margret
Die Musterfamilie	Wendler, Horst-Ulrich
Die Musterfrauen	Böttcher, Wolfgang
Der Musterschüler	Kahlau, Heinz
Die Mutprobe	Nawrath, Marta
Die Mutter	Brecht, Bertolt
Mutter Courage und ihre Kinder	Brecht, Bertolt
Mutter Riba	Hauptmann, Elisabeth
Muttermilchpumpe	Schneider, Peter M.
Muzelkopp	Preuß, Gunter
Mysterium buffo	Baierl, Helmut

N

Na, diese Musketiere	Bläss, Helmut
Nabucco	Kuba
Der Nachbar des Herrn Pansa	Rücker, Günther
Nachbarn	Freyer, Paul Herbert
Die nachgeholte Hochzeitsreise	Stolper, Armin
Nachlaß	Hornawsky, Gerd
Nachruf	Bez, Helmut
Der Nächste	Kuhnert, Reinhard Frieder
Die Nacht der Linden	Matusche, Alfred
Die Nacht, in der der Chef geschlachtet wurde	Kipphardt, Heinar
Nacht mit Kompromissen	Kerndl, Rainer
Eine Nacht mit Marie Isabell	Lommer, Horst
Nachtasyl	Kirsch, Rainer
Nachtfrost	Wendt, Albert
Die Nachtigall	Kaltofen, Günter
Die Nachtigall	Knauth, Joachim
Die Nachtigall	Schreiber, Helmut
Nachtlogis	Pfeiffer, Hans
Der Nachtpatient	Malink, Peter
Nachts, wenn die Katzen grau sind	Salchow, Werner
Die Nachtschwalbe	Wolf, Friedrich
Nachtwache	Bieler, Manfred
Nackenstützen für Badewannen	Eidam, Klaus
Der nackte König	Wagner-Regeny, Rudolf
Die nackte Wahrheit	Kahlow, Heinz
Die Nackten	Drewniok, Heinz
Nacktes Gras	Matusche, Alfred
Namensgebung	Enders, Horst
Der Namensvetter	Drewniok, Heinz
Napoleon	Groß, Jürgen
Napoleon in Jaffa	Zweig, Arnold
Narkose	Felkel, Günter
Das Narrenparadies	Dudow, Slatan
Nashorn und Giraffe	Günther, Horst
Nasreddin in Buchara	Eidam, Klaus
Das Natternkrönlein	Bergner, Edith
Das Naturkind	Stolper, Armin
Nausikaa	Mickel, Karl
Nebenan wohnen andere Leute	Korf, Rudolf
Der Neinsager	Brecht, Bertolt
Neptuns Damen	Wangenheim, Friedel von
Netze an Bord	Krautz, Bodo
Neue Bekanntschaft	Groß, Jürgen
Neue Häuser	Matusche, Alfred
Das neue Kanaan	Zweig, Arnold
Das neue Kapitel	Enders, Horst
Der neue Kontinent	Hammel, Claus
Der neue Menoza	Hein, Christoph
Die neue Straße von Katzgraben	Strittmatter, Erwin
Der neue Struwelpeter	Schmidt, Hans-Dieter
Die neuen Leiden des jungen W.	Plenzdorf, Ulrich
Ein neuer Sommernachtstraum	Köllinger, Bernd

Neuland unterm Pflug	Knauth, Joachim
Neun Miniaturen	Strahl, Rudi
Nibelungen	Braun, Volker
Nie wieder...	Czech-Kuckhoff, Ilse
Der Niedergang des Kleinhandels	Schlesinger, Klaus
Night Step	Hauser, Harald
Nina Nina tam kartina	Buhss, Werner
Niobe	Berg, Jochen
Niobe am Sipylos	Berg, Jochen
Nitschewo	Hauser, Harald
Noahs Jeep	Budjuhn, Horst
Noch einen Löffel Gift, Liebling?	Hacks, Peter
Nochmal ein Ding drehen	Strahl, Rudi
Nöhr	Saeger, Uwe
Nonnenmacher	Liebig, Dieter
Nordische Hochzeit	Schaller, Rudolf
Das Notwendige und das Ueber- flüssige	Schneider, Rolf
Die Novembernacht	Czechowski, Heinz
Der Nullmensch	Bigott, Gabriele
Numa	Hacks, Peter
Nun könntest du auch etwas tun	Tasche, Elke
Nur die Liebe...	Stockhaus, Heinz
Die Nürnberger Nachtigall	Lindner, Otto

O

O die Mama	Böttcher, Wolfgang
O, diese Kinder	Kramer, Heinz
O la la Mademoiselle	Eidam, Klaus
Oben und unten	Hanell, Robert
Oberon	Seeger, Horst
Oberst Hagenachs Gäste	Vogt, Helmut
Das oberste Gesetz	Bagdahn, Alfred
Der Ochse von Kulm	Eidam, Klaus
Octavius und Kleopatra	Schneider, Rolf
Odysseus	Collin, Christian
Odysseus' Heimkehr	Schütz, Stefan
Oedipus	Stahl, Heidemarie
Oedypus, Tyrann	Müller, Heiner
Oel	Felkel, Günter
Die Offensive	Kleineidam, Horst
Ohne Dich war es Nacht	Zuchardt, Renate
Ohne uns	Herzog, Alfred
Öl	Felkel, Günter
Old Fritz	Kunad, Rainer
Old-Germans-Story	Selber, Martin
Oliver Cromells Sendung	Gilbricht, Walter
Der Olle Henry	Schubert, Dieter
Omphale	Hacks, Peter
Onkel Schmittka aus Sibirien	Malink, Peter
Onkel Toms Hütte	Schmidt, Hans-Dieter
Opposition der Erde	Gentz, Friedrich
Optimistische Tragödie	Hauptmann, Elisabeth
Optimistische Tragödie	Wolf, Friedrich

Orestes	Berg, Jochen
Orfeus	Seidemann, Burkhart
Originalanregung aus Betrieben der DDR	Fensch, Eberhard
Orpheus in der Unterwelt	Bartsch, Kurt
Orpheus in der Unterwelt	Eidam, Klaus
Orpheus in der Unterwelt	Neef, Wilhelm
Orpheus und der Bürgermeister	Seitz, Robert
Orpheus und Euridice	Swarowsky, Hans
Oskar Kasuskes letzter Gang	Stave, John
Ossel kommt	Schlossarek, Erich
Ossoki – Ossokin	Hein, Christoph
Der Osteresel	Wiede, Anna E.
Othello	Schaller, Rudolf
Ottokar Dommas Elternabend	Häuser, Otto
Der Ozeanflug	Brecht, Bertolt

P

Pabst Urban VIII.	Brasch, Thomas
Paddy Glück	Brock, Rudolf Peter
Palmyra	Gosse, Peter
Panchito und die Beulenpest	Brasch, Thomas
Pandora	Hacks, Peter
Pannemann, der Ehestifter	Meissner, Hildegard
Die Pantherfrau	Kirsch, Rainer
Papa Mama	Trolle, Lothar
Der Papiertiger	Brasch, Thomas
Die Päpstin	Lask, Berta
Paragraph 218	Wolf, Friedrich
Die Pariserin	Focke, Gerd
Die Parteibraut	Groß, Jürgen
Party	Wefelmeyer, Bernd
Pässe nach Deutschland	Gentz, Friedrich
Die Passion des Johannes Hörder	Forest, Jean Kurt
Pathetique ‹Pathetische Sonate›	Kirsch, Rainer
Patrioten	Wolf, Friedrich
Patrique, Patrique	Wander, Fred
Pauken und Trompeten	Brecht, Bertolt
Paul und Maria	Dechant, Lutz
Pause für Wanzka	Schmidt, Hans-Dieter
Das Pawlow Haus	Weindich, Günter
Pazifik 1960	Richter, Kurt Dietmar
Pellkartoffel	Hentschel, Sibylle
Persische Episode ‹Persische Späße›	Neher, Caspar
Die Pest	Denger, Alfred
Peter der Froschkönig	Reissinger, Horst
Peter kehrt heim	Wolf, Friedrich
Peter Kiewe	Goertz, Heinrich
Peter Schlemihl	Thilmann, Johannes Paul
Peter und der Kaktus	Koeppel, Jochen
Der Pfad der Irrenden	Freyer, Paul Herbert
Der Pfahl	Gerlach, Harald
Pfarrer Koldehoff	Lange, Hertmut

Prinzessin Hochmut	Kaden, Stefan
Die Prinzessin mit dem goldenen Stern	Bauer, Andreas
Prinzessin Rosinchen	Bortfeldt, Kurt
Prinzessin Tausendschön	Lindner, Otto
Die Prinzessin und der Schweinehirt	Bernhardy, Werner
Die Prinzessin und der Schweinehirt	Ensikat, Peter
Die Prinzessin und der Schweinehirt	Müller, Dietmar
Die Prinzessin von Sansibar	Scheer, Maximilian
Prinzessin Zartfuß und die sieben Elefanten	Wendt, Albert
Die Prinzipalin	Zuchardt, Karl
Der private Frieden	Bartsch, Kurt
Die Probe	Bauer, Werner
Professor Hudebraach	Wangenheim, Inge von
Der Professor kommt um sechs	Janowski, Maurycy
Professor Mamlock	Wolf, Friedrich
Prognose	Matusche, Alfred
Projekt Goliath	Lange, Friedrich
Prometheus	Müller, Heiner
Prometheus	Vogt, Helmut
Prometheus	Wagner-Regeny, Rudolf
Der Prozeß der Jeanne d'Arc zu Rouen 1431	Brecht, Bertolt
Der Prozeß der Karin Lenz	Neutsch, Erik
prozeß in nürnberg	Schneider, Rolf
Prozeß Richard Waverley	Schneider, Rolf
Prozeß Wedding	Hauser, Harald
Die Prüfungen Hiobs	Herrmann, Klaus
Der Prüfungsaufsatz	Schlossarek, Erich
Puffi	Trommer, Rudolf
Puppenhokuspokus	Lange, Hanns
Der Puppenschuster	Pederzani, Hans Albert
Das Puppenspiel von Dr. Faustus	Schröder, Carl
Puppenzirkus	Lange, Hanns
Purpurstaub	Baierl, Helmut
Pygmalia	Wendler, Otto Bernhard

Q

Quadriga	Müller, Heiner
Die quälenden Wände	Lebrecht, Georg
Quartett	Müller, Heiner
Quartett mit Schlagern	Schmidt, Hans-Dieter
Der Querkopf	Kilz, Hans Otto

R

R. Hot bzw. Die Hitze	Körner, Thomas
Rächer, Retter und Rapiere	Lang, Ottomar
Ramayana	Endler, Adolf
Ratcliff rechnet ab	Streubel, Manfred

Die Ratten von Hameln	Wiede, Anna E.
Der Räuberhase	Könner, Alfred
Rauhweiler	Jakobs, Karl-Heinz
Ravensbrücker Ballade	Zinner, Hedda
Der Rebell	Reif, Guido
Rebell Jan Cuska	Malink, Peter
Rebell Stülpner	Kurzbach, Herbert
Rebellion der Söhne	Kleineidam, Horst
Die Regentrude	Brosch, Alwin
Die Regentrude	Kunkel, Erhard
Der Regenwettermann	Matusche, Alfred
Regenwürmer	Waschinsky, Peter
Regina	Neef, Wilhelm
Regina B. - Ein Tag in ihrem Leben	Pfaff, Siegfried
Regine	Schlossarek, Erich
Reifeprüfung	Finck, Wolfgang
Reineke Fuchs	Deicke, Günther
Reineke Fuchs	Griesbach, Rudi
Reingefallen	Borde-Klein, Ingeborg
Die Reise	Müller, Heiner
Eine Reise auf den Mond	Irmer, Hans-Joachim
Die Reise in das Märchenland	Kaltofen, Günter
Reise mit Joujou	Eidam, Klaus
Die Reise nach Afrika	Wendler, Horst-Ulrich
Reise nach dem Süden	Schneider, Peter M.
Reise um die Erde in 80 Tagen	Kunkel, Erhard
Reisefieber	Borde-Klein, Ingeborg
Reiter der Nacht	Deicke, Günther
Requiem für Patrice Lumumba	Mickel, Karl
Revisor	Groß, Jürgen
Das Restaurant in Shanghai	Pfeiffer, Hans
Revolte der Gefühle	Gorrish, Walter
Rheinsberg	Wendler, Horst-Ulrich
Die Rheumakur	Kypke, Peter Günther
Der Richter von Hohenburg	Köhler, Siegfried
Rigoletto	Seeger, Horst
Rinaldo Rinaldini	Focke, Gerd
Ringtausch	Fries, Hans Joachim
Risiko	Angermüller, Horst
Ritter Blaubart	Seeger, Horst
Der Ritter Fortune	Knauth, Joachim
Ritualmord in Ungarn	Zweig, Arnold
Robby Kruse	Schmidt, Hans-Dieter
Robert Bottenschuh	Viertel, Martin
Robert und Bertram	Lang, Ottomar
Robin Hood	Rahn, Karlheinz
Die Robinsoninsel	Wiener, C. U.
Rockballade	Knaup, Andreas
Rodaer Ballade	Gerlach, Harald
Rokkok soll sterben	Lindner, Otto
Roland und Regine	Schlossarek, Erich
Rom	Hammel, Claus
Romeo und Julia	Schaller, Rudolf
Rook in Düwels Kök	Liebenberg, Günter
Rosa Laub	Lewin, Waldtraut

Rosebud	Müller, Heiner
Die Rosenbergs	Scheer, Meximilian
Rosie träumt	Hacks, Peter
Eine Rosine in der Sonne	Anderson, Edith
Rostocker Billerbogen	Czerwenka, Rudi
Roswitha	Heiduczek, Werner
Rote Nelken	Hocke, Wolfgang
Rote Rosen für mich	Hacks, Peter
Der rote Veit	Baierl, Helmut
Rotkäppchen	Tiefensee, Siegfried
Rotkäppchen von Grünau	Bejach, Peter
Rotter: Ein deutsches Märchen	Brasch, Thomas
Das Rübchen	Ensikat, Peter
‹Das› Rübchen	Richter, Manfred
Rückspiele	Baierl, Helmut
Rumpelstilz	Lindow, Rainer
Rumpelstilzchen	Czechowski, Heinz
Rumpelstilzchen	Kaltofen, Günter
Rumpelstilzchen	Richter, Peter
Rumpelstilzchen	Schrader, Richard
Rumpelstilzchen	Stäcker, Hans-Dieter
Rund ist die Welt	Eidam, Klaus
Die Rundköpfe und die Spitzköpfe	Brecht, Bertolt
Die Russen kommen	Koerbl, Jürg-Michael
Russische Eröffnung	Müller, Heiner
Russisches Roulette	Schreyer, Wolfgang
Ruzante	Stolper, Armin

S

's ist Feierabend	Leonhardt, Arne
S.M.S. Prinzregent Luitpold	Schlotterbeck, Anna
Saatzeit	Schönrock, Hans
Sabellicus	Kunad, Rainer
Die Sache mit dem Fußball	Koeppel, Jochen
Die Sache Päker	Corrinth, Curt
Die Säge im Langenmoor	Sakowski, Helmut
Der Salamander	Wander, Fred
Salto Mortale	Herrmann, Klaus
Salut an alle. Marx	Kaltofen, Günter
Salzberger	Jakobs, Karl-Heinz
Samson	Griesbach, Rudi
Samson	Stahl, Heidemarie
Sappa	Schütz, Stefan
Sappho in Paris	Fries, Hans Joachim
Sarajewo 1914	May, Ferdinand
Satanische Komödie	Lucke, Hans
Satyros	Brasch, Thomas
Sätze über eine Frau	Trolle, Lothar
Die Säulen des Memnon	Knaup, Andreas
Der Sauwetterwind	Wendt, Albert
Die Schafsquelle	Wolf, Friedrich
Schalmeienstunde	Rücker, Günther
Scharf nachwaschen	Wiener, C. U.

Schneeweißchen und Rosenrot	Borowski, S. A.
Schneeweißchen und Rosenrot	Foellbach, Lena
Schneeweißchen und Rosenrot	Greef, Hertha
Schneeweißchen und Rosenrot	Günther, Horst
Schneeweißchen und Rosenrot	Pasch, Albert
Schneeweißchen und Rosenrot	Richter, Siegfried
Schneewittchen	Auenmüller, Hans
Schneewittchen	Eidam, Klaus
Schneewittchen	Griesbach, Rudi
Schneewittchen	Kaltofen, Günter
Schneewittchen	Waschinsky, Peter
Schneewittchen	Weidermann, Werner
Der Schneider von Ulm	Honigmann, Barbara
Das Schneiderlein	Lorenz, Hartmut
Schnurps Ferienabenteuer	Pillep, Peter
Schöne Ferien	Strahl, Rudi
Die schöne Galathee	Böttcher, Wolfgang
Die schöne Helena	Degenhardt, Jürgen
Die schöne Helena	Hacks, Peter
Die Schöne und das Tier	Müller, Dietmar
Die Schöne und der Papagei	Müller, Dietmar
Eine schöne und lustige neue Aktion vom ernsthaften Narren Hans Clauert	Kuhnert, Reinhard Frieder
Die Schöpfung	Honigmann, Barbara
Der Schornsteinfeger und seine Frau	Stolper, Armin
Die Schrankkomödie	Wolf, Friedrich
Schreie im Kamin	Liebenberg, Günter
Schritt der Millionen	Salchow, Werner
Schritte	Wendt, Albert
Die Schuhe der Zarin	Gay, Fritz
Die Schuhe unterm Bett	Gilbricht, Walter
Der Schuhu und die fliegende Prinzessin	Hacks, Peter
Schuld sind die anderen	Pfeiffer, Hans
Schuldspiel	Saeger, Uwe
Die Schule der Frauen	Kirsch, Rainer
Die Schule der Polzins	Sakowski, Helmut
Schulleiter Fleming	Horn, Heinz
Schüsse, Küsse	Spickermann, Adolf
Der Schuster und der Hahn	Stolper, Armin
Der Schützenkönig	Lindner, Otto
Schwanda, der Dudelsackpfeifer	Deicke, Günther
Schwarzbrot	Welk, Ehm
Der Schwarze, der Weiße und die Frau	Griesbach, Rudi
Der schwarze Engel	Pastowski, Klaus Manfred
Die schwarze Kabale	Deicke, Günther
Die schwarze Kugel	Pastowski, Klaus Manfred
Die schwarze Madonna	Heinze, Herbert
Die schwarze Mühle	Kaltofen, Günter
Die schwarze Perle	Degenhardt, Jürgen
Der schwarze Pfad	Mahrholz, Otto
Die schwarze Sonne	Wolf, Friedrich

Schwarze Vögel	Köllinger, Bernd
Schwarzer Freitag	Noack, Siegfried
Das schwedische Zündholz	Just, Gustav
Das schwedische Zündholz	Pfeiffer, Hans
Das schweigende Dorf	Neef, Wilhelm
Die Schweine	Schütz, Stefan
Der Schweinehirt	Bernhardy, Werner
Der Schweinehirt	Brasch, Thomas
Der Schweinehirt	Brock, Rudolf Peter
Der Schweinehirt	Müller, Dietmar
Die Schweinekirmes	Dancker, Susanne
Schwejk	Lebinsky, Horst
Schwejk im zweiten Weltkrieg	Brecht, Bertolt
Schweyk	Kunad, Rainer
Schwielenhans	Bergner, Edith
Schwierigkeiten beim Hören von Musik	Berg, Jochen
Schwitzbad	Kirsch, Rainer
Schwitzbad und Tod Majakowskis	Seyppel, Joachim
Die Schwitzkur	Lange, Hanns
Sechse kommen durch die ganze Welt	Noack, Christian
Sechse kommen durch die Welt	Hocke, Wolfgang
Sechse kommen durch die Welt	Knaup, Andreas
Sedanfeier	Kipphardt, Heinar
Seemann, Tod und Teufel	Schneider, Peter M.
Seemannsliebe	Freitag, Manfred
Das Seepferdchen	Däbritz, Fritz
Segel am Horizont	Leonhard, Rudolf
Das Segel des Colon	Korn, Vilmos
Sehr jung, sehr blond und das gewisse Etwas	Strahl, Rudi
Die Seidels	Schütz, Stefan
Seilfahrt	Schneider, Hannsjörg
Seine Kinder	Kerndl, Rainer
Sekondeleutnant Aberdehr	Hawemann, Horst
Sektion Rahnstetten	Corrinth, Curt
Sekundenoper	Richter, Kurt Dietmar
Ein seltener Fall von Liebe	Nowotny, Joachim
Die seltsame Reise des Alois Fingerlein	Kerndl, Rainer
Ein Semester Zärtlichkeit	Heiduczek, Werner
Die Sendung Samaels	Zweig, Arnold
Seneca	Schütz, Stefan
Seneca‹s Tod›	Hacks, Peter
Senftenberger Erzählungen	Lange, Hartmut
Senora Sempre widerfährt Gerechtigkeit	Kuhnert, Reinhard Frieder
Sensation in London	Bauer, Andreas
Senta	Lask, Berta
Servus Peter	Bez, Helmut
Sganarelle	Wagner-Regeny, Rudolf
Shakespeare dringend gesucht	Kipphardt, Heinar
Shakespeareana	Neef, Wilhelm
Showboat	Eidam, Klaus
Sie geht, sie geht nicht	Brasch, Thomas

Sie haben aber Glück!	Richter, Kurt Dietmar
Sie hatten sonst keinen Raum in der Herberge	Hüllweck, Karl
Sie sind zauberhaft, Madame	Bez, Helmut
Sie tragen wieder Ritterkreuz	Focke, Gerd
Sieben auf einen Streich	Wendler, Otto Bernhard
Sieben Scheffel Salz	Pitschmann, Siegfried
Die sieben Todsünden ‹der Kleinbürger›	Brecht, Bertolt
Sieben Wünsche	Müller, Armin
7000 ‹Siebentausend›	Wangenheim, Gustav von
Das siebte Kreuz	Jaksch, Bärbel
Siebtens: Stiehl ein bißchen weniger	Knauth, Joachim
Die Sieger	Grabner, Hasso
Signal auf Rot	Focke, Gerd
Signal Stalingrad	Sauer, Günther
Die silberne Flöte	Merckel, Rudolf
Der silberne Pfeil	Eidam, Klaus
Simplex Deutsch	Braun, Volker
Simplizius Simplizissimus	Drewniok, Heinz
Sind wir das?	Bauer, Werner
Das singende Pferdchen	Bergner, Edith
Das singende springende Löweneckerchen	Honigmann, Barbara
Sisyphos	Gersch, Tilmann
Sitting Bull	Amberger, Wolfgang
Sitzenbleiben	Kühne, Hans J.
Skandal um Meegeren	Focke, Gerd
Der Smaragdring	Corrinth, Curt
So ein Theater	Eckert, Holger
So eine reizende Familie	Foellbach, Lena
So fing es an	Wolf, Friedrich
So long, Cello	Weissig, Bernd
So scharf wird nie ein Mann	Schleif, Klaus
So wie neulich	Schneidereit, Otto
Der Sohn des Blitzes	Müller, Helmut
Der Sohn des Sheriffs	Knietzsch, Karl C.
Die Söhne Garibaldis	Claudius, Eduard
Der Soldat und das Feuerzeug	Benecke, Heinz-Martin
Der Soldat und das Feuerzeug	Kirsch, Rainer
Soldaten	Flegel, Walter
Die Soldaten	Kipphardt, Heinar
Die Soldaten	Knauth, Joachim
Sommer in Heidkau	Sakowski, Helmut
Sommer in Sans Souci	Schlossarek, Erich
Sommer, See und schwarze Betten	Liebenberg, Günter
Ein Sommer und so weiter	Schleinitz, Karl Heinz
Der Sommerbürger	Baierl, Helmut
Ein Sommernachtstraum	Schaller, Rudolf
Sommersonnabendsonntag	Hall, Heinz
Sonnen am Horizont	Günther, Jens-Uwe
Die Sonnenfinsternis	Schlott, Ulrich
Der Sonnenstaat	Braun, Volker
Die Sonnenuhr	Wiede, Anna E.

Sonniges Wetter	Troche, Peter
Die Sorgen und die Macht	Hacks, Peter
Sorgenkinder	Freitag, Franz
Sozialistischer Frühling	Freitag, Franz
Spanische Tugenden	Matthus, Siegfried
Spanisches Capriccio	Röttger, Heinz
Spartacus	Lang, Ottomar
Spartakus	Brecht, Bertolt
Spartanische Suppe	Gilbricht, Walter
Spätere Heirat nicht ausge-schlossen	Strahl, Rudi
Der Spatzenturm	Günther, Lothar
Spectacle Cressida	Schütz, Stefan
Spektakel in Seltensow	Völkel, Ulrich
Spektakel 2 ‹Zwei›	Bartsch, Kurt; Hein, Christoph; Lang, Alexander; Lebrecht, Georg; Müller, Heiner; Weicker, Regina
Der Spiegel	Körner-Schrader, Paul
Spiel ins Leben	Zinner, Hedda
Das Spiel vom argen Schalk Till Eulenspiegel	Pasch, Albert
Das Spiel vom Dr. Faust	Schwaen, Kurt
Das Spiel vom Herrn und vom Jockel	Zweig, Arnold
Das Spiel vom kleinen Propheten Jona	Zweig, Arnold
Das Spiel vom Leben und Tod des Peter Göring	Brasch, Thomas
Das Spiel vom Mädchen Ming-Ming	Korb, Irene
Das Spiel vom Prinzenraub	Findeisen, Kurt Arnold
Das Spiel vom Pumphut	Findeisen, Kurt Arnold
Das Spiel vom Sergeanten Grischa	Zweig, Arnold
Das Spiel vom tapferen Schneiderlein	Otte, Volkmar
Das Spiel von der verlorenen Zeit	Wendler, Horst-Ulrich
Das Spiel von Irgendwer	Bergner, Edith
Das Spiel von Liebe und Zufall	Hartmann, Gerhard
Spiel vor dem Feind	Hawemann, Horst
Die Spieldose	Hanell, Robert
Der Spielmann ist da	Ebert, Günther
Spielwiese	Bohne, Monika
Spione des Kaisers	Kunzelmann, Gerhard Heinz
Das Spitzentuch der Königin	Neef, Wilhelm
Sprengstoff für Santa Ines	Borde-Klein, Ingeborg
Der Sprung über den Leierkasten	Wendler, Otto Bernhard
Spuk auf Frankenhöhe	Hauser, Harald
Spuk in der Bibliothek	Ensikat, Peter
Spuk um Mitternacht	Wendler, Otto Bernhard
Spur der Steine	Neutsch, Erik
Der Staatsstreich	Sauer, Günther
Der Stab	Herzog, Alfred
Stadelmann	Lucke, Hans
Die Stadt der Kinder	Groß, Jürgen

Stadt ohne Liebe	Streubel, Manfred
Stadthauptmann Karst	Auenmüller, Hans
Stalin als Herakles	Lange, Hartmut
Standpunkte	Mehlhausen, Kurt
Der starke Hans ‹und seine Brüder›	Rainer, Wolfgang
Der stärkere Gesetz	Freese, Rudolf
Die Stärkeren	Fabian, Gerhard
Das starrsinnige Weib	Burger, Hanus
Start in die Unsterblichkeit	Zuchardt, Karl
Stasch	Schütz, Stefan
Staschek	Lange, Hartmut
Der staunenswerte Aufstieg des Alois Piontek	Kipphardt, Heinar
Stefan und Franziska	Drewniok, Heinz
Steffel und der Zauberhut	Gabriel, Gerhard
Der Stein des Anstoßes	Strahl, Rudi
Der Stein des Glücks	Kirsch, Rainer
Steine im Weg	Sakowski, Helmut
Die steinerne Blume	Borowski, S. A.
Der steinerne Gast	Müller, Heiner
Der steinerne Mühlmann	Probst, Anneliese
Eine Stelle hinterm Komma	Schlossarek, Erich
Die Stellung ist kampflos zu halten	Kollhoff, Helga
Die sterblichen Götter	Knauth, Joachim
Ein Stern erster Größe	Kleineidam, Horst
Ein Stern in Stockholm	Hall, Heinz
Stern ohne Himmel	Ossowski, Leonie
Der Stern wird rot	Baierl, Helmut
Sterne, Geld und Vagabunden	Bauer, Andreas
Die Sterne vom Himmel runter	Lange, Katrin
Der Sternenbaum	Lindner, Otto
Der Stiefelgeist	Könner, Alfred
Der Stilze Rumpel	Wendler, Otto Bernhard
Die Stimme seines Herrn	Trolle, Lothar
Stirb, du Narr	Zuchardt, Karl
Stoffel und der Zauberhut	Güttinger, Hans
Der Stolperhahn	Wendt, Albert
...stolz auf 18 Stunden	Baierl, Helmut
Strafsache Pfeifer	Schweickert, W. K.
Die Straße	Gerlach, Harald
Die Straße hinauf	Freyer, Paul Herbert
Der Streit um den Sergeanten Grischa	Zweig, Arnold
Der Streit um die Puppe	Küchenmeister, Claus
Der Streit um J. S. Bach	Baierl, Helmut
Der Streit zwischen Kaiser und Bäcker	Noack, Christian
Strephart	Berg, Jochen
Der Strick	Bartsch, Kurt
Ein Strom, der Liebe heißt	Hall, Heinz
Ein Student kommt an	Drescher, Piet
Studenten	Bonn, Karl Heinrich
Studentenkomödie	Wangenheim, Gustav von
Stufen	Gerlach, Harald

Ein Stuhl bleibt leer	Schirmer, Bernd
Die Stühle	Lang, Alexander
Die Stühle des Herrn Szmil	Kipphardt, Heinar
Die stumme Schönheit	Tasche, Elke
Die Stumme von Portici	Neef, Wilhelm
Der stumme Zeuge	Pijet, Georg Waldemar
Die Stunde Null	Küchenmeister, Claus
Der Sturm	Schaller, Rudolf
Sturm aus den Sonnen	Hamm, Christoph
Die Sturmflut	Blach, Erich
Sturmvögel	Horn, Rudolf
Sturz nach oben	Bortfeldt, Kurt
Stützpunkt Trufanowa	Enders, Horst
Südseemärchen	Bortfeldt, Kurt
Der Sündenbock	Strahl, Rudi
Susanna	Kurzbach, Paul
Susanna im Bade	Müller, Dietmar
Susanne	Kleineidam, Horst
System Kuckuck	Eidam, Klaus
Szenen	Gerlach, Harald
Szenen aus dem Thüringer Wald	Drewniok, Heinz
Szenen keiner Ehe	Groß, Jürgen

T

Der Tag ist noch nicht zu Ende	Richter, Manfred
Die Tage der Commune	Brecht, Bertolt
Ein Tagebuch für Anne Frank	Deicke, Günther
Tagesbefehl 333	Dornberger, Paul
Tai Yang erwacht	Wolf, Friedrich
Taillenweite 68	Lucke, Hans
Tamar	Wolf, Friedrich
Tambari	Wefelmeyer, Bernd
Der Tambour und sein Herr König	Knauth, Joachim
Tandem	Freitag, Manfred
Tanker Nebraska	Hauptmann, Elisabeth
Die Tannenkippe	Kühne, Hans J.
Tante Eugenie und der Mond	Morgner, Martin
Der tapfere kleine Schneider	Eidam, Klaus
Das tapfere Schneiderlein	Auenmüller, Hans
Das tapfere Schneiderlein	Bergner, Edith
Das tapfere Schneiderlein	Bernhardy, Werner
Das tapfere Schneiderlein	Däbritz, Fritz
Das tapfere Schneiderlein	Eckert, Holger
Das tapfere Schneiderlein	Ensikat, Peter
Das tapfere Schneiderlein	Gay, Fritz
Das tapfere Schneiderlein	Geng, Heinz
Das tapfere Schneiderlein	Gerlach, Wolfgang Rainer
Das tapfere Schneiderlein	Kaltofen, Günter
Das tapfere Schneiderlein	Kunkel, Erhard
Das tapfere Schneiderlein	Lebinsky, Horst
Das tapfere Schneiderlein	Schneidereit, Otto
Das tapfere Schneiderlein	Schwarz-Marell, Gisela
Das tapfere Schneiderlein	Tradowsky, Walter
Der tapfere Zinnsoldat	Brosch, Alwin

Tarelkins Tod	Müller, Heiner
Der Tartüff	Lange, Hartmut
Tartuffe	Friedrich, Karl
Tatort Klassenzimmer	Streubel, Manfred
Tatort Lehrerzimmer	Lange, Rainer R.
Tatort Warenhaus	Blankenfeld, Martin
Der taube Acker	Krengel-Strudthoff, Inge
Das taubengraue Haus	Wander, Fred
Tausend Dollar Lösegeld	Korb, Irene
Die tausend Tapferen	Felkel, Günter
Tauwetter	Pijet, Georg Waldemar
Teamwork	Drewniok, Heinz
Techtelmechtel	Bauer, Andreas
Teddy Honigmaul und der Zauberer	Kirsch, Rainer
Teddys größter Weihnachtswunsch	Pillep, Peter
Die Teefrau	Wendt, Albert
Die Teegesellschaft	Lübke, Alfred
Tendako	Stephan, Klaus
Terra incognita	Kuba
Terrorfalle	Geiger, Erich
Terzett	Bez, Helmut
Das Testament eines Fuchses	Schuster, Uwe
Testfahrt nach Thule	Streubel, Manfred
Teton-Tatanka, Tochter der Dakota	Menschel, Helmut
Der Teufel im Haus	Salchow, Werner
Der Teufel mit den 3 goldenen Haaren	Günther, Horst
Des Teufels drei goldene Haare	Wendler, Horst-Ulrich
Des Teufels goldene Haare	Schulze, Gernot
Des Teufels Lustschloß	Arnold, Hans Dieter
Teufelskarl	Paffrath, Elifius
Der Teufelskreis	Zinner, Hedda
Die Teufelsmühle	Lorenz, Hartmut
Teuflische Wünsche	Bejach, Peter
Theater eines Gesichts	Wendler, Otto Bernhard
Theater über Theater	Wolf, Klaus Martin
Ein Theater wird vorgestellt	Berg, Jochen
Der Theatergraf von Remplin	Meincke, Wilhelm
Theaterkrise	Zehlen, Petra
Thersites und Helena	Lommer, Horst
Thomas Müntzer	Kurzbach, Paul
Thomas Müntzer	Lask, Berta
Thomas Müntzer	Pfeiffer, Hans
Thomas Mün‹t›zer, der Mann mit der Regenbogenfahne	Wolf, Friedrich
Thomas Müntzer in Mühlhausen	Wendler, Horst-Ulrich
Thyl Ulenspiegel, Geist von Flandern	Liljeberg, Jörg
Einen Tick hat schließlich jeder	Waterstradt, Berta
Der Tiefstapler	Erpenbeck, Fritz
Tiergeschichten	Wolf, Friedrich
Das Tierhäuschen	Bobrowski, Johannes
Till	Gerlach, Harals
Till	Günther, Egon
Till Eulenspiegel	Jirschim, Susanne

Till Eulenspiegel	Lorenz, Hartmut
Till Eulenspiegel	Wolf, Gerhard
Till Eulenspiegel in Bernburg	Rainer, Wolfgang
Till Eulenspiegels Streiche	Kaltofen, Günter
Tilla und der Burgvogt	Krug, Hans-Herrmann
Tilman Riemenschneider	Müller, Harald
Timbu Limbu und die Schneemüller	Schneider, Elke
Timur und sein Trupp	Braun, Klaus Dieter
Tinka	Braun, Volker
Tinko	Schmidt, Hans-Dieter
Tischlein, deck dich	Bodeit, Gerhard
Tischlein, deck dich	Kaltofen, Günter
Tischlein, deck dich	Rainer, Wolfgang
Tischlein, deck dich	Wilde, Erika
Tobias Ahoi!	Kendzia, Marie-Louise
Tochter der Dakota	Menschel, Helmut
Tod am Morgen	Eidam, Klaus
Tod, Auferstehung, Leben eines Genossenschaftsbauern	Trolle, Lothar
Der Tod des Archimedes	Schneider, Peter M.
Der Tod des Chefs	Schreyer, Wolfgang
Der Tod des Matrosen Hassein	Gilbricht, Walter
Der Tod einer Kleinbürgerin	Roehricht, Karl Hermann
Der Tod Tatanka Yotankas	Schmidt-Behrens, Friedrich
Tod und Leben des Martin Röder	Drewniok, Heinz
Der todesmüde Tod	Hüllweck, Karl
Die Todesspirale	Fischborn, Gottfried
‹Ein› ‹Der› Todestag	Strahl, Rudi
Tödliche Tinte	Wieland, Günter
Toleranz	Wangenheim, Gustav von
Die tolle Lisette	Stockhaus, Heinz
Ein toller Tag	Keisch, Henryk
Tölpelhans und die gelehrten Brüder	Baierl, Helmut
Tom Sawyers ‹großes› Abenteuer	Heym, Stefan
Tomaten und Stahl	Kilz, Hans Otto
Torquato Tasso	Kahlau, Heinz
Der tote Hund	Brecht, Bertolt
Der Tote kommt zu Gast	Eckert, Holger
Das tote Tal	Kipphardt, Heinar
Die tote Zeit	Herrmann, Klaus
Die Toten rufen	Lask, Berta
Totleben	Braun, Volker
Die Tragikomödie von Calisto und Melibea	Mickel, Karl
Die Tragödie des Coriolan	Brecht, Bertolt
Die Tragödie vom Tod der liebeskranken Melisande	Lebrecht, Georg
Tragödie von heute	Leonhard, Rudolf
Der Traktor	Müller, Heiner
Der Trampelpfad - Szenen keiner Ehe	Groß, Jürgen
Trampelpfade	Groß, Jürgen
Trampen nach Norden	Holtz-Baumert, Gerhard
Transportpaule	Gratzik, Paul

Die Trauben werden nicht süßer	Denger, Alfred
Die Trauerrede	Strahl, Rudi
Träume vom Glück	Bejach, Peter
Traumtanz	Venus, Frieder
Die traurige Geschichte von Friedrich dem Großen	Lang, Alexander
Treffpunkt Herz	Bejach, Peter
Treibjagd	Pijet, Georg Waldemar
Der treue Prinz von Behramgur	Dornberger, Paul
Die Trickbetrügerin und andere merkwürdige Begebenheiten	Hacks, Peter
Der Triebriemen	Lange, Friedrich
Tristan und Isold	Flechsig, Horst
Trockenkursus	Bortfeldt, Kurt
Trojaner	Corrinth, Curt
Das trojanische Pferd	Wolf, Friedrich
Trombis Erdenreise	Borde-Klein, Ingeborg
Das Trommelmädchen	Selber, Martin
Trommeln in der Nacht	Brecht, Bertolt
Ein Trompeter kommt	Kohlhaase, Wolfgang
Trotzki in Coyoacan	Lange, Hartmut
Trufanowa	Enders, Horst
Trütschler	Lindner, Otto
Tschapai...Tschapai...Tschapajew	Hawemann, Horst
Tschintschraka	Ensikat, Peter
Tschüß bis Freitag	Damm-Wendler, Ursula
Der Tuchkauf zu Tratting	Tiefensee, Siegfried
Der Tüchtige	Drewniok, Heinz
Der tugendhafte Taugenichts	Braun, Volker
Tuppi Schleife und die drei Grobiane	Borde-Klein, Ingeborg
Turandot	Brecht, Bertolt
Tyl Claas ‹Tyl Klaas›	Kurzbach, Paul

U

Überall ist Heiterkeit	Drewniok, Heinz
Der Überläufer	Dornberger, Paul
Überlegungen zu Feliks D.	Hammel, Claus
Der überlistete Dieb	Günther, Jens-Uwe
Die Uhr geht nach	Hacks, Peter
Uhr im Ohr	Schweickert, W. K.
Eine Uhr schlug dreimal	Zoch, Georg
Das Uhrenständchen	Billing, Gerd
Ulysses daheim	Gilbricht, Walter
Um neun an der Achterbahn	Hammel, Claus
Die Umkehr ‹des Abtrünnigen›	Zweig, Arnold
Die Umsiedlerin	Müller, Heiner
Umtausch gestattet	Kleemann, Roderich
Der Umweg	Kuhnert, Reinhard Frieder
Umwege: Bilder aus dem Leben des jungen Motorenschlossers Michael Runa	Gratzik, Paul
Umzug ins Glück	Böttcher, Wolfgang
Der Unbedingte	Wolf, Friedrich

Die unbefleckte Empfängnis	Müller, Heiner
Die unbekannte Schöne	Morgner, Martin
Unberufen toi, toi, toi	Blankenstein, Walter
Unbesiegbares Vietnam	Kuba
Und das Licht leuchtet in der Finsternis	Wolf, Friedrich
Und das soll Liebe sein	Abraham, Peter
Und der August, der bist du	Hladik, Rita
Und lieben, Götter, welch ein Glück	Hacks, Peter
Und plötzlich: Ein Clown	Strahl, Rudi
Und Rosie träumt	Hacks, Peter
...und wachsen wird der junge Wind	Bergner, Edith
Und weil wir uns lieben	Schmidt, Gerhard
Und wen verurteilen Sie?	Herzog, Alfred
Undine	Eschner, Eugen
Der ungehorsame Prophet	Voss, Helmut
Die ungewöhnliche Königstochter	Gröschke, Gerhard
Das Unglück auf dem Theater	Brasch, Thomas
Unkel Jakob und Unkel Jochen	Korf, Rudolf
Eine unmögliche Frau	Bejach, Peter
Eine unmögliche Geschichte	Schubert, Helga
Die Unperson	Seyppel, Joachim
Unruhe im Dorf	Stürzebecher, Friedrich
Unruhige Tage	Gratzik, Paul
Die unschuldige Sünderin	Küchenmeister, Claus
Unser Drache Kasimir	Streubel, Manfred
Unser kleiner Trompeter	Pederzani, Hans Albert
Unser Leben im Lied	Seeger, Bernhard
Unser täglich Brot	Kubsch, Hermann Werner
Unsere Großeltern nannten es Liebe	Krengel-Strudthoff, Inge
Die unsichtbare Front	Weindich, Günter
Unsterbliche Flamme	Felkel, Günter
Unter der Egge	Bischoff, Karl-Heinrich
Unter sieben Brücken	Koch, Jurij
Der Untergang des Egoisten Fatzer	Müller, Heiner
Der Untergang des Egoisten <Johann> Fatzer	Brecht, Bertolt
Unterm Rock der Teufel	Djacenko, Boris
Unterm Wind der Jahre	Seeger, Bernhard
Untermieter	Wieland, Günter
Unternehmen Rakete	Höher, Wolfgang
Der unterschlagene Ehemann	Schmidt, Konrad
Untersuchungshaft	Lucke, Hans
Unterwegs	Müller, Heiner
Das Untier von Samarkand	Hacks, Peter
Upstand in't Ollenheim	Böttcher, Wolfgang
Urfaust	Brecht, Bertolt
Urlaub ins Glück	Eidam, Klaus
Urlaub mit Engel	Bez, Helmut
Das Urteil	Wangenheim, Gustav von
Das Urteil	Zinner, Hedda
Ut Großmuddings Honigpott	Korf, Rudolf

V

Van Gogh	Matusche, Alfred
Variante B	Bortfeldt, Kurt
Varianten einer Szene	Kipphardt, Heinar
Vasantasena	Ensikat, Peter
Der Vater bin ich	Wohlgemuth, Joachim
Vater sein dagegen sehr	Paffrath, Elifius
Veilchen für Dolly	Bürger, Ernst
Vendetta	Billing, Gerd
Venezianisches Glas	Kuhn, Fritz
Der Verbesserungsvorschlag	Bauer, Werner
Verbotene Umklammerung	Schubert, Helga
Das verbummelte Leben	Wendt, Albert
Die Verbündeten	Kantorowicz, Alfred
Der Verdacht	Pijet, Georg Waldemar
Verdacht auf Dieter	Reichwald, Fritz
Verdammtes Gift	Schmidt-Behrens, Friedrich
Verflixter Alltag	Damm-Wendler, Ursula
Der vergessene Weihnachtsauftrag	Pillep, Peter
Die vergifteten Hunde	Hirsch, Rudolf
Der vergötterte Waldteufel	Brasch, Thomas
Das Verhör des Lukullus	Brecht, Bertolt
Die verkehrte Welt	Bez, Helmut
Verkommenes Ufer Medeamaterial *Landschaft mit Argonauten*	Müller, Heiner
Der verlegene Magistrat	Rahn, Karlheinz
Verlieb dich nicht in eine Heilige	Wiener, C. U.
Die Verliebten	Schuster, Uwe
Verlobt ist nicht verheiratet	Allihn, Jochen
Der verlorene Blick	Collin, Christian
Der verlorene Schlaf	Böttcher, Wolfgang
Der verlorene Sohn	Kleineidam, Horst
Der verlorene Vater	Bortfeldt, Kurt
Verrat in der Nacht	Pijet, Georg Waldemar
Der verratene Rebell	Kerndl, Rainer
Der verrückte Jourdain	Geissler, Fritz
Ein verrückter Einfall	Focke, Gerd
Ver-rückt-wärts	Baumgart, Peter
Die versäumte Verpflichtung	Kuberski, Angela
Die Verschworenen	Sakowski, Helmut
Verschwörung um Hannes	Freitag, Franz
Die verschwundene Brieftasche	Salchow, Werner
Die verschwundene Partitur	Wiener, C. U.
Der verspielte Scheidungsgrund	Gassauer, Karl
Versuch mit Üpsilon	Reich, Konrad
Die Versuchung des Forschers	Schumacher, Ernst
Die Versuchung des Sabellicus	Kunad, Rainer
Die vertauschten Brüder	Wangenheim, Gustav von
Verteidigung	Sabo, Wolf
Die Verurteilung des Lukullus	Brecht, Bertolt
Die Verwandlung	Schneider, Frank
Der verwunschene Berg	Köhler, Erich
Das verzauberte Ich	Gerster, Ottmar
Victory-Day	Enders, Horst

Viel Lärm um Nichts	Schaller, Rudolf
Die vier Jahreszeiten	Borde-Klein, Ingeborg
Die vier Musketiere	Damm-Wendler, Ursula
Vier Szenen	Gerlach, Harald
34 ‹Vierunddreißig› Sätze über eine Frau	Trolle, Lothar
Der vierzehnte Sommer	Kerndl, Rainer
Vietnam Rhapsodie	Groß, Jürgen
Vietnamesische Legende	Köhler, Erich
Vietnamesische Schulstunde	Stolper, Armin
Villa Matuschek	Lebrecht, Georg
Villon kommt über Paris	Günther, Jens-Uwe
Vincent	Kunad, Rainer
Viola vor dem Tor	Wogatzki, Benito
Visionen aus der Realität	Schumacher, Ernst
Die Vögel	Bartsch, Kurt
Die Vögel	Hacks, Peter
Ein Vogel wollte Hochzeit machen	Hocke, Wolfgang
Der Vogelkopp	Wendt, Albert
Die Vogelscheuche	Stolper, Armin
Der Vogelscheuchenmann	Pijet, Georg Waldemar
Der Vogtländer	Baierl, Helmut
Das Volksbuch vom Herzog Ernst	Hacks, Peter
Volksfreunde	Wangenheim, Gustav von
Vollpension	Kuhnert, Reinhard Frieder
Volpone	Hauptmann, Elisabeth
Vom Aberheiner	Hahnfeld, Ingrid
Vom Äffchen, das eine Brille trug	Tiefense, Siegfried
Vom braven Schüler Ottokar Domma	Häuser, Otto
Vom Fischer und seiner Frau	Frenzel, Klaus
Vom Fischer und seiner Frau	Richter, Peter
Vom freien Leben träumt Jan Hus	Schütz, Stefan
Vom Furz	Hein, Christoph
Vom hungrigen Hennecke	Hein, Christoph
Vom Kalaf und Prinzessin Turandot	Otte, Volkmar
Vom Katerchen, das Stiefel trug	Bohne, Monika
Vom König Midas	Kunert, Günter
Vom Mäuschen, Vögelchen und der Bratwurst	Borde-Klein, Ingeborg
Vom Peter, der auszog, das Fürchten zu lernen	Wendler, Horst-Ulrich
Vom Peter, der nicht singen konnte	Methe, Hubertus
Vom Werden der Vernunft	Lange, Hartmut
Von einem, der auszog, das Fürchten zu lernen	Kirsch, Rainer
Von einem, der auszog, das Fürchten zu lernen	Knaup, Andreas
Von einem, der auszog, das Gruseln zu lernen	Böttcher, Wolfgang
Von einem, der auszog, das Gruseln zu lernen	Müller, Dietmar
Von Gaunern und Narren	Wendler, Horst-Ulrich
Von Leichtgläubigen und Denkfaulen	Wendler, Horst-Ulich
Von List, Torheit und Betrug	Wendler, Horst-Ulrich

W

Was wird denn hier gespielt?	Solga, Norbert
Die Weber von Lyon	Neef, Wilhelm
Wechsel	Berg, Jochen
Weder der Teufel los noch Stille	Schütz, Stefan
Weder Katz noch Maus	Könner, Alfred
Der Weg in die Zukunft	Lask, Berta
Der Weg ins Leben	Stauder, Josef
Der Weg nach Füssen	Becher, Johannes R.
Der Weg nach Palermo	Röttger, Heinz
Der Weg zu Dir	Seelig, Käthe
Der Weg zum Vesuv	Jungnickel, Rudolf
Der Weg zum Wir	Pastowski, Klaus Manfred
Der Weg zurück	Wendler, Horst-Ulrich
Wege übers Land	Sakowski, Helmut
Ein Wegweiser	Baierl, Helmut
Die Weiberbrigade	Müller, Inge
Der Weiberheld	Wilde, Erika
Weiberkomödie	Müller, Heiner
Weiberlist	Bauer, Werner
Die Weibermühle	Griesbach, Rudi
Die Weibervolksversammlung	Knauth, Joachim
Weiberzwist und Liebeslist	Sakowski, Helmut
Weihe der Jugend	Lask, Berta
Weihnachten im Wald	Borde-Klein, Ingeborg
Der Weihnachtsauftrag	Pillep, Peter
Die Weihnachtsgans Auguste	Wefelmeyer, Bernd
Weihnachtslegende	Polonski, Georg
‹Die› Weihnachtsmänner	Wendt, Albert
Die Weihnachtsüberraschung	Pillep, Peter
Das Weihnachtswunder	Zweig, Arnold
Weil wir keine Kinder sind	Weindich, Günter
Die Weise von Liebe und Tod des Cornets Christoph Rilke	Matthus, Siegfried
Der weiße Dakota	Schmidt-Behrens, Friedrich
Die weiße Königin	Czech-Kuckhoff, Ilse
Weiße Nächte	Seeger, Horst
Die weiße Rose	Zimmermann, Ingo
Weiße Rose	Zimmermann, Udo
Die weiße Schlange	Philipp, Horst
Weißes Blut	Hauser, Harald
Weißt du, wo du zu Hause bist?	Focke, Gerd
Welche Art zu leben lohnt sich?	Matusche, Alfred
Welche von den Frauen?	Matusche, Alfred
Die Welle	Felkel, Günter
Welt und Traum des Hieronymus Bosch	Schuder, Rosemarie
Die Weltidee zu Schiffe	Hacks, Peter
Die Weltreise im Zimmer	Kunert, Günter
Der Weltuntergang	Dudow, Slatan
Weltuntergang Berlin	Trolle, Lothar
Wem die Glocke schlägt	Pfeiffer, Hans
Wem die Mütze paßt	Ensikat, Peter
Wem gehören die Sterne?	Hauser, Harald
Wenn das Eis bricht	Lange, Friedrich
Wenn der Thunfisch tickt	Denger, Alfred

Wenn der Wacholder blüht	Deicke, Günther
Wenn Figaro Hochzeit macht	Keisch, Henryk
Wenn Georgie kommt...	Drewniok, Heinz
Wenn man Freunde hat	Freyer, Paul Herbert
Wenn wir zusammenstehen	Wendler, Horst-Ulrich
Wer braucht Geld?	Schneidereit, Otto
Wer die Wahl hat	Knauth, Joachim
Wer dreht schon Tauben den Hals um?	Brennecke, Wolf D.
Wer einmal aus dem Blechnapf frißt	Hammel, Claus
Wer fängt Hugo?	Borde-Klein, Ingeborg
Wer hat Angst vorm schwarzen Mann?	Otte, Volkmar
Wer ist der Dümmste?	Wangenheim, Gustav von
Wer ist hier von gestern?	Hastedt, Regina
Wer lacht, lebt länger	Schneidereit, Otto
Wer seine Frau lieb hat	Stauder, Josef
Wer zuletzt lacht...	Wendler, Horst-Ulrich
Der Werbeoffizier	Brecht, Bertolt
Das Werk	Selber, Martin
Westerplatte	Gerlach, Harald
Die Wette des Mr. Fogg	Bez, Helmut
Die Wette des Serapion	Stahl, Heidemarie
Wetten, daß...	Bejach, Peter
Das Wetter von Kiebitzwinkel	Denger, Alfred
Der Wettlauf	Borde-Klein, Ingeborg
Der Wettlauf zwischen dem Hasen und dem Igel	Leidner, Susanne
Der Wettlauf zwischen Hase und Igel	Hocke, Wolfgang
Der Wettlauf zwischen Hase und Igel	Schmidt, Hans-Dieter
Der Widerspenstigen Zähmung	Matusche, Alfred
Wie der kleine Elefant zu seinem Rüssel kam	Stäcker, Hans-Dieter
Wie der König zum Mond wollte	Knauth, Joachim
Wie die ersten Menschen	Strahl, Rudi
Wie die Wilden	Böttcher, Wolfgang
Wie du mir, so ich dir	Stolper, Armin
Wie ein Theaterstück entsteht	Bigott, Gabriele
Wie es euch gefällt	Müller, Heiner
Wie halten Sie's zu Hause?	Wendler, Horst-Ulrich
Wie Hund und Katze	Ebert, Günther
Wie Klauke die vier besiegt	Borde-Klein, Ingeborg
Wie man Karriere macht	Heiduczek, Werner
Wie man Minister wird	Schütz, Stefan
Wie man sich bettet	Kuhnert, Reinhard Frieder
Wie oft soll man heiraten?	Peter, Hans
Wie Recke, Katze und Maus den Teufel besiegen	Maaß, Joachim
Wie stehn die Fronten?	Wolf, Friedrich
Wie Tiere des Waldes	Wolf, Friedrich
Wie werd ich dich, mein Junge, pflegen?	Schuchart, R. Ottmar
Wieder übern Regenbogen	Vogel, Roderich

Y

Ein Yankee an König Artus' Hof	Hammel, Claus
Yankee Doodle	Müller, Helmut
Yesterday	Müller, Ernst Dietrich

Z

Die Zähmung der Widerspenstigen	Schaller, Rudolf
Das Zahngeschwür	Brasch, Thomas
Die Zange	Ret, Joachim
Zäpfel Kerns Abenteuer	Eidam, Klaus
Zapotcatki	Brezan, Jurij
Zauber der Melodie	Degenhardt, Jürgen
Die Zauberburg	Holger, Eckert
Der Zauberer von Smaragdenstadt	Solga, Norbert
Das Zauberfaß	Richter, Manfred
Die Zaubergans	Martens, Leo
Das Zauberkochbuch	Damm-Wendler, Ursula
Das Zauberpferdchen	Köhler, Erich
Der Zauberring	Probst, Anneliese
Der Zauberring	Winter, Klaus
Zaubersprüche	Lewin, Waldtraut
Die Zaubersuppe	Hofmeier, Anni
ZAZA	Bieler, Manfred
Zehn Tage, die die Welt erschütterten	Hamm, Christoph
Zehn Tage, die die Welt erschütterten	Müller, Heiner
Die Zeit der Hoffnung	Freyer, Paul Herbert
Zeit der Störche	Keyn, Ulf
Zeit der Störche	Otto, Herbert
Zeit der Störche	Pörschmann, Jürgen
Der Zeitfaktor	Stolper, Armin
Zeitgenossen	Stolper, Armin
Zement	Müller, Heiner
Die Zensurenschlacht	Kuhnert, Reinhard Frieder
Der zerbrochene Krug	Geissler, Fritz
Der zerbrochene Krug	Wagner-Regeny, Rudolf
Die Zermalmten	Pijet, Georg Waldemar
Zeuge Kretschmar	Müller-Glösa, Otto
Der Zeuge wird zum Richter	Wegerdt, Friedrich
Der Zigeunerbaron	Schneidereit, Otto
Zille-Heinrich	Kahlau, Heinz
Zimmer 13 ‹dreizehn›	Erpenbeck, Fritz
Ein Zimmer mit Frühstück – für Musiker	Strahl, Rudi
Zimmer Nr. 13	Erpenbeck, Fritz
Die Zimmerleute	Wornar, Jan
Zirkus von hinten	Koerbl, Jürg-Michael
Zugvögel nisten spät	Günther, Lothar
Zum Glück hat sie Pech	Böttcher, Wolfgang
Zum Sterben geboren	Weiß, Rudolf
Zur letzten Rettung	Claus, Manfred
Zwecks späterer Heirat	Fries, Hans Joachim

Zwei Ärzte	Pfeiffer, Hans
Zwei Hände	Krengel-Strudthoff, Inge
Zwei Herren aus Verona	Hauptmann, Elisabeth
Zwei in einer kleinen Stadt	Kerndl, Rainer
Zwei Ohrfeigen	Schneidereit, Otto
Zwei Physiker	Stolper, Armin
Zwei Schleier, drei Freier	Böttcher, Wolfgang
Zwei Sonnen über dem Feld	Bodeit, Gerhard
2 : 1 ‹Zwei zu eins› für Irmgard	Stauder, Josef
Zweimal Helden	Brennecke, Wolf D.
2 x ‹Zweimal› Katharina	Schöbel, Hildegard
2 x ‹Zweimal› klingeln	Neubert, Kurt
2 x ‹Zweimal› Madeleine	Allihn, Jochen
Die zweite Entscheidung	Zimmermann, Ingo
Die zweite Erschaffung der Welt	Hammel, Claus
Das zweite Gesicht	Fricke, Jürgen
Die zweite Hochzeit	Baierl, Helmut
Das zweite Urteil	Mickel, Karl
Zwerg Nase	Herz, Joachim
Zwerg Nase	Kaltofen, Günter
Zwerg Nase	Stolzenbach, Beatrice
Zwerg Nase	Wendler, Horst-Ulrich
Die Zwerge	Lang, Alexander
Die Zwickmühle	Preil, Hans Joachim
Zwiesprache halten	Bez, Helmut
Die Zwillinge	Freitag, Franz
Zwillingskomödie	Bortfeldt, Kurt
Der Zwillingssoldat	Berthold, Siegfried
Zwischen Dünen und Daunen	Kahlow, Heinz
Zwischen Gestern und Morgen	Stockhaus, Heinz
Ein Zwischenfall	Budjuhn, Horst
Zwischenfall auf Norderney	Vogt, Helmut
Zwischenspiel	Lange, Hartmut
Die zwölf Geschworenen	Budjuhn, Horst
Zyankali	Wolf, Friedrich